NAOKI URASAWA'S
20th CENTURY BOYS

VOL 06
FINAL HOPE

Story & Art by
NAOKI URASAWA

With the cooperation of
Takashi NAGASAKI

PROFILES

NAOKI URASAWA'S 20th CENTURY BOYS

Fourteen years on from December 31, 2000, or Bloody New Year's Eve... Kanna is now 17 and living in a once again peaceful Neo Tokyo—but the shadow of the Friends, who run this new world, looms ominously. What is Japan's—and the rest of the world's—destiny in this new millennium? And where are Kenji and his companions?

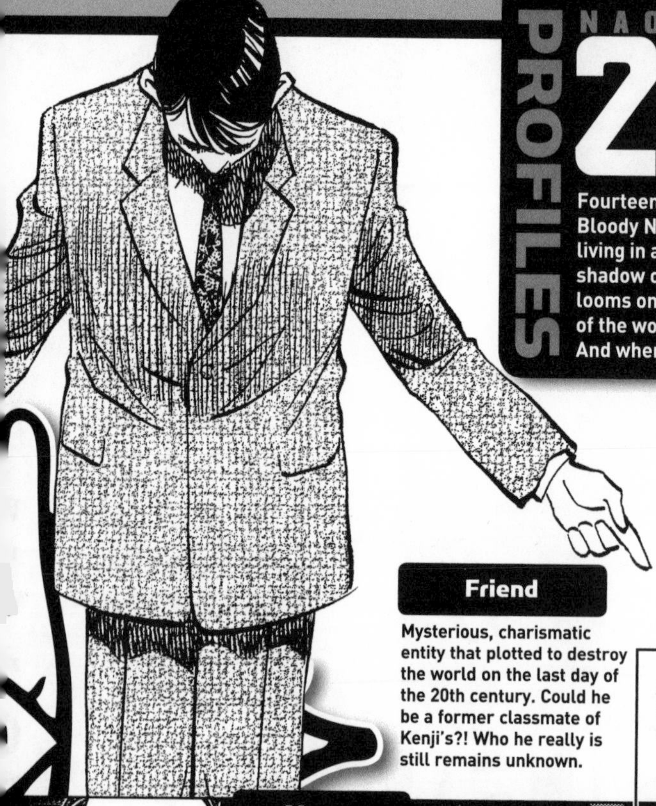

Friend

Mysterious, charismatic entity that plotted to destroy the world on the last day of the 20th century. Could he be a former classmate of Kenji's?! Who he really is still remains unknown.

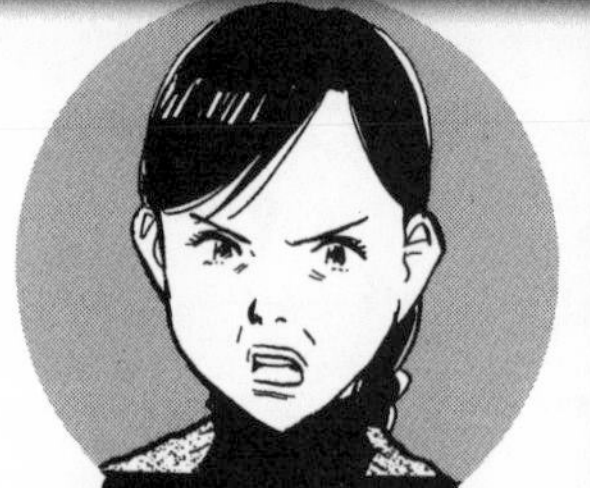

Yukiji

Acting as Kanna's guardian in Tokyo in accordance with Kenji's wishes ever since Bloody New Year's Eve.

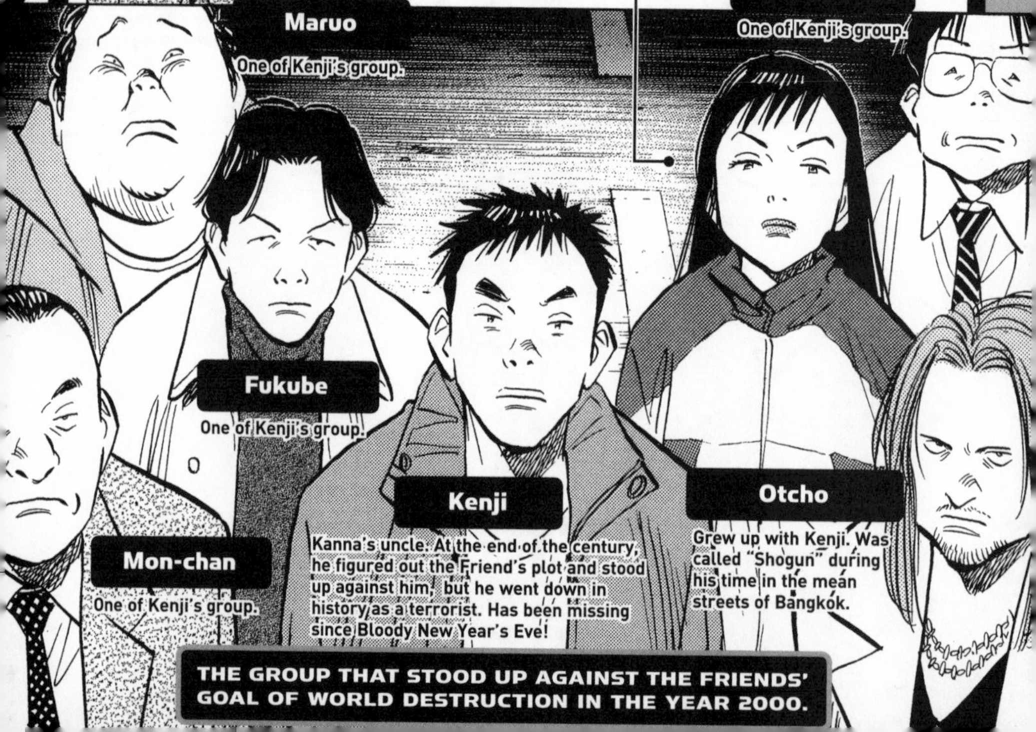

Yoshitsune

One of Kenji's group.

Maruo

One of Kenji's group.

Fukube

One of Kenji's group.

Otcho

Grew up with Kenji. Was called "Shogun" during his time in the mean streets of Bangkok.

Kenji

Kanna's uncle. At the end of the century, he figured out the Friend's plot and stood up against him, but he went down in history as a terrorist. Has been missing since Bloody New Year's Eve!

Mon-chan

One of Kenji's group.

THE GROUP THAT STOOD UP AGAINST THE FRIENDS' GOAL OF WORLD DESTRUCTION IN THE YEAR 2000.

Chono Shohei

Freshman detective assigned to the Kabuki-cho Police Station in Shinjuku who aims to emulate his grandfather, the fabled detective Cho-san. Very motivated but very ineffective.

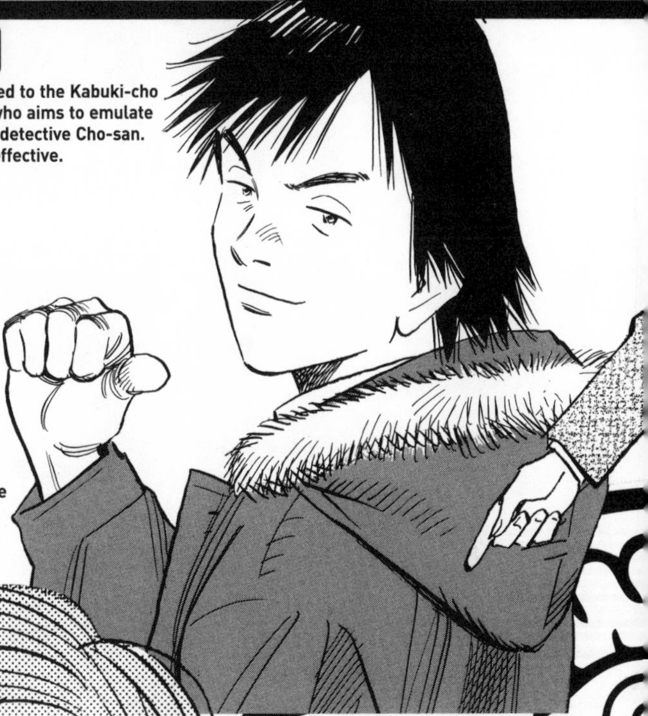

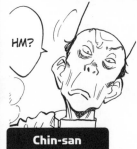

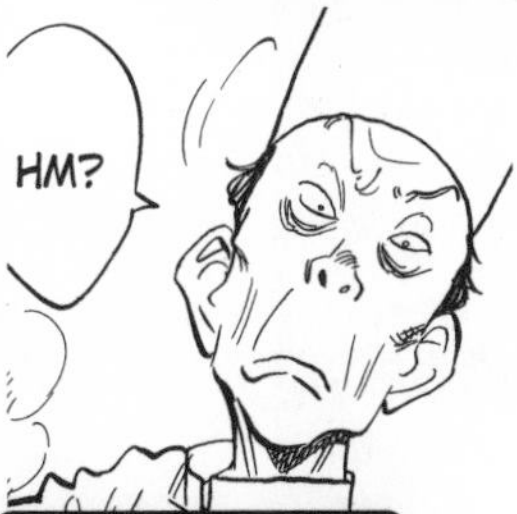
HM?

Chin-san

Owner-chef of Chin Po Ro, the Chinese restaurant where Kanna works.

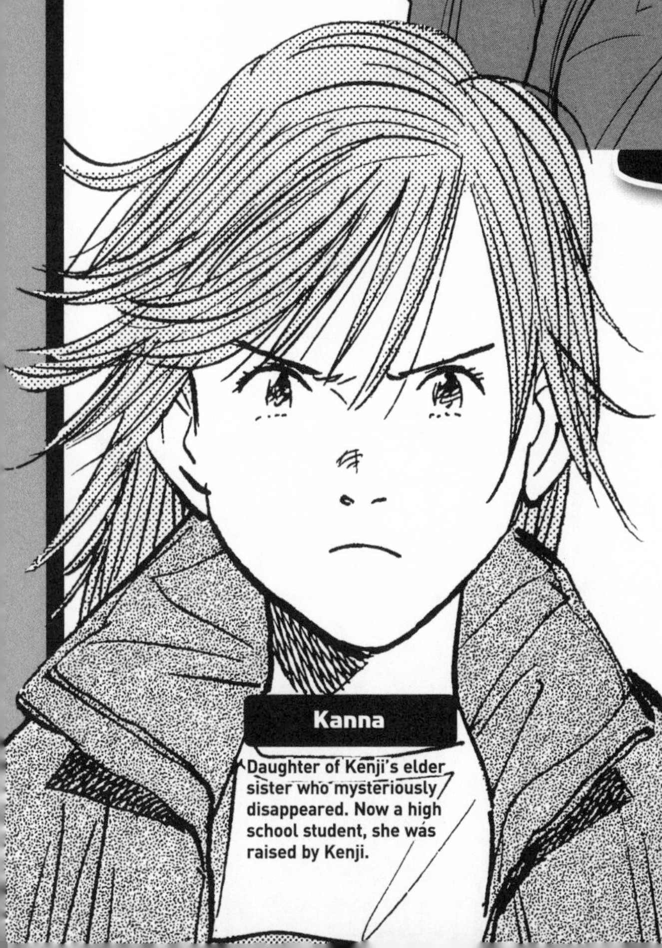

Kanna

Daughter of Kenji's elder sister who mysteriously disappeared. Now a high school student, she was raised by Kenji.

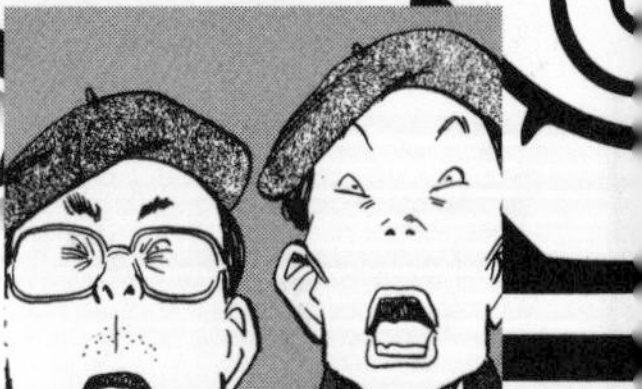

Ujiko Ujio

Ujiki and Kaneko, a manga artist duo who are Kanna's next-door neighbors.

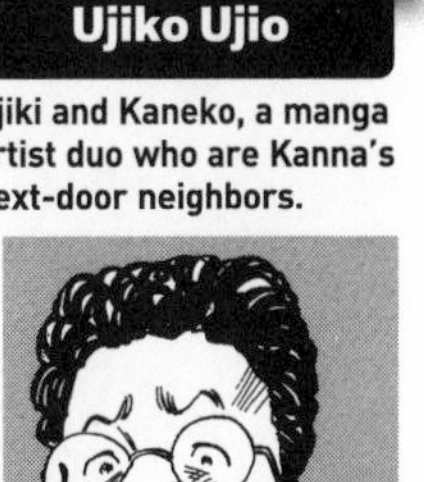

Kakuta

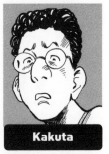

A manga artist friend of Ujiko Ujio.

CONTENTS

VOL 06
FINAL HOPE

NAOKI URASAWA'S

20 CENTURY BOYS

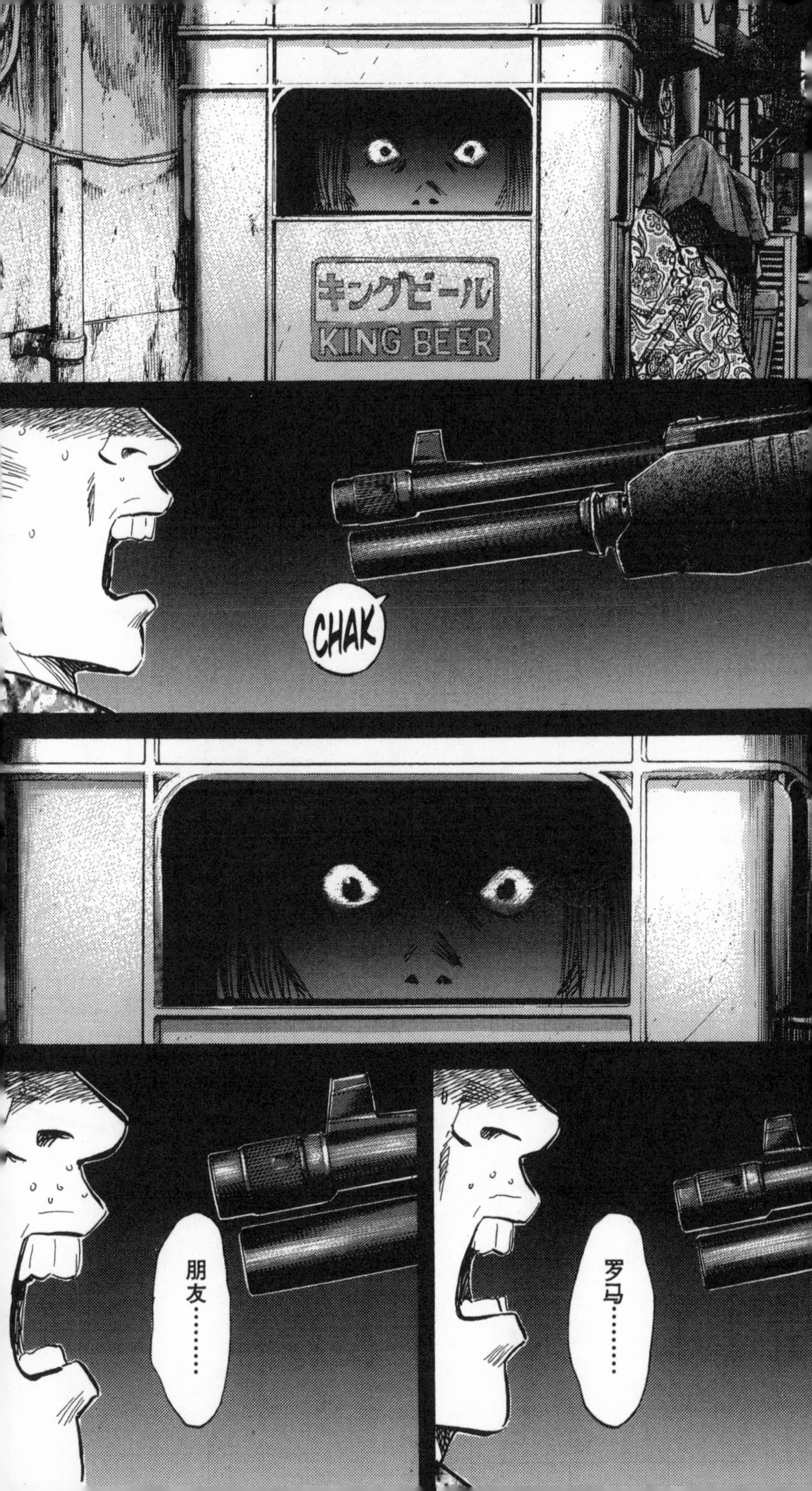
キングビール
KING BEER
CHAK
罗马……
朋友……

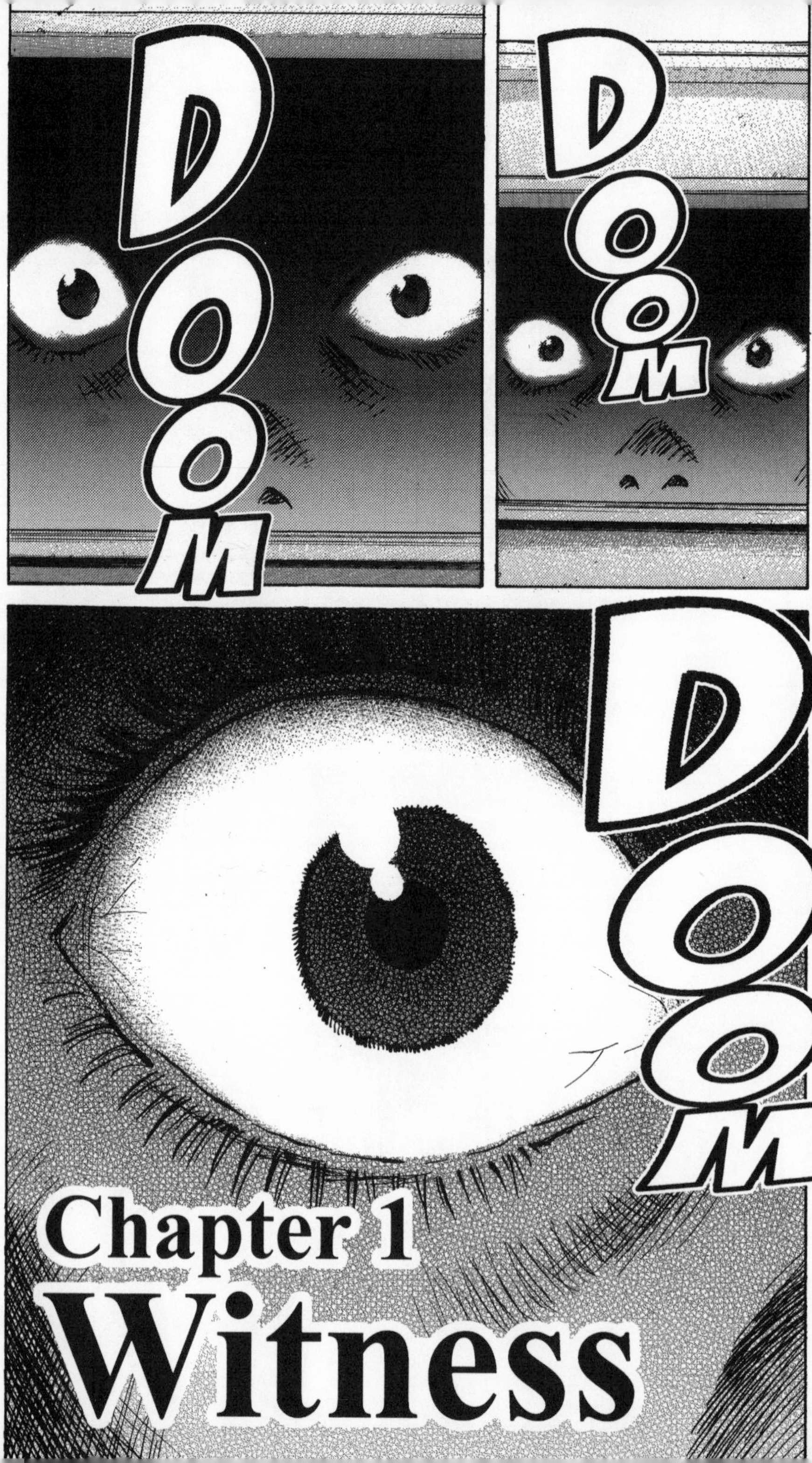
DOOOM
DOOOM
DOOOM
Chapter 1
Witness

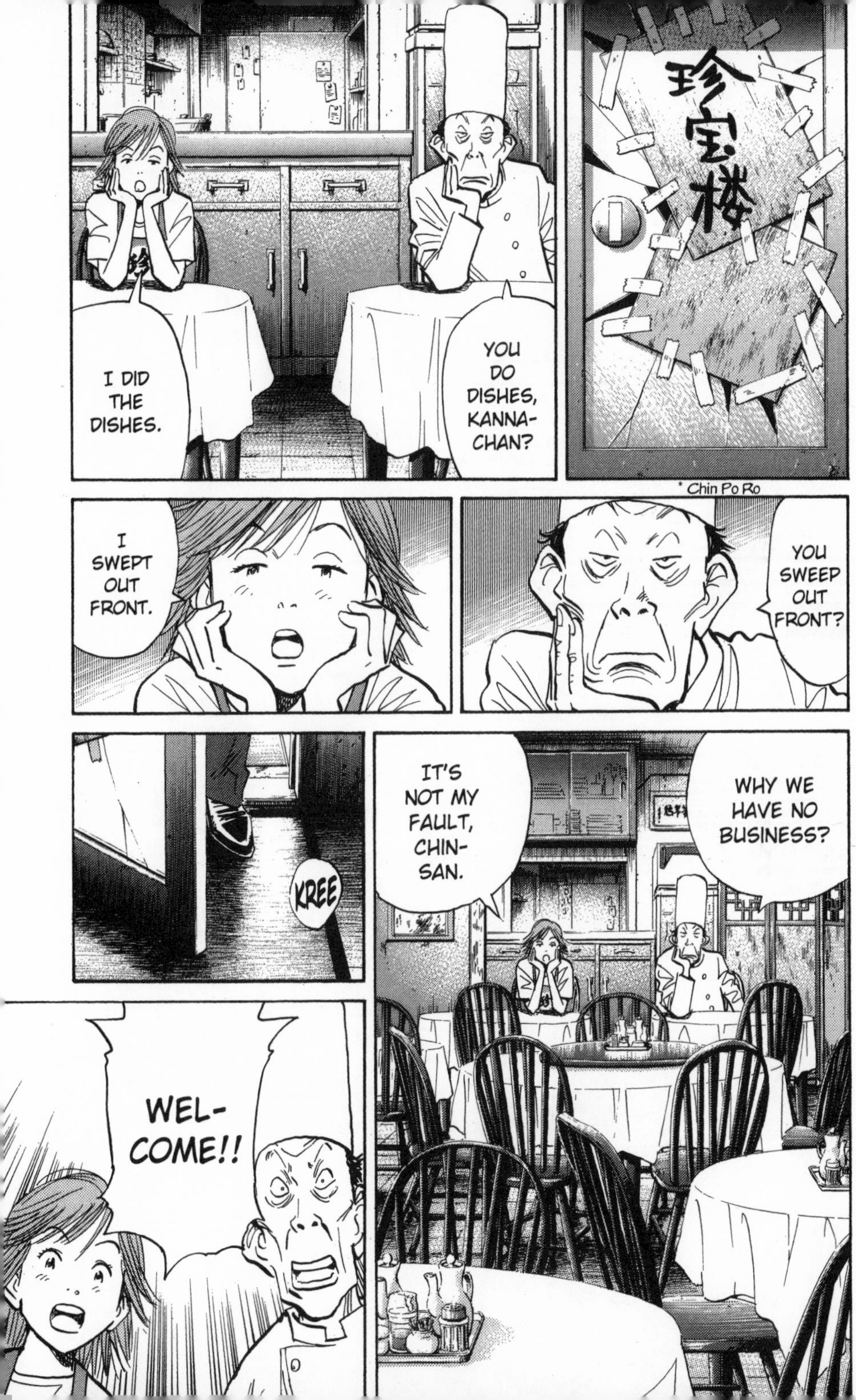
珍宝楼
* Chin Po Ro
YOU DO DISHES, KANNA-CHAN?
I DID THE DISHES.
YOU SWEEP OUT FRONT?
I SWEPT OUT FRONT.
WHY WE HAVE NO BUSINESS?
IT'S NOT MY FAULT, CHIN-SAN.
KREE
WEL-COME!!

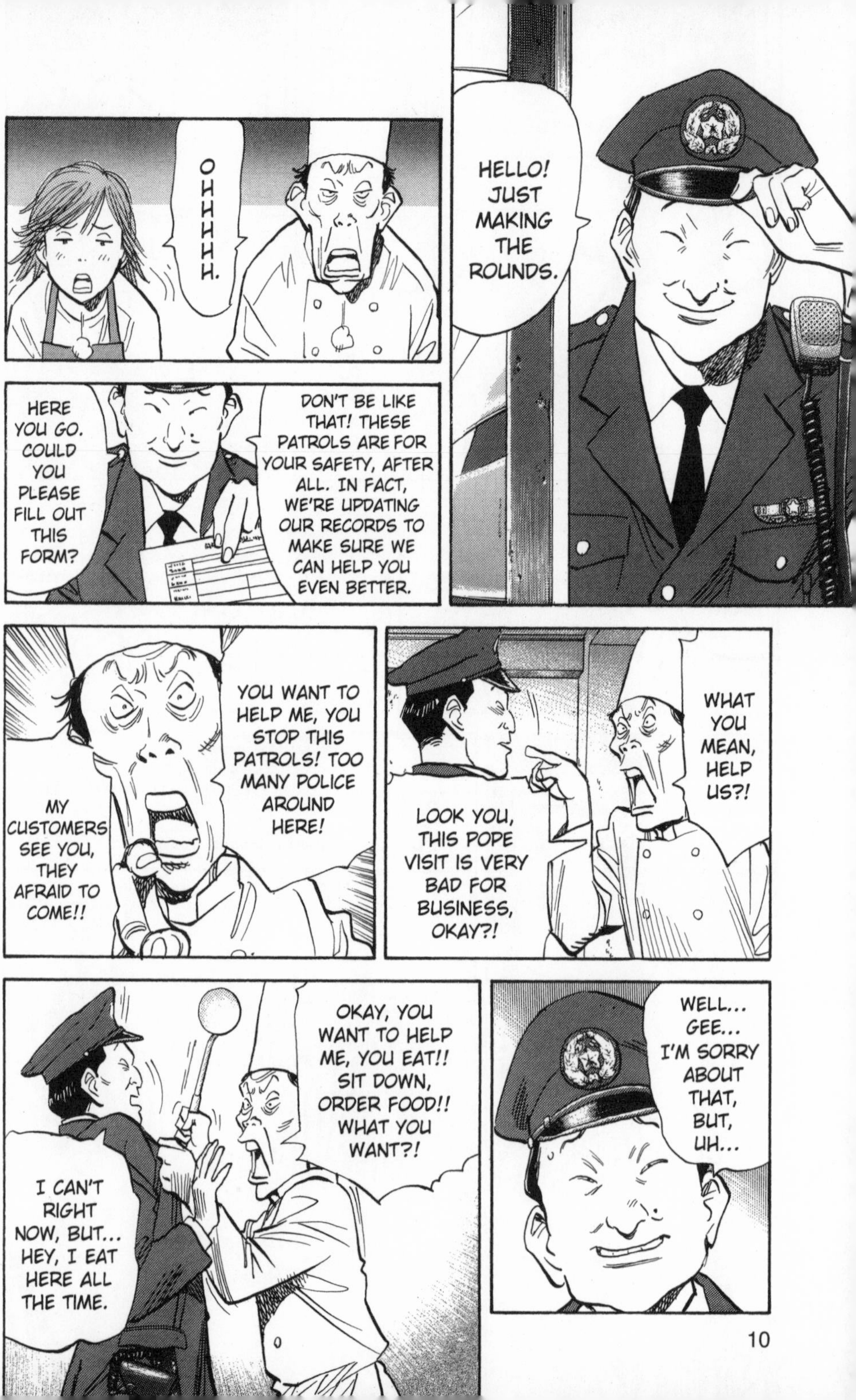
HELLO! JUST MAKING THE ROUNDS.
OHHHHH.
DON'T BE LIKE THAT! THESE PATROLS ARE FOR YOUR SAFETY, AFTER ALL. IN FACT, WE'RE UPDATING OUR RECORDS TO MAKE SURE WE CAN HELP YOU EVEN BETTER.
HERE YOU GO. COULD YOU PLEASE FILL OUT THIS FORM?
WHAT YOU MEAN, HELP US?!
LOOK YOU, THIS POPE VISIT IS VERY BAD FOR BUSINESS, OKAY?!
YOU WANT TO HELP ME, YOU STOP THIS PATROLS! TOO MANY POLICE AROUND HERE!
MY CUSTOMERS SEE YOU, THEY AFRAID TO COME!!
WELL... GEE... I'M SORRY ABOUT THAT, BUT, UH...
OKAY, YOU WANT TO HELP ME, YOU EAT!! SIT DOWN, ORDER FOOD!! WHAT YOU WANT?!
I CAN'T RIGHT NOW, BUT... HEY, I EAT HERE ALL THE TIME.

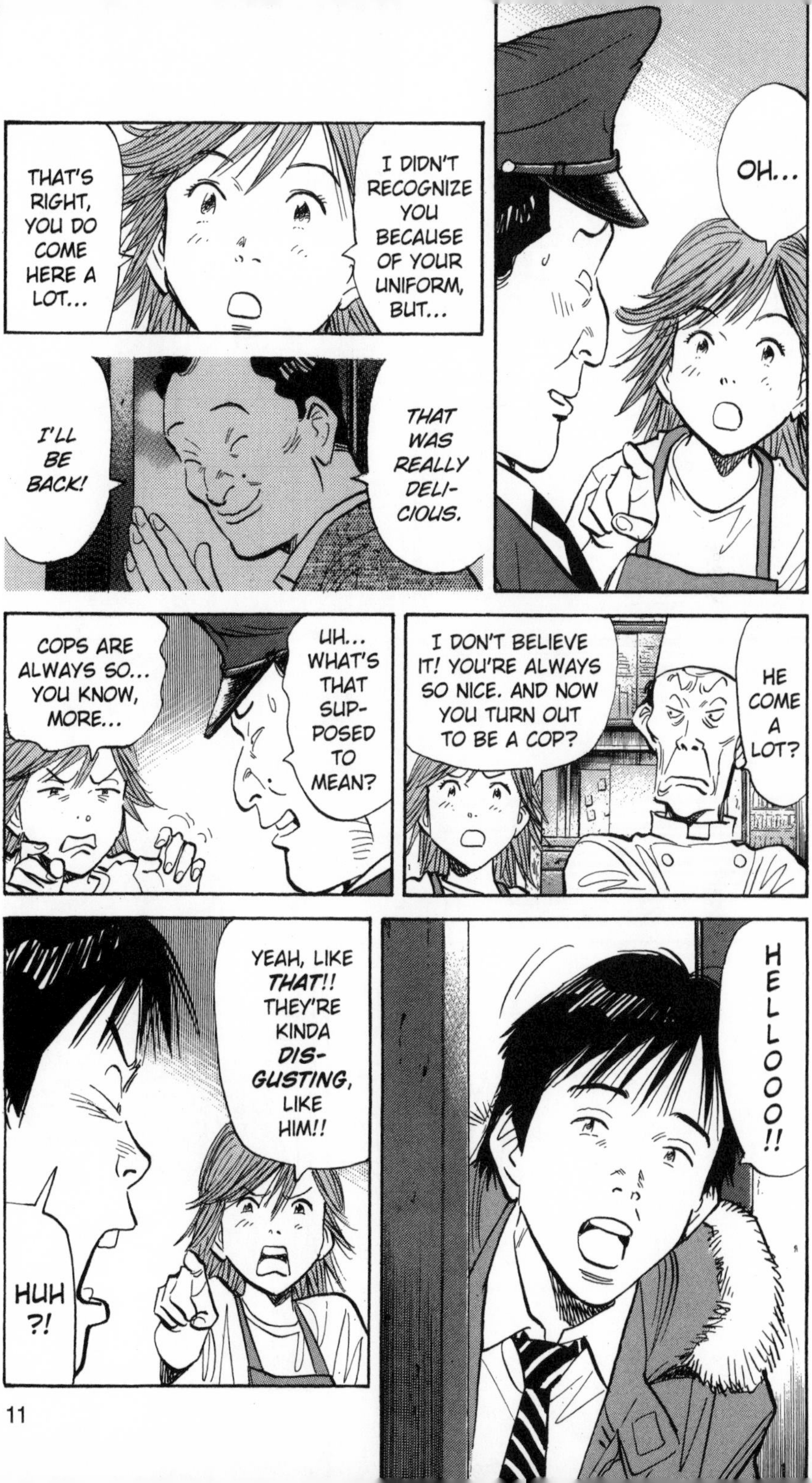
OH...
I DIDN'T RECOGNIZE YOU BECAUSE OF YOUR UNIFORM, BUT...
THAT'S RIGHT, YOU DO COME HERE A LOT...
THAT WAS REALLY DELI-CIOUS.
I'LL BE BACK!
HE COME A LOT?
I DON'T BELIEVE IT! YOU'RE ALWAYS SO NICE. AND NOW YOU TURN OUT TO BE A COP?
UH... WHAT'S THAT SUP-POSED TO MEAN?
COPS ARE ALWAYS SO... YOU KNOW, MORE...
HELLOOOO!!
YEAH, LIKE *THAT*!! THEY'RE KINDA *DIS-GUSTING*, LIKE HIM!!
HUH ?!

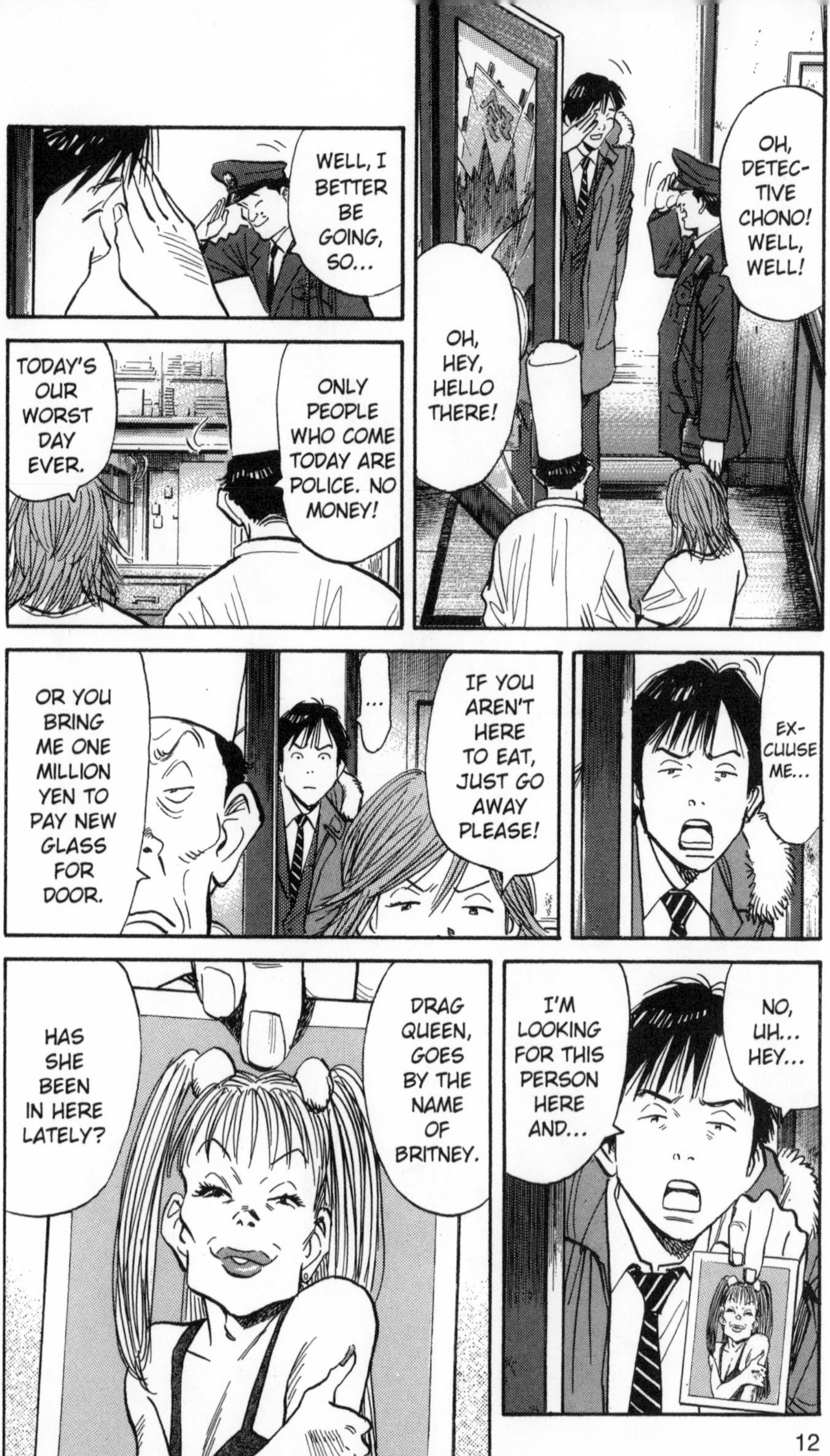

OH, DETECTIVE CHONO! WELL, WELL!
OH, HEY, HELLO THERE!
WELL, I BETTER BE GOING, SO...
ONLY PEOPLE WHO COME TODAY ARE POLICE. NO MONEY!
TODAY'S OUR WORST DAY EVER.
EX-CUUSE ME...
IF YOU AREN'T HERE TO EAT, JUST GO AWAY PLEASE!
...
OR YOU BRING ME ONE MILLION YEN TO PAY NEW GLASS FOR DOOR.
NO, UH... HEY...
I'M LOOKING FOR THIS PERSON HERE AND...
DRAG QUEEN, GOES BY THE NAME OF BRITNEY.
HAS SHE BEEN IN HERE LATELY?

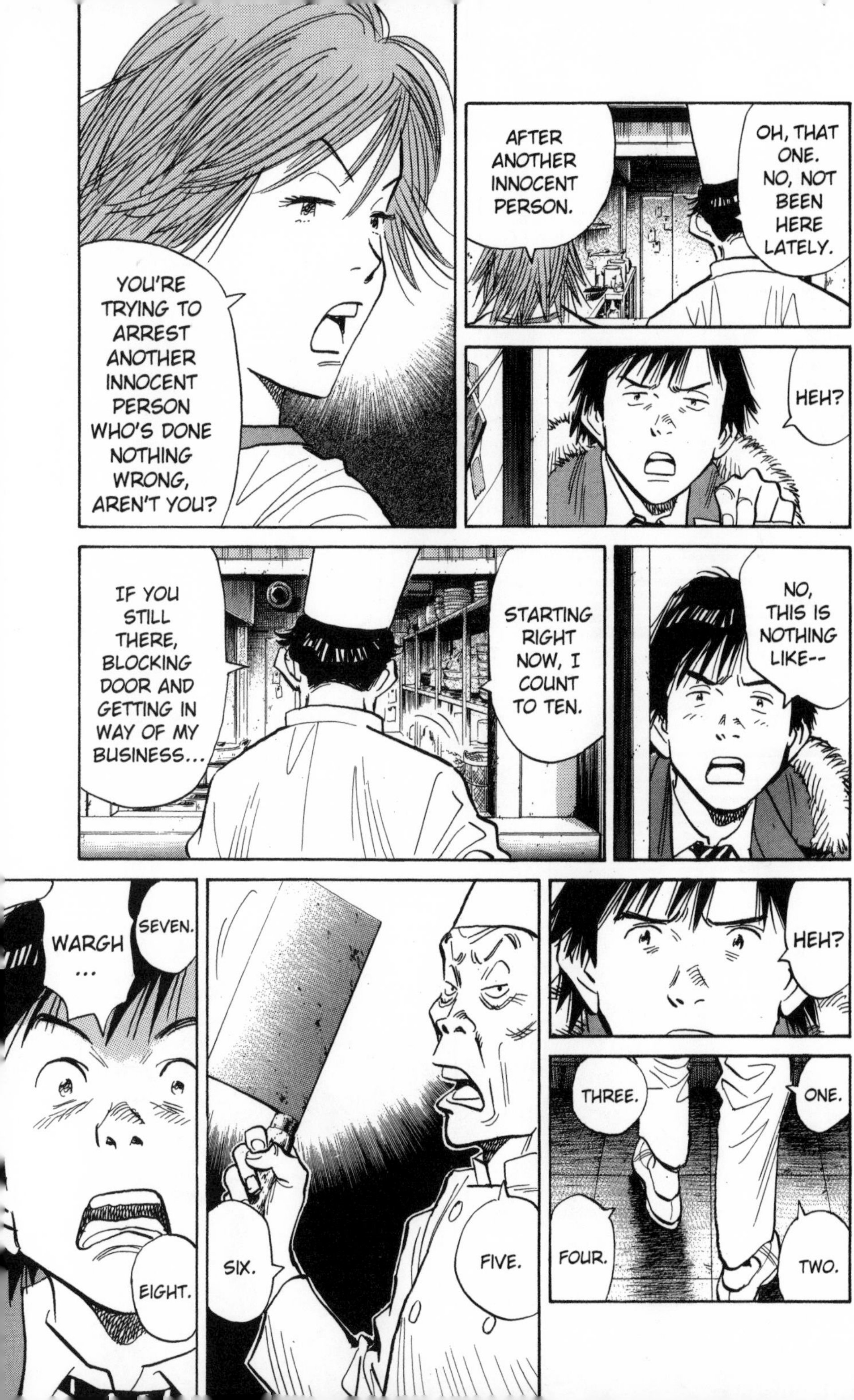

OH, THAT ONE. NO, NOT BEEN HERE LATELY.
AFTER ANOTHER INNOCENT PERSON.
HEH?
YOU'RE TRYING TO ARREST ANOTHER INNOCENT PERSON WHO'S DONE NOTHING WRONG, AREN'T YOU?
NO, THIS IS NOTHING LIKE--
STARTING RIGHT NOW, I COUNT TO TEN.
IF YOU STILL THERE, BLOCKING DOOR AND GETTING IN WAY OF MY BUSINESS...
HEH?
ONE.
THREE.
TWO.
FOUR.
FIVE.
SIX.
SEVEN.
WARGH ...
EIGHT.

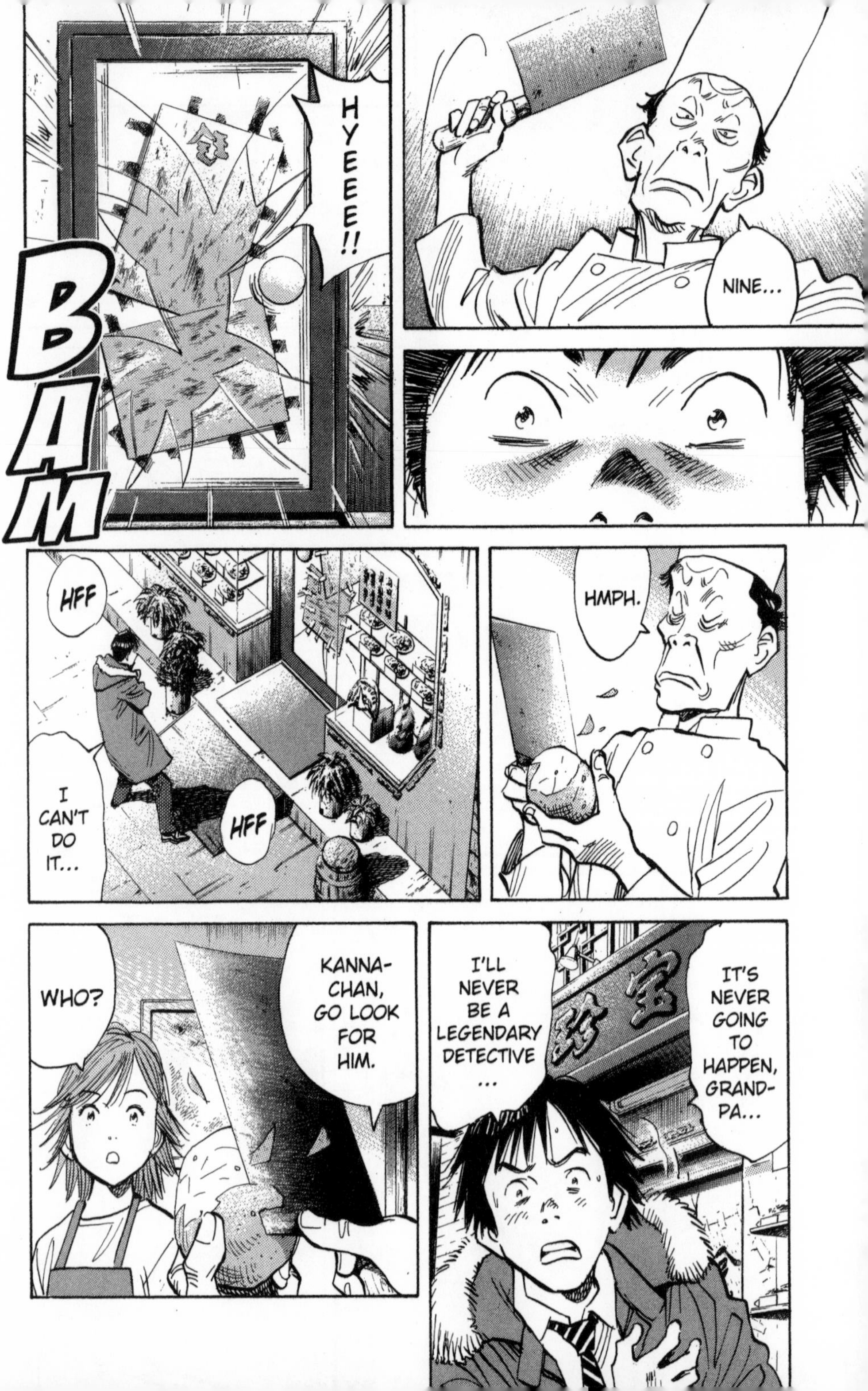
NINE...
HYEEE!!
BAM
HMPH.
HFF
I CAN'T DO IT...
HFF
IT'S NEVER GOING TO HAPPEN, GRAND-PA...
I'LL NEVER BE A LEGENDARY DETECTIVE...
KANNA-CHAN, GO LOOK FOR HIM.
WHO?

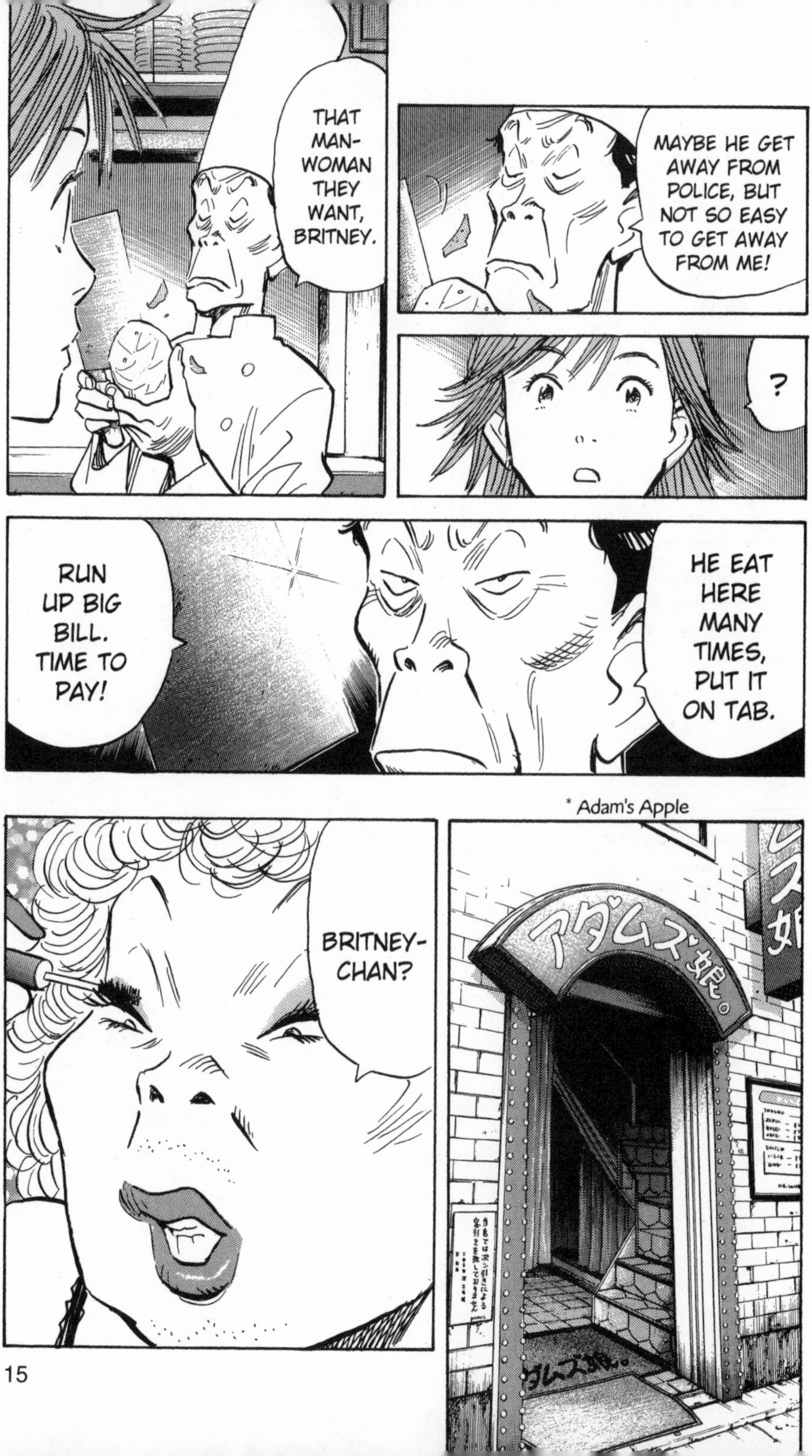
MAYBE HE GET AWAY FROM POLICE, BUT NOT SO EASY TO GET AWAY FROM ME!
?
THAT MAN-WOMAN THEY WANT, BRITNEY.
HE EAT HERE MANY TIMES, PUT IT ON TAB.
RUN UP BIG BILL. TIME TO PAY!
* Adam's Apple
アダムズ姫
BRITNEY-CHAN?

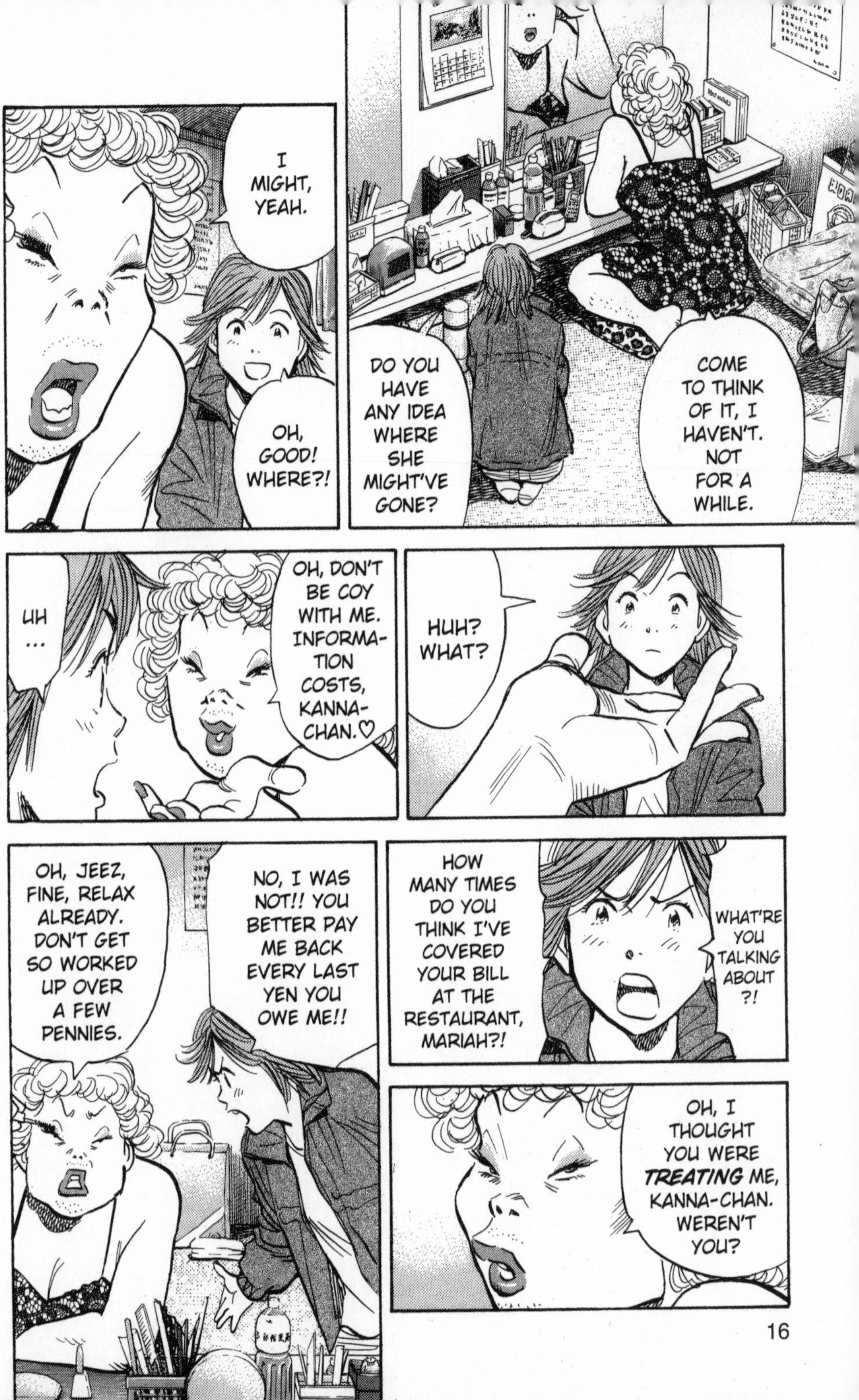
COME TO THINK OF IT, I HAVEN'T. NOT FOR A WHILE.
DO YOU HAVE ANY IDEA WHERE SHE MIGHT'VE GONE?
I MIGHT, YEAH.
OH, GOOD! WHERE?!
HUH? WHAT?
OH, DON'T BE COY WITH ME. INFORMATION COSTS, KANNA-CHAN.♡
UH ...
WHAT'RE YOU TALKING ABOUT ?!
HOW MANY TIMES DO YOU THINK I'VE COVERED YOUR BILL AT THE RESTAURANT, MARIAH?!
OH, I THOUGHT YOU WERE *TREATING* ME, KANNA-CHAN. WEREN'T YOU?
NO, I WAS NOT!! YOU BETTER PAY ME BACK EVERY LAST YEN YOU OWE ME!!
OH, JEEZ, FINE, RELAX ALREADY. DON'T GET SO WORKED UP OVER A FEW PENNIES.

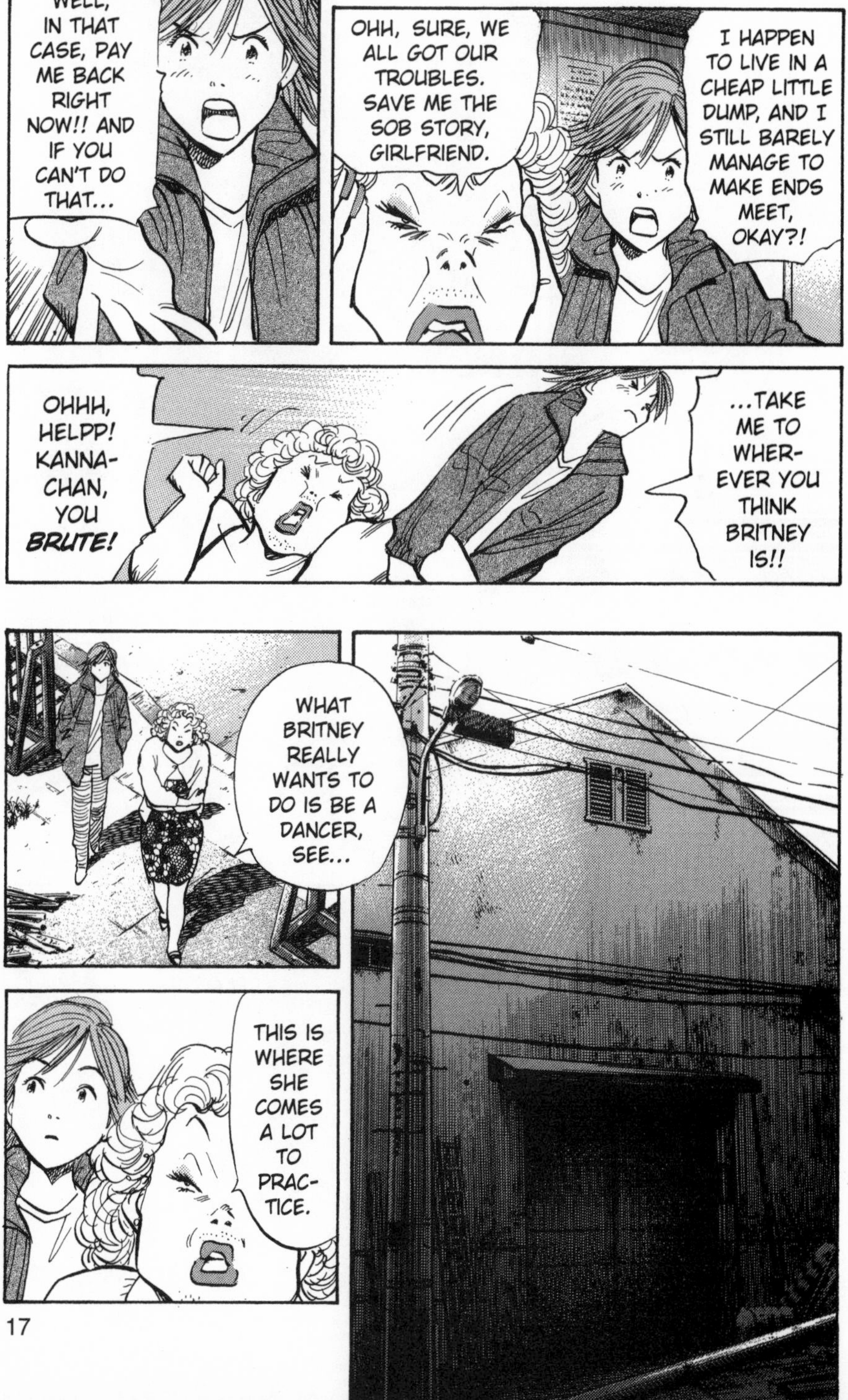
I HAPPEN TO LIVE IN A CHEAP LITTLE DUMP, AND I STILL BARELY MANAGE TO MAKE ENDS MEET, OKAY?!
OHH, SURE, WE ALL GOT OUR TROUBLES. SAVE ME THE SOB STORY, GIRLFRIEND.
WELL, IN THAT CASE, PAY ME BACK RIGHT NOW!! AND IF YOU CAN'T DO THAT...
...TAKE ME TO WHER-EVER YOU THINK BRITNEY IS!!
OHHH, HELPP! KANNA-CHAN, YOU *BRUTE!*
WHAT BRITNEY REALLY WANTS TO DO IS BE A DANCER, SEE...
THIS IS WHERE SHE COMES A LOT TO PRAC-TICE.

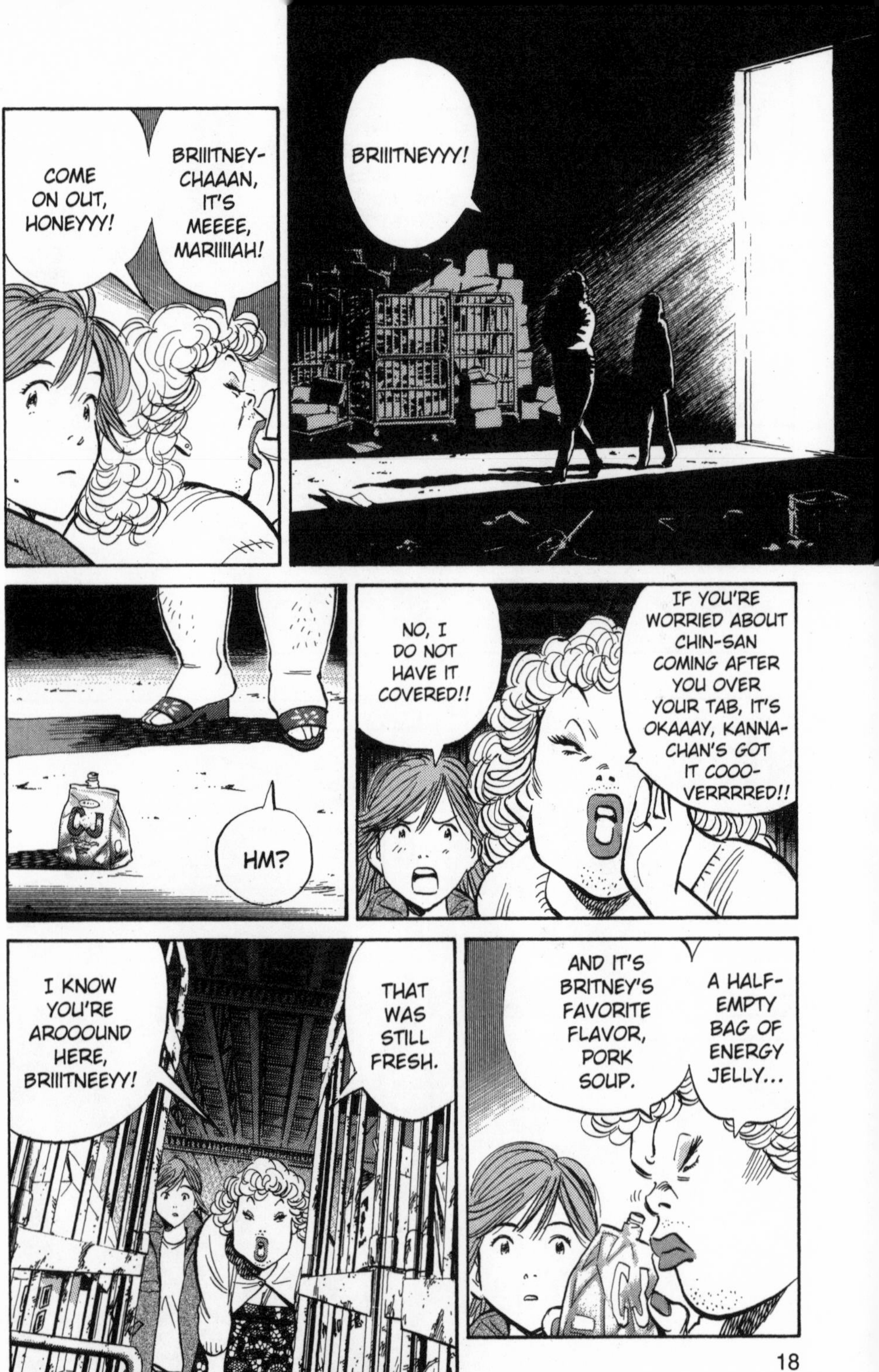
BRIIITNEYYY!
BRIIITNEY-CHAAAN, IT'S MEEEE, MARIIIIAH!
COME ON OUT, HONEYYY!
IF YOU'RE WORRIED ABOUT CHIN-SAN COMING AFTER YOU OVER YOUR TAB, IT'S OKAAAY, KANNA-CHAN'S GOT IT COOO-VERRRRED!!
NO, I DO NOT HAVE IT COVERED!!
CJ
HM?
A HALF-EMPTY BAG OF ENERGY JELLY...
AND IT'S BRITNEY'S FAVORITE FLAVOR, PORK SOUP.
THAT WAS STILL FRESH.
I KNOW YOU'RE AROOOUND HERE, BRIIITNEEYY!

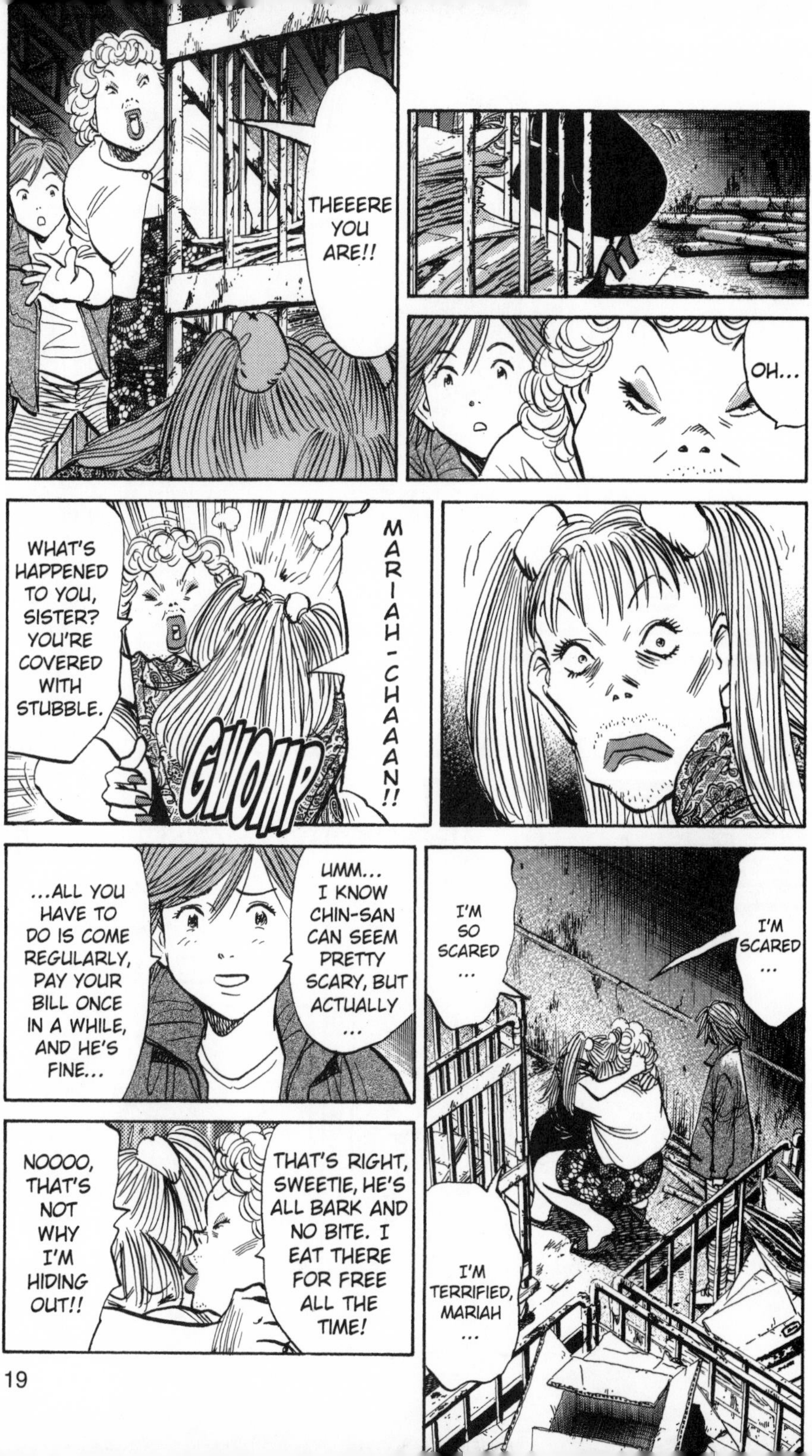
OH...
THEEERE YOU ARE!!
MARIAH-CHAAAAN!!
GWOMP
WHAT'S HAPPENED TO YOU, SISTER? YOU'RE COVERED WITH STUBBLE.
I'M SCARED...
I'M SO SCARED...
I'M TERRIFIED, MARIAH...
UMM... I KNOW CHIN-SAN CAN SEEM PRETTY SCARY, BUT ACTUALLY...
...ALL YOU HAVE TO DO IS COME REGULARLY, PAY YOUR BILL ONCE IN A WHILE, AND HE'S FINE...
THAT'S RIGHT, SWEETIE, HE'S ALL BARK AND NO BITE. I EAT THERE FOR FREE ALL THE TIME!
NOOOO, THAT'S NOT WHY I'M HIDING OUT!!

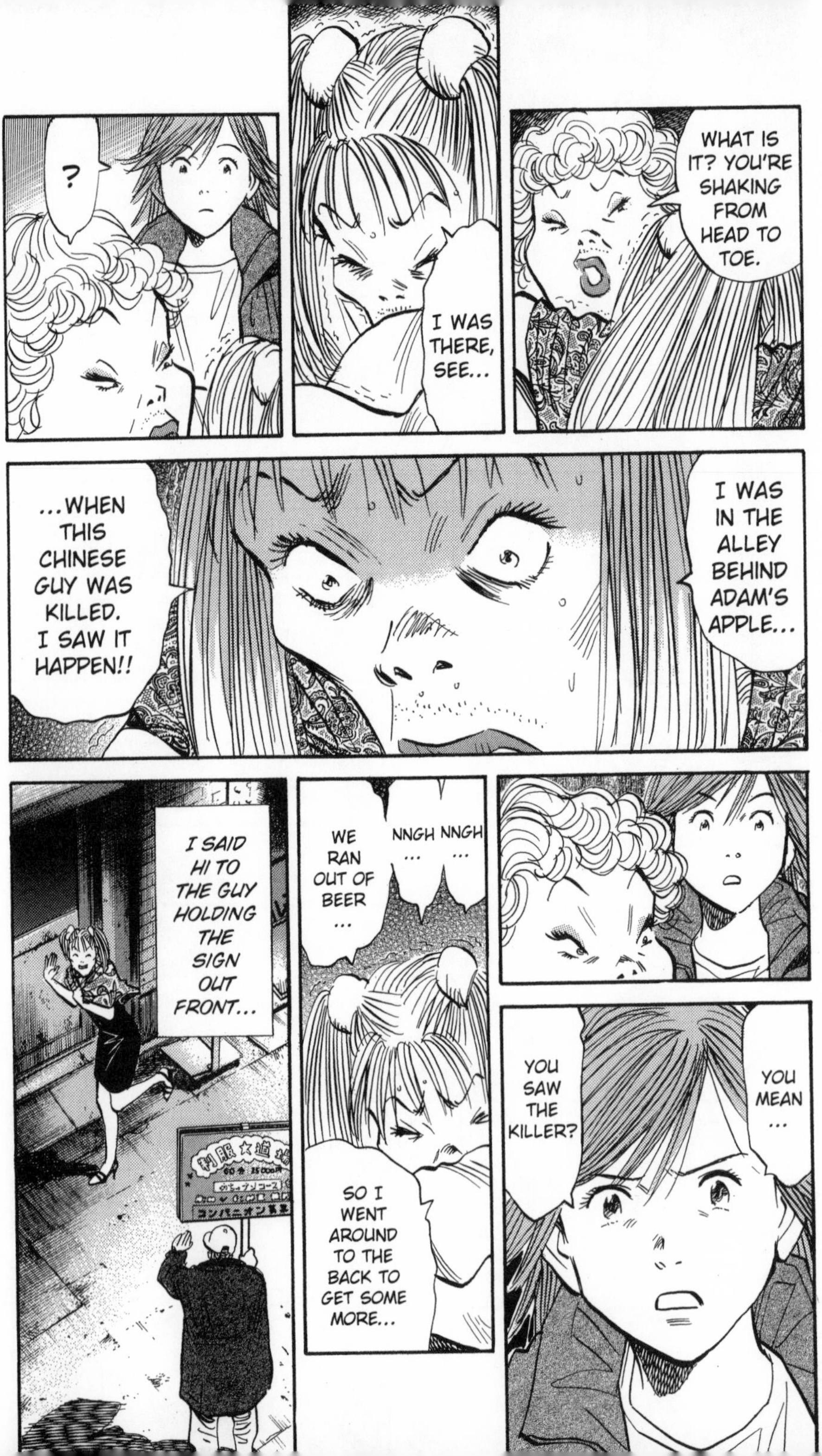
WHAT IS IT? YOU'RE SHAKING FROM HEAD TO TOE.
I WAS THERE, SEE...
?
I WAS IN THE ALLEY BEHIND ADAM'S APPLE...
...WHEN THIS CHINESE GUY WAS KILLED. I SAW IT HAPPEN!!
YOU MEAN...
YOU SAW THE KILLER?
NNGH...
NNGH...
WE RAN OUT OF BEER...
SO I WENT AROUND TO THE BACK TO GET SOME MORE...
I SAID HI TO THE GUY HOLDING THE SIGN OUT FRONT...

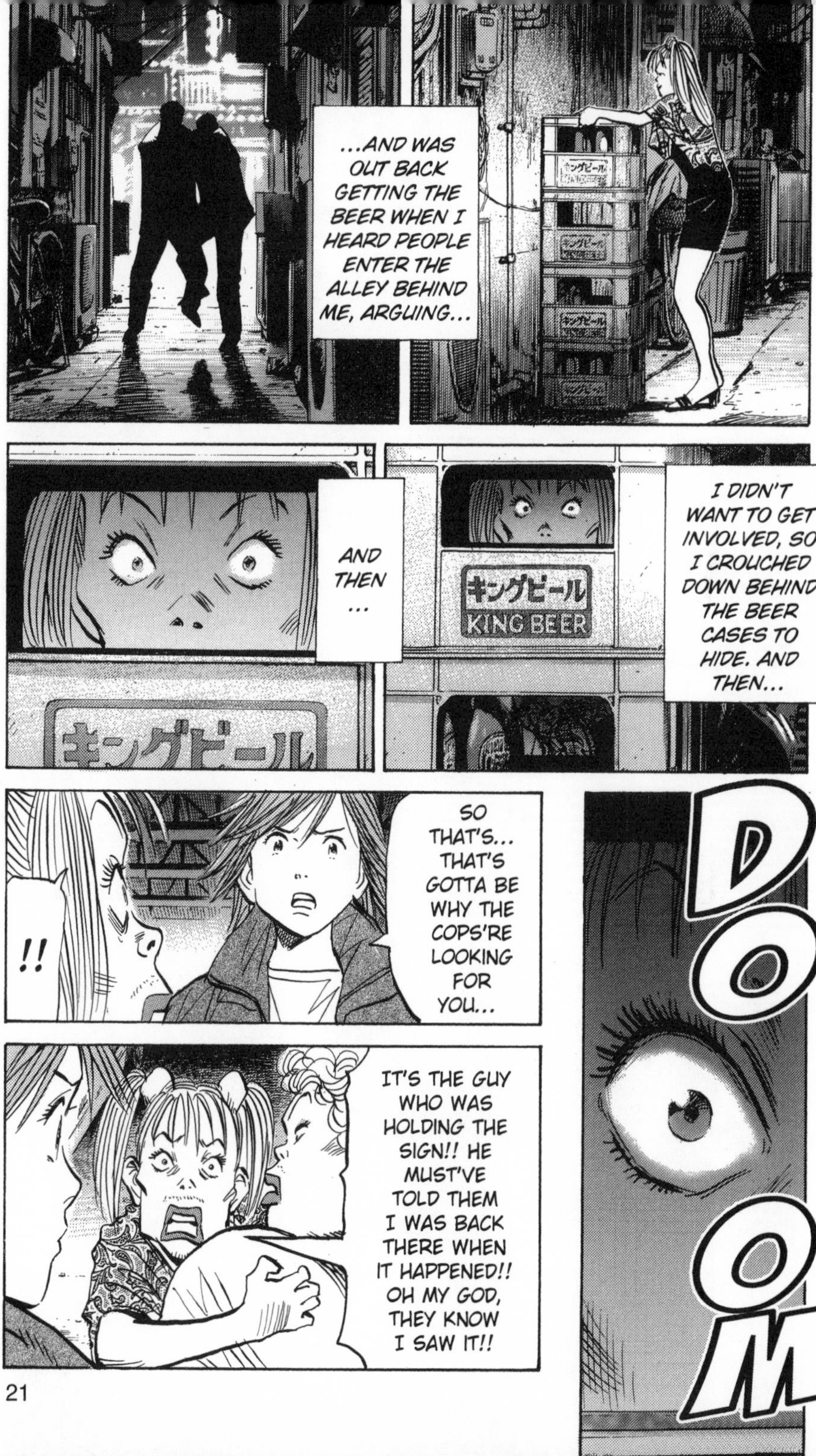
...AND WAS OUT BACK GETTING THE BEER WHEN I HEARD PEOPLE ENTER THE ALLEY BEHIND ME, ARGUING...
キングビール
I DIDN'T WANT TO GET INVOLVED, SO I CROUCHED DOWN BEHIND THE BEER CASES TO HIDE. AND THEN...
キングビール
KING BEER
AND THEN...
キングビール
DOOM
SO THAT'S... THAT'S GOTTA BE WHY THE COPS'RE LOOKING FOR YOU...
!!
IT'S THE GUY WHO WAS HOLDING THE SIGN!! HE MUST'VE TOLD THEM I WAS BACK THERE WHEN IT HAPPENED!! OH MY GOD, THEY KNOW I SAW IT!!

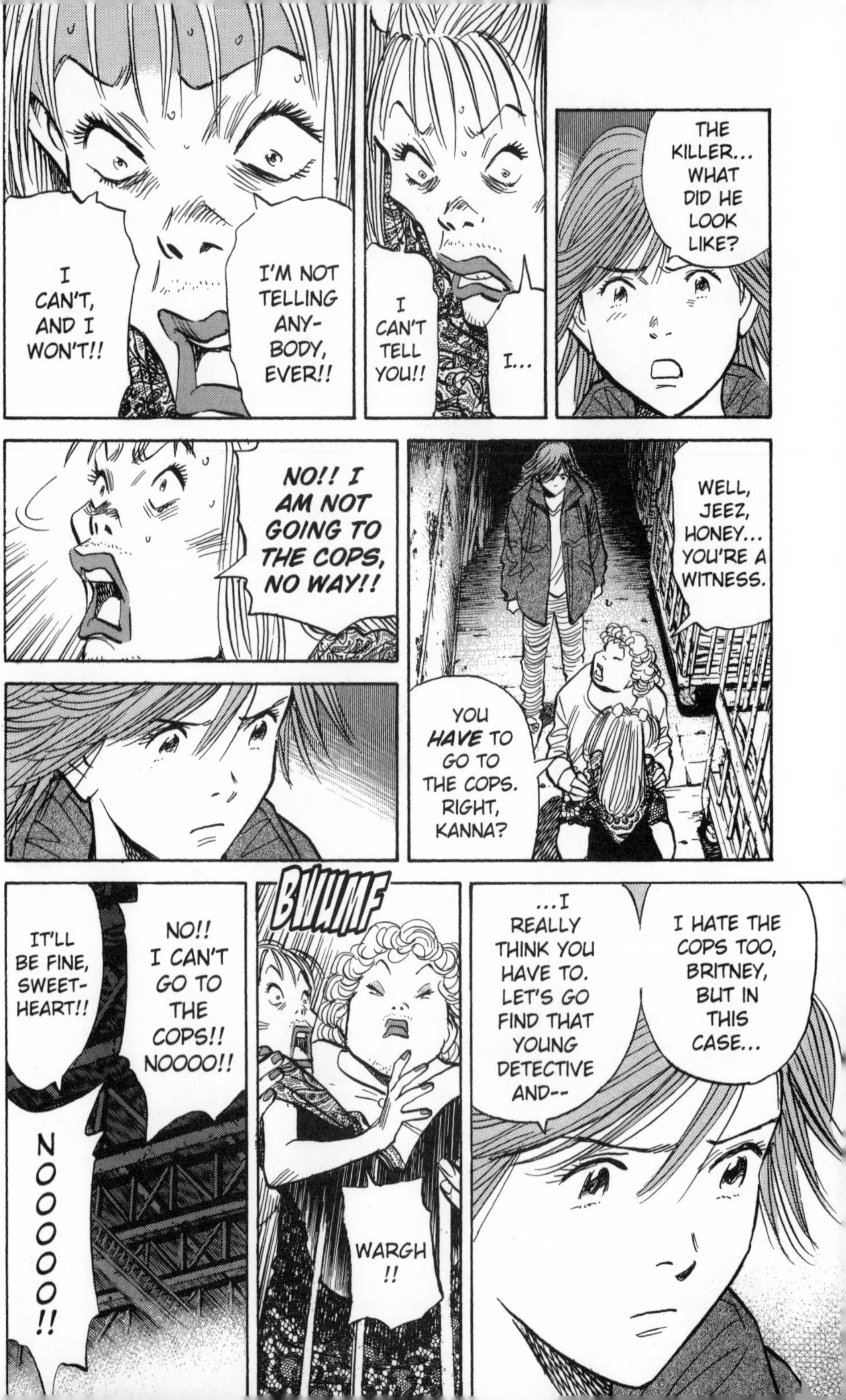
THE KILLER... WHAT DID HE LOOK LIKE?
I...
I CAN'T TELL YOU!!
I'M NOT TELLING ANY-BODY, EVER!!
I CAN'T, AND I WON'T!!
WELL, JEEZ, HONEY... YOU'RE A WITNESS.
YOU *HAVE* TO GO TO THE COPS. RIGHT, KANNA?
NO!! I AM NOT GOING TO THE COPS, NO WAY!!
I HATE THE COPS TOO, BRITNEY, BUT IN THIS CASE...
...I REALLY THINK YOU HAVE TO. LET'S GO FIND THAT YOUNG DETECTIVE AND--
BWUMF
WARGH !!
NO!! I CAN'T GO TO THE COPS!! NOOOO!!
IT'LL BE FINE, SWEET-HEART!!
NOOOOOO!!

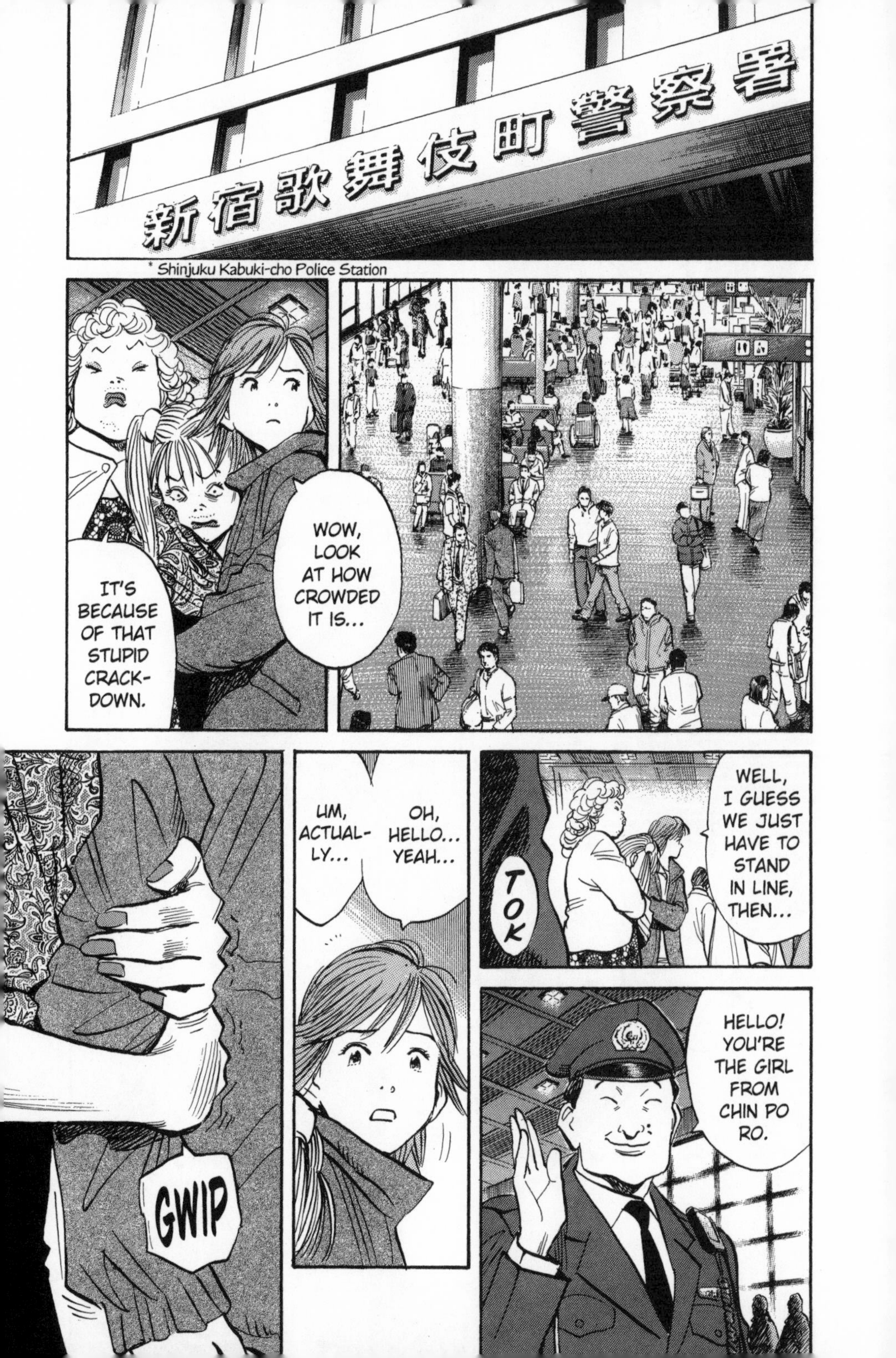
新宿歌舞伎町警察署
WOW, LOOK AT HOW CROWDED IT IS...
IT'S BECAUSE OF THAT STUPID CRACK-DOWN.
WELL, I GUESS WE JUST HAVE TO STAND IN LINE, THEN...
TOK
HELLO! YOU'RE THE GIRL FROM CHIN PO RO.
OH, HELLO... YEAH...
UM, ACTUALLY...
GWIP
* Shinjuku Kabuki-cho Police Station

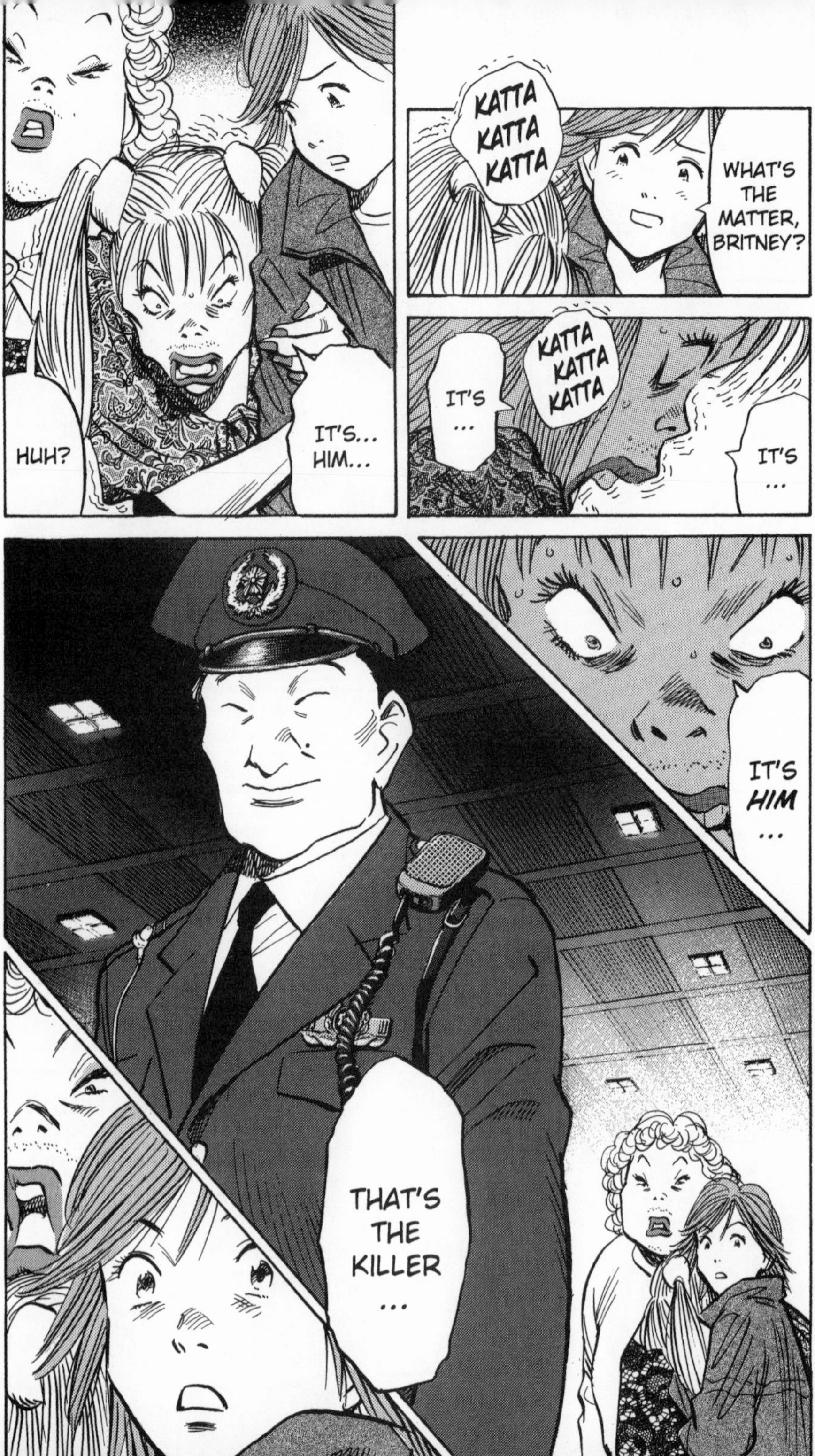
WHAT'S THE MATTER, BRITNEY?
KATTA KATTA KATTA
IT'S ...
KATTA KATTA KATTA
IT'S ...
IT'S... HIM...
HUH?
IT'S *HIM* ...
THAT'S THE KILLER ...

Chapter 2 The Killer

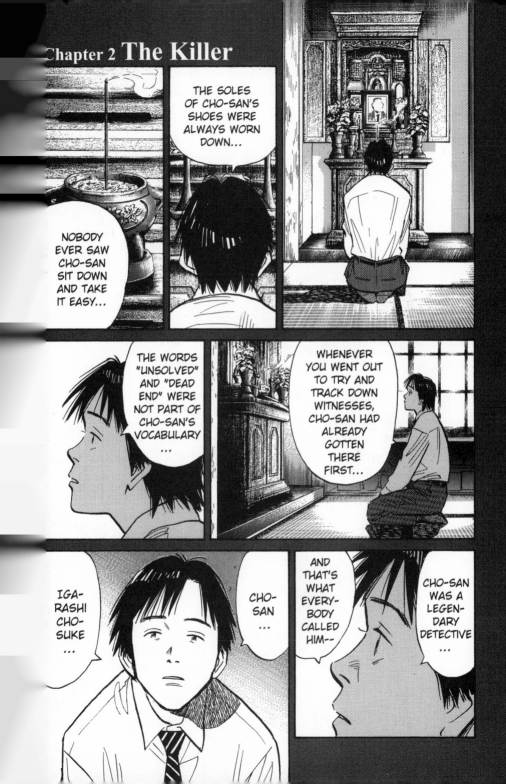

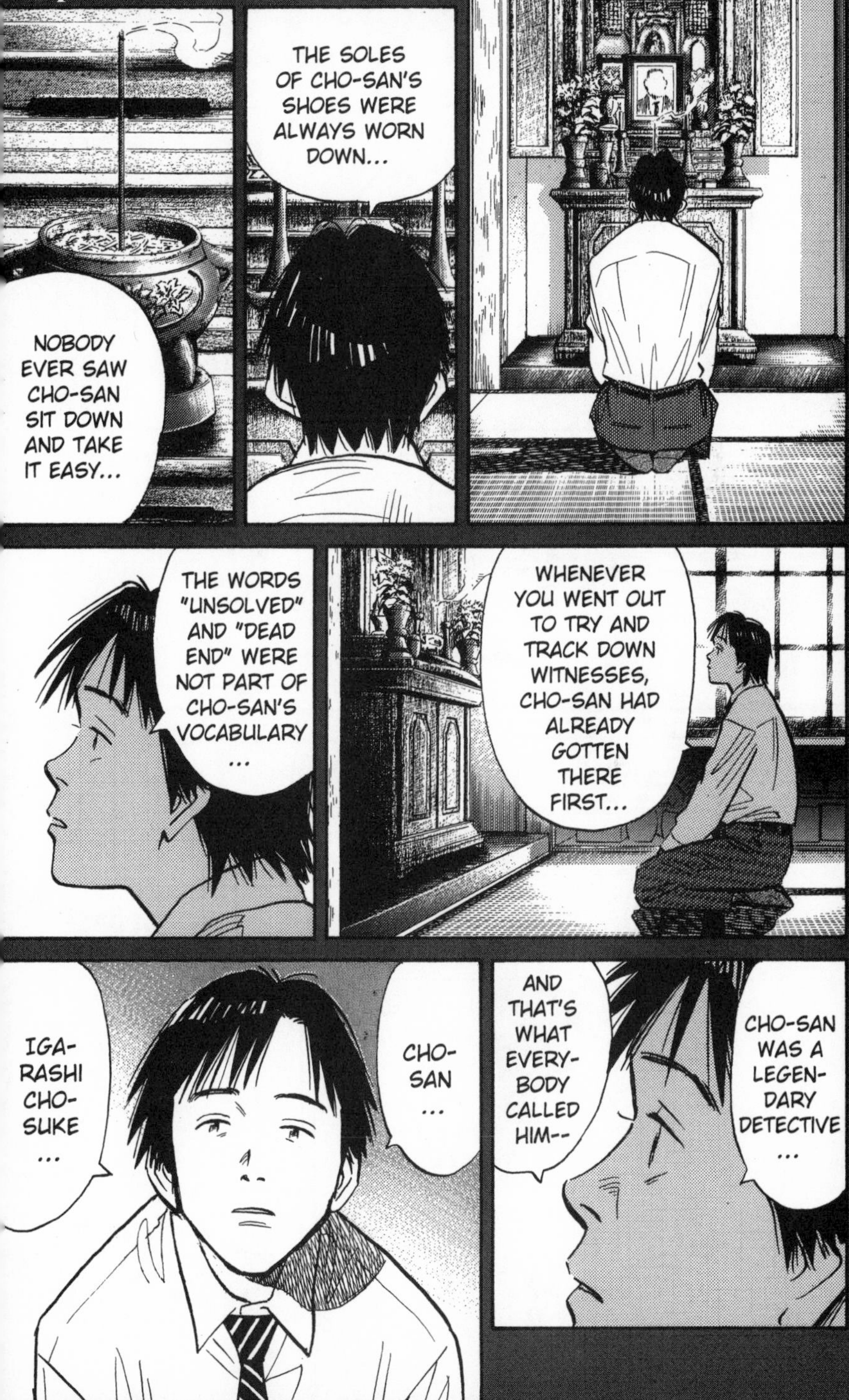
THE SOLES OF CHO-SAN'S SHOES WERE ALWAYS WORN DOWN...
NOBODY EVER SAW CHO-SAN SIT DOWN AND TAKE IT EASY...
WHENEVER YOU WENT OUT TO TRY AND TRACK DOWN WITNESSES, CHO-SAN HAD ALREADY GOTTEN THERE FIRST...
THE WORDS "UNSOLVED" AND "DEAD END" WERE NOT PART OF CHO-SAN'S VOCABULARY...
CHO-SAN WAS A LEGENDARY DETECTIVE...
AND THAT'S WHAT EVERYBODY CALLED HIM--
CHO-SAN...
IGARASHI CHOSUKE...

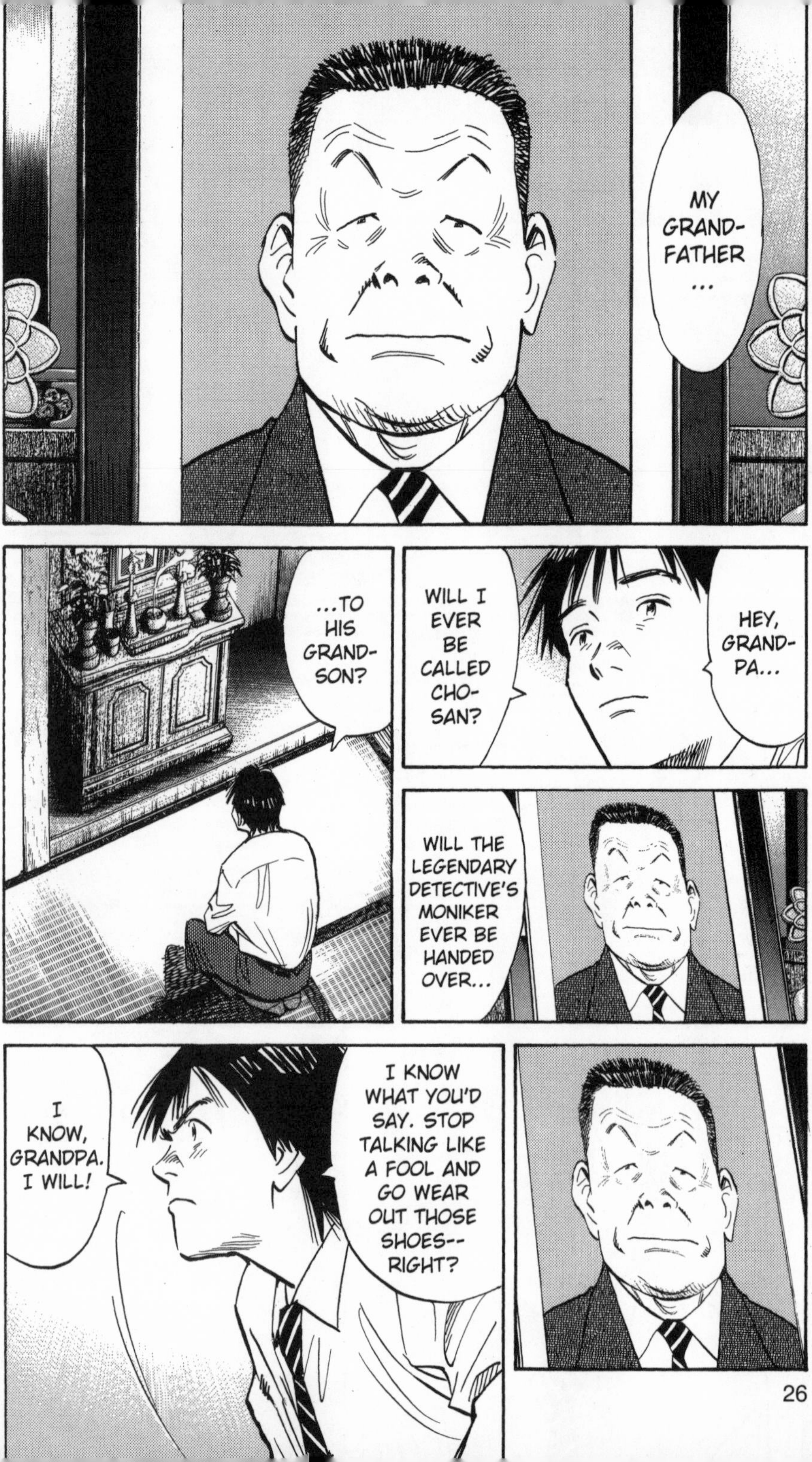

MY GRAND-FATHER...
HEY, GRAND-PA...
WILL I EVER BE CALLED CHO-SAN?
WILL THE LEGENDARY DETECTIVE'S MONIKER EVER BE HANDED OVER...
...TO HIS GRAND-SON?
I KNOW WHAT YOU'D SAY. STOP TALKING LIKE A FOOL AND GO WEAR OUT THOSE SHOES--RIGHT?
I KNOW, GRANDPA. I WILL!

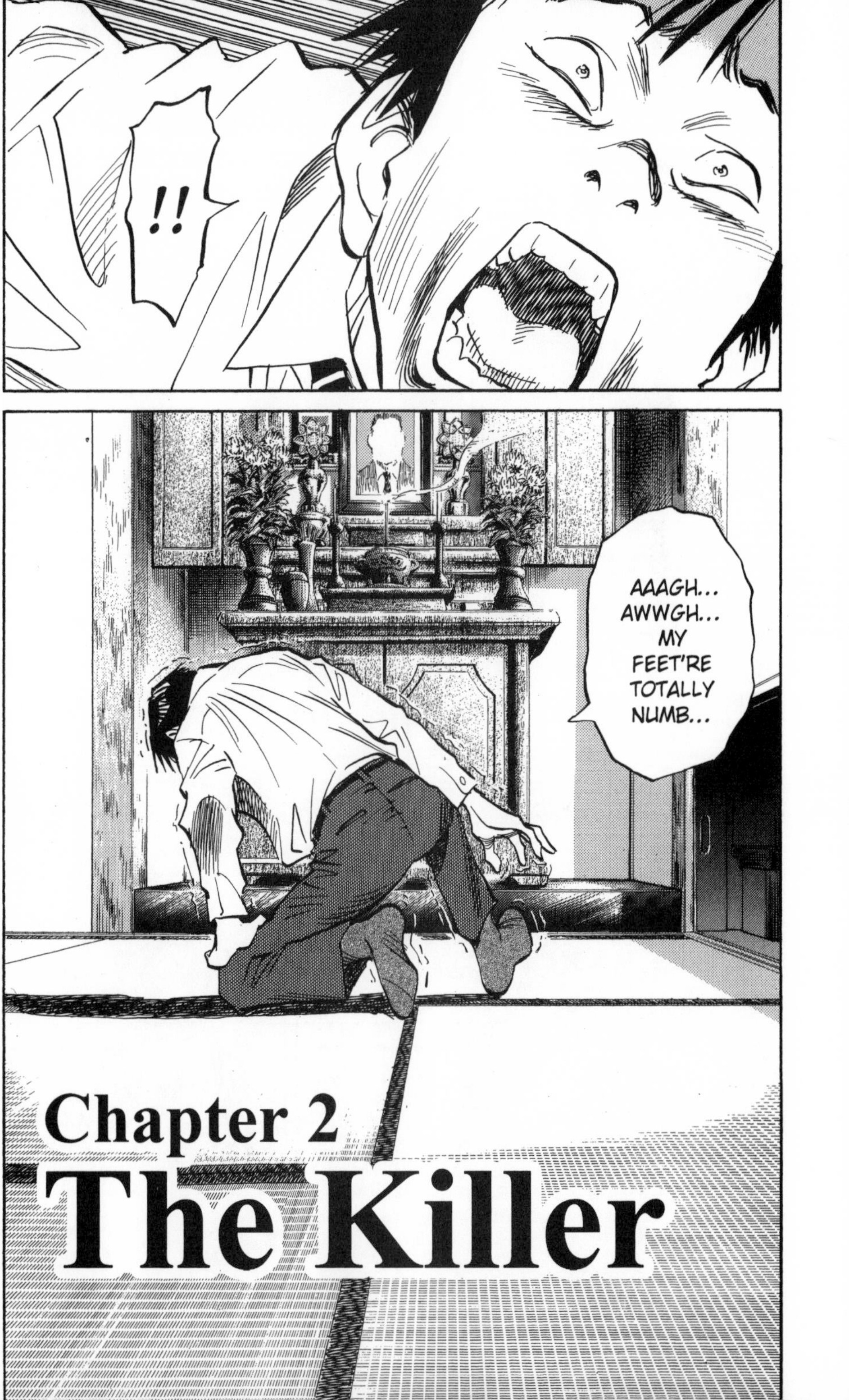
!!
AAAGH... AWWGH... MY FEET'RE TOTALLY NUMB...
Chapter 2
The Killer

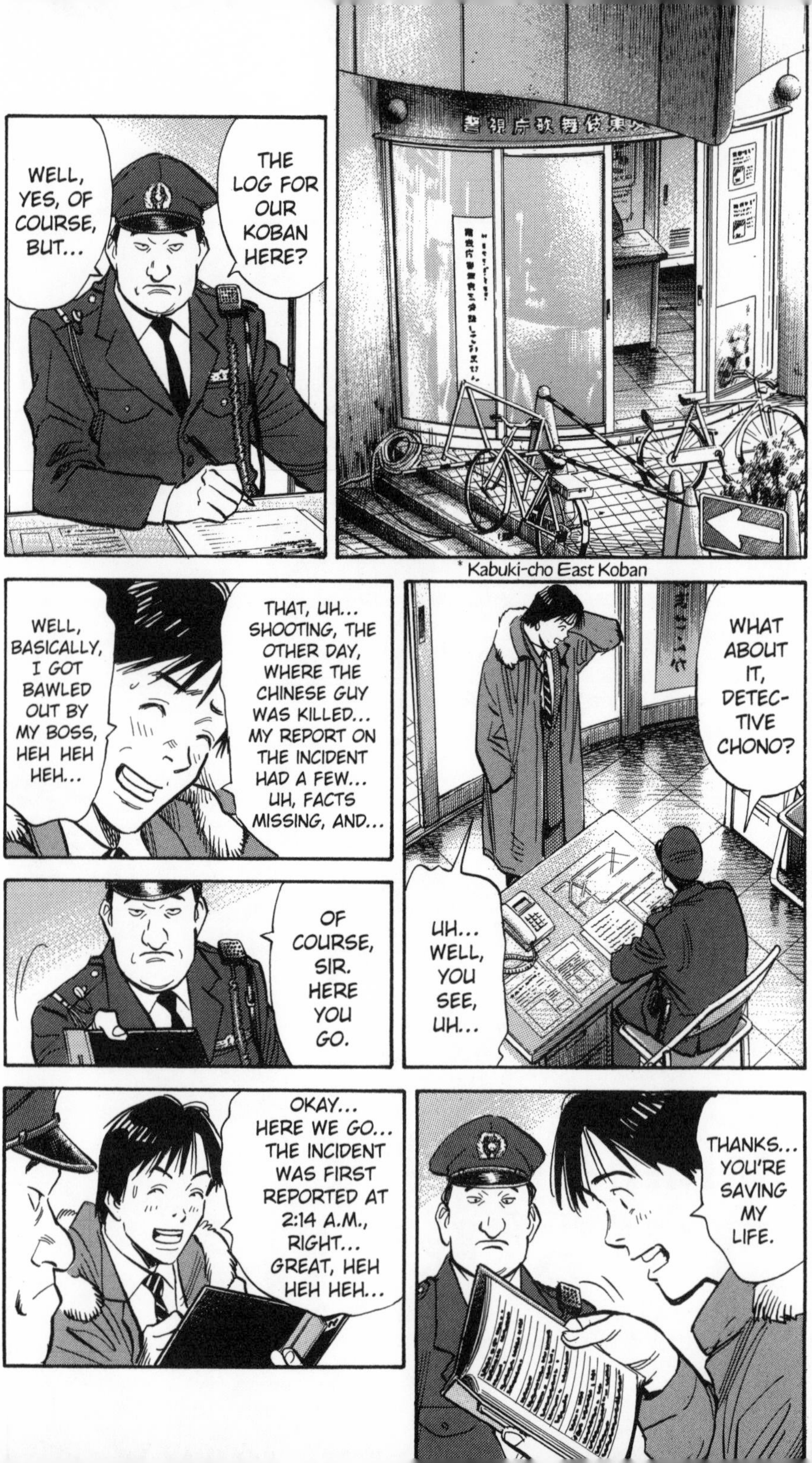

* Kabuki-cho East Koban
THE LOG FOR OUR KOBAN HERE?
WELL, YES, OF COURSE, BUT...
WHAT ABOUT IT, DETECTIVE CHONO?
UH... WELL, YOU SEE, UH...
THAT, UH... SHOOTING, THE OTHER DAY, WHERE THE CHINESE GUY WAS KILLED... MY REPORT ON THE INCIDENT HAD A FEW... UH, FACTS MISSING, AND...
WELL, BASICALLY, I GOT BAWLED OUT BY MY BOSS, HEH HEH HEH...
OF COURSE, SIR. HERE YOU GO.
THANKS... YOU'RE SAVING MY LIFE.
OKAY... HERE WE GO... THE INCIDENT WAS FIRST REPORTED AT 2:14 A.M., RIGHT... GREAT, HEH HEH HEH...

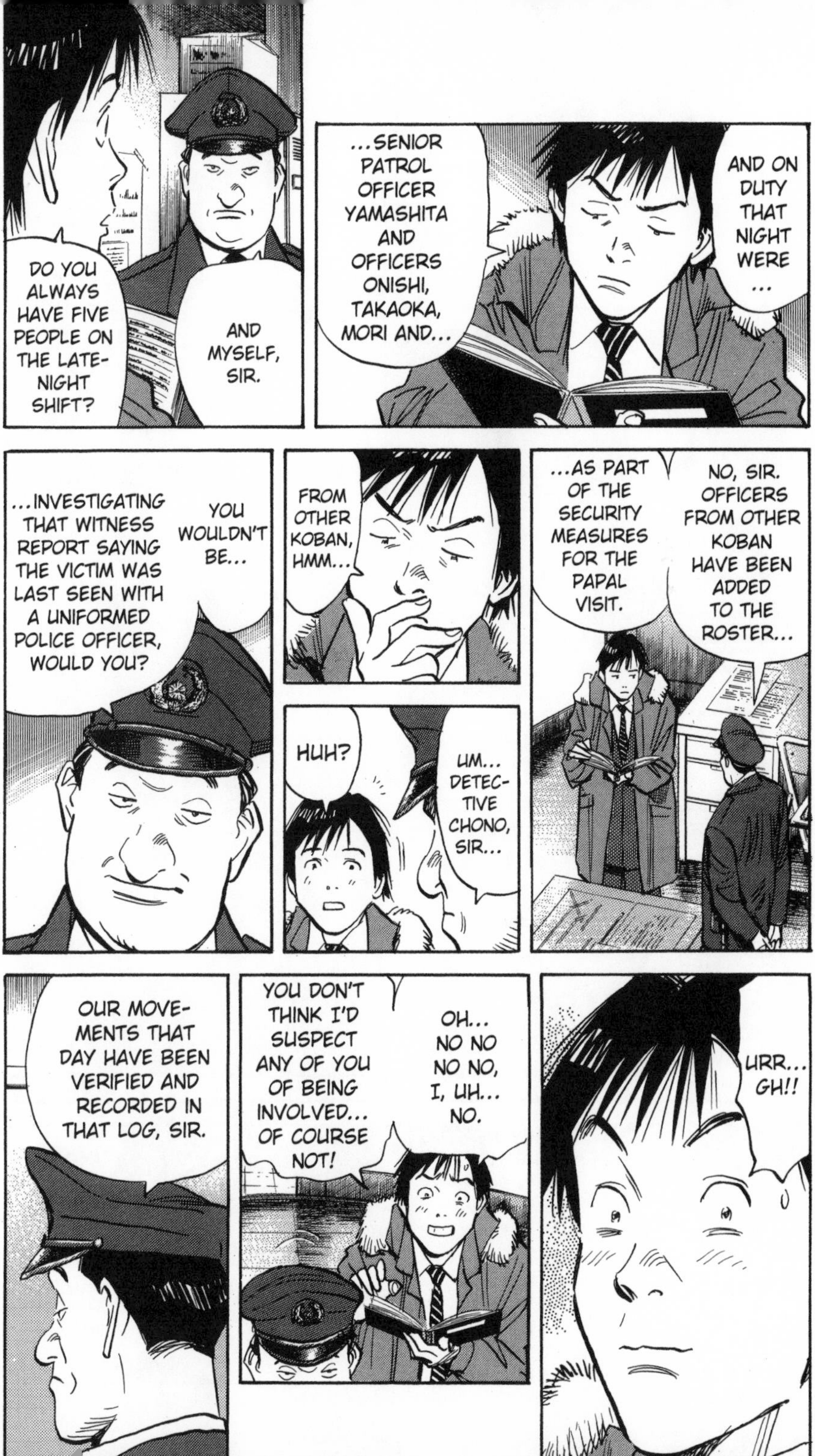
AND ON DUTY THAT NIGHT WERE...
...SENIOR PATROL OFFICER YAMASHITA AND OFFICERS ONISHI, TAKAOKA, MORI AND...
AND MYSELF, SIR.
DO YOU ALWAYS HAVE FIVE PEOPLE ON THE LATE-NIGHT SHIFT?
NO, SIR. OFFICERS FROM OTHER KOBAN HAVE BEEN ADDED TO THE ROSTER...
...AS PART OF THE SECURITY MEASURES FOR THE PAPAL VISIT.
FROM OTHER KOBAN, HMM...
UM... DETECTIVE CHONO, SIR...
HUH?
YOU WOULDN'T BE...
...INVESTIGATING THAT WITNESS REPORT SAYING THE VICTIM WAS LAST SEEN WITH A UNIFORMED POLICE OFFICER, WOULD YOU?
URR...GH!!
OH... NO NO NO NO, I, UH... NO.
YOU DON'T THINK I'D SUSPECT ANY OF YOU OF BEING INVOLVED... OF COURSE NOT!
OUR MOVEMENTS THAT DAY HAVE BEEN VERIFIED AND RECORDED IN THAT LOG, SIR.

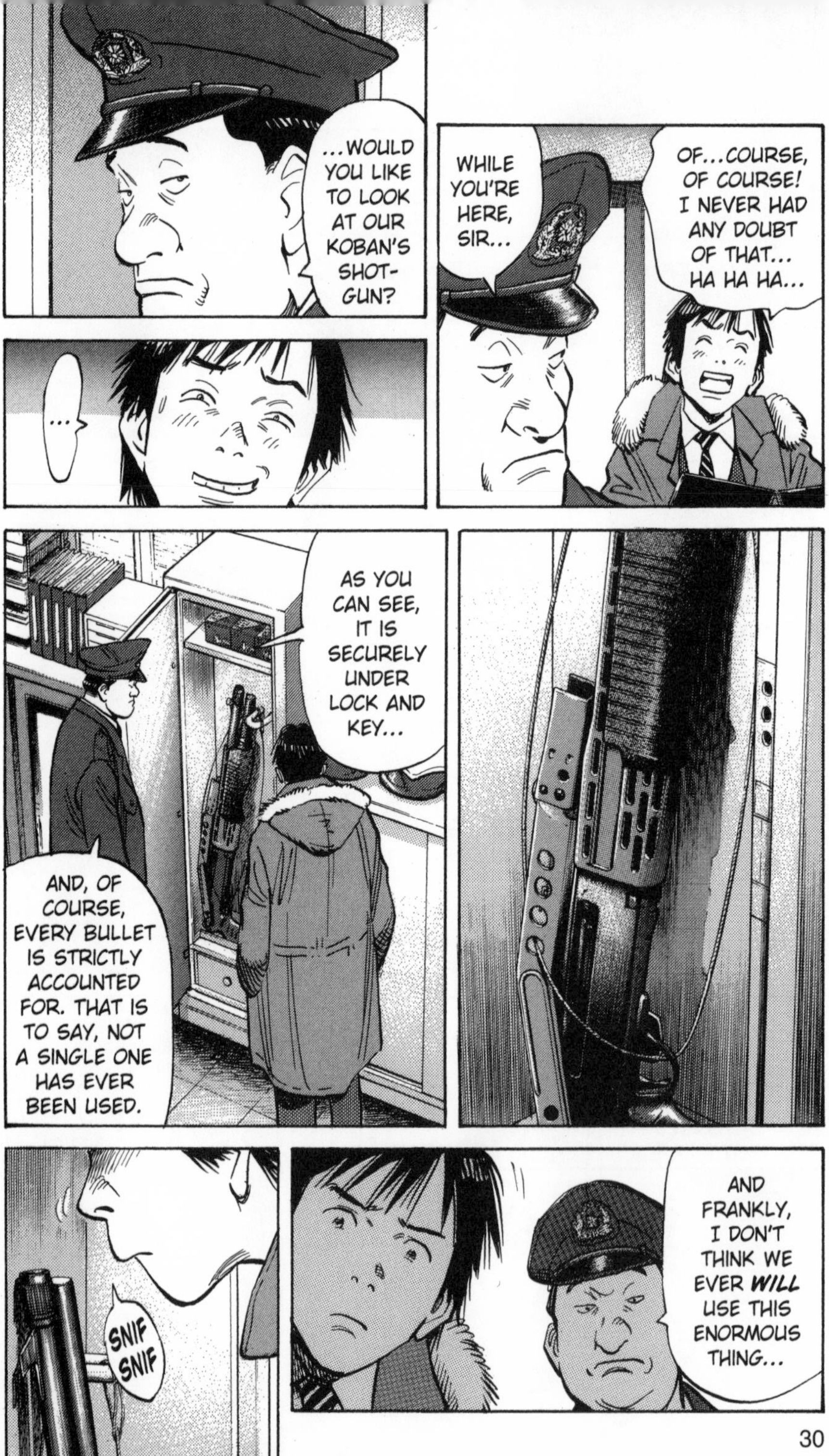

OF...COURSE, OF COURSE! I NEVER HAD ANY DOUBT OF THAT... HA HA HA...
WHILE YOU'RE HERE, SIR...
...WOULD YOU LIKE TO LOOK AT OUR KOBAN'S SHOT-GUN?
...
AS YOU CAN SEE, IT IS SECURELY UNDER LOCK AND KEY...
AND, OF COURSE, EVERY BULLET IS STRICTLY ACCOUNTED FOR. THAT IS TO SAY, NOT A SINGLE ONE HAS EVER BEEN USED.
AND FRANKLY, I DON'T THINK WE EVER *WILL* USE THIS ENORMOUS THING...
SNIF SNIF

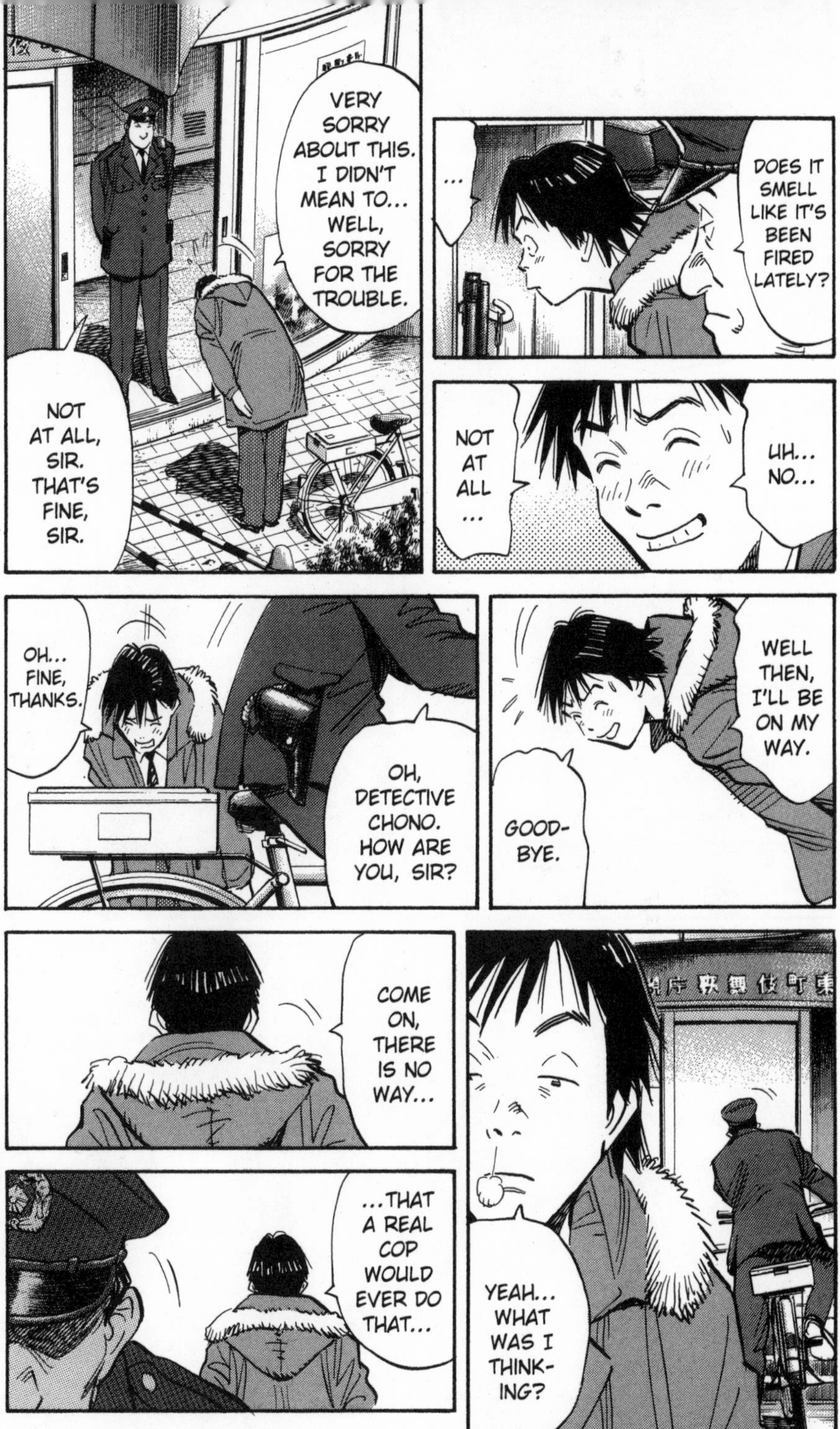
DOES IT SMELL LIKE IT'S BEEN FIRED LATELY?
...
UH... NO...
NOT AT ALL ...
VERY SORRY ABOUT THIS. I DIDN'T MEAN TO... WELL, SORRY FOR THE TROUBLE.
NOT AT ALL, SIR. THAT'S FINE, SIR.
WELL THEN, I'LL BE ON MY WAY.
GOOD-BYE.
OH, DETECTIVE CHONO. HOW ARE YOU, SIR?
OH... FINE, THANKS.
YEAH... WHAT WAS I THINK-ING?
COME ON, THERE IS NO WAY...
...THAT A REAL COP WOULD EVER DO THAT...

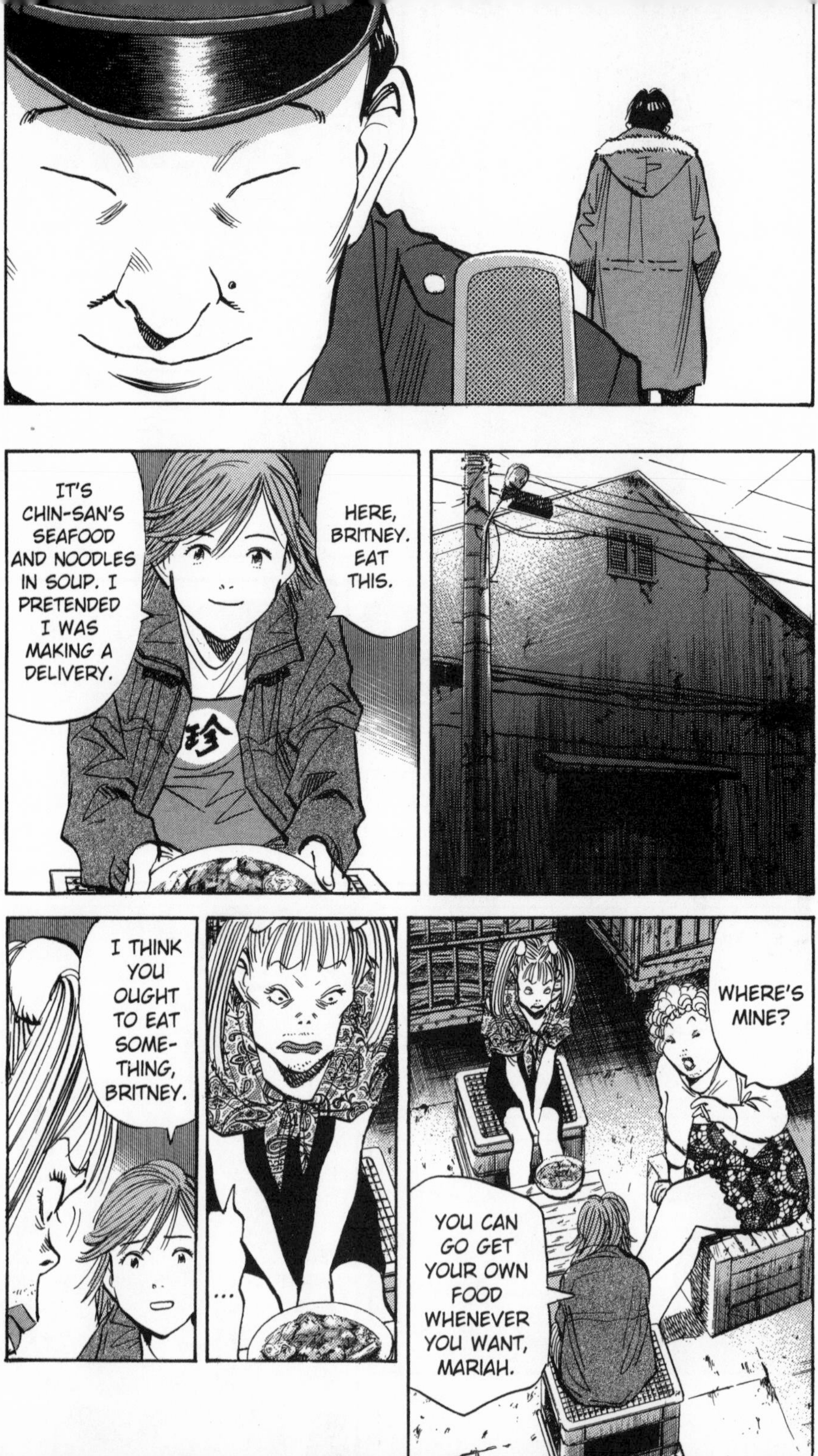
HERE, BRITNEY. EAT THIS.
IT'S CHIN-SAN'S SEAFOOD AND NOODLES IN SOUP. I PRETENDED I WAS MAKING A DELIVERY.
WHERE'S MINE?
YOU CAN GO GET YOUR OWN FOOD WHENEVER YOU WANT, MARIAH.
...
I THINK YOU OUGHT TO EAT SOMETHING, BRITNEY.

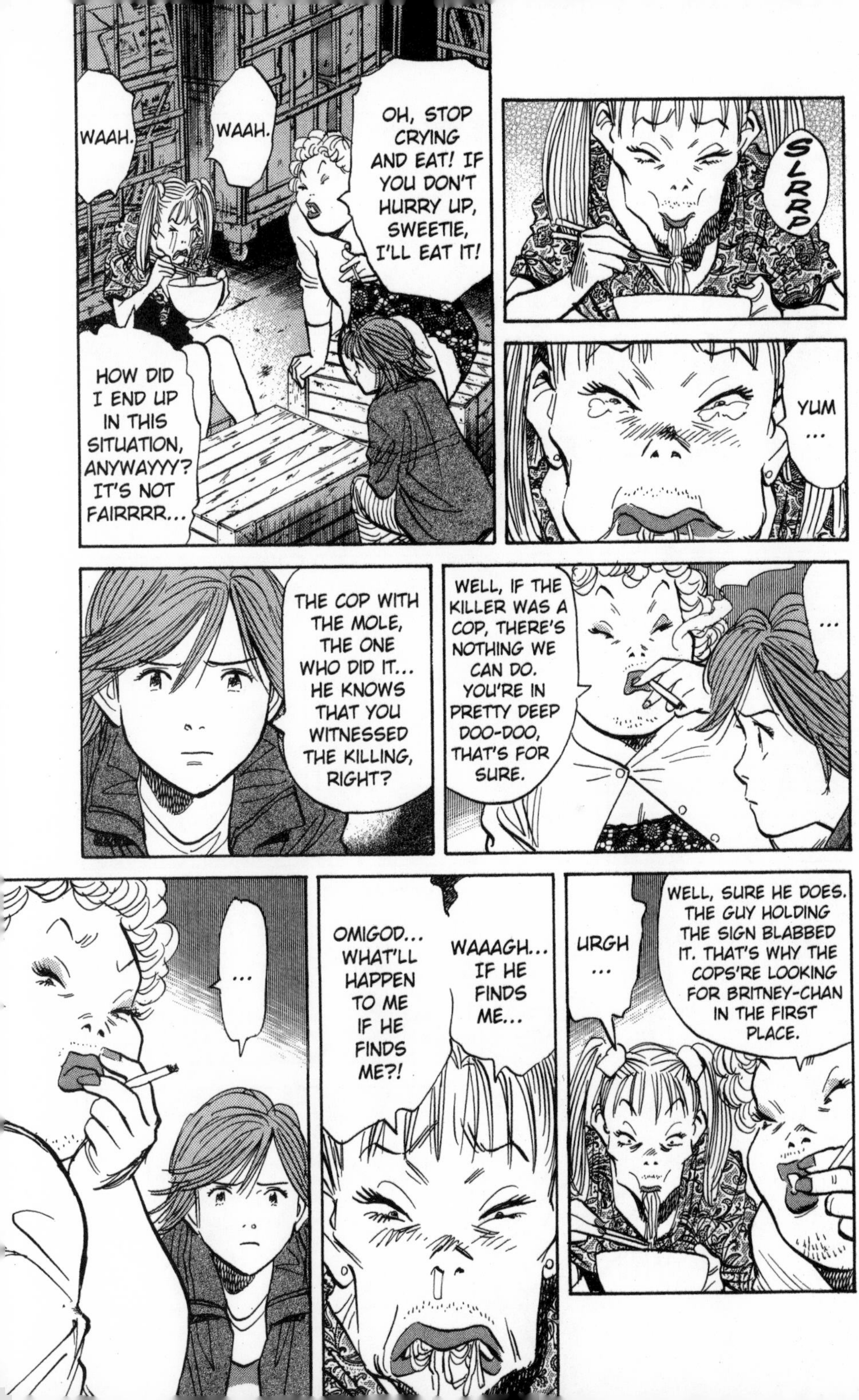
SLRRP
YUM ...
OH, STOP CRYING AND EAT! IF YOU DON'T HURRY UP, SWEETIE, I'LL EAT IT!
WAAH.
WAAH.
HOW DID I END UP IN THIS SITUATION, ANYWAYYY? IT'S NOT FAIRRRR...
...
WELL, IF THE KILLER WAS A COP, THERE'S NOTHING WE CAN DO. YOU'RE IN PRETTY DEEP DOO-DOO, THAT'S FOR SURE.
THE COP WITH THE MOLE, THE ONE WHO DID IT... HE KNOWS THAT YOU WITNESSED THE KILLING, RIGHT?
WELL, SURE HE DOES. THE GUY HOLDING THE SIGN BLABBED IT. THAT'S WHY THE COPS'RE LOOKING FOR BRITNEY-CHAN IN THE FIRST PLACE.
URGH ...
WAAAGH... IF HE FINDS ME...
OMIGOD... WHAT'LL HAPPEN TO ME IF HE FINDS ME?!
...

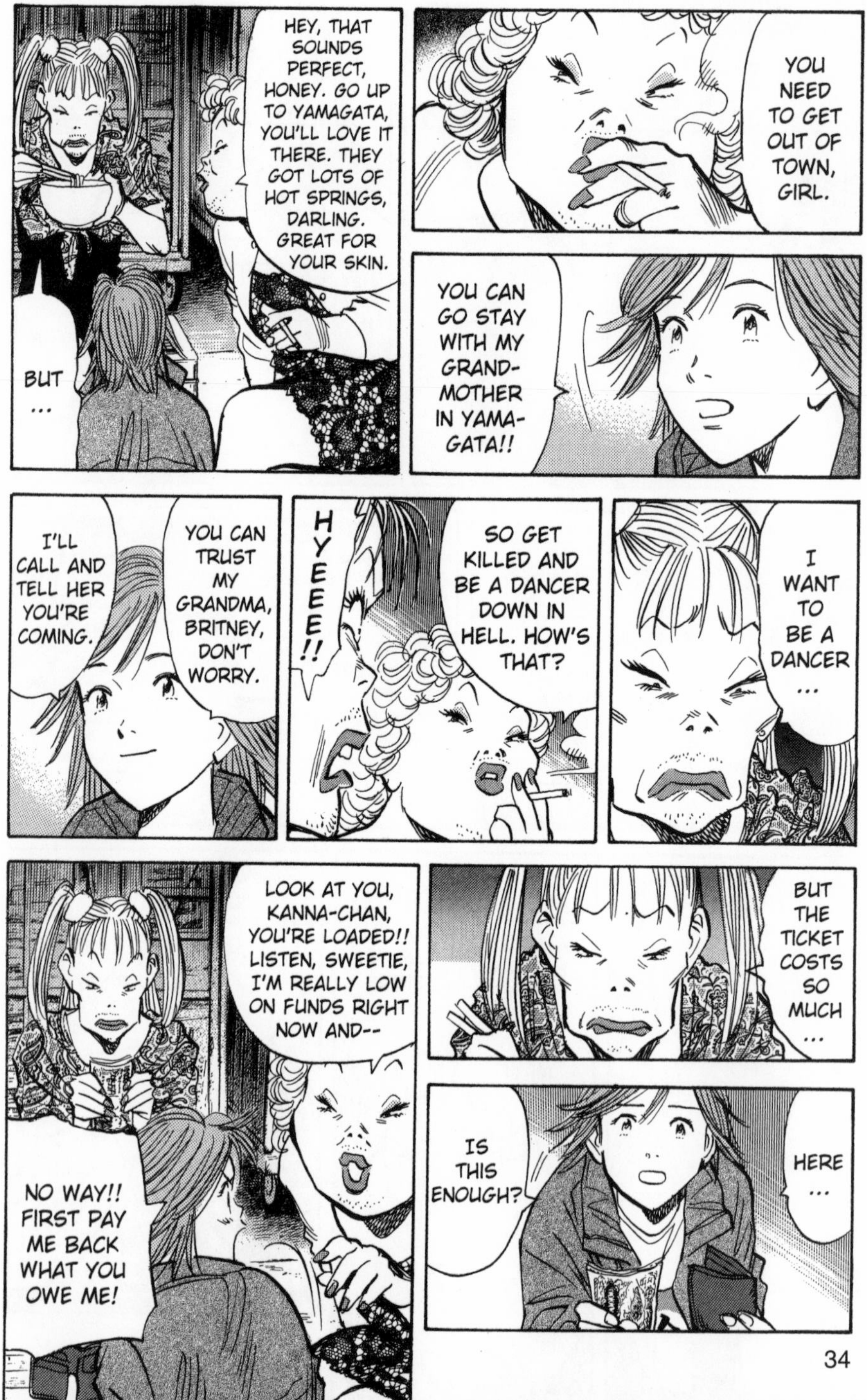
YOU NEED TO GET OUT OF TOWN, GIRL.
YOU CAN GO STAY WITH MY GRAND-MOTHER IN YAMA-GATA!!
HEY, THAT SOUNDS PERFECT, HONEY. GO UP TO YAMAGATA, YOU'LL LOVE IT THERE. THEY GOT LOTS OF HOT SPRINGS, DARLING. GREAT FOR YOUR SKIN.
BUT ...
I WANT TO BE A DANCER ...
SO GET KILLED AND BE A DANCER DOWN IN HELL. HOW'S THAT?
HYEEEE!!
YOU CAN TRUST MY GRANDMA, BRITNEY, DON'T WORRY.
I'LL CALL AND TELL HER YOU'RE COMING.
BUT THE TICKET COSTS SO MUCH ...
HERE ...
IS THIS ENOUGH?
LOOK AT YOU, KANNA-CHAN, YOU'RE LOADED!! LISTEN, SWEETIE, I'M REALLY LOW ON FUNDS RIGHT NOW AND--
NO WAY!! FIRST PAY ME BACK WHAT YOU OWE ME!

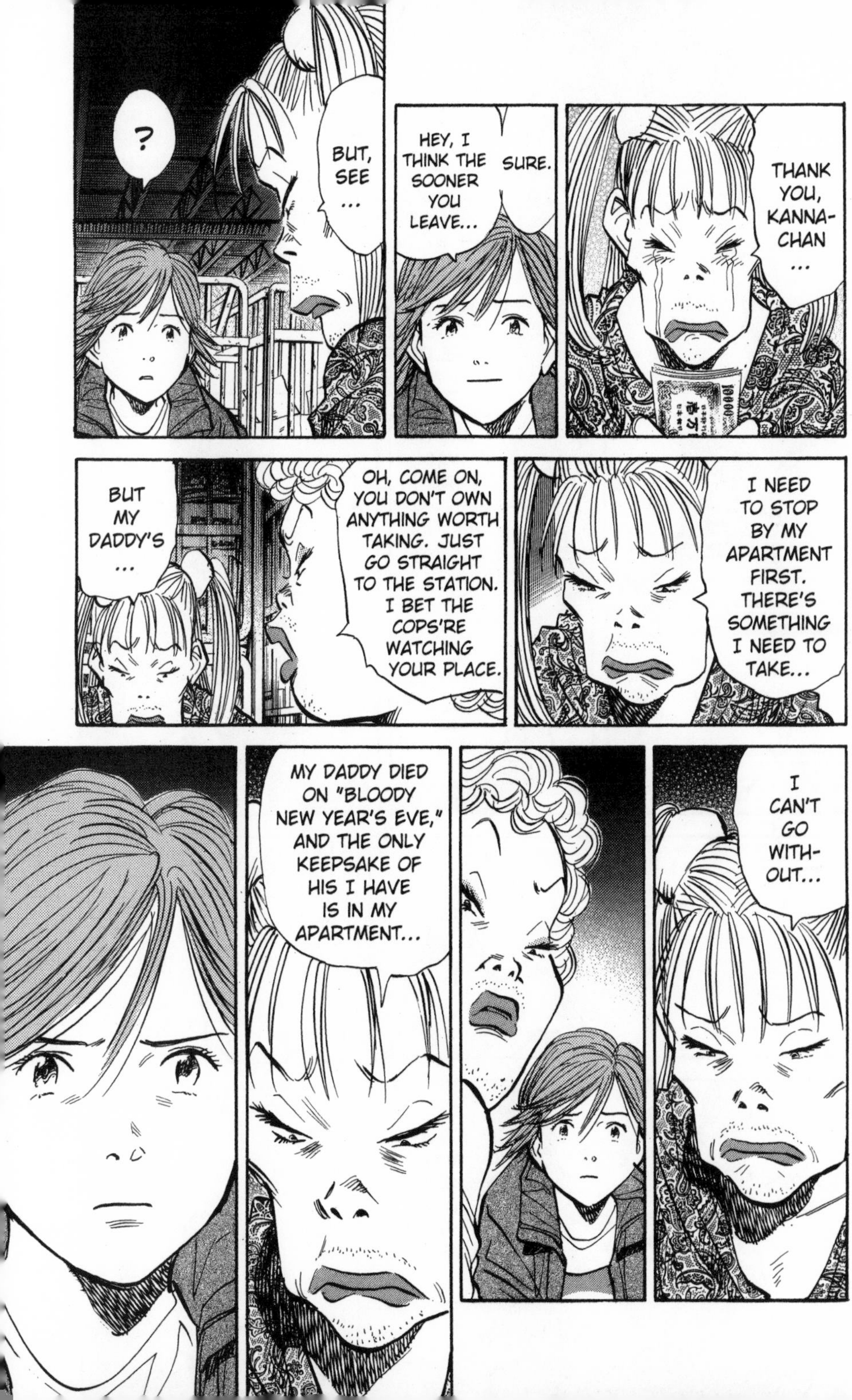
THANK YOU, KANNA-CHAN...
SURE.
HEY, I THINK THE SOONER YOU LEAVE...
BUT, SEE...
?
I NEED TO STOP BY MY APARTMENT FIRST. THERE'S SOMETHING I NEED TO TAKE...
OH, COME ON, YOU DON'T OWN ANYTHING WORTH TAKING. JUST GO STRAIGHT TO THE STATION. I BET THE COPS'RE WATCHING YOUR PLACE.
BUT MY DADDY'S...
I CAN'T GO WITH-OUT...
MY DADDY DIED ON "BLOODY NEW YEAR'S EVE," AND THE ONLY KEEPSAKE OF HIS I HAVE IS IN MY APARTMENT...

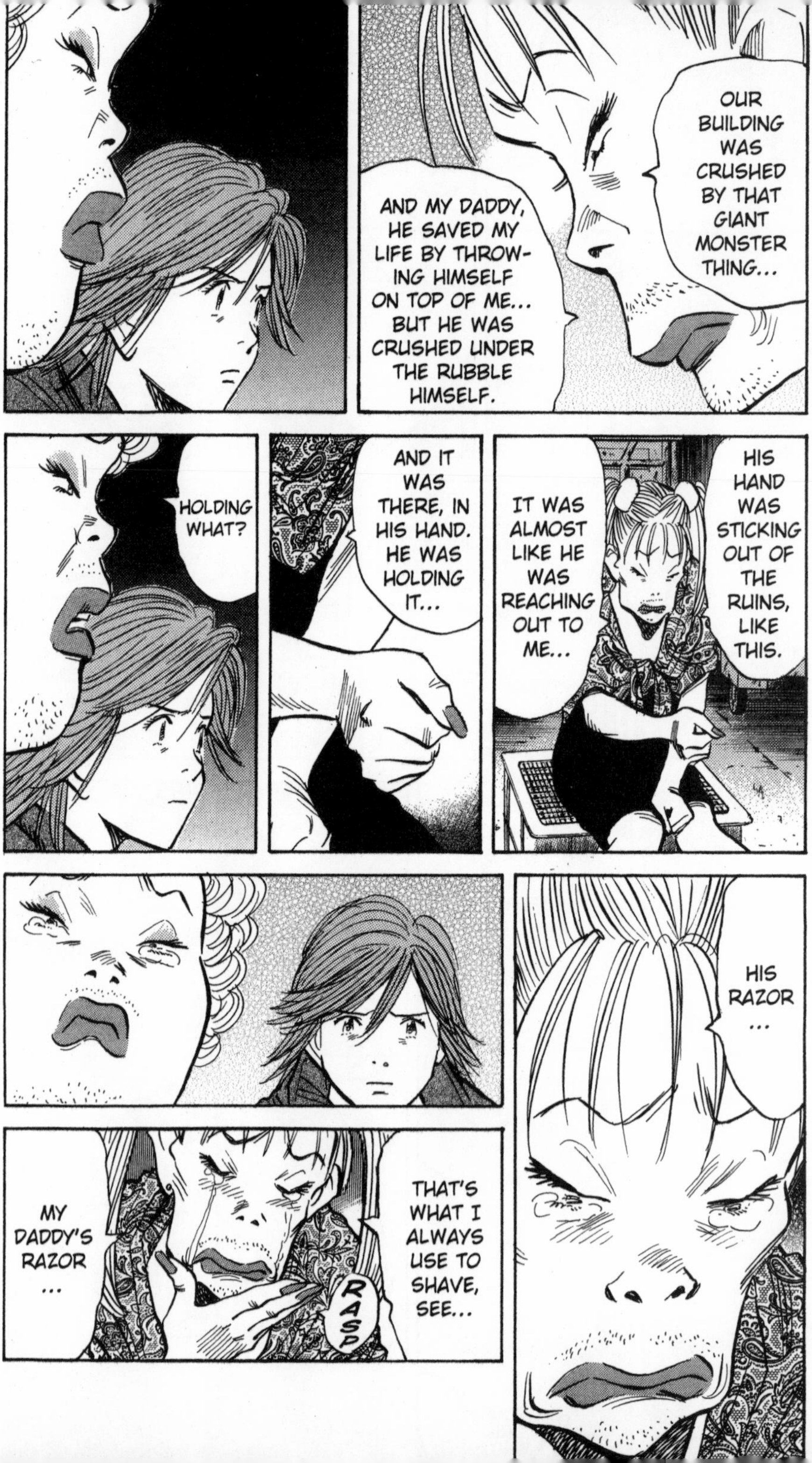
OUR BUILDING WAS CRUSHED BY THAT GIANT MONSTER THING...
AND MY DADDY, HE SAVED MY LIFE BY THROWING HIMSELF ON TOP OF ME... BUT HE WAS CRUSHED UNDER THE RUBBLE HIMSELF.
HIS HAND WAS STICKING OUT OF THE RUINS, LIKE THIS.
IT WAS ALMOST LIKE HE WAS REACHING OUT TO ME...
AND IT WAS THERE, IN HIS HAND. HE WAS HOLDING IT...
HOLDING WHAT?
HIS RAZOR ...
THAT'S WHAT I ALWAYS USE TO SHAVE, SEE...
RASP
MY DADDY'S RAZOR ...

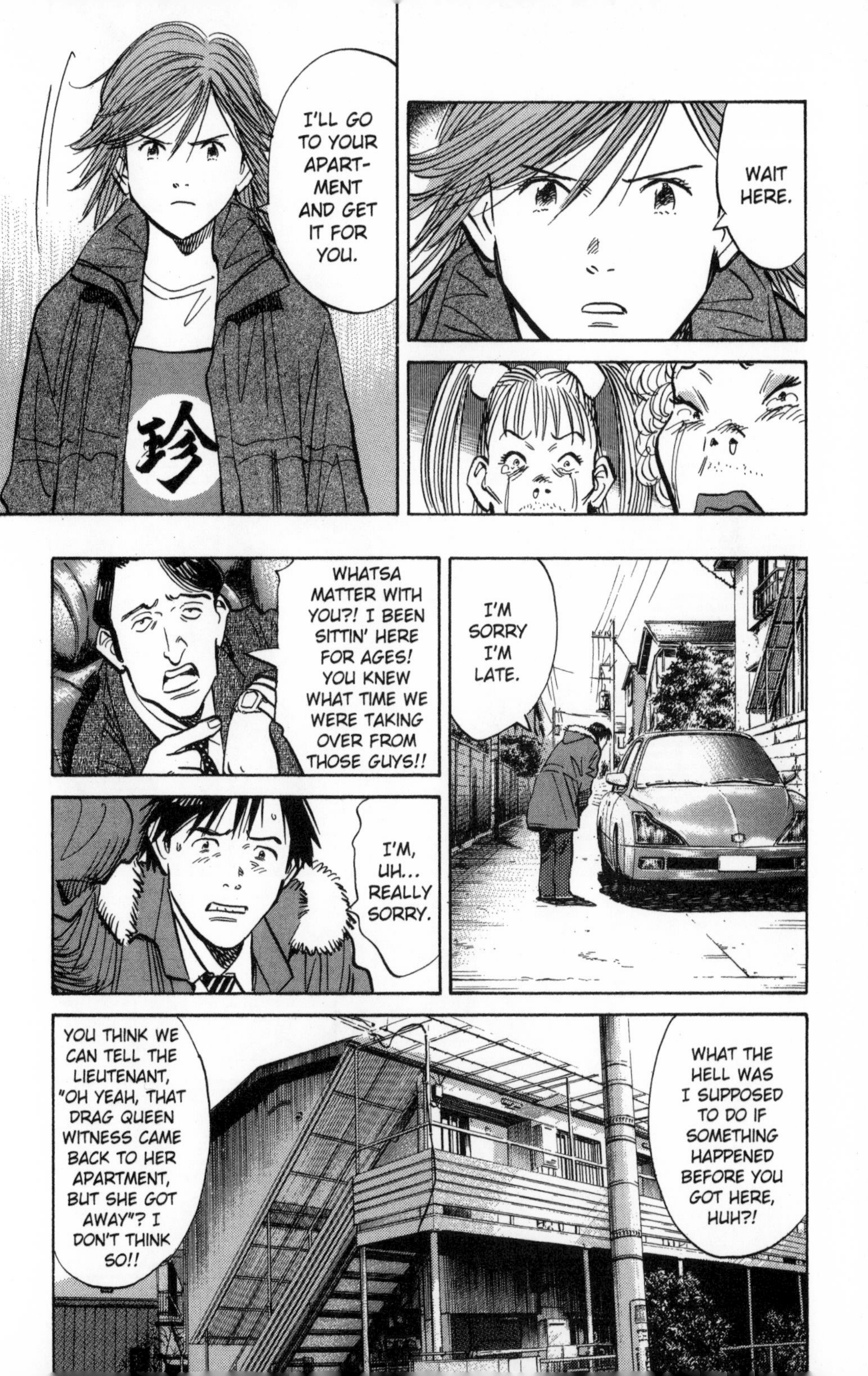
WAIT HERE.
I'LL GO TO YOUR APARTMENT AND GET IT FOR YOU.
I'M SORRY I'M LATE.
WHATSA MATTER WITH YOU?! I BEEN SITTIN' HERE FOR AGES! YOU KNEW WHAT TIME WE WERE TAKING OVER FROM THOSE GUYS!!
I'M, UH... REALLY SORRY.
WHAT THE HELL WAS I SUPPOSED TO DO IF SOMETHING HAPPENED BEFORE YOU GOT HERE, HUH?!
YOU THINK WE CAN TELL THE LIEUTENANT, "OH YEAH, THAT DRAG QUEEN WITNESS CAME BACK TO HER APARTMENT, BUT SHE GOT AWAY"? I DON'T THINK SO!!

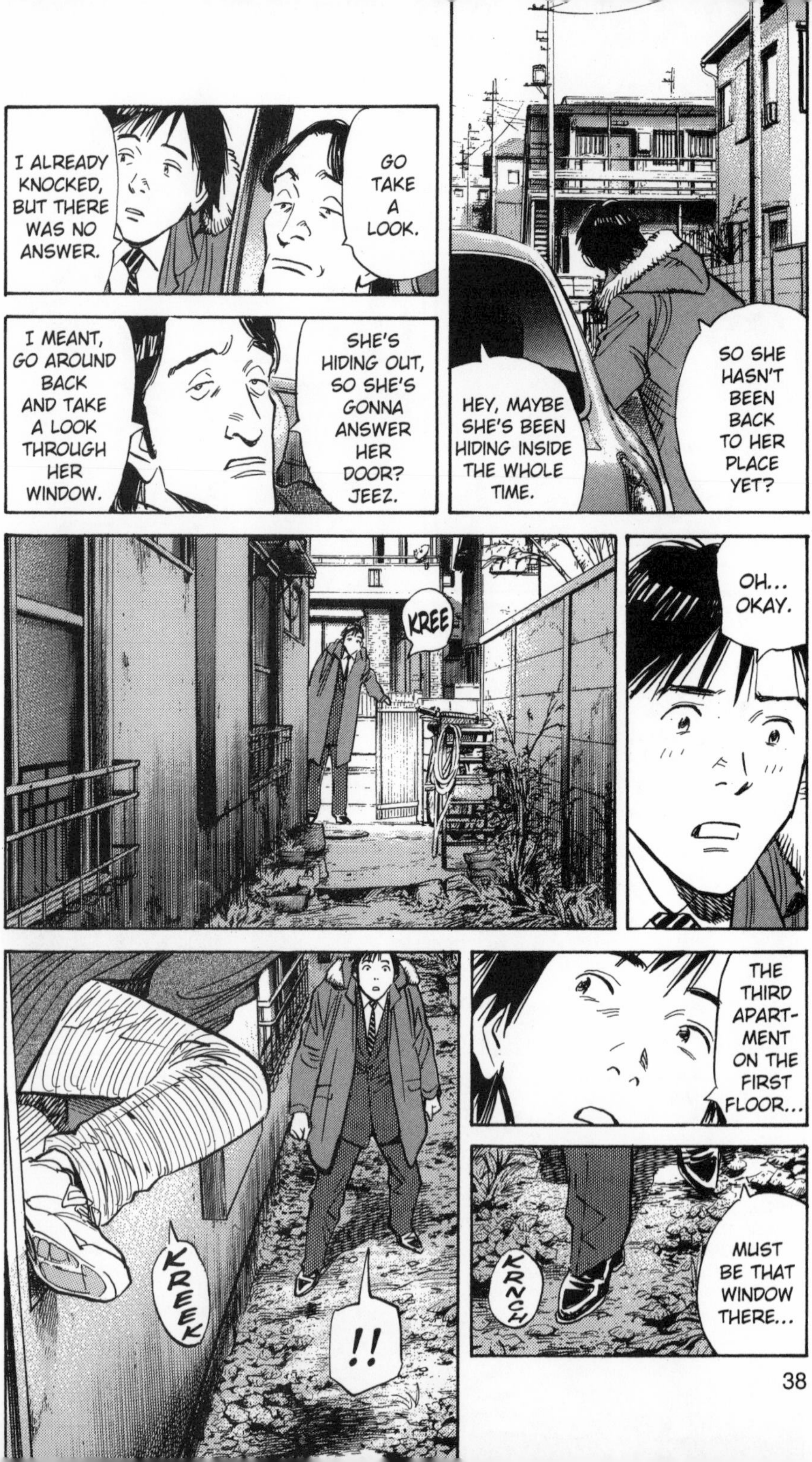
SO SHE HASN'T BEEN BACK TO HER PLACE YET?
HEY, MAYBE SHE'S BEEN HIDING INSIDE THE WHOLE TIME.
GO TAKE A LOOK.
I ALREADY KNOCKED, BUT THERE WAS NO ANSWER.
SHE'S HIDING OUT, SO SHE'S GONNA ANSWER HER DOOR? JEEZ.
I MEANT, GO AROUND BACK AND TAKE A LOOK THROUGH HER WINDOW.
OH... OKAY.
KREE
THE THIRD APART-MENT ON THE FIRST FLOOR...
KRNCH
MUST BE THAT WINDOW THERE...
KREEK
!!

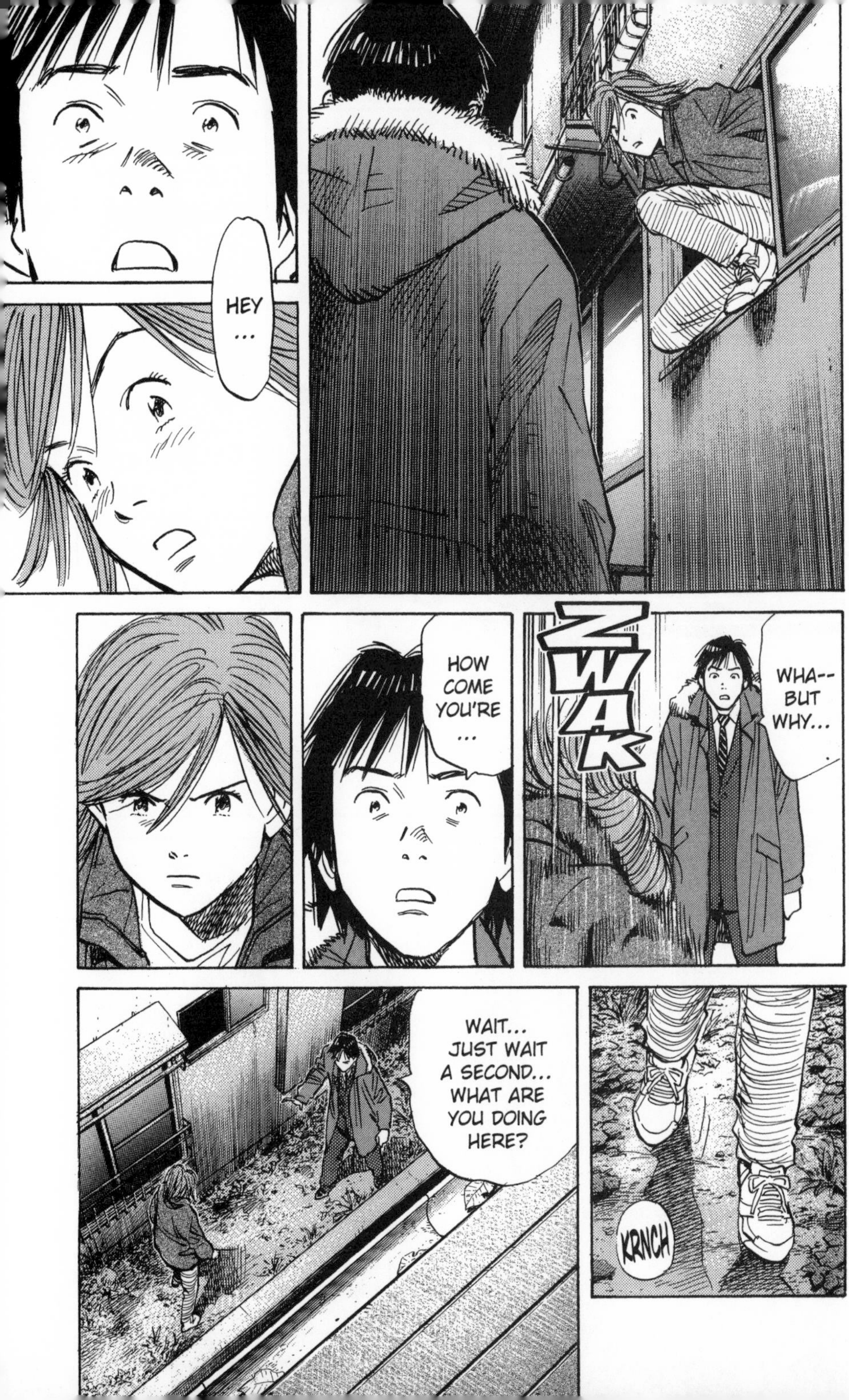
HEY ...
ZWAK
WHA-- BUT WHY...
HOW COME YOU'RE ...
KRNCH
WAIT... JUST WAIT A SECOND... WHAT ARE YOU DOING HERE?

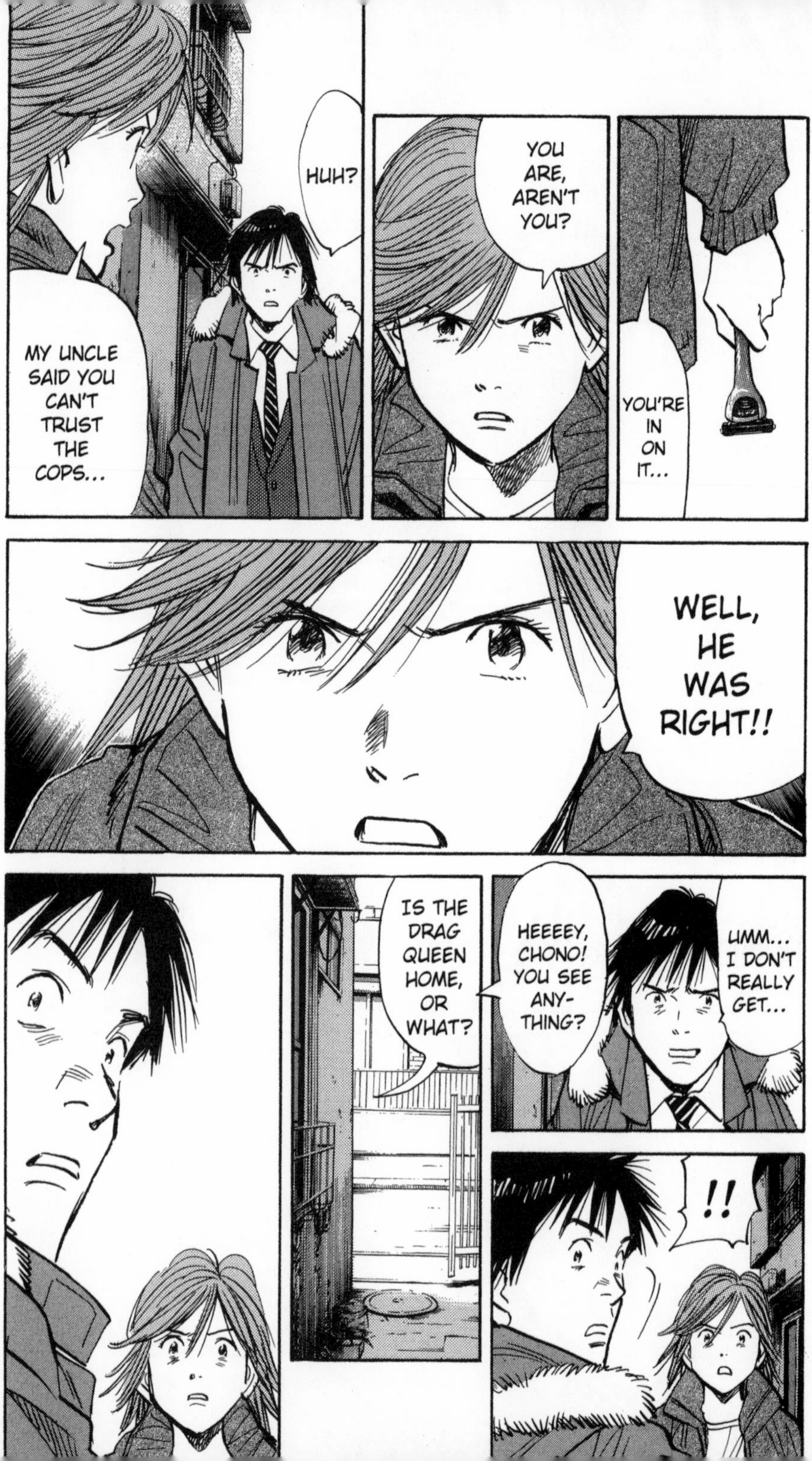
YOU'RE IN ON IT...
YOU ARE, AREN'T YOU?
HUH?
MY UNCLE SAID YOU CAN'T TRUST THE COPS...
WELL, HE WAS RIGHT!!
UMM... I DON'T REALLY GET...
HEEEEY, CHONO! YOU SEE ANY-THING?
!!
IS THE DRAG QUEEN HOME, OR WHAT?

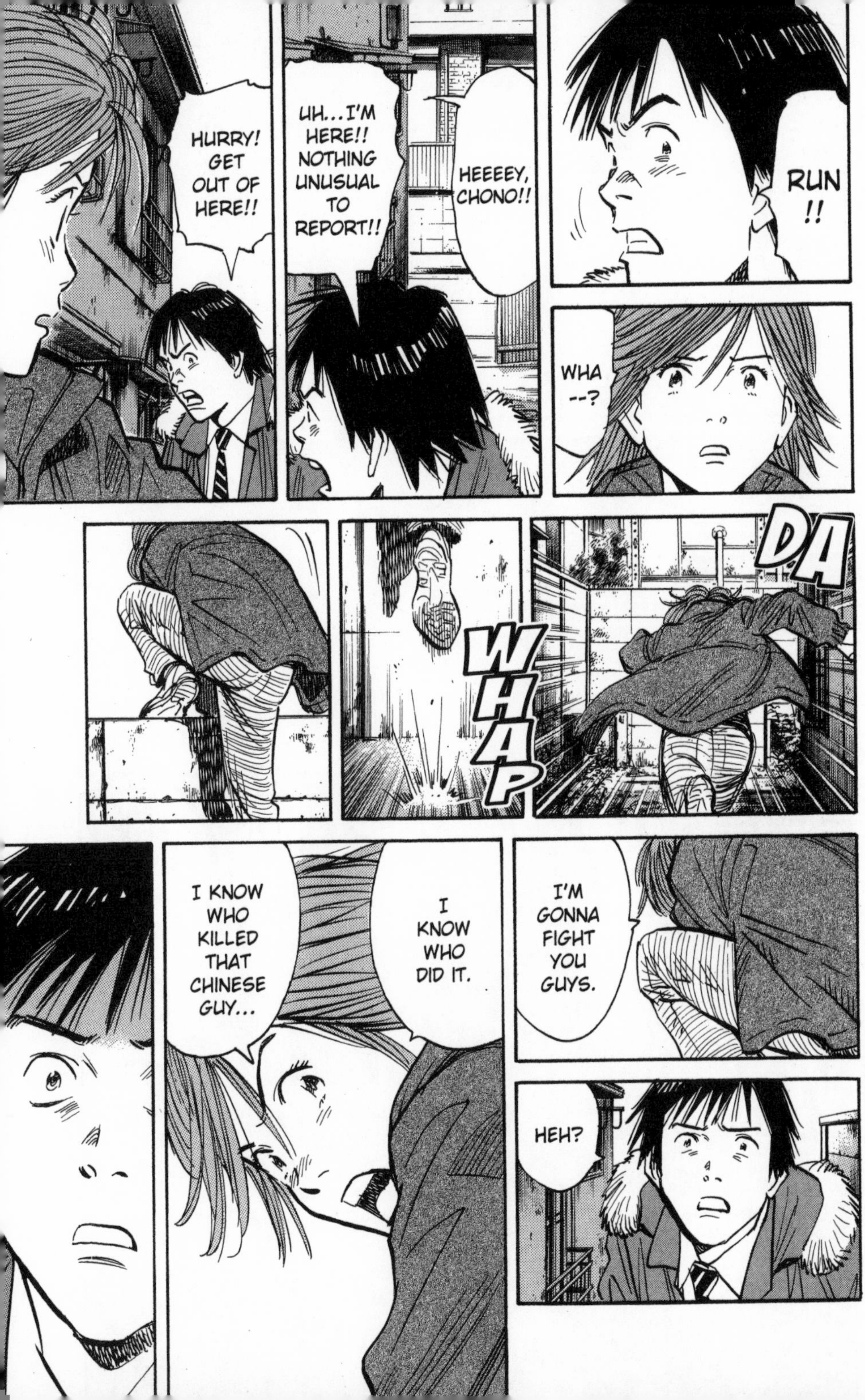
RUN!!
WHA--?
HEEEEY, CHONO!!
UH...I'M HERE!! NOTHING UNUSUAL TO REPORT!!
HURRY! GET OUT OF HERE!!
DA
WHAP
I'M GONNA FIGHT YOU GUYS.
HEH?
I KNOW WHO DID IT.
I KNOW WHO KILLED THAT CHINESE GUY...

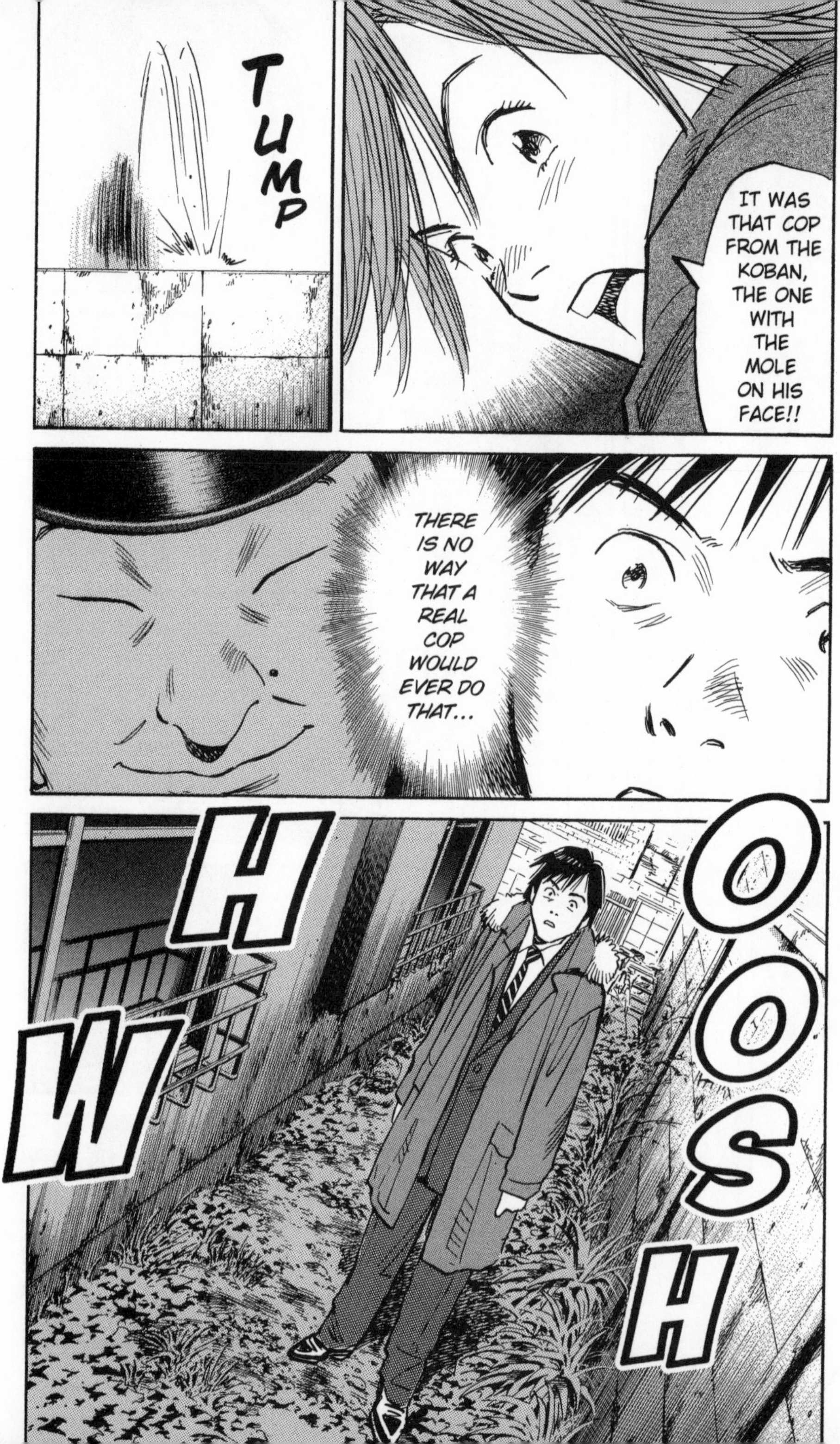
IT WAS THAT COP FROM THE KOBAN, THE ONE WITH THE MOLE ON HIS FACE!!
TUMP
THERE IS NO WAY THAT A REAL COP WOULD EVER DO THAT...
WHOOSH

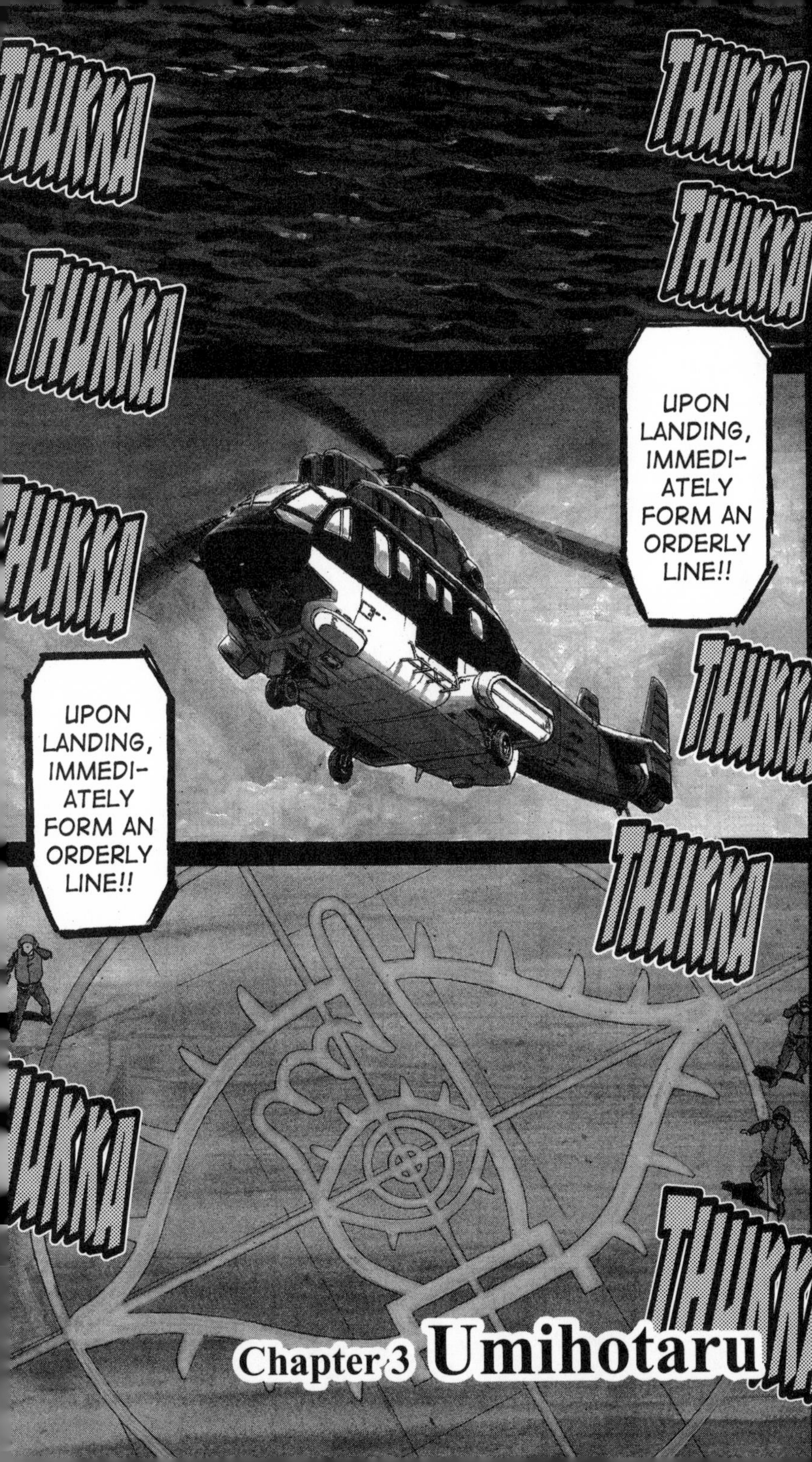
THUKKA
THUKKA
THUKKA
THUKKA
UPON LANDING, IMMEDIATELY FORM AN ORDERLY LINE!!
UPON LANDING, IMMEDIATELY FORM AN ORDERLY LINE!!
THUKKA
THUKKA
THUKKA
THUKKA
THUKKA

Chapter 3 Umihotaru

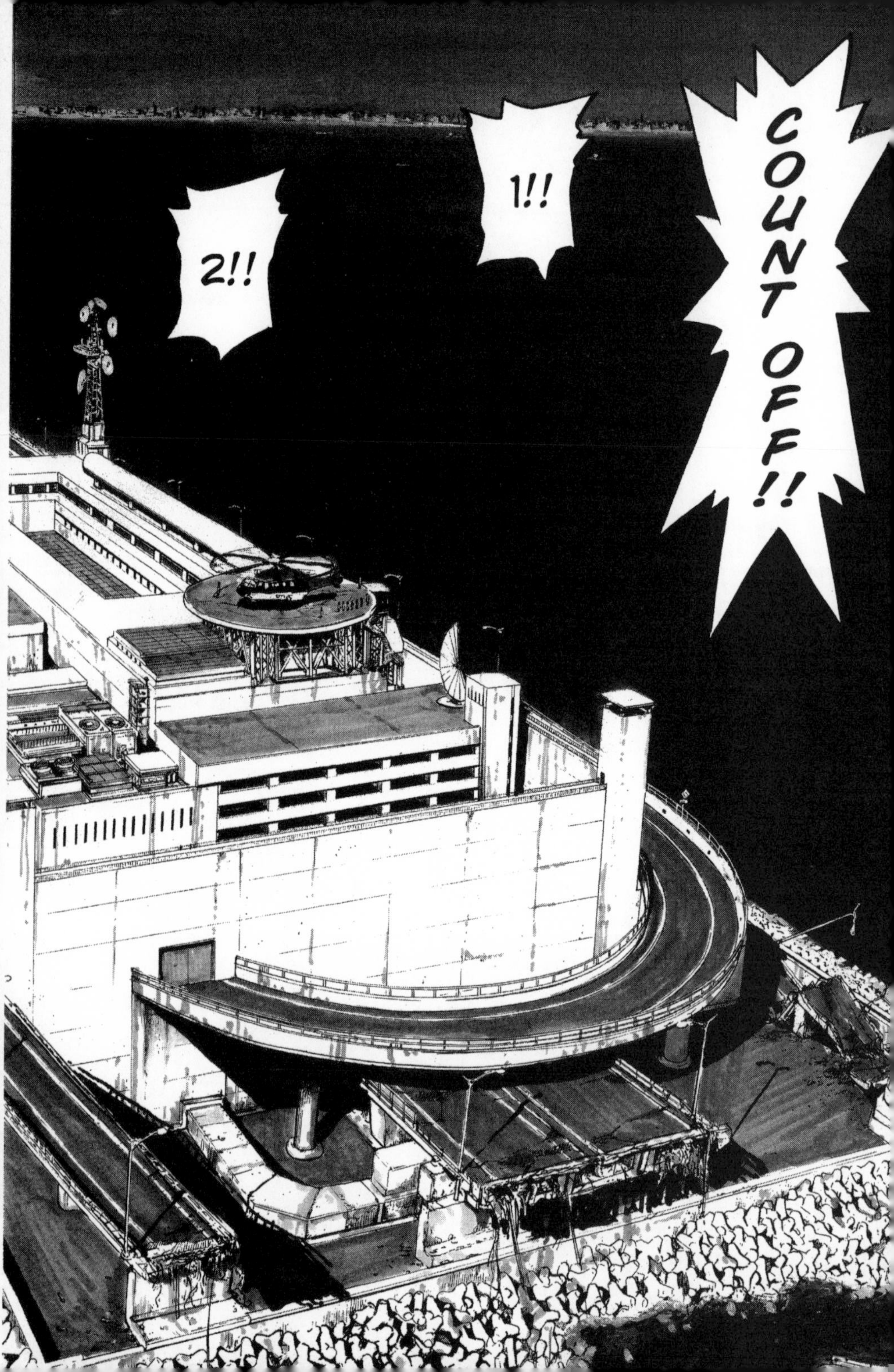
COUNT OFF!!
1!!
2!!

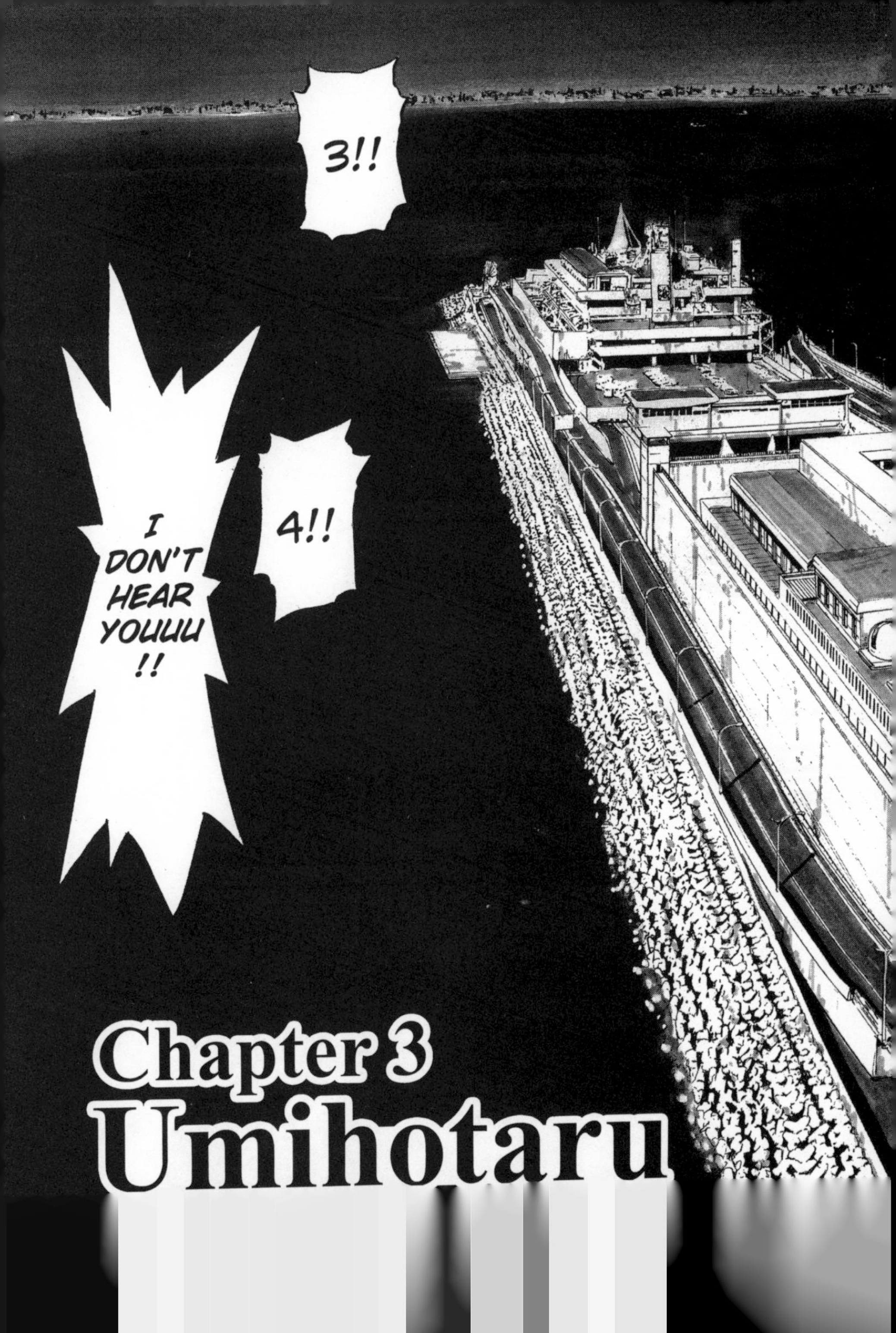
3!!
4!!
I DON'T HEAR YOUUU!!

Chapter 3
Umihotaru

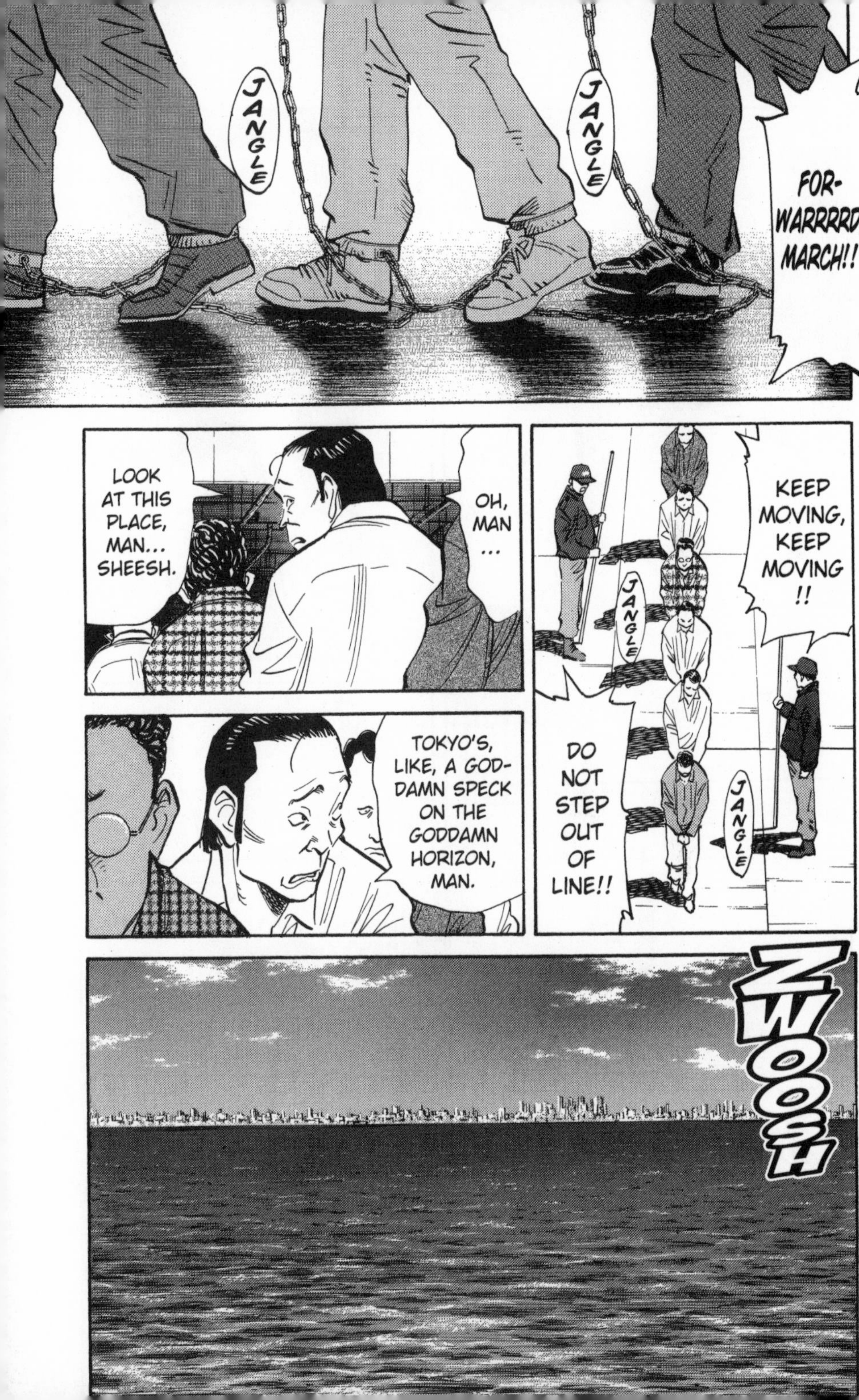
FOR-WARRRRD, MARCH!!
JANGLE
JANGLE
KEEP MOVING, KEEP MOVING!!
JANGLE
DO NOT STEP OUT OF LINE!!
JANGLE
OH, MAN...
LOOK AT THIS PLACE, MAN... SHEESH.
TOKYO'S, LIKE, A GOD-DAMN SPECK ON THE GODDAMN HORIZON, MAN.
ZWOOSH

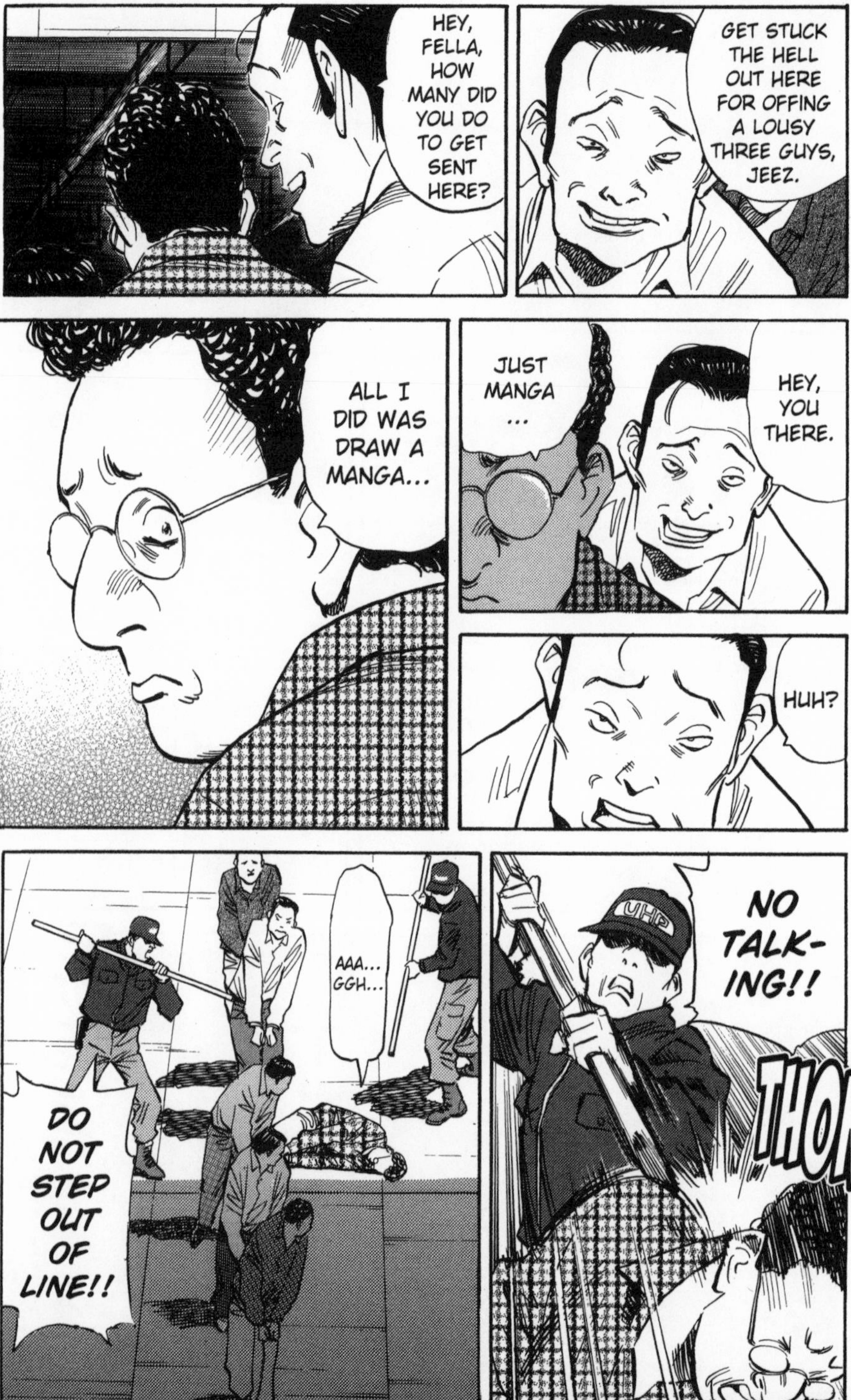
GET STUCK THE HELL OUT HERE FOR OFFING A LOUSY THREE GUYS, JEEZ.
HEY, FELLA, HOW MANY DID YOU DO TO GET SENT HERE?
HEY, YOU THERE.
JUST MANGA ...
HUH?
ALL I DID WAS DRAW A MANGA...
NO TALK-ING!!
THOK
AAA... GGH...
DO NOT STEP OUT OF LINE!!

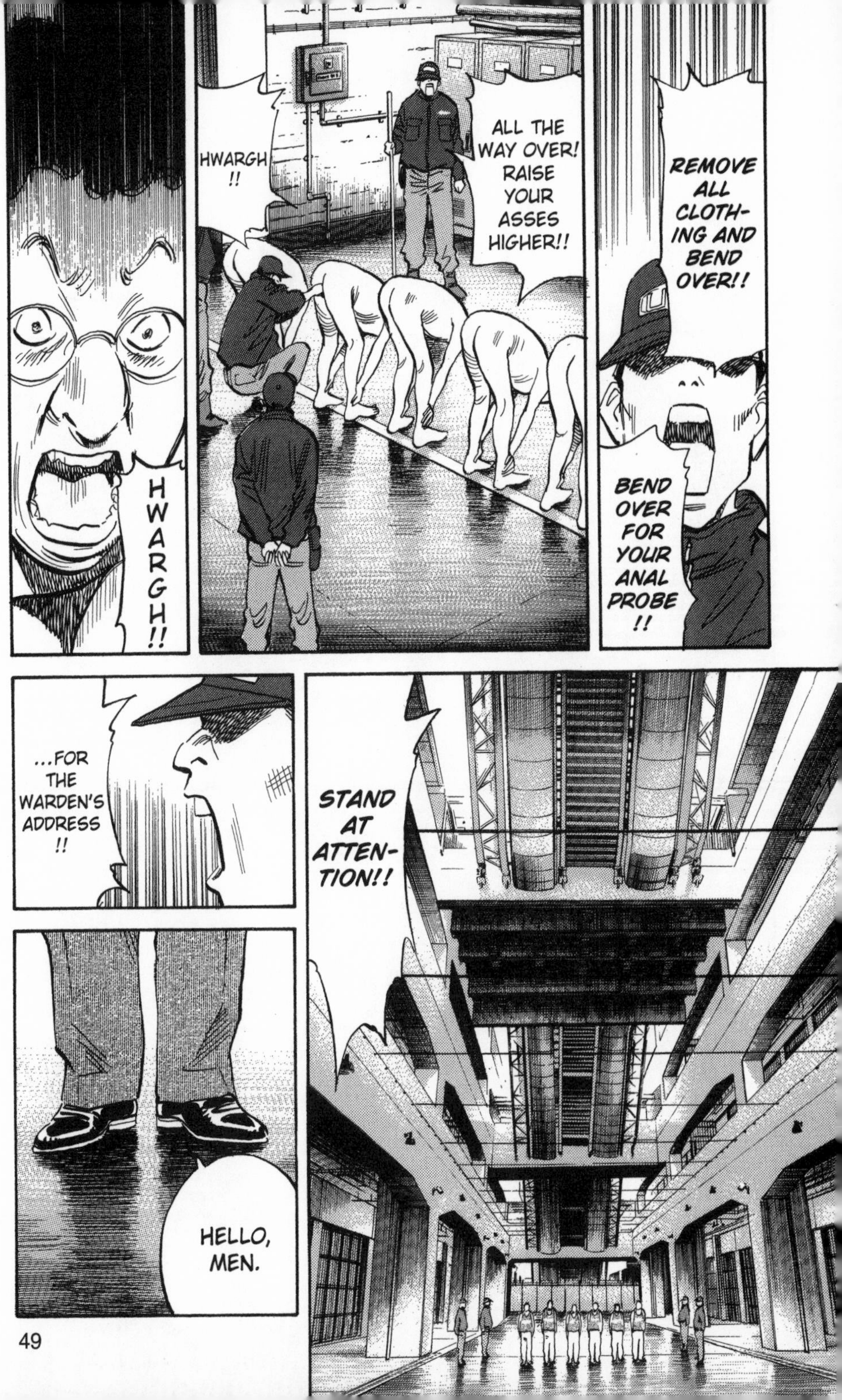
REMOVE ALL CLOTHING AND BEND OVER!!
BEND OVER FOR YOUR ANAL PROBE!!
ALL THE WAY OVER! RAISE YOUR ASSES HIGHER!!
HWARGH!!
HWARGH!!
STAND AT ATTENTION!!
...FOR THE WARDEN'S ADDRESS!!
HELLO, MEN.

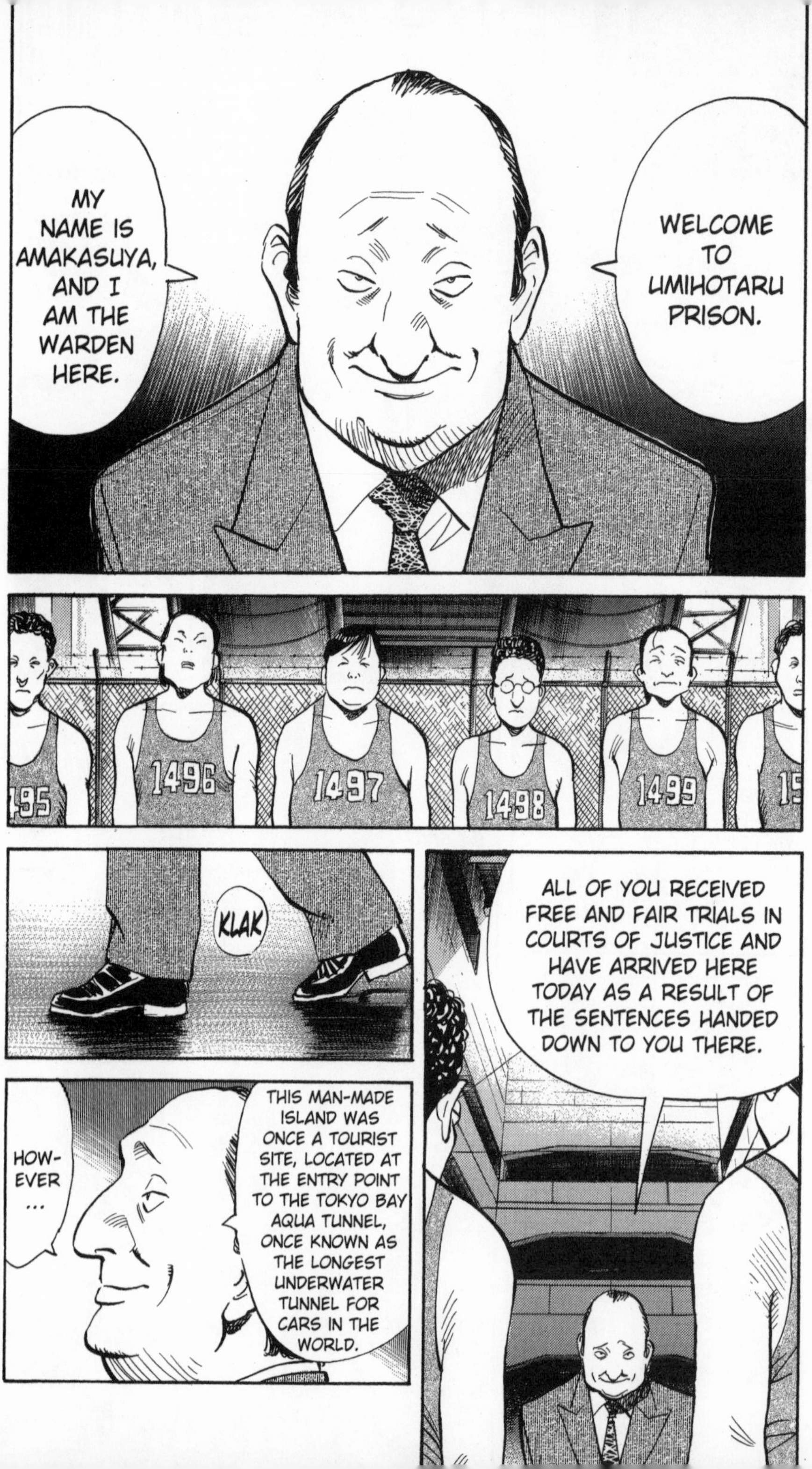
WELCOME TO UMIHOTARU PRISON.
MY NAME IS AMAKASUYA, AND I AM THE WARDEN HERE.
1496
1497
1498
1499
ALL OF YOU RECEIVED FREE AND FAIR TRIALS IN COURTS OF JUSTICE AND HAVE ARRIVED HERE TODAY AS A RESULT OF THE SENTENCES HANDED DOWN TO YOU THERE.
KLAK
THIS MAN-MADE ISLAND WAS ONCE A TOURIST SITE, LOCATED AT THE ENTRY POINT TO THE TOKYO BAY AQUA TUNNEL, ONCE KNOWN AS THE LONGEST UNDERWATER TUNNEL FOR CARS IN THE WORLD.
HOW-EVER ...

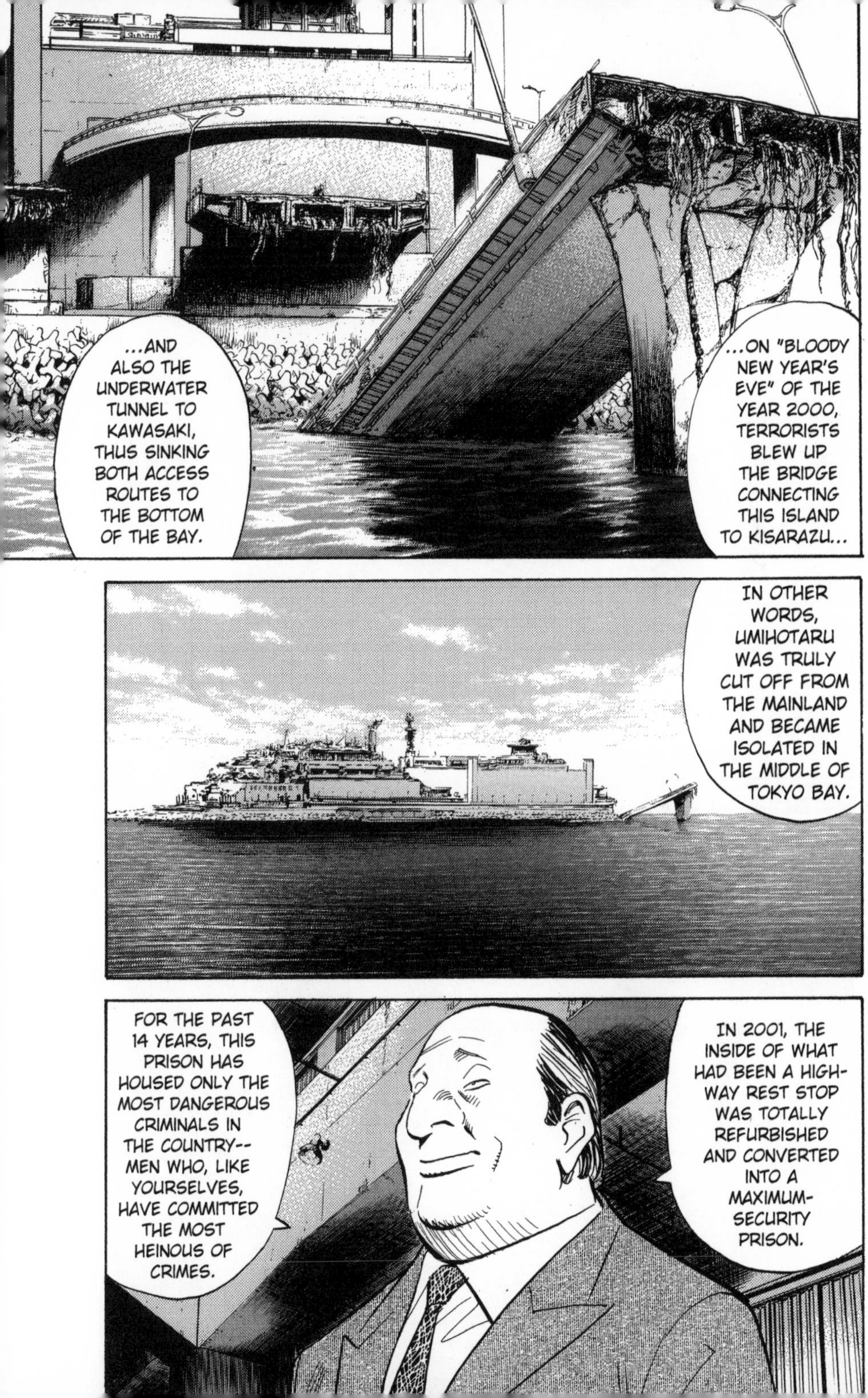
...ON "BLOODY NEW YEAR'S EVE" OF THE YEAR 2000, TERRORISTS BLEW UP THE BRIDGE CONNECTING THIS ISLAND TO KISARAZU...
...AND ALSO THE UNDERWATER TUNNEL TO KAWASAKI, THUS SINKING BOTH ACCESS ROUTES TO THE BOTTOM OF THE BAY.
IN OTHER WORDS, UMIHOTARU WAS TRULY CUT OFF FROM THE MAINLAND AND BECAME ISOLATED IN THE MIDDLE OF TOKYO BAY.
IN 2001, THE INSIDE OF WHAT HAD BEEN A HIGH-WAY REST STOP WAS TOTALLY REFURBISHED AND CONVERTED INTO A MAXIMUM-SECURITY PRISON.
FOR THE PAST 14 YEARS, THIS PRISON HAS HOUSED ONLY THE MOST DANGEROUS CRIMINALS IN THE COUNTRY--MEN WHO, LIKE YOURSELVES, HAVE COMMITTED THE MOST HEINOUS OF CRIMES.

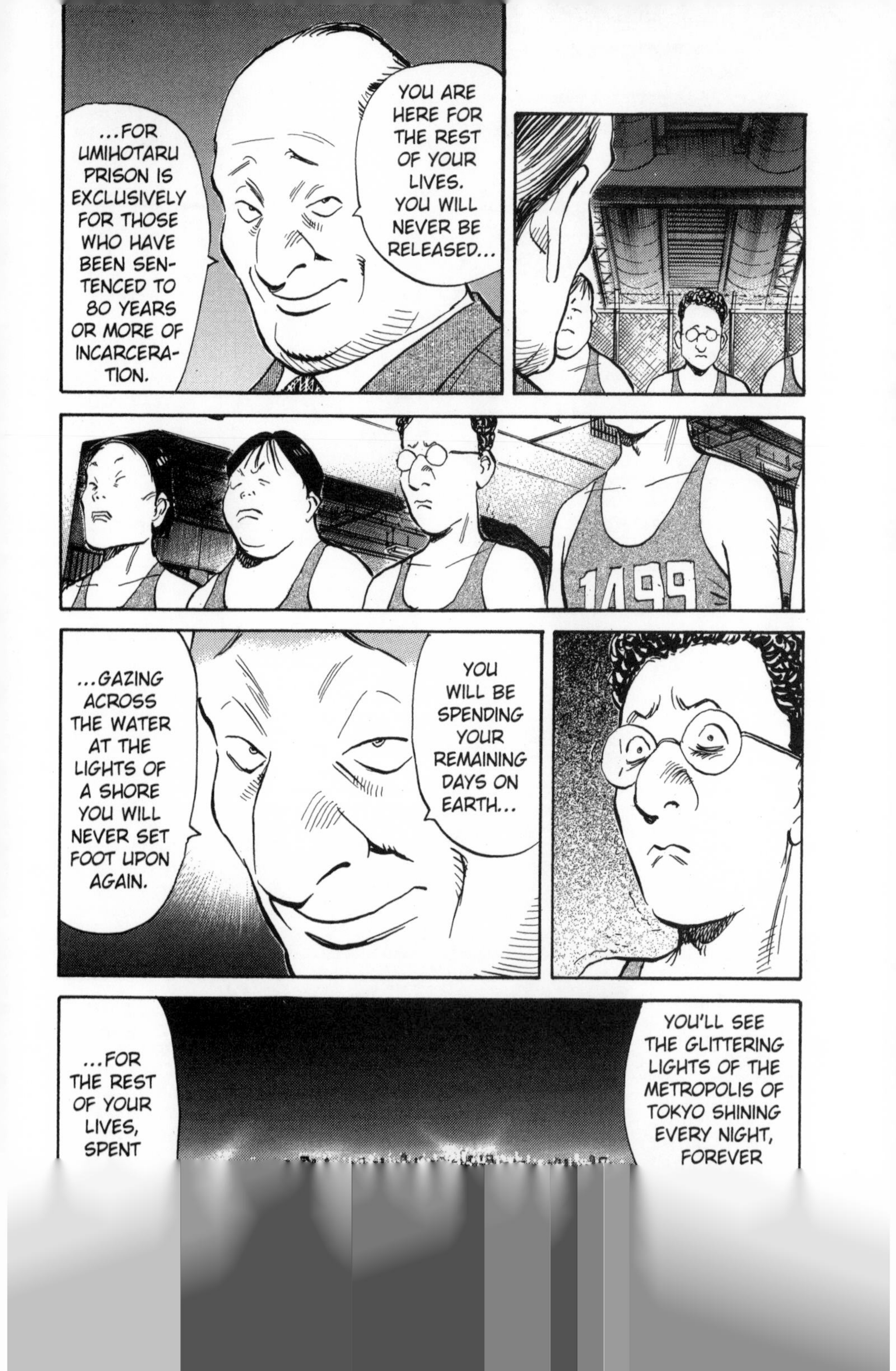
YOU ARE HERE FOR THE REST OF YOUR LIVES. YOU WILL NEVER BE RELEASED...
...FOR UMIHOTARU PRISON IS EXCLUSIVELY FOR THOSE WHO HAVE BEEN SEN-TENCED TO 80 YEARS OR MORE OF INCARCERA-TION.
YOU WILL BE SPENDING YOUR REMAINING DAYS ON EARTH...
...GAZING ACROSS THE WATER AT THE LIGHTS OF A SHORE YOU WILL NEVER SET FOOT UPON AGAIN.
YOU'LL SEE THE GLITTERING LIGHTS OF THE METROPOLIS OF TOKYO SHINING EVERY NIGHT, FOREVER
...FOR THE REST OF YOUR LIVES, SPENT

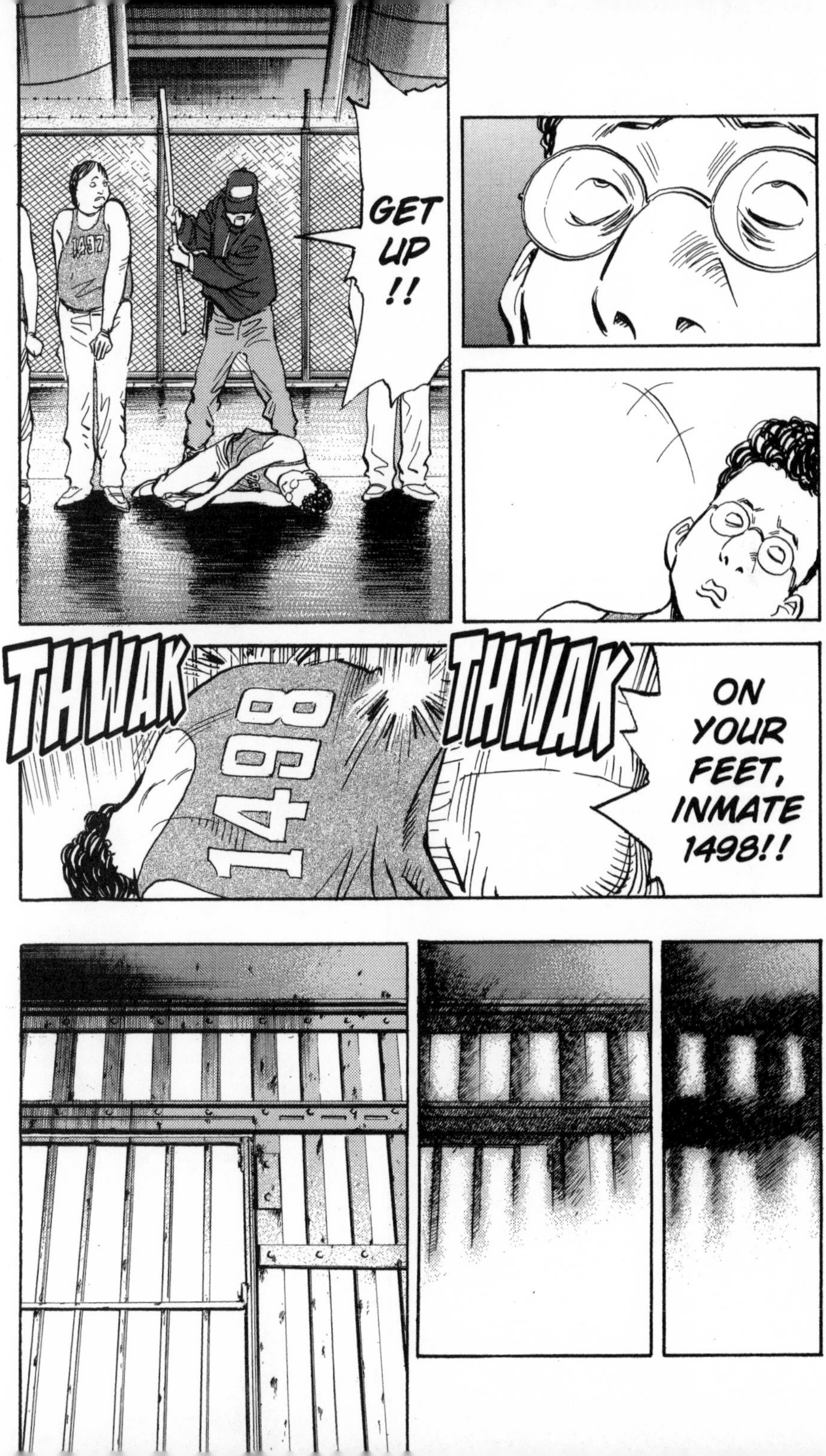
GET UP !!
ON YOUR FEET, INMATE 1498!!
THWAK
THWAK

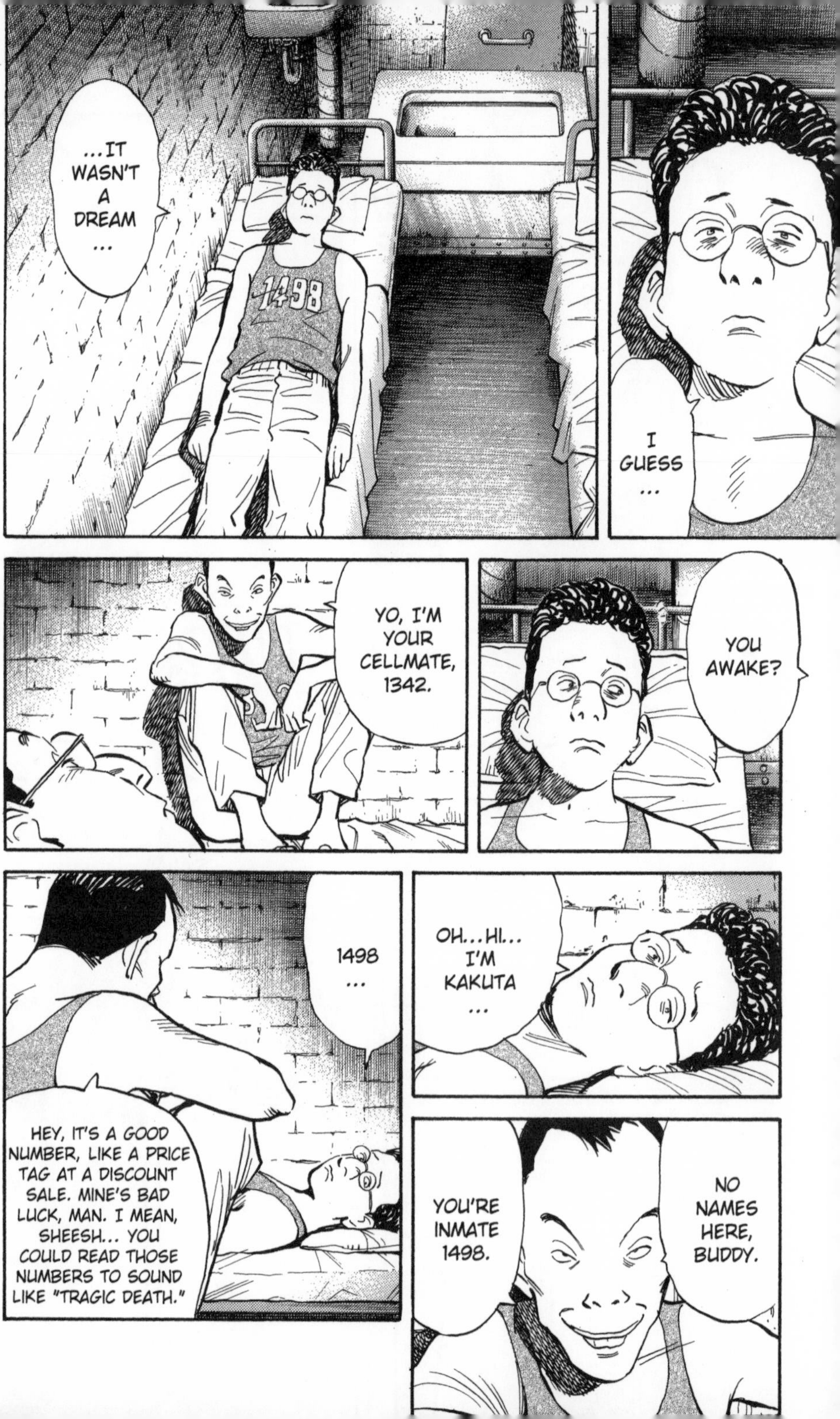
I GUESS ...
...IT WASN'T A DREAM ...
YOU AWAKE?
YO, I'M YOUR CELLMATE, 1342.
OH...HI... I'M KAKUTA ...
NO NAMES HERE, BUDDY.
YOU'RE INMATE 1498.
1498 ...
HEY, IT'S A GOOD NUMBER, LIKE A PRICE TAG AT A DISCOUNT SALE. MINE'S BAD LUCK, MAN. I MEAN, SHEESH... YOU COULD READ THOSE NUMBERS TO SOUND LIKE "TRAGIC DEATH."

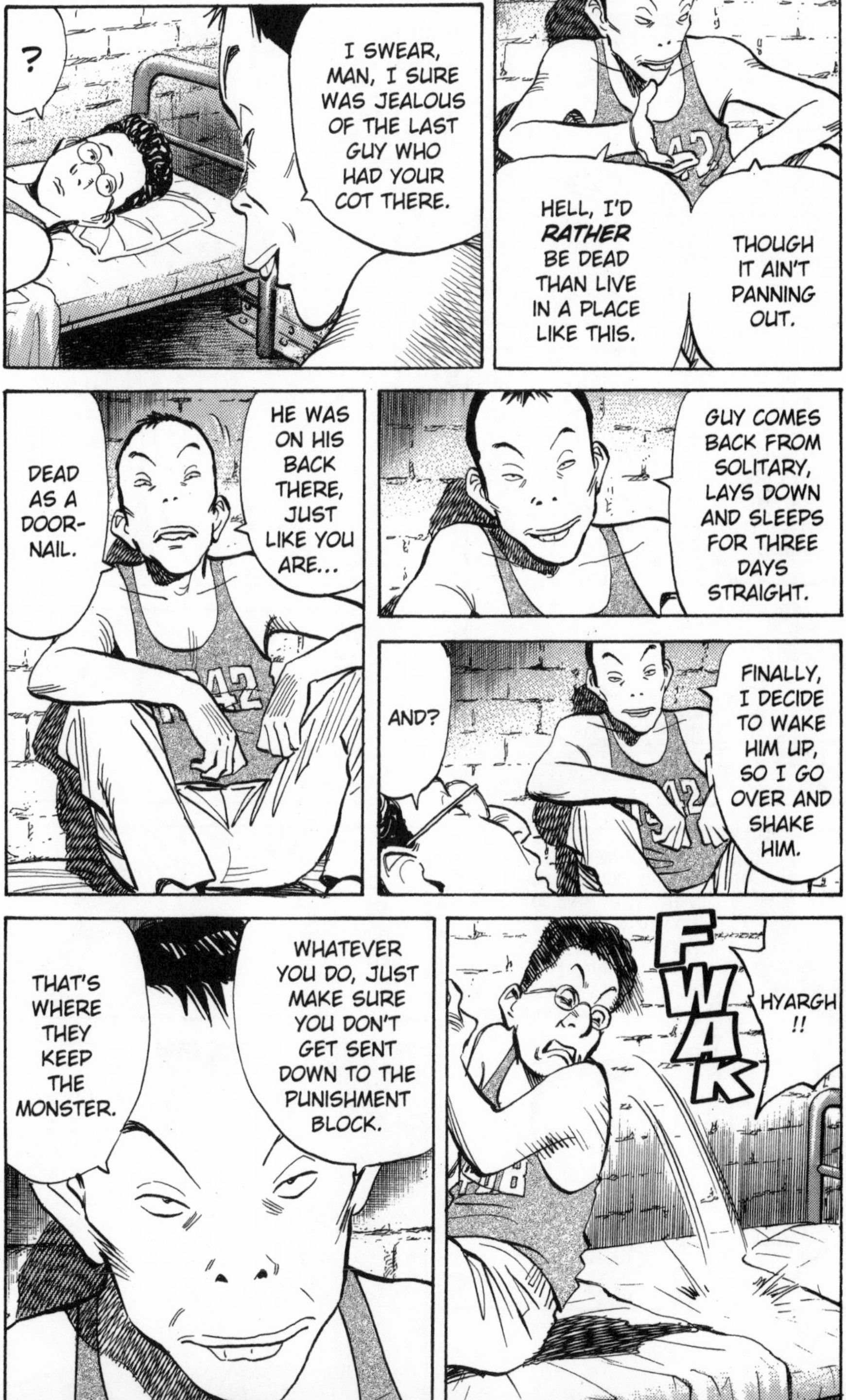
HELL, I'D *RATHER* BE DEAD THAN LIVE IN A PLACE LIKE THIS.
THOUGH IT AIN'T PANNING OUT.
I SWEAR, MAN, I SURE WAS JEALOUS OF THE LAST GUY WHO HAD YOUR COT THERE.
?
GUY COMES BACK FROM SOLITARY, LAYS DOWN AND SLEEPS FOR THREE DAYS STRAIGHT.
FINALLY, I DECIDE TO WAKE HIM UP, SO I GO OVER AND SHAKE HIM.
AND?
HE WAS ON HIS BACK THERE, JUST LIKE YOU ARE...
DEAD AS A DOOR-NAIL.
HYARGH !!
FWAK
WHATEVER YOU DO, JUST MAKE SURE YOU DON'T GET SENT DOWN TO THE PUNISHMENT BLOCK.
THAT'S WHERE THEY KEEP THE MONSTER.

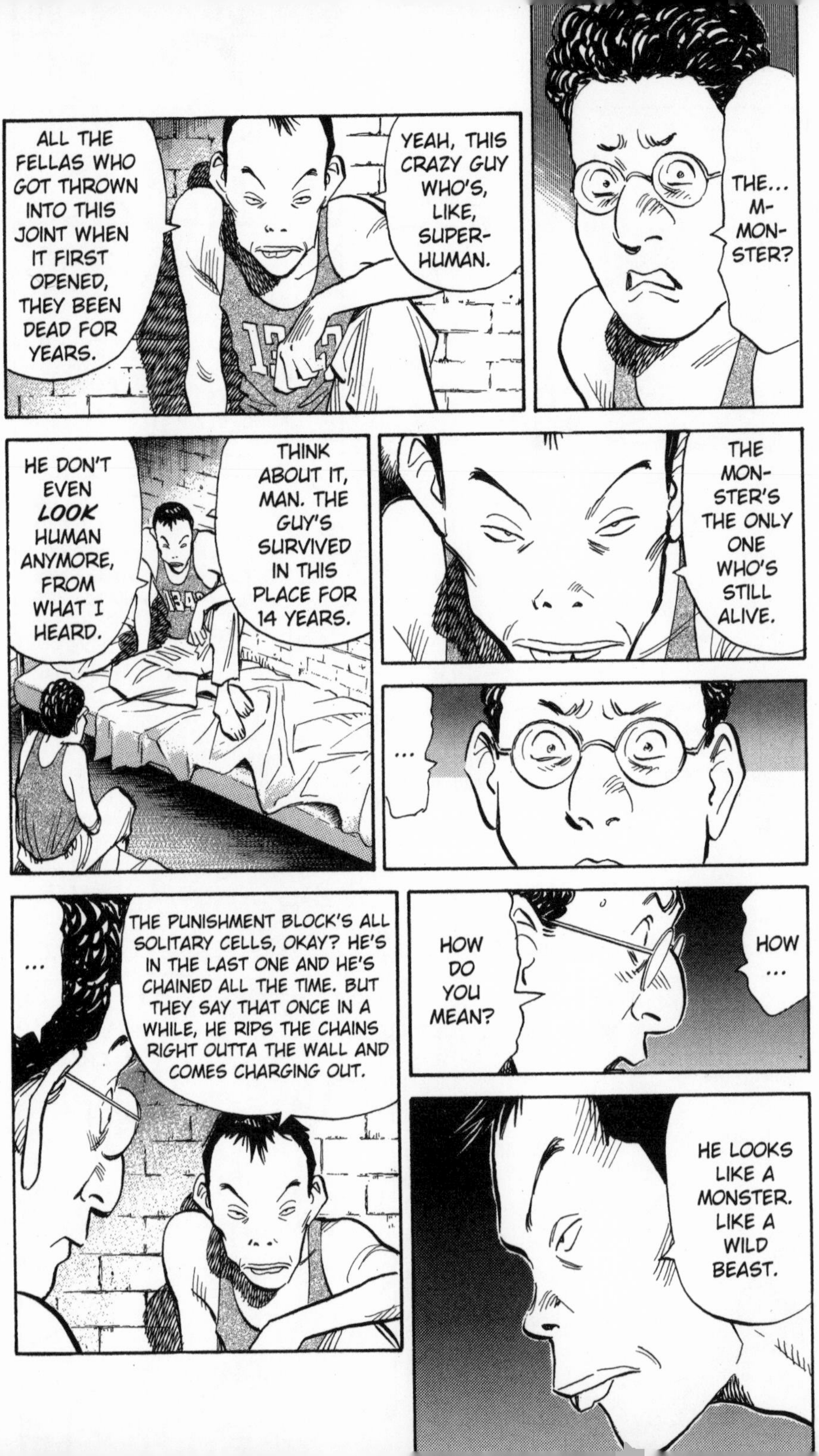
THE... M-MONSTER?
YEAH, THIS CRAZY GUY WHO'S, LIKE, SUPER-HUMAN.
ALL THE FELLAS WHO GOT THROWN INTO THIS JOINT WHEN IT FIRST OPENED, THEY BEEN DEAD FOR YEARS.
THE MONSTER'S THE ONLY ONE WHO'S STILL ALIVE.
...
THINK ABOUT IT, MAN. THE GUY'S SURVIVED IN THIS PLACE FOR 14 YEARS.
HE DON'T EVEN *LOOK* HUMAN ANYMORE, FROM WHAT I HEARD.
HOW ...
HOW DO YOU MEAN?
HE LOOKS LIKE A MONSTER. LIKE A WILD BEAST.
THE PUNISHMENT BLOCK'S ALL SOLITARY CELLS, OKAY? HE'S IN THE LAST ONE AND HE'S CHAINED ALL THE TIME. BUT THEY SAY THAT ONCE IN A WHILE, HE RIPS THE CHAINS RIGHT OUTTA THE WALL AND COMES CHARGING OUT.
...

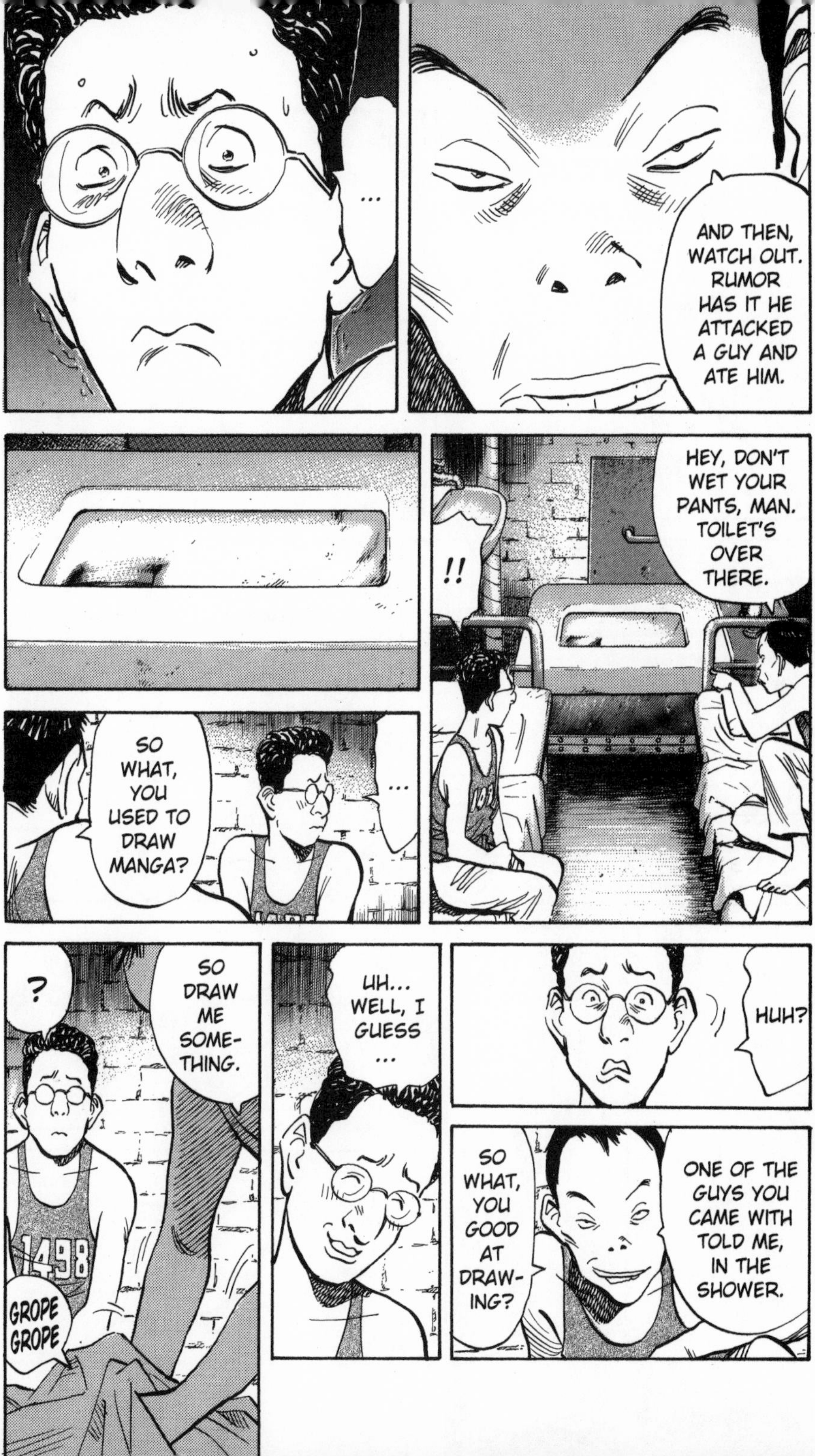
AND THEN, WATCH OUT. RUMOR HAS IT HE ATTACKED A GUY AND ATE HIM.
...
HEY, DON'T WET YOUR PANTS, MAN. TOILET'S OVER THERE.
!!
SO WHAT, YOU USED TO DRAW MANGA?
...
HUH?
ONE OF THE GUYS YOU CAME WITH TOLD ME, IN THE SHOWER.
SO WHAT, YOU GOOD AT DRAW-ING?
UH... WELL, I GUESS ...
SO DRAW ME SOME-THING.
?
GROPE GROPE

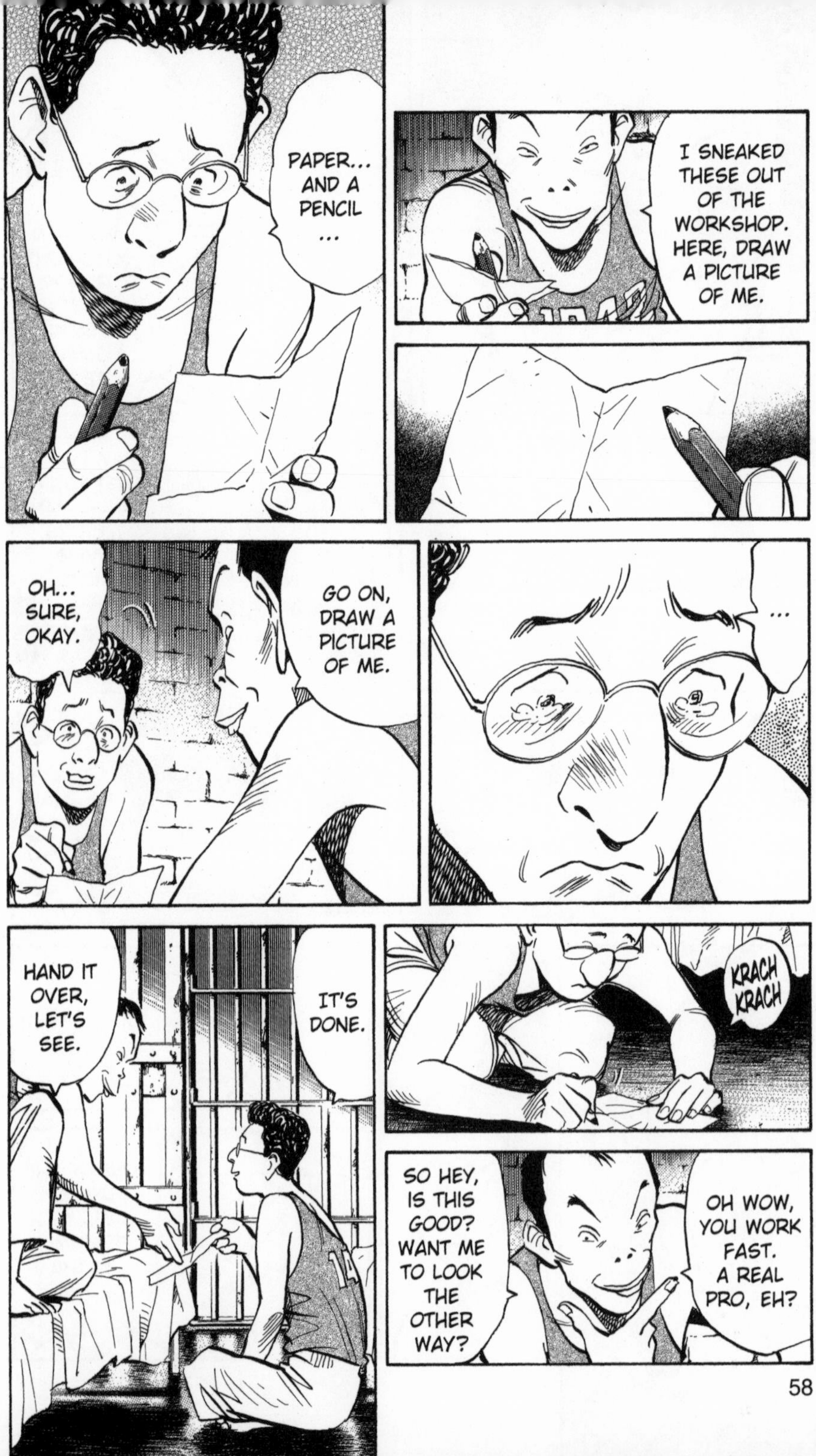
I SNEAKED THESE OUT OF THE WORKSHOP. HERE, DRAW A PICTURE OF ME.
PAPER... AND A PENCIL ...
...
GO ON, DRAW A PICTURE OF ME.
OH... SURE, OKAY.
KRACH KRACH
OH WOW, YOU WORK FAST. A REAL PRO, EH?
SO HEY, IS THIS GOOD? WANT ME TO LOOK THE OTHER WAY?
IT'S DONE.
HAND IT OVER, LET'S SEE.

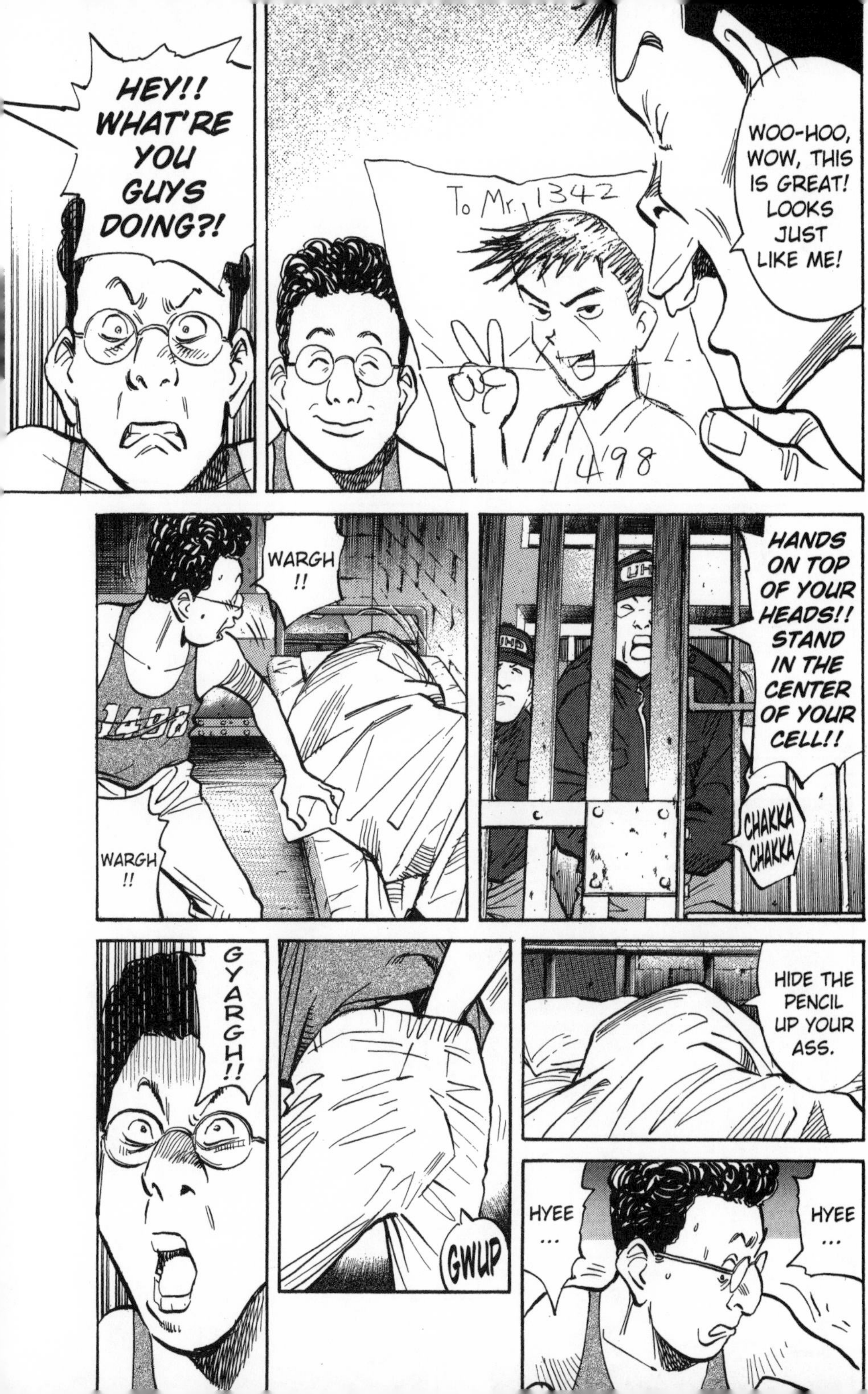
To Mr. 1342
4'98
WOO-HOO, WOW, THIS IS GREAT! LOOKS JUST LIKE ME!
HEY!! WHAT'RE YOU GUYS DOING?!
HANDS ON TOP OF YOUR HEADS!! STAND IN THE CENTER OF YOUR CELL!!
CHAKKA CHAKKA
WARGH !!
WARGH !!
HIDE THE PENCIL UP YOUR ASS.
HYEE ...
HYEE ...
GWUP
GYARGH!!

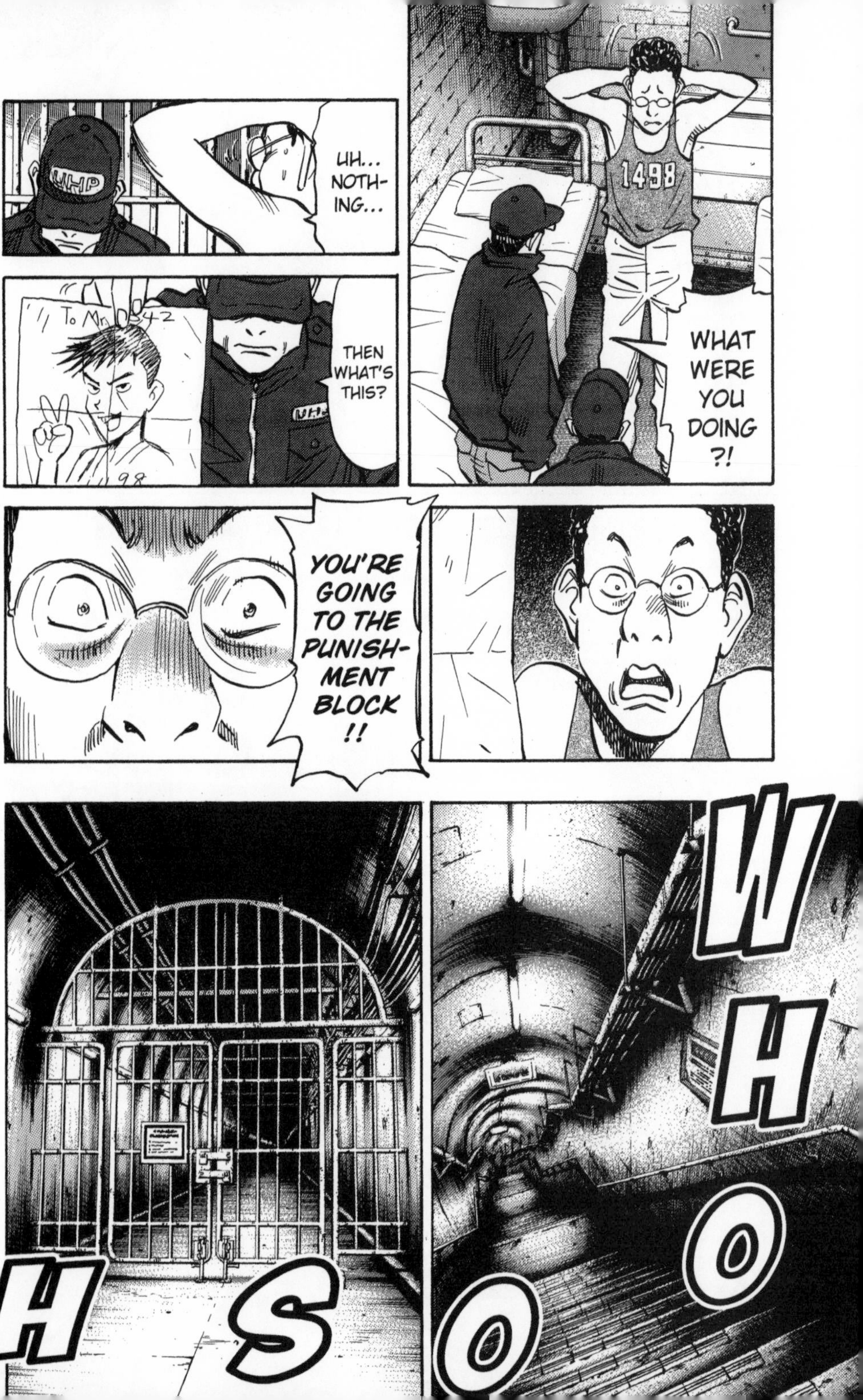
WHAT WERE YOU DOING?!
UH... NOTHING...
THEN WHAT'S THIS?
YOU'RE GOING TO THE PUNISHMENT BLOCK!!
WHOOSH

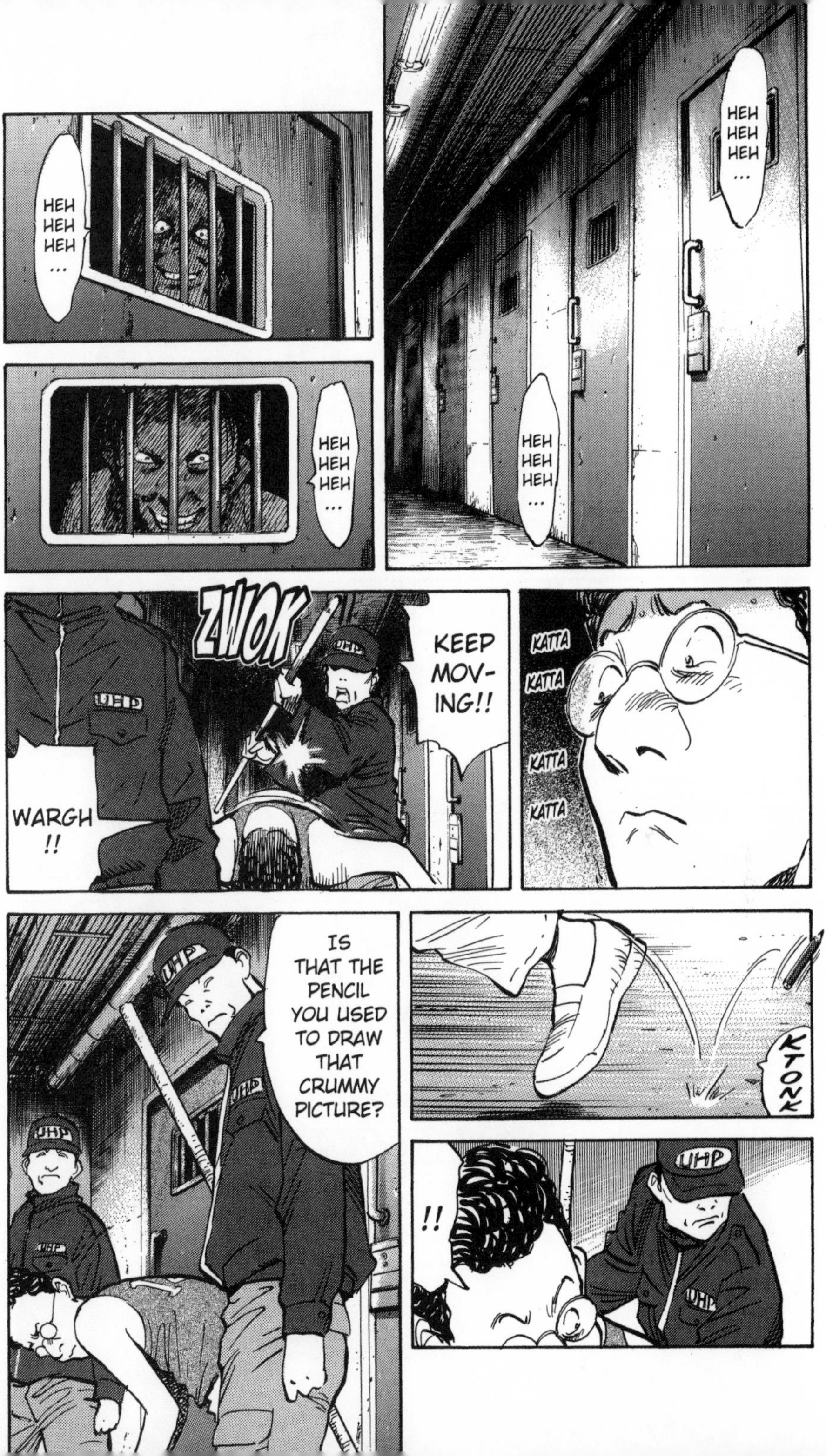
HEH HEH HEH ...
HEH HEH HEH ...
HEH HEH HEH ...
HEH HEH HEH ...
KATTA
KATTA
KATTA
KATTA
ZWOK
KEEP MOV-ING!!
WARGH !!
KTONK
!!
IS THAT THE PENCIL YOU USED TO DRAW THAT CRUMMY PICTURE?

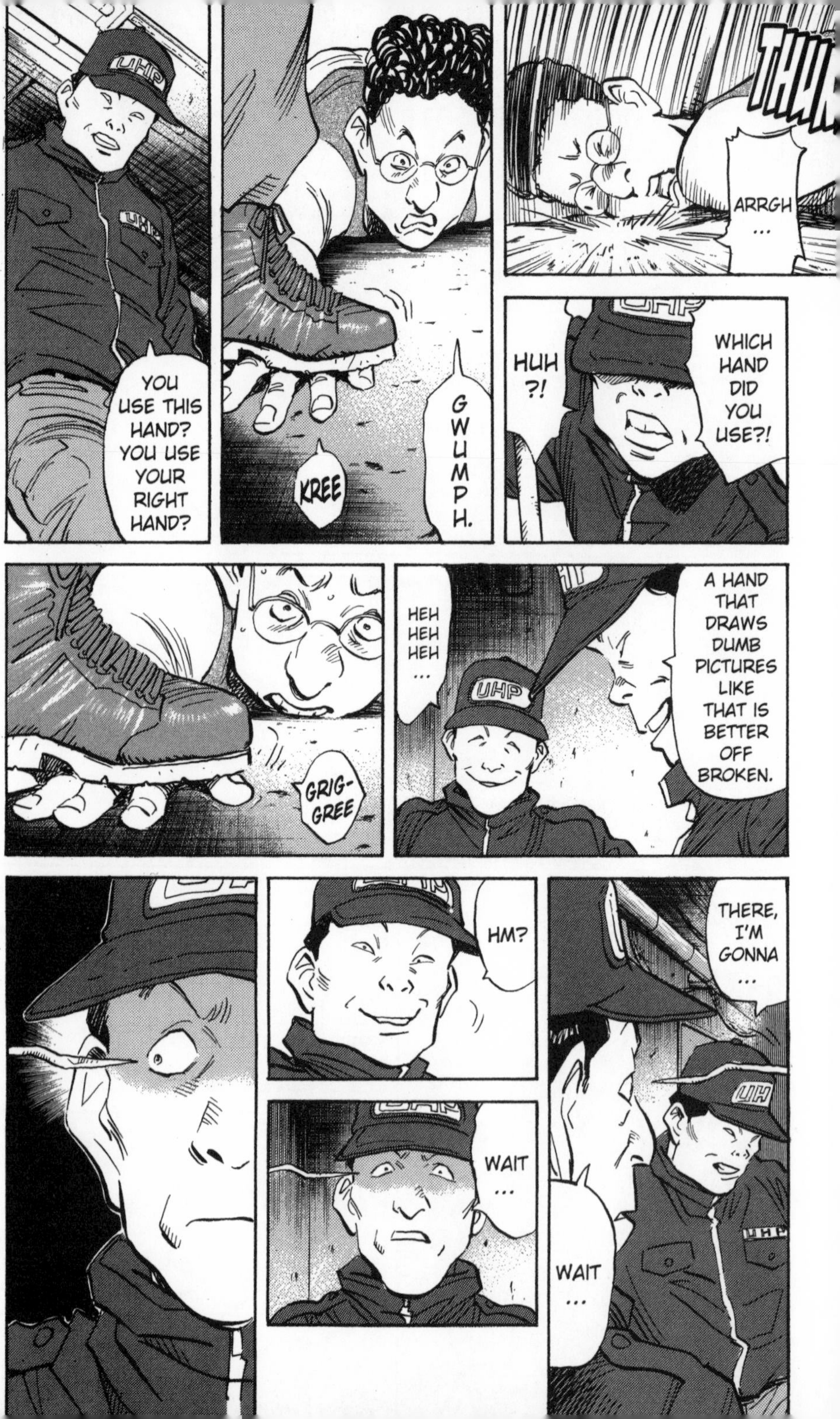
THU
ARRGH ...
WHICH HAND DID YOU USE?!
HUH ?!
GWUMPH.
KREE
YOU USE THIS HAND? YOU USE YOUR RIGHT HAND?
A HAND THAT DRAWS DUMB PICTURES LIKE THAT IS BETTER OFF BROKEN.
HEH HEH HEH ...
GRIG-GREE
THERE, I'M GONNA ...
WAIT ...
HM?
WAIT ...

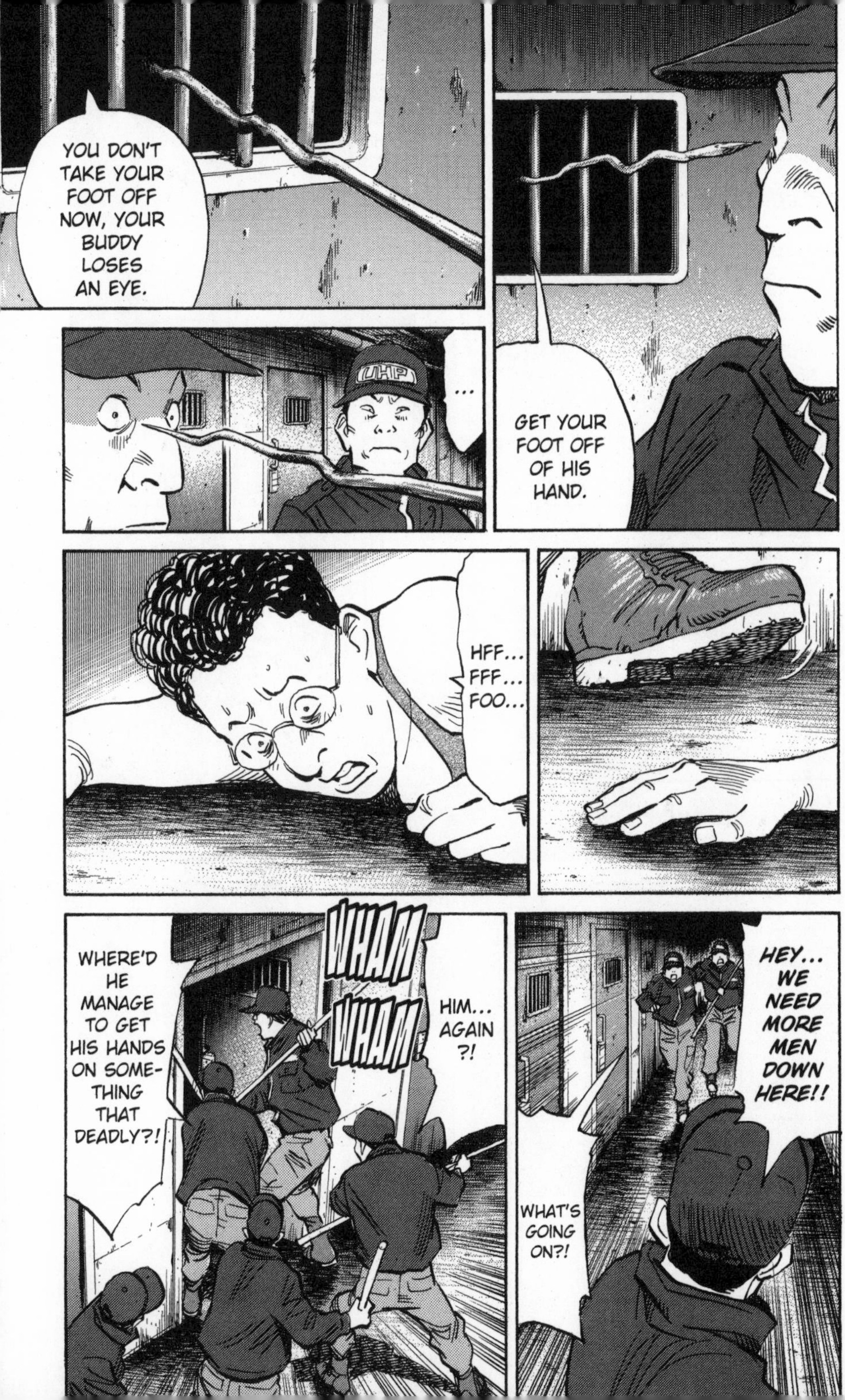
GET YOUR FOOT OFF OF HIS HAND.
YOU DON'T TAKE YOUR FOOT OFF NOW, YOUR BUDDY LOSES AN EYE.
...
HFF... FFF... FOO...
HEY... WE NEED MORE MEN DOWN HERE!!
WHAT'S GOING ON?!
WHAM WHAM
HIM... AGAIN ?!
WHERE'D HE MANAGE TO GET HIS HANDS ON SOME-THING THAT DEADLY?!

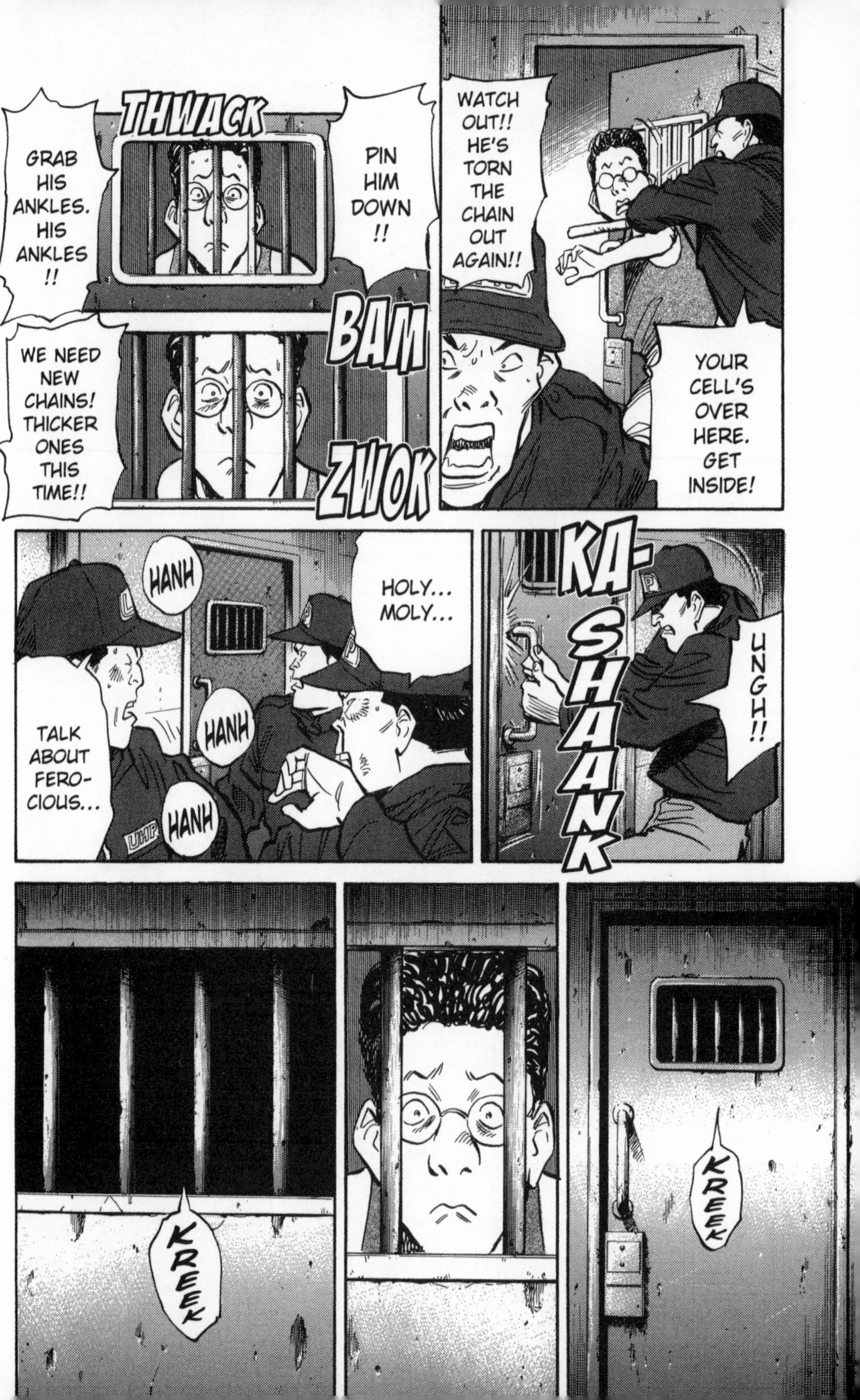
WATCH OUT!! HE'S TORN THE CHAIN OUT AGAIN!!
BAM
ZWOK
YOUR CELL'S OVER HERE. GET INSIDE!
THWACK
PIN HIM DOWN!!
GRAB HIS ANKLES. HIS ANKLES!!
WE NEED NEW CHAINS! THICKER ONES THIS TIME!!
KA-SHAAANK
UNGH!!
HOLY... MOLY...
HANH
HANH
HANH
TALK ABOUT FEROCIOUS...
KREEK
KREEK

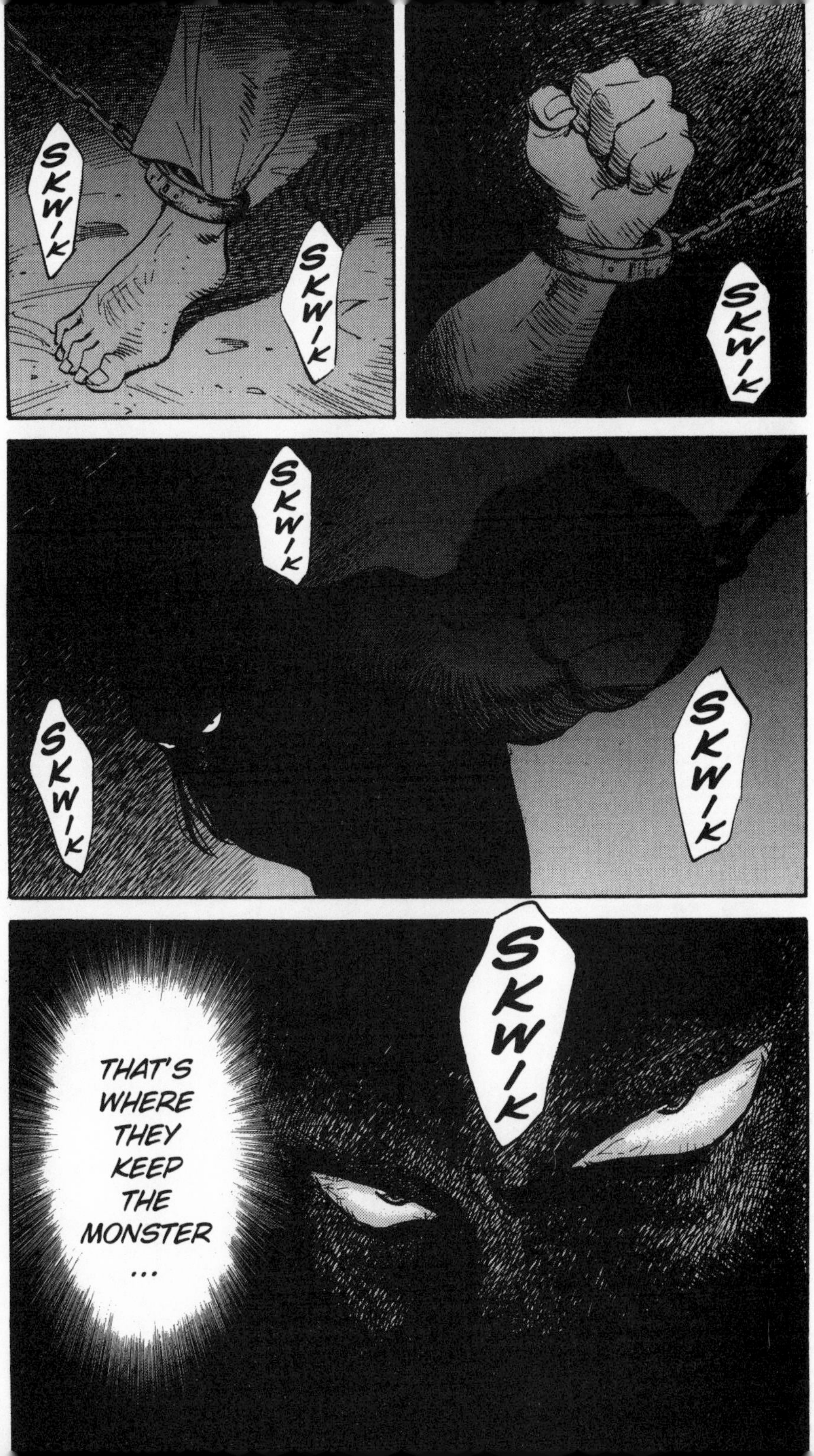
SKWIK
SKWIK
SKWIK
SKWIK
SKWIK
SKWIK
SKWIK
THAT'S WHERE THEY KEEP THE MONSTER ...

20世紀少年
Twentieth Century Boys

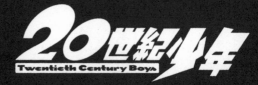

Chapter 4 The Monster

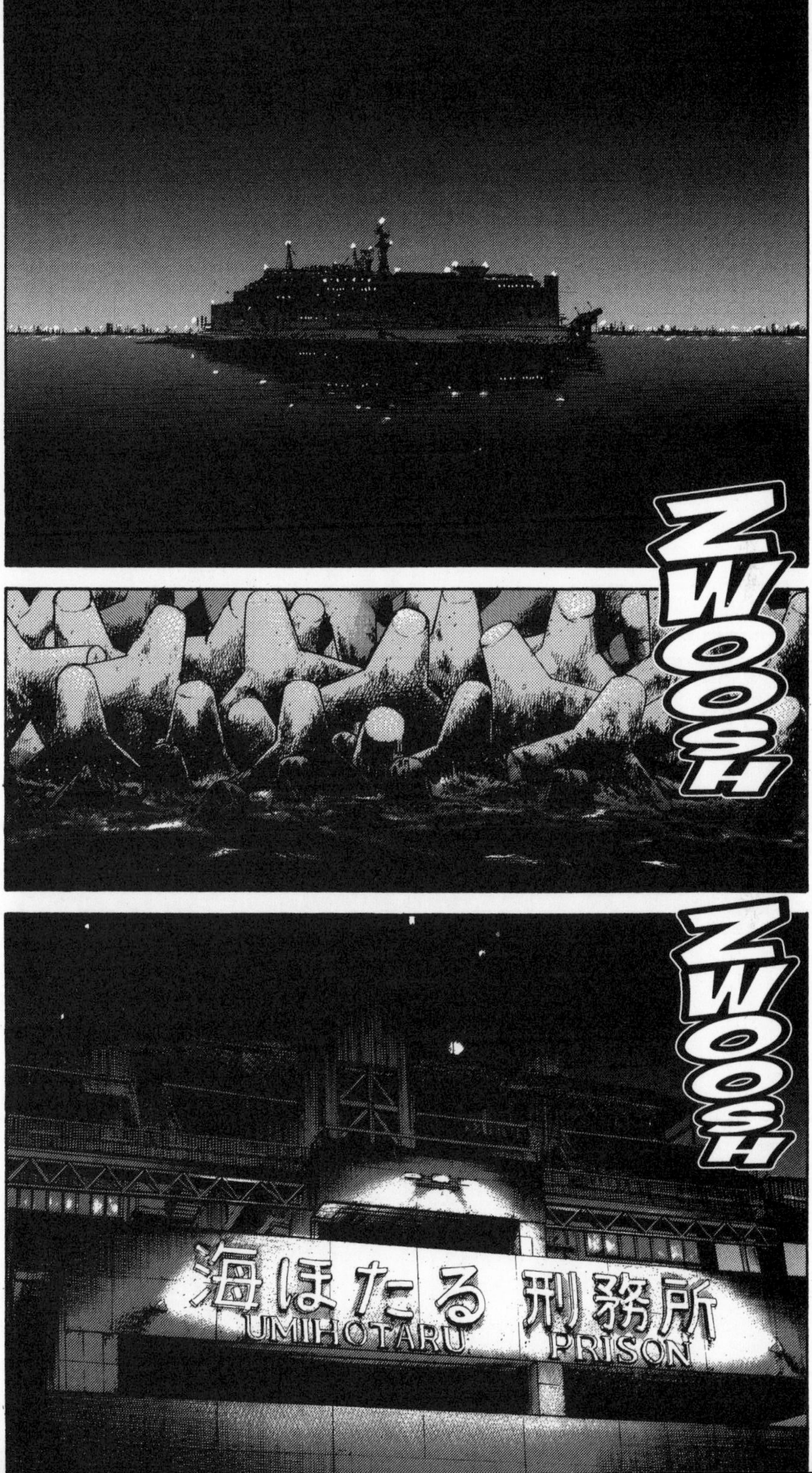
ZWOOSH
ZWOOSH
海ほたる 刑務所
UMIHOTARU PRISON

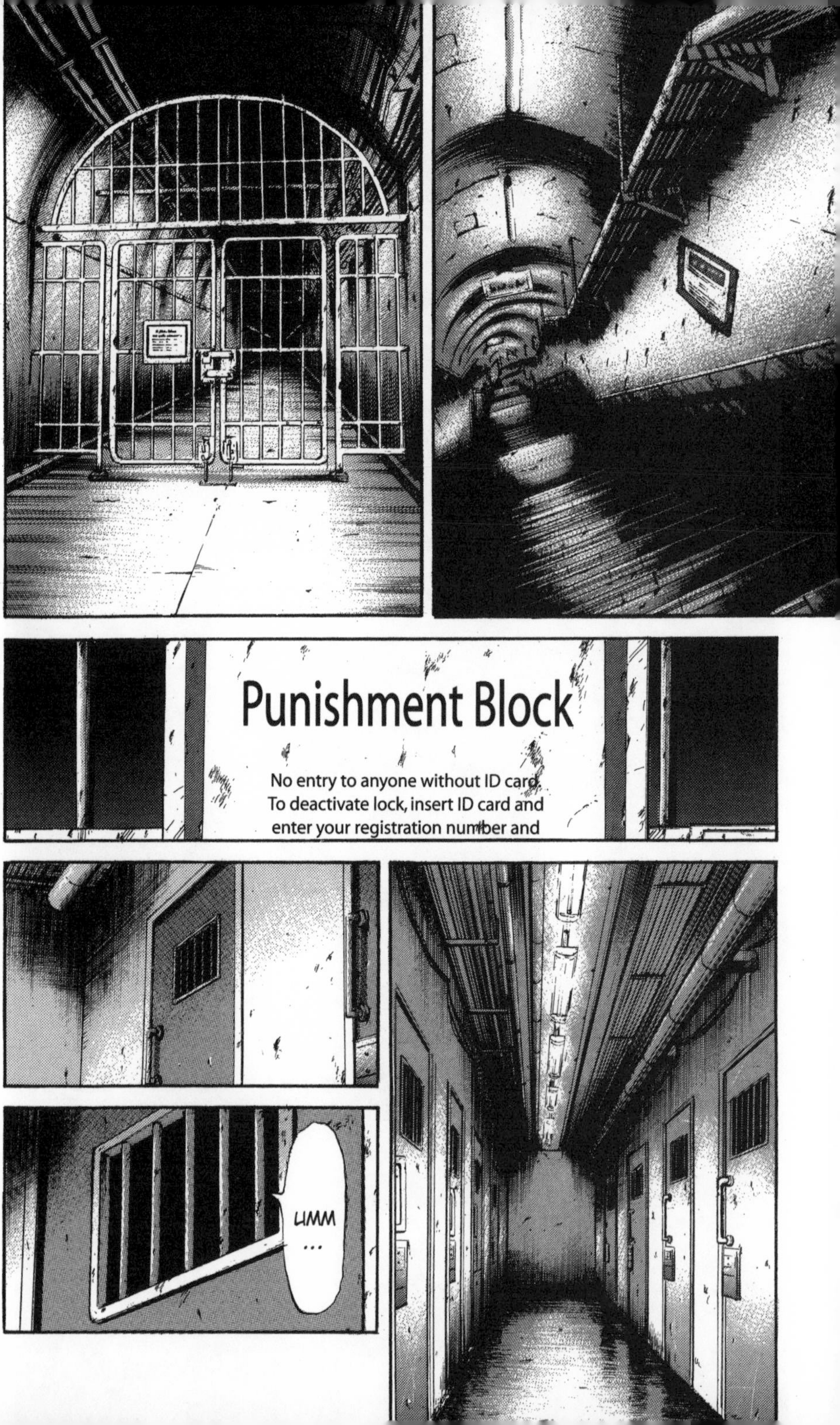
Punishment Block
No entry to anyone without ID card.
To deactivate lock, insert ID card and
enter your registration number and
UMM ...

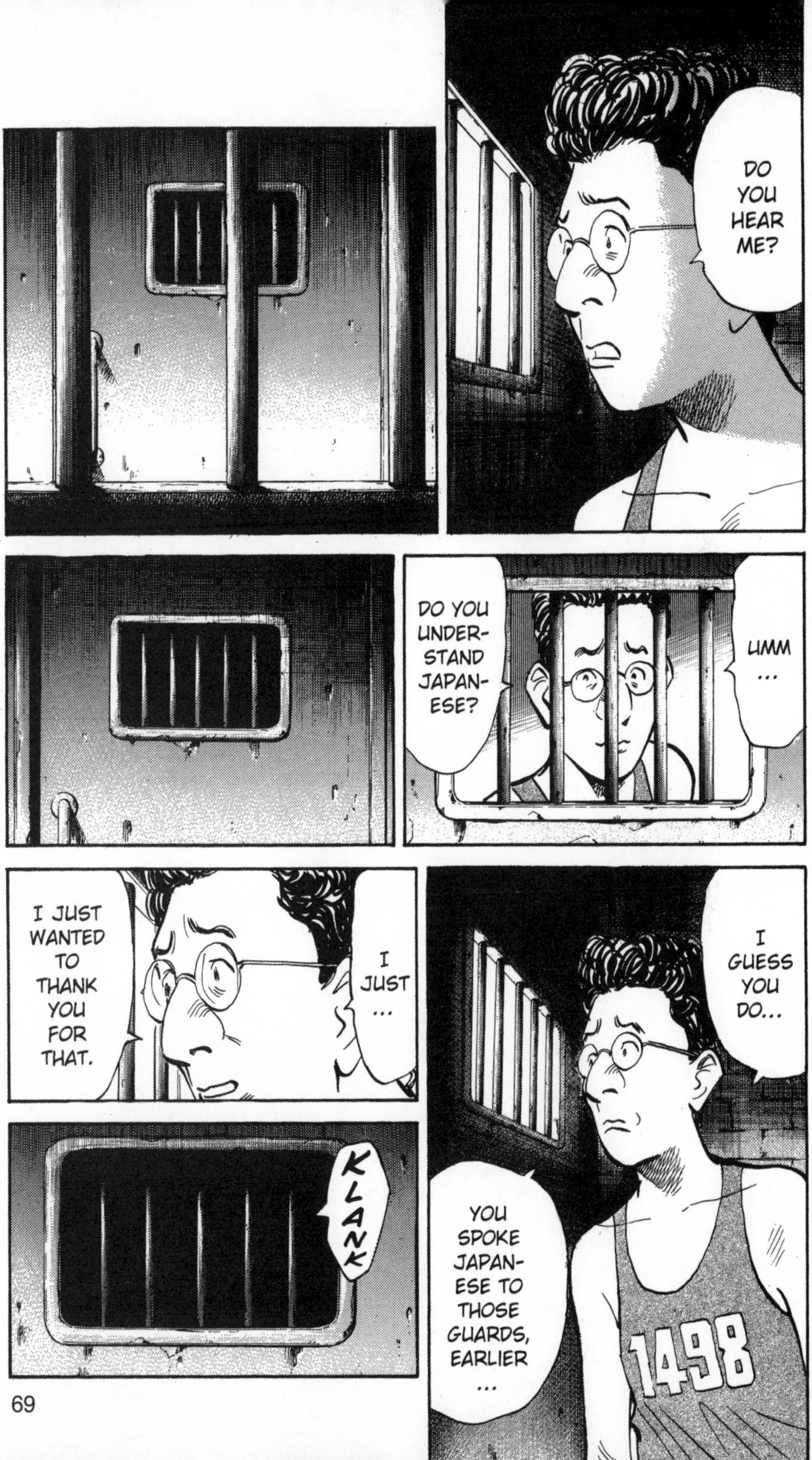
DO YOU HEAR ME?
UMM...
DO YOU UNDERSTAND JAPANESE?
I GUESS YOU DO...
YOU SPOKE JAPANESE TO THOSE GUARDS, EARLIER...
I JUST...
I JUST WANTED TO THANK YOU FOR THAT.
KLANK

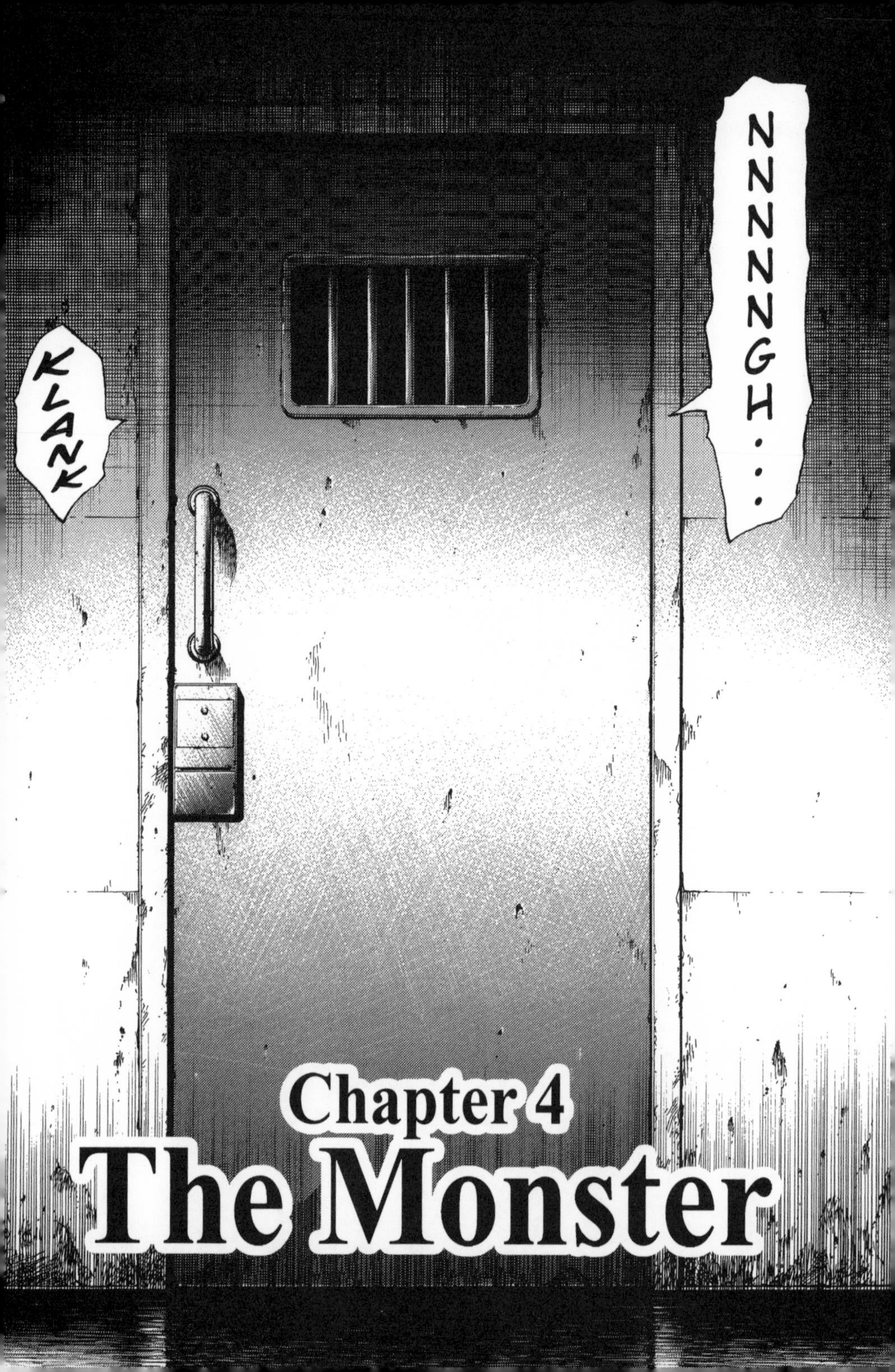
NNNNNGH...
KLANK

Chapter 4
The Monster

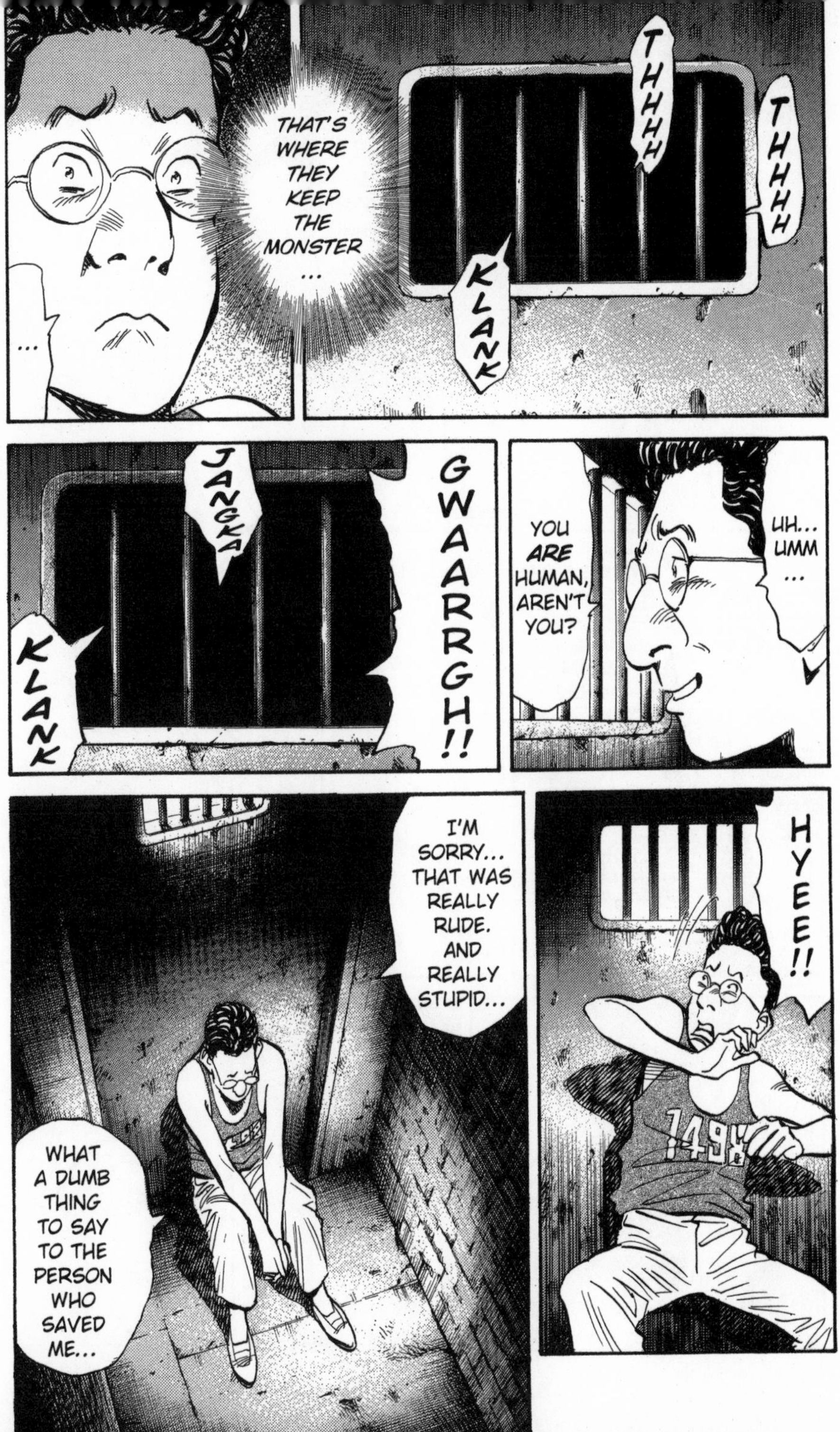
THHHH
THHHH
KLANK
THAT'S WHERE THEY KEEP THE MONSTER...
...
UH... UMM...
YOU ARE HUMAN, AREN'T YOU?
GWAARRRGH!!
JANGKA
KLANK
HYEEE!!
I'M SORRY... THAT WAS REALLY RUDE. AND REALLY STUPID...
WHAT A DUMB THING TO SAY TO THE PERSON WHO SAVED ME...

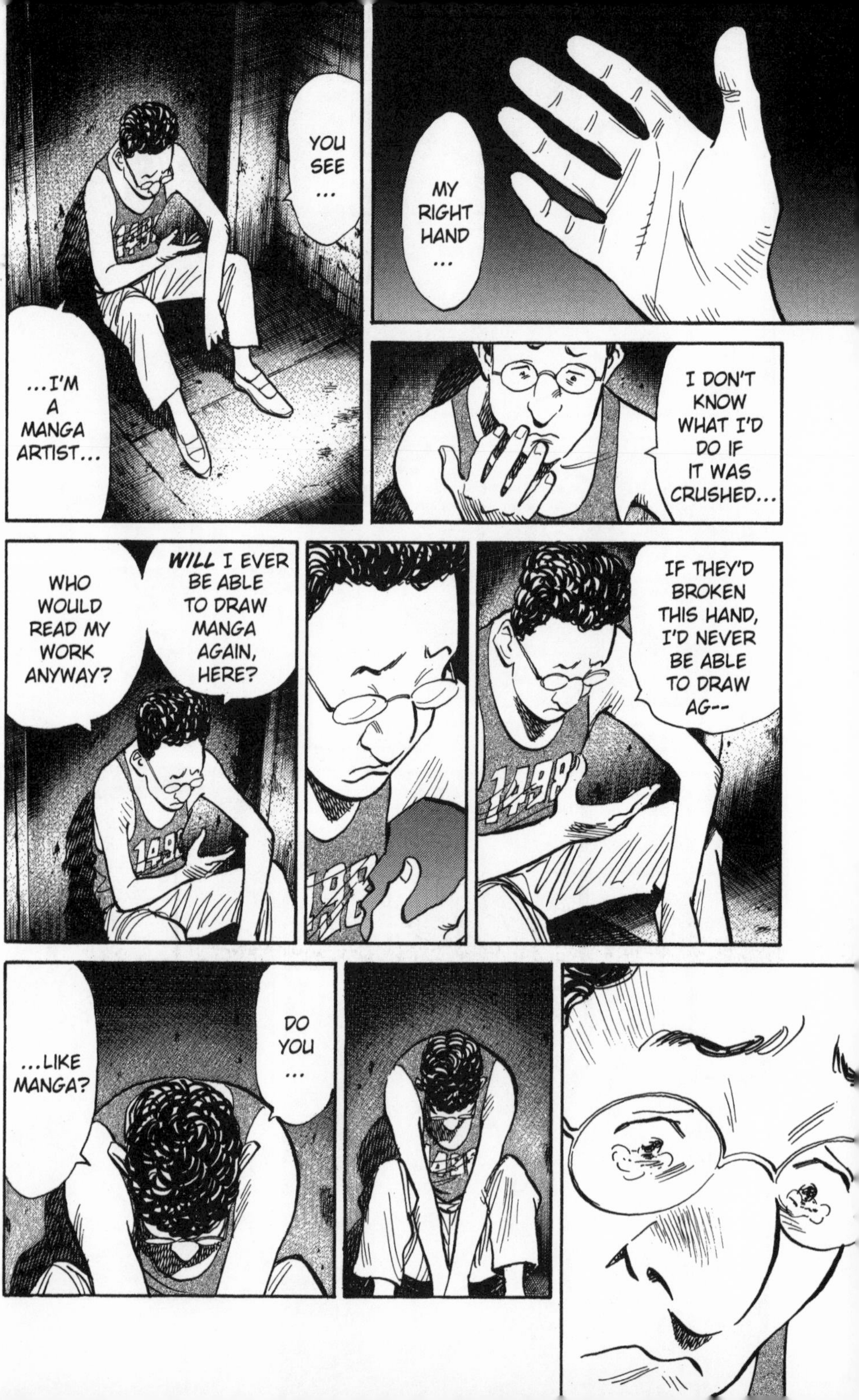
MY RIGHT HAND ...
I DON'T KNOW WHAT I'D DO IF IT WAS CRUSHED...
YOU SEE ...
...I'M A MANGA ARTIST...
IF THEY'D BROKEN THIS HAND, I'D NEVER BE ABLE TO DRAW AG--
WILL I EVER BE ABLE TO DRAW MANGA AGAIN, HERE?
WHO WOULD READ MY WORK ANYWAY?
DO YOU ...
...LIKE MANGA?

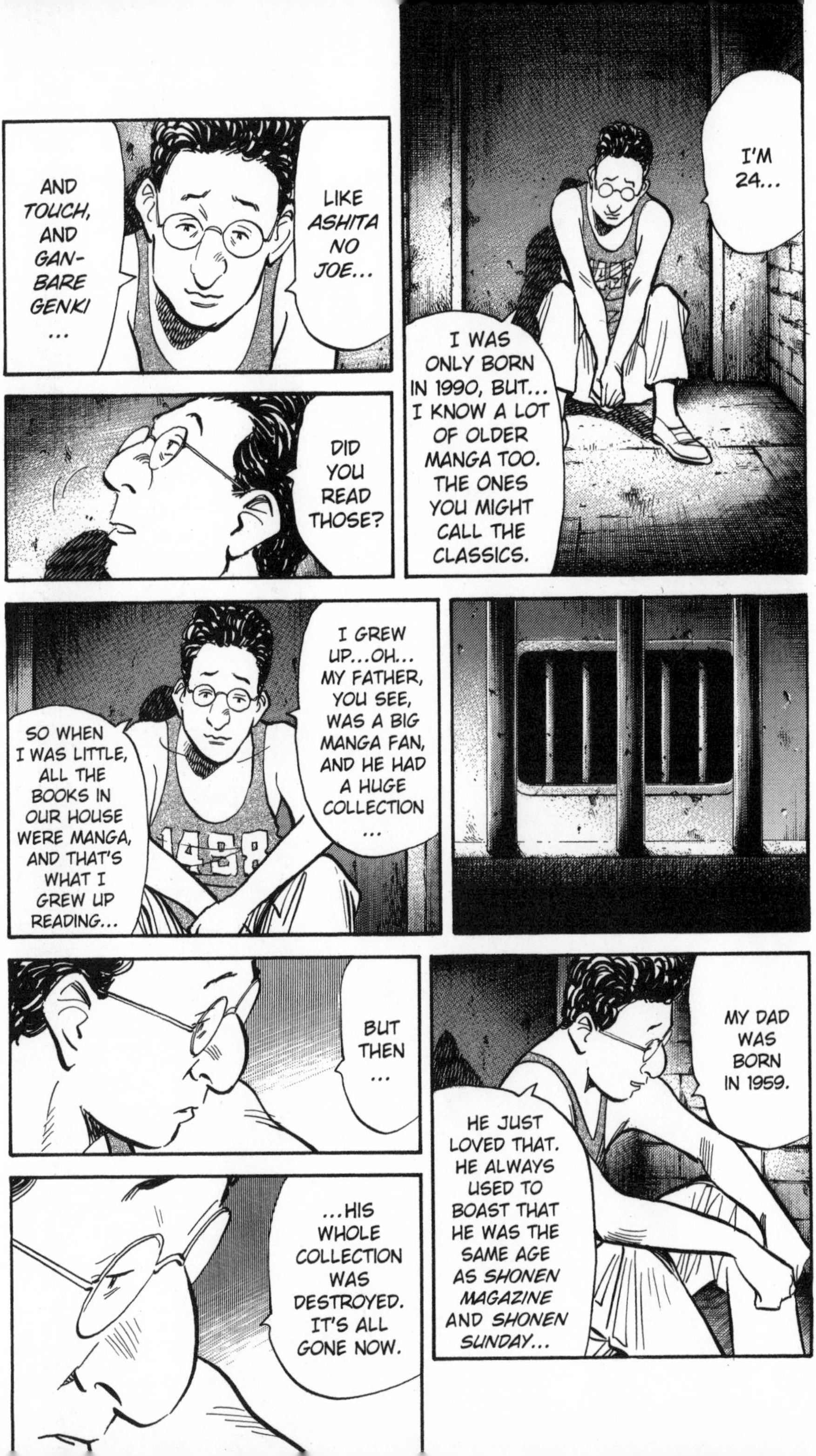
I'M 24...
I WAS ONLY BORN IN 1990, BUT... I KNOW A LOT OF OLDER MANGA TOO. THE ONES YOU MIGHT CALL THE CLASSICS.
LIKE *ASHITA NO JOE*...
AND *TOUCH*, AND *GAN-BARE GENKI* ...
DID YOU READ THOSE?
I GREW UP...OH... MY FATHER, YOU SEE, WAS A BIG MANGA FAN, AND HE HAD A HUGE COLLECTION ...
SO WHEN I WAS LITTLE, ALL THE BOOKS IN OUR HOUSE WERE MANGA, AND THAT'S WHAT I GREW UP READING...
MY DAD WAS BORN IN 1959.
HE JUST LOVED THAT. HE ALWAYS USED TO BOAST THAT HE WAS THE SAME AGE AS *SHONEN MAGAZINE* AND *SHONEN SUNDAY*...
BUT THEN ...
...HIS WHOLE COLLECTION WAS DESTROYED. IT'S ALL GONE NOW.

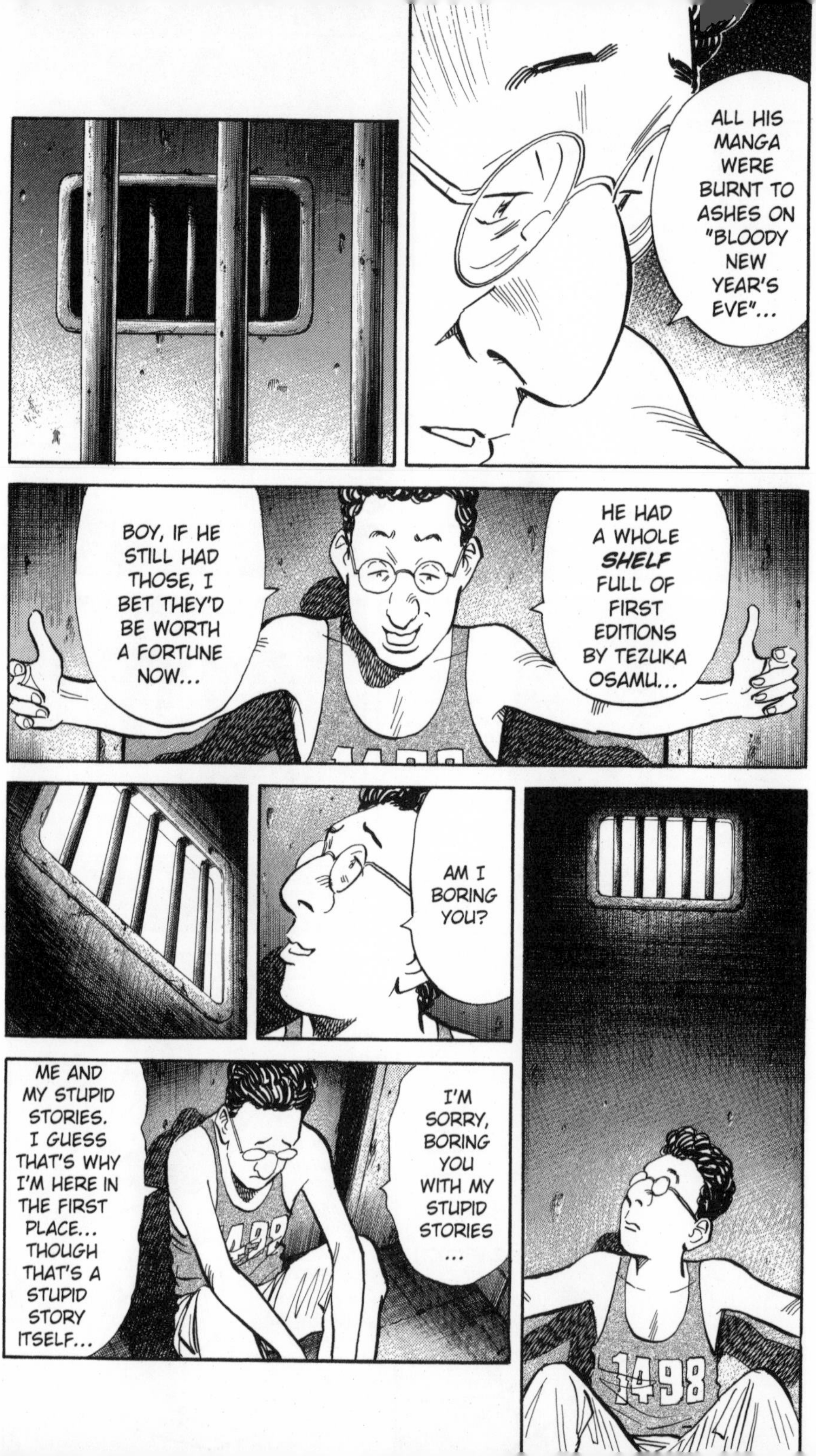
ALL HIS MANGA WERE BURNT TO ASHES ON "BLOODY NEW YEAR'S EVE"...
HE HAD A WHOLE ***SHELF*** FULL OF FIRST EDITIONS BY TEZUKA OSAMU...
BOY, IF HE STILL HAD THOSE, I BET THEY'D BE WORTH A FORTUNE NOW...
AM I BORING YOU?
I'M SORRY, BORING YOU WITH MY STUPID STORIES...
ME AND MY STUPID STORIES. I GUESS THAT'S WHY I'M HERE IN THE FIRST PLACE... THOUGH THAT'S A STUPID STORY ITSELF...

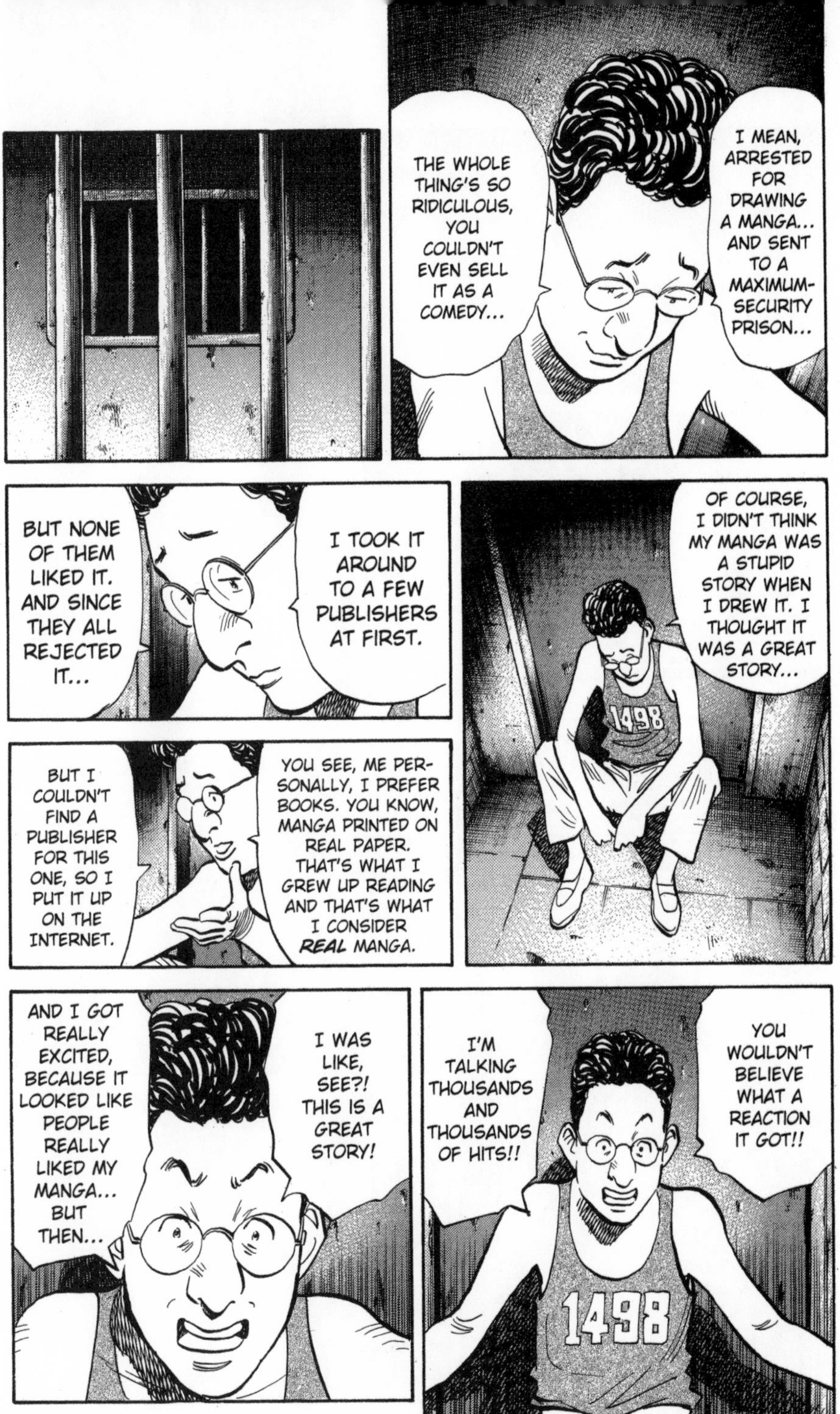
I MEAN, ARRESTED FOR DRAWING A MANGA... AND SENT TO A MAXIMUM-SECURITY PRISON...
THE WHOLE THING'S SO RIDICULOUS, YOU COULDN'T EVEN SELL IT AS A COMEDY...
OF COURSE, I DIDN'T THINK MY MANGA WAS A STUPID STORY WHEN I DREW IT. I THOUGHT IT WAS A GREAT STORY...
1498
I TOOK IT AROUND TO A FEW PUBLISHERS AT FIRST.
BUT NONE OF THEM LIKED IT. AND SINCE THEY ALL REJECTED IT...
YOU SEE, ME PERSONALLY, I PREFER BOOKS. YOU KNOW, MANGA PRINTED ON REAL PAPER. THAT'S WHAT I GREW UP READING AND THAT'S WHAT I CONSIDER ***REAL*** MANGA.
BUT I COULDN'T FIND A PUBLISHER FOR THIS ONE, SO I PUT IT UP ON THE INTERNET.
YOU WOULDN'T BELIEVE WHAT A REACTION IT GOT!!
I'M TALKING THOUSANDS AND THOUSANDS OF HITS!!
1498
I WAS LIKE, SEE?! THIS IS A GREAT STORY!
AND I GOT REALLY EXCITED, BECAUSE IT LOOKED LIKE PEOPLE REALLY LIKED MY MANGA... BUT THEN...

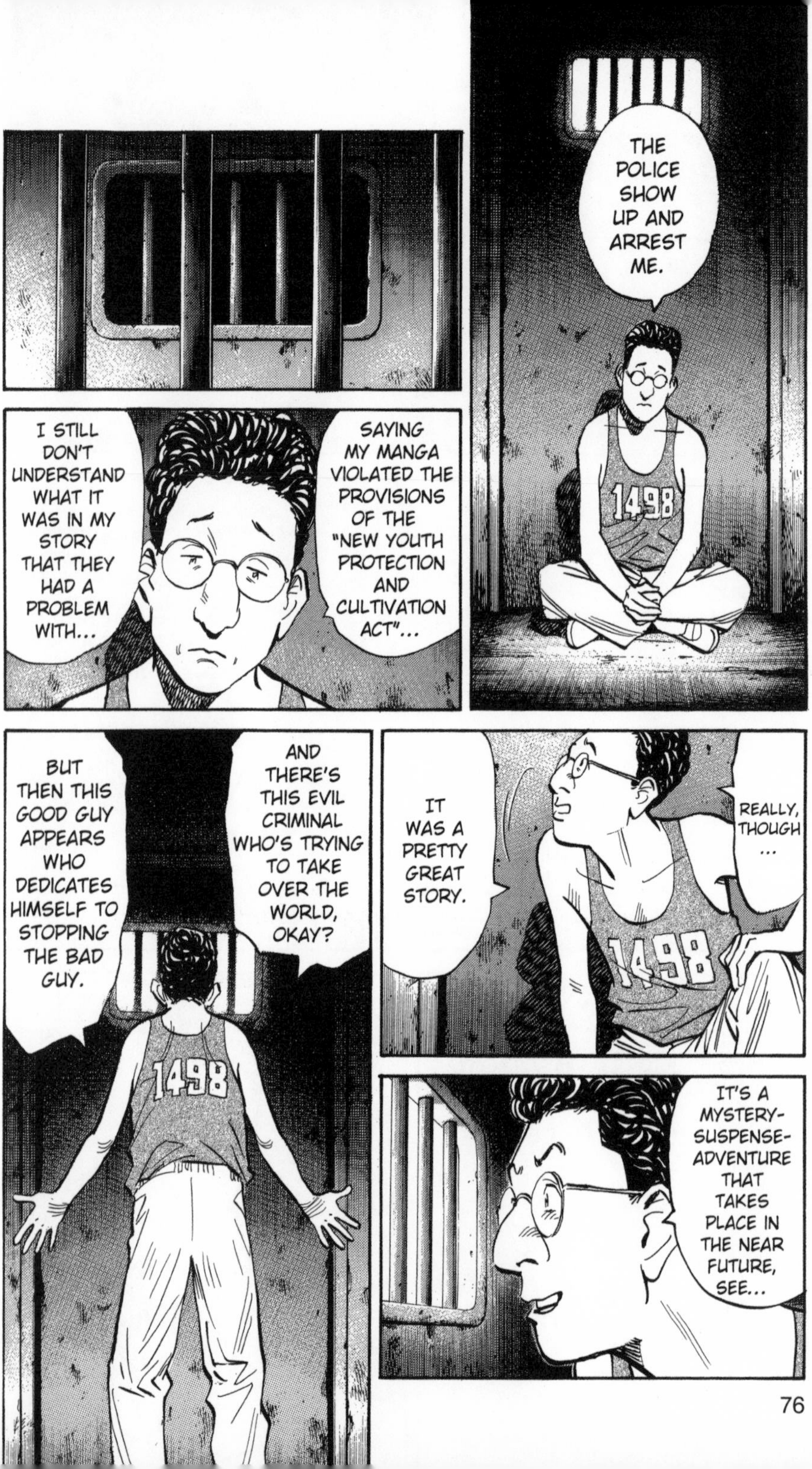
THE POLICE SHOW UP AND ARREST ME.
SAYING MY MANGA VIOLATED THE PROVISIONS OF THE "NEW YOUTH PROTECTION AND CULTIVATION ACT"...
I STILL DON'T UNDERSTAND WHAT IT WAS IN MY STORY THAT THEY HAD A PROBLEM WITH...
REALLY, THOUGH ...
IT WAS A PRETTY GREAT STORY.
IT'S A MYSTERY-SUSPENSE-ADVENTURE THAT TAKES PLACE IN THE NEAR FUTURE, SEE...
AND THERE'S THIS EVIL CRIMINAL WHO'S TRYING TO TAKE OVER THE WORLD, OKAY?
BUT THEN THIS GOOD GUY APPEARS WHO DEDICATES HIMSELF TO STOPPING THE BAD GUY.

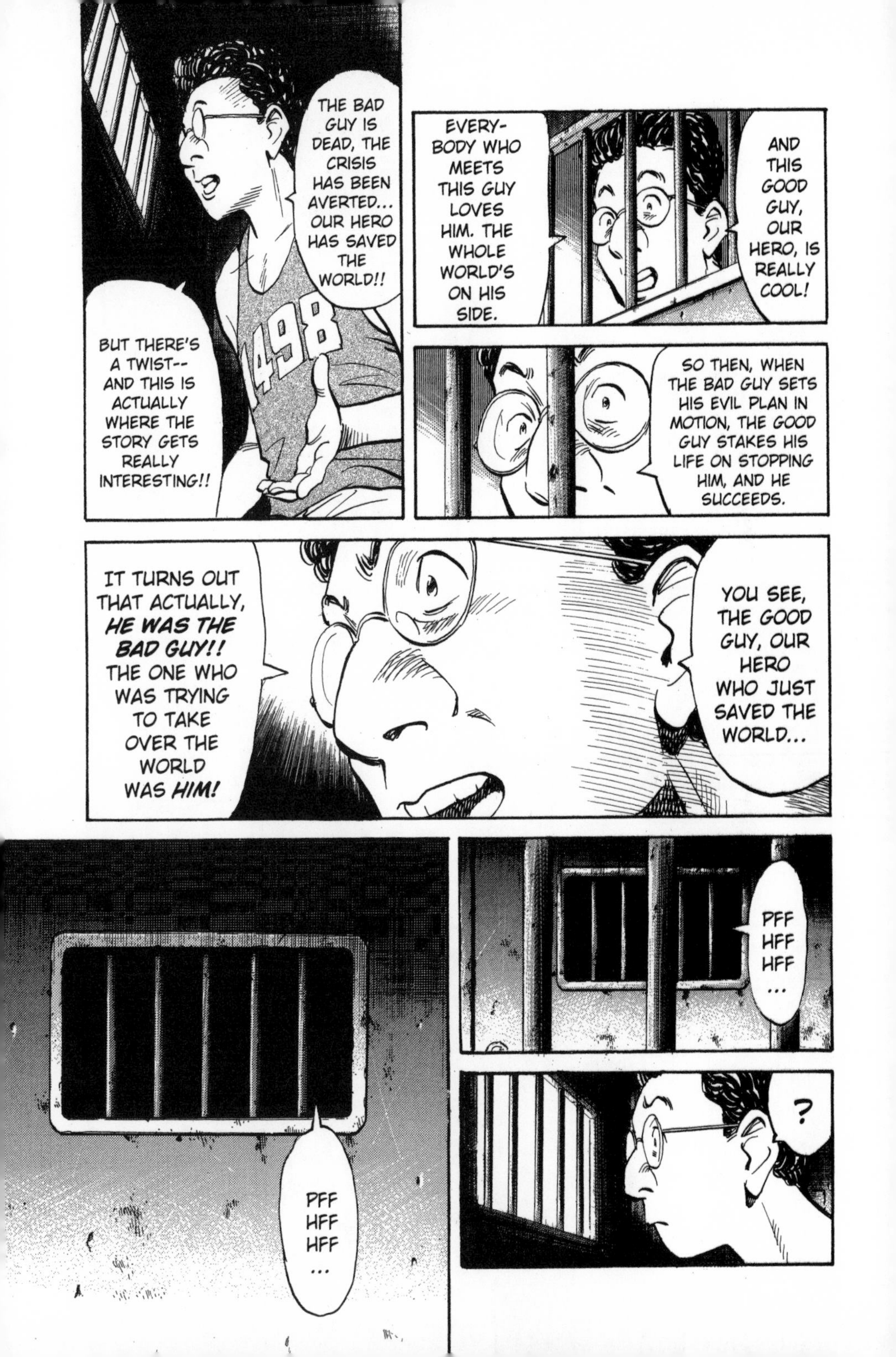
AND THIS GOOD GUY, OUR HERO, IS REALLY COOL!
EVERY-BODY WHO MEETS THIS GUY LOVES HIM. THE WHOLE WORLD'S ON HIS SIDE.
SO THEN, WHEN THE BAD GUY SETS HIS EVIL PLAN IN MOTION, THE GOOD GUY STAKES HIS LIFE ON STOPPING HIM, AND HE SUCCEEDS.
THE BAD GUY IS DEAD, THE CRISIS HAS BEEN AVERTED... OUR HERO HAS SAVED THE WORLD!!
BUT THERE'S A TWIST-- AND THIS IS ACTUALLY WHERE THE STORY GETS REALLY INTERESTING!!
YOU SEE, THE GOOD GUY, OUR HERO WHO JUST SAVED THE WORLD...
IT TURNS OUT THAT ACTUALLY, HE WAS THE BAD GUY!! THE ONE WHO WAS TRYING TO TAKE OVER THE WORLD WAS HIM!
PFF HFF HFF ...
?
PFF HFF HFF ...

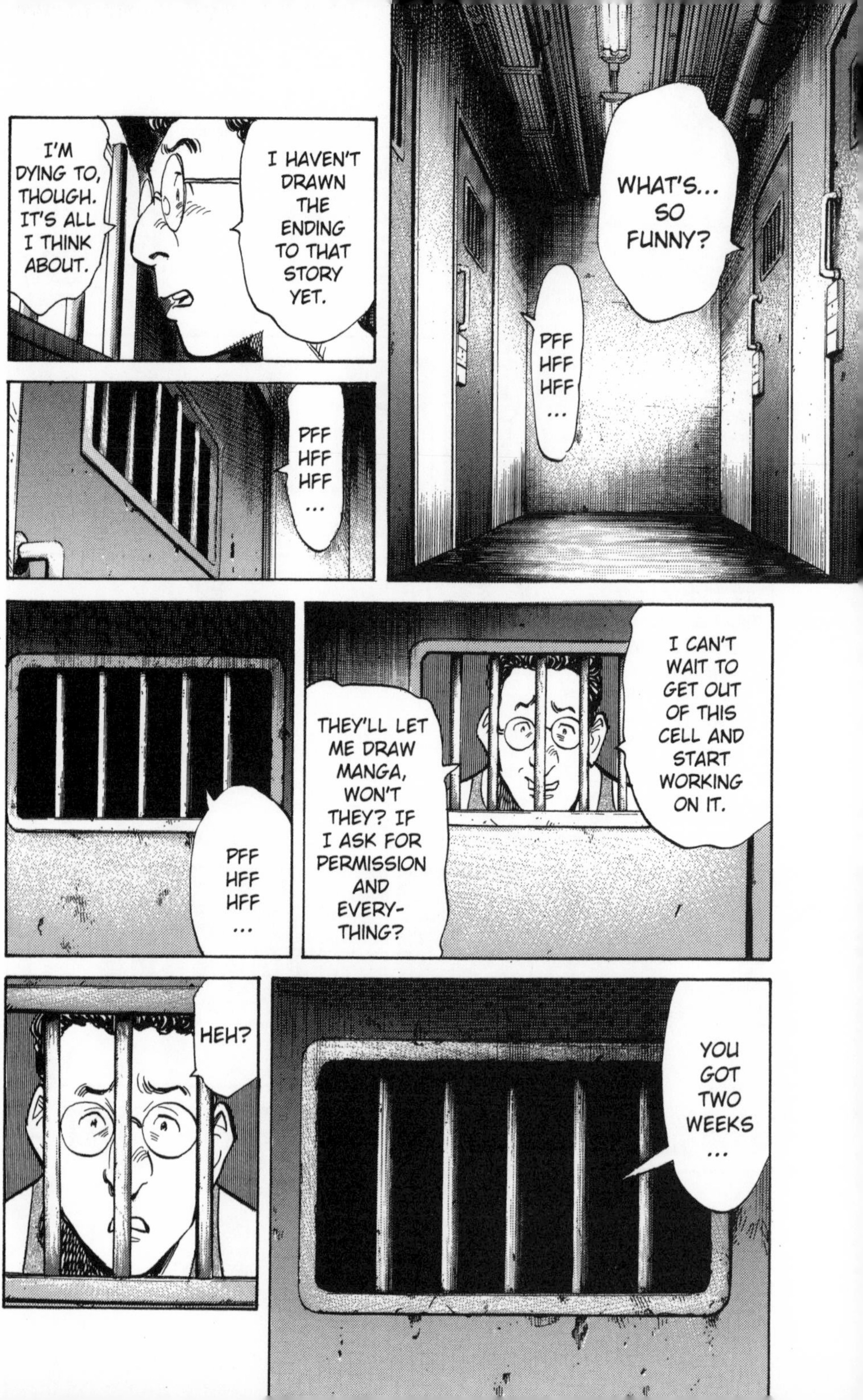
WHAT'S... SO FUNNY?
PFF HFF HFF...
I HAVEN'T DRAWN THE ENDING TO THAT STORY YET.
I'M DYING TO, THOUGH. IT'S ALL I THINK ABOUT.
PFF HFF HFF...
I CAN'T WAIT TO GET OUT OF THIS CELL AND START WORKING ON IT.
THEY'LL LET ME DRAW MANGA, WON'T THEY? IF I ASK FOR PERMISSION AND EVERY-THING?
PFF HFF HFF...
YOU GOT TWO WEEKS...
HEH?

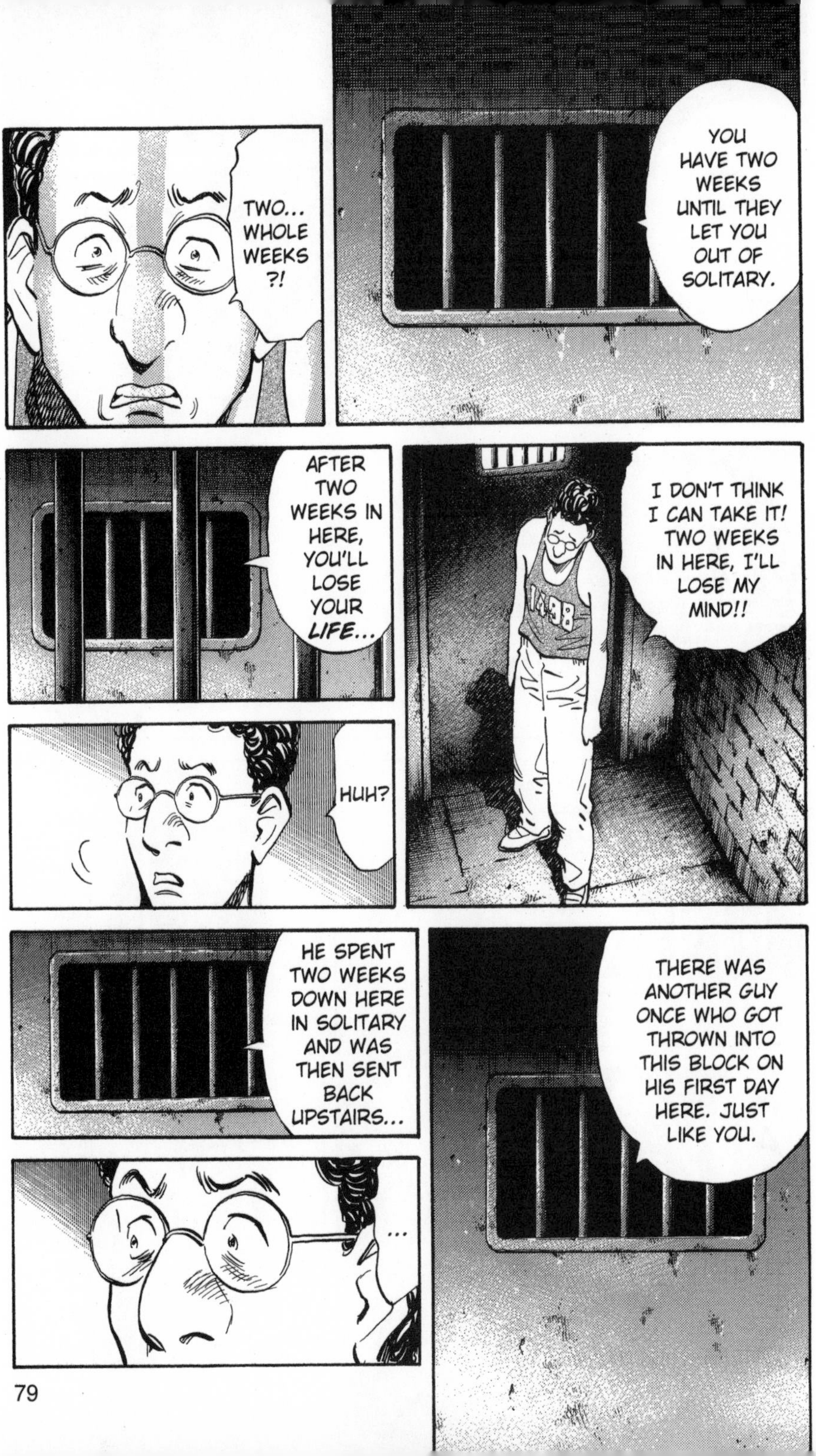
YOU HAVE TWO WEEKS UNTIL THEY LET YOU OUT OF SOLITARY.
TWO... WHOLE WEEKS ?!
I DON'T THINK I CAN TAKE IT! TWO WEEKS IN HERE, I'LL LOSE MY MIND!!
AFTER TWO WEEKS IN HERE, YOU'LL LOSE YOUR *LIFE*...
HUH?
THERE WAS ANOTHER GUY ONCE WHO GOT THROWN INTO THIS BLOCK ON HIS FIRST DAY HERE. JUST LIKE YOU.
HE SPENT TWO WEEKS DOWN HERE IN SOLITARY AND WAS THEN SENT BACK UPSTAIRS...
...

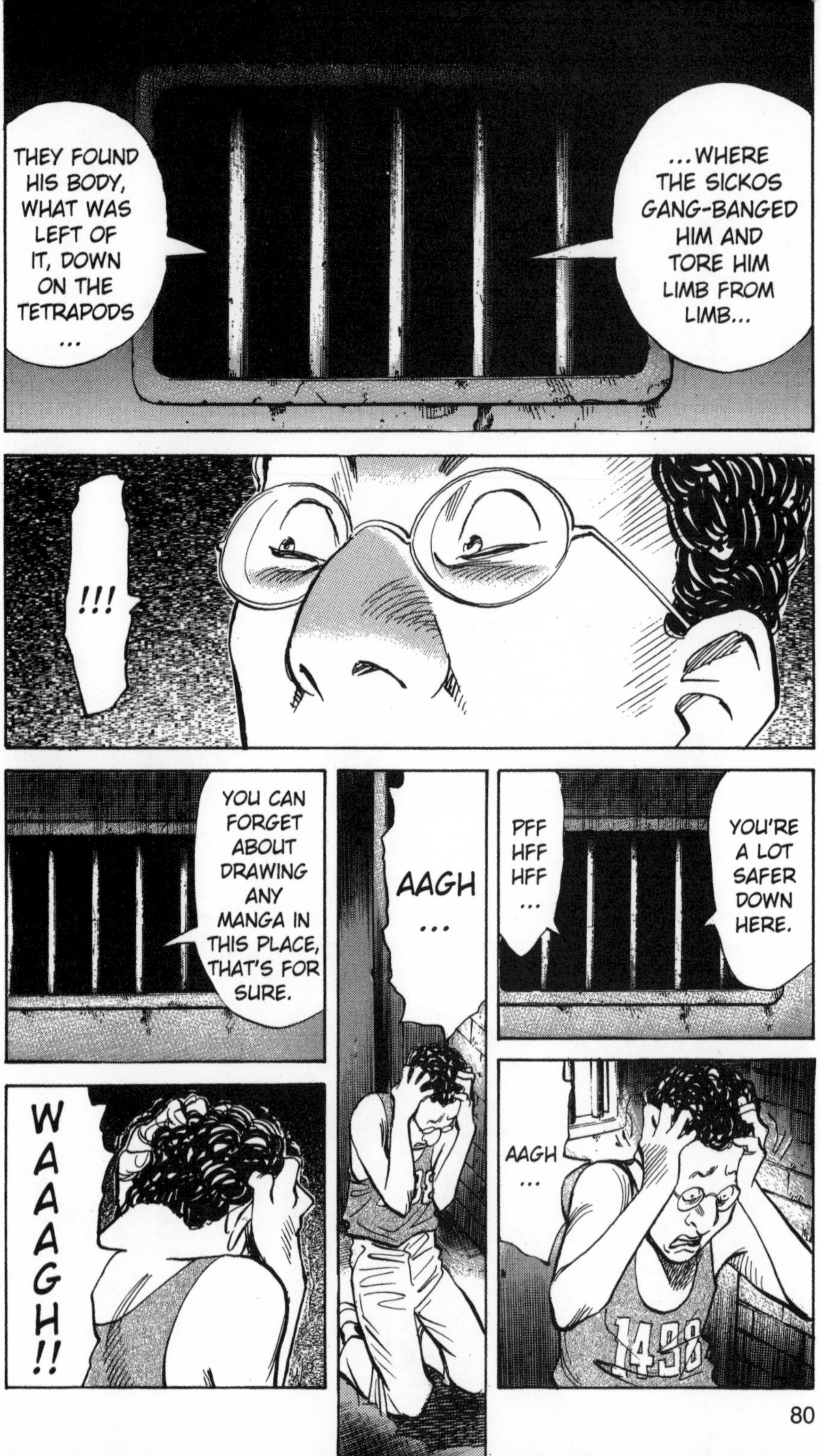

THEY FOUND HIS BODY, WHAT WAS LEFT OF IT, DOWN ON THE TETRAPODS ...
...WHERE THE SICKOS GANG-BANGED HIM AND TORE HIM LIMB FROM LIMB...
!!!
YOU'RE A LOT SAFER DOWN HERE.
PFF HFF HFF ...
AAGH ...
AAGH ...
YOU CAN FORGET ABOUT DRAWING ANY MANGA IN THIS PLACE, THAT'S FOR SURE.
WAAAAGH!!

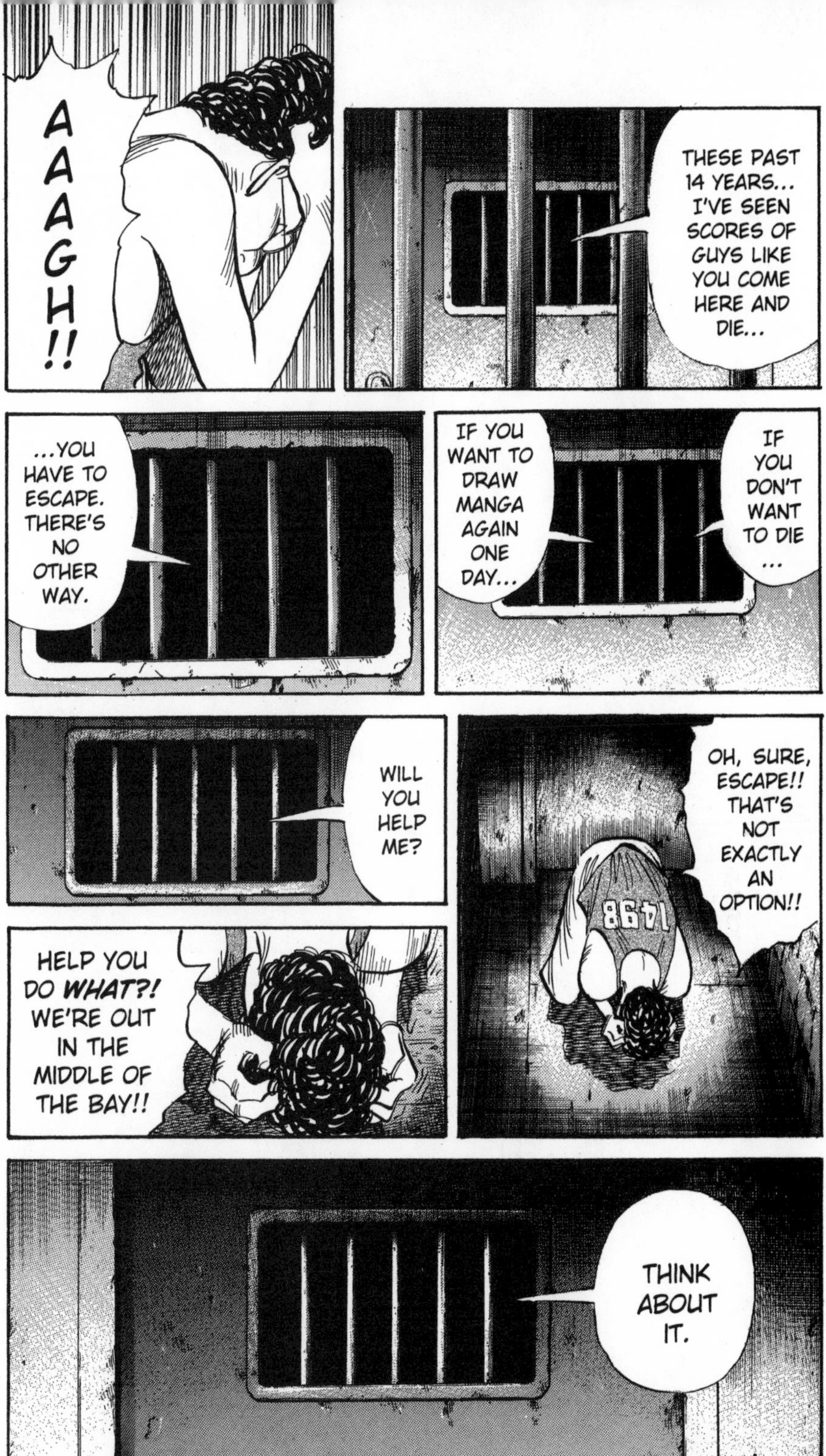
THESE PAST 14 YEARS... I'VE SEEN SCORES OF GUYS LIKE YOU COME HERE AND DIE...
AAAAGH!!
IF YOU DON'T WANT TO DIE ...
IF YOU WANT TO DRAW MANGA AGAIN ONE DAY...
...YOU HAVE TO ESCAPE. THERE'S NO OTHER WAY.
OH, SURE, ESCAPE!! THAT'S NOT EXACTLY AN OPTION!!
WILL YOU HELP ME?
HELP YOU DO ***WHAT?!*** WE'RE OUT IN THE MIDDLE OF THE BAY!!
THINK ABOUT IT.

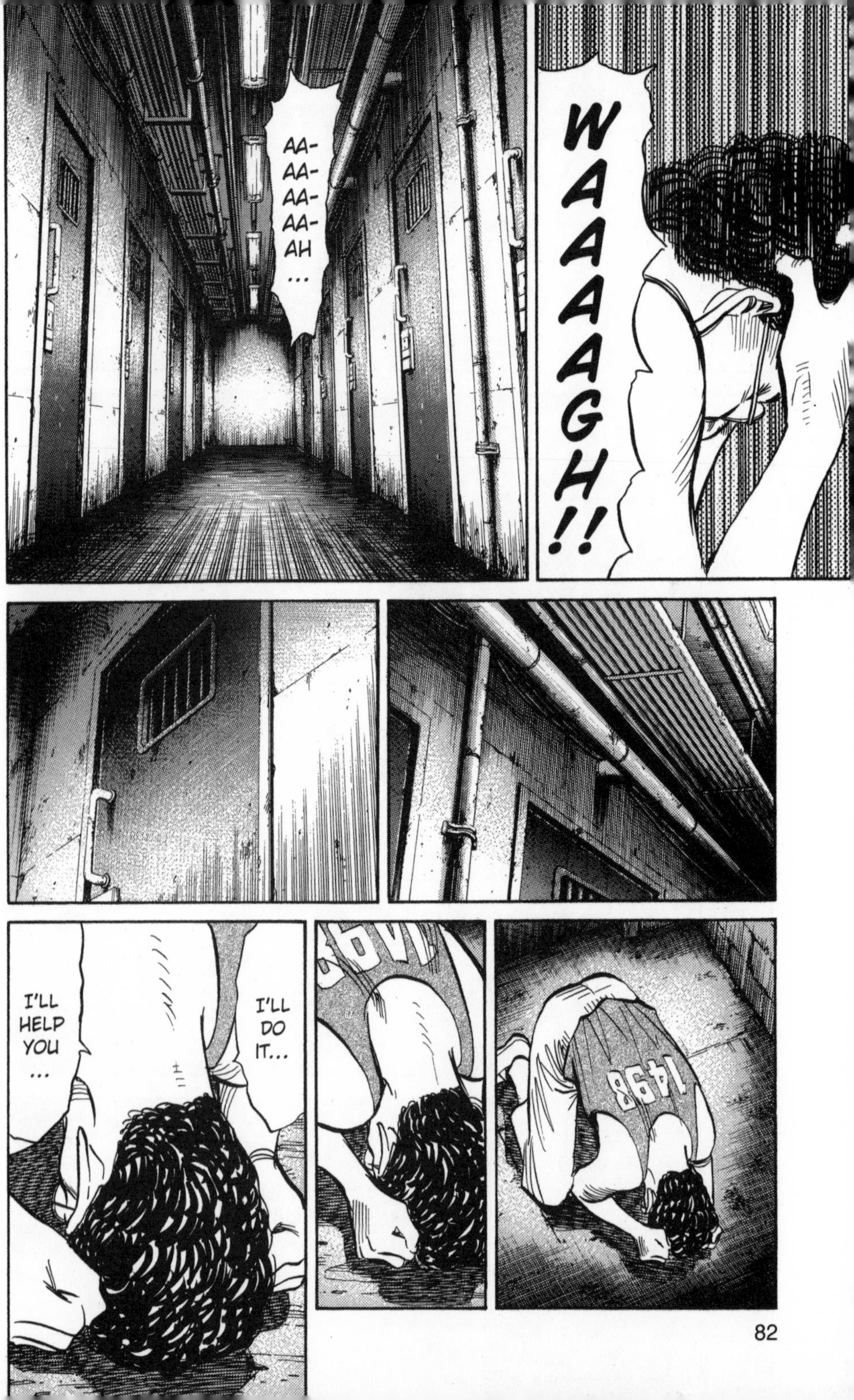
WAAAAAGH!!
AA-AA-AA-AA-AH...
1498
I'LL DO IT...
I'LL HELP YOU...

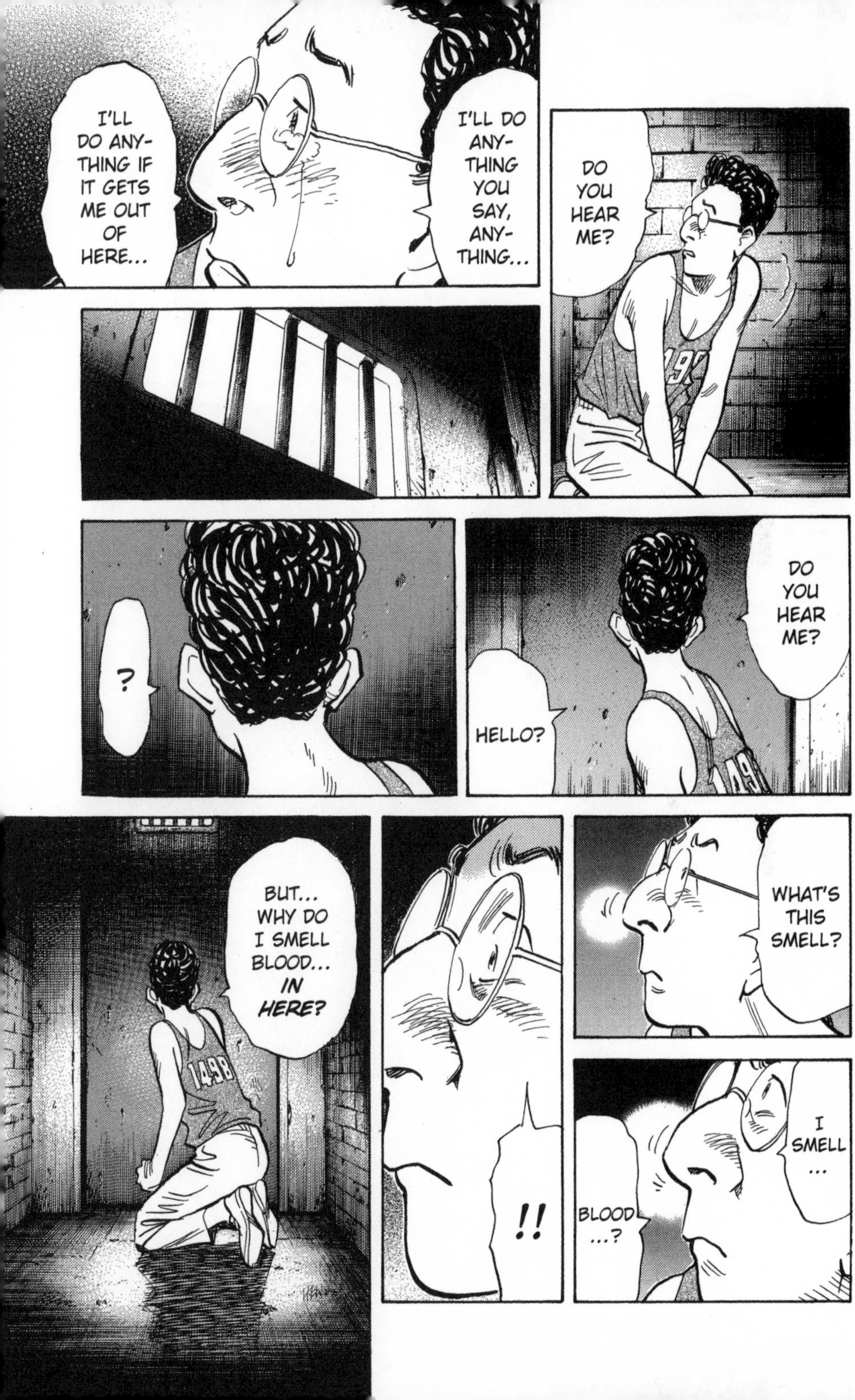
DO YOU HEAR ME?
I'LL DO ANYTHING YOU SAY, ANYTHING...
I'LL DO ANYTHING IF IT GETS ME OUT OF HERE...
DO YOU HEAR ME?
HELLO?
?
WHAT'S THIS SMELL?
I SMELL ...
BLOOD ...?
!!
BUT... WHY DO I SMELL BLOOD... *IN HERE?*

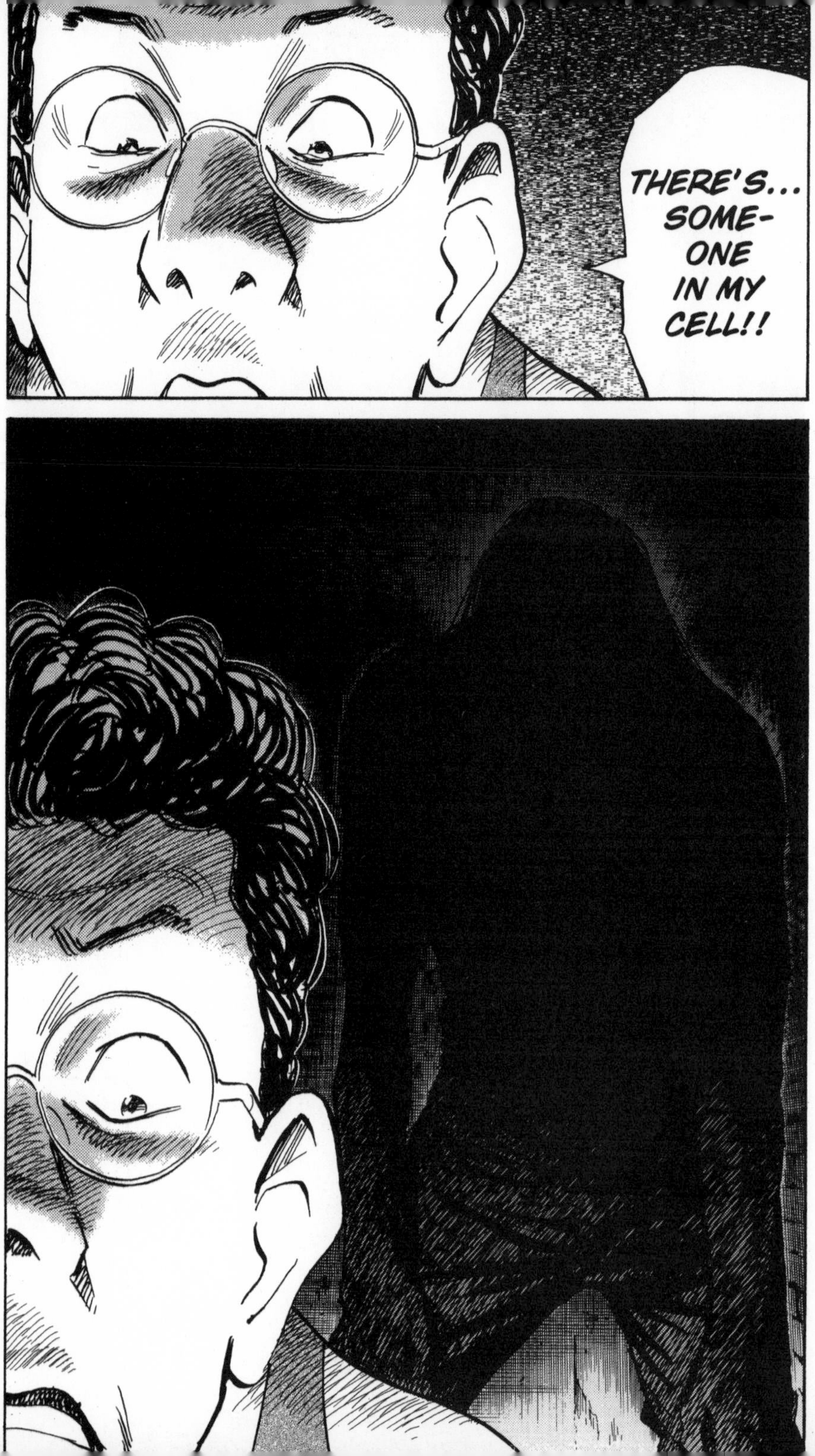
THERE'S... SOME-ONE IN MY CELL!!

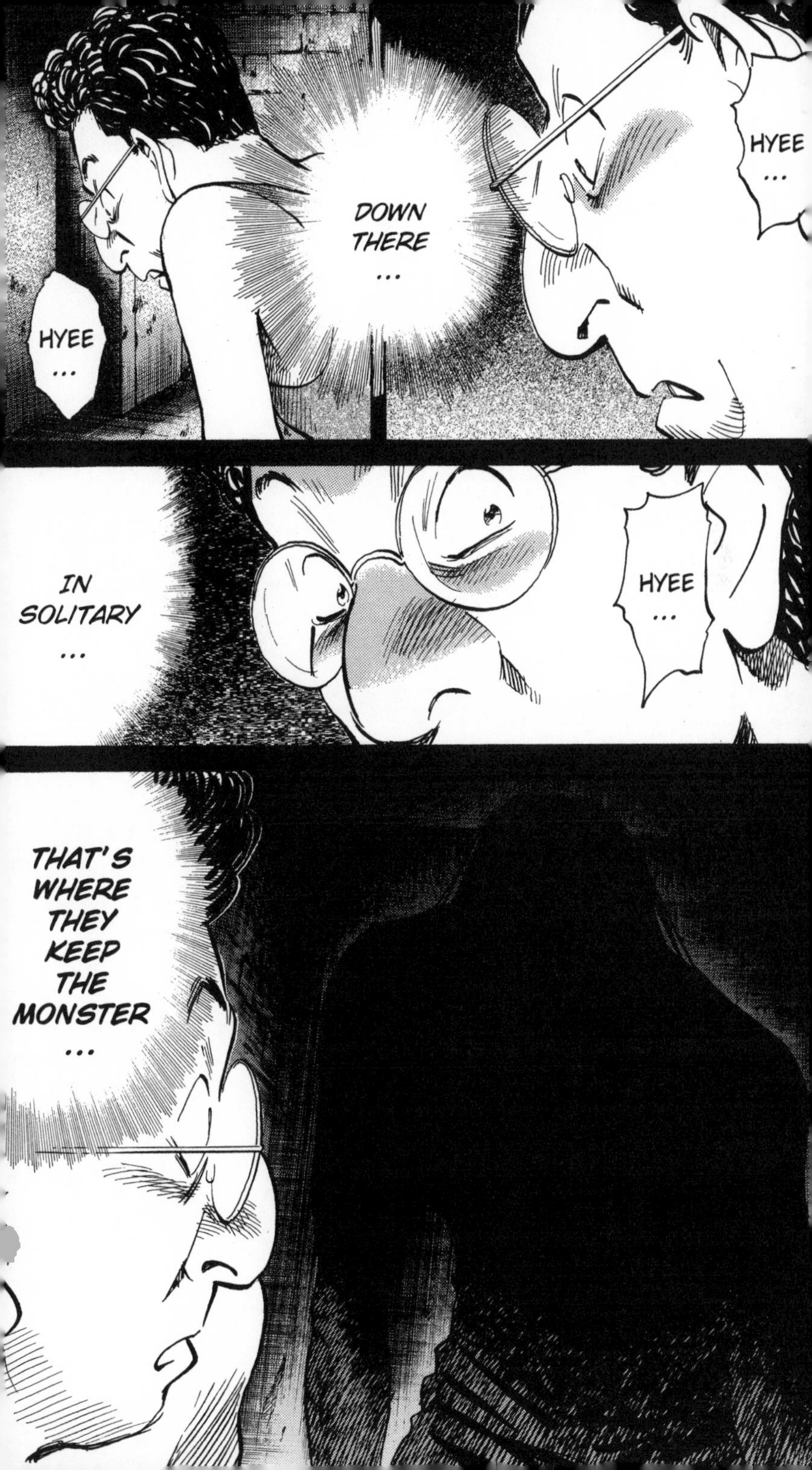
HYEE ...
DOWN THERE ...
HYEE ...
HYEE ...
IN SOLITARY ...
THAT'S WHERE THEY KEEP THE MONSTER ...

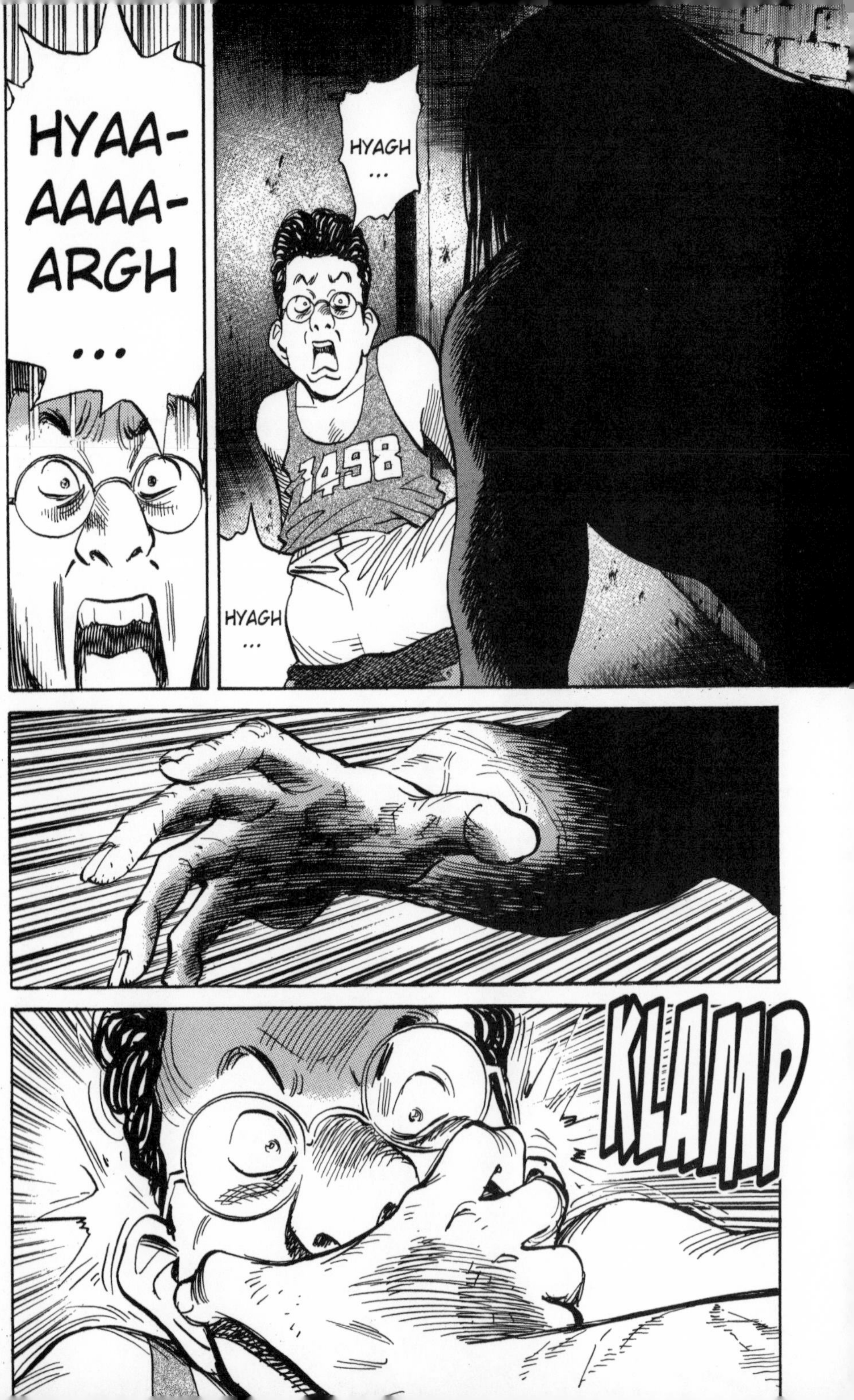
HYAGH ...
HYAGH ...
HYAA-AAAA-ARGH ...
KLAMP

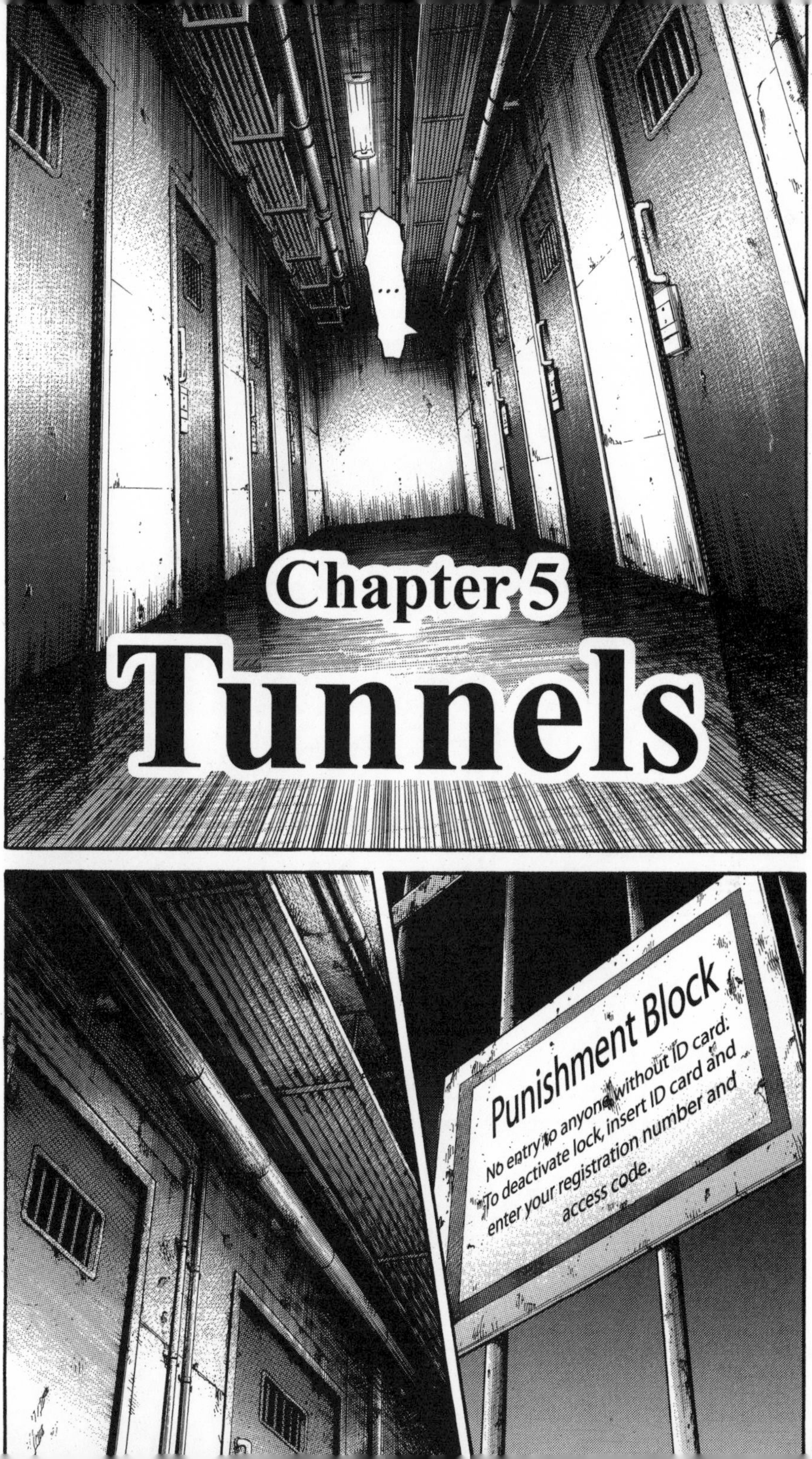
...
Chapter 5
Tunnels
Punishment Block
No entry to anyone without ID card.
To deactivate lock, insert ID card and enter your registration number and access code.

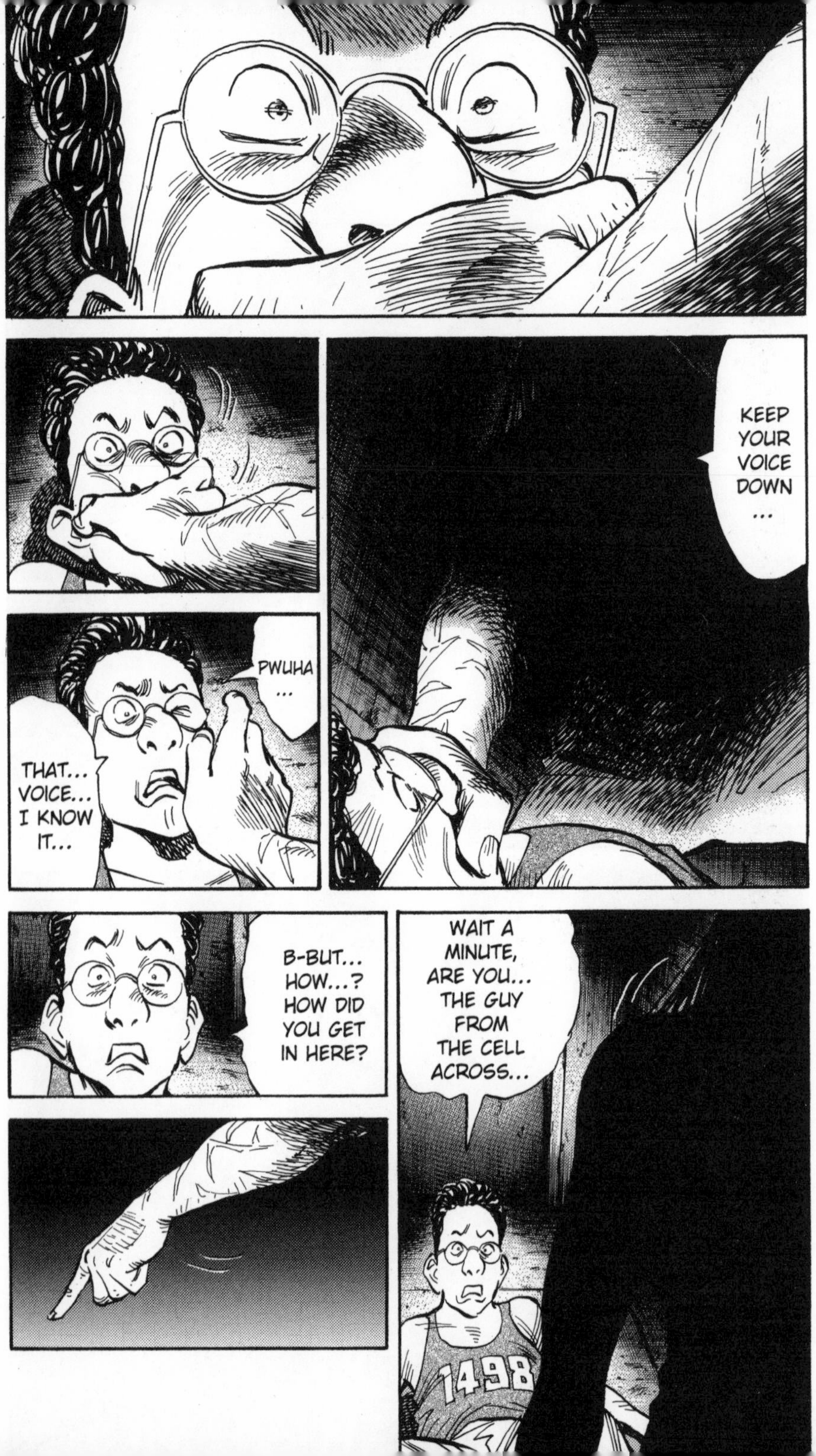
KEEP YOUR VOICE DOWN ...
PWUHA ...
THAT... VOICE... I KNOW IT...
WAIT A MINUTE, ARE YOU... THE GUY FROM THE CELL ACROSS...
1498
B-BUT... HOW...? HOW DID YOU GET IN HERE?

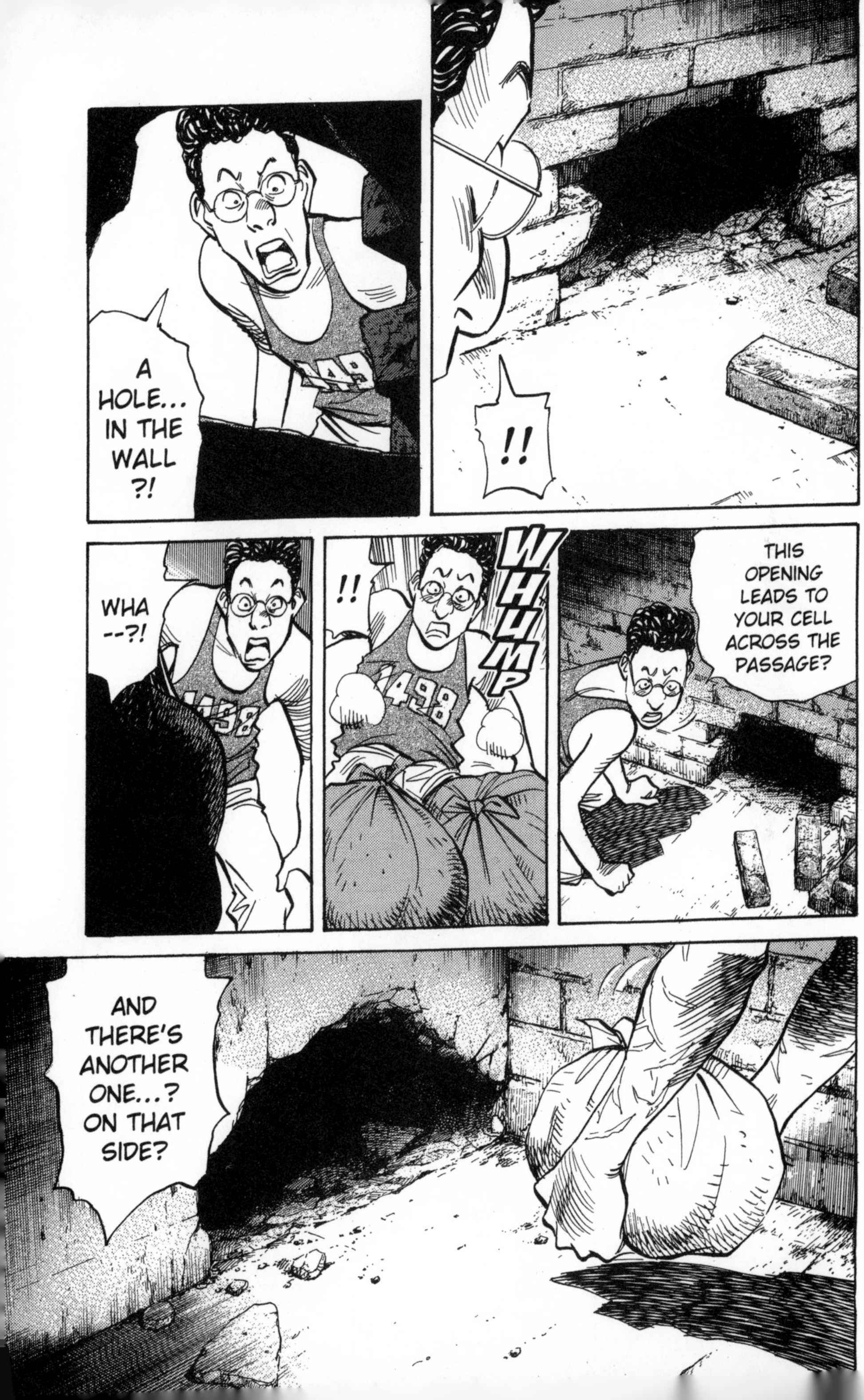
!!
A HOLE... IN THE WALL ?!
THIS OPENING LEADS TO YOUR CELL ACROSS THE PASSAGE?
WHUMP
!!
WHA --?!
AND THERE'S ANOTHER ONE...? ON THAT SIDE?

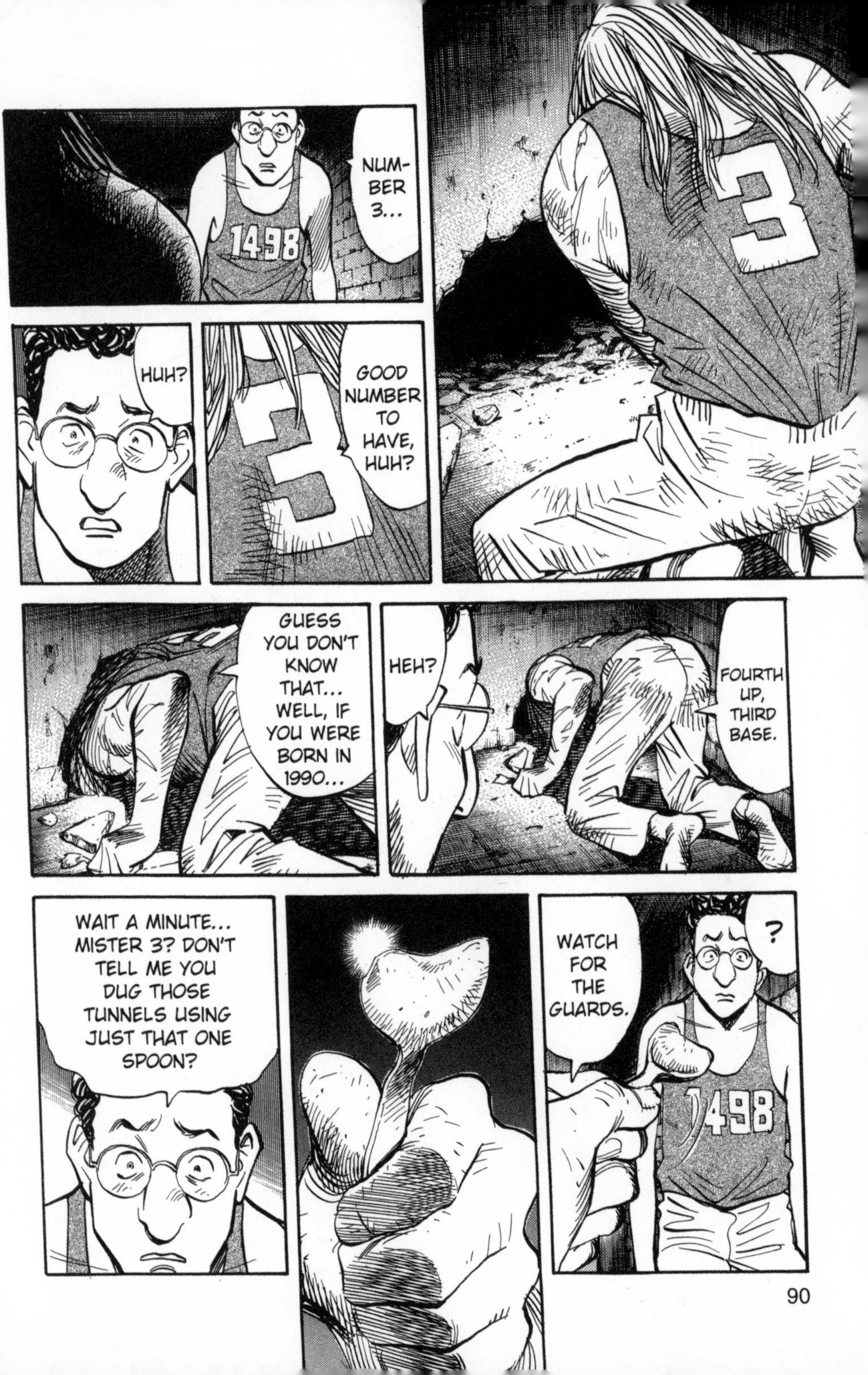
NUM-BER 3...
GOOD NUMBER TO HAVE, HUH?
HUH?
FOURTH UP, THIRD BASE.
HEH?
GUESS YOU DON'T KNOW THAT... WELL, IF YOU WERE BORN IN 1990...
?
WATCH FOR THE GUARDS.
WAIT A MINUTE... MISTER 3? DON'T TELL ME YOU DUG THOSE TUNNELS USING JUST THAT ONE SPOON?

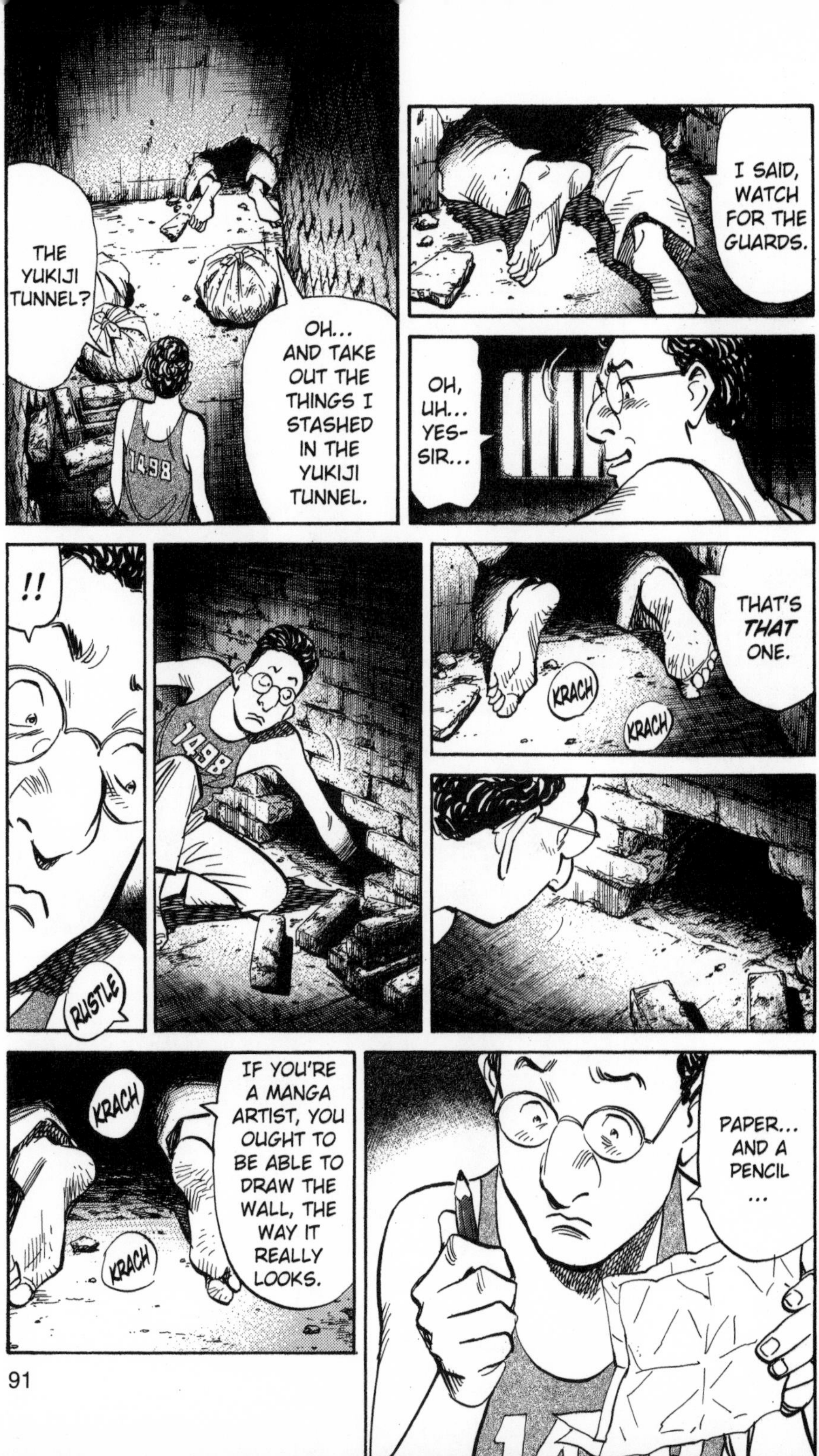
I SAID, WATCH FOR THE GUARDS.
OH, UH... YES-SIR...
OH... AND TAKE OUT THE THINGS I STASHED IN THE YUKIJI TUNNEL.
THE YUKIJI TUNNEL?
THAT'S *THAT* ONE.
KRACH
KRACH
!!
RUSTLE
PAPER... AND A PENCIL ...
KRACH
IF YOU'RE A MANGA ARTIST, YOU OUGHT TO BE ABLE TO DRAW THE WALL, THE WAY IT REALLY LOOKS.
KRACH

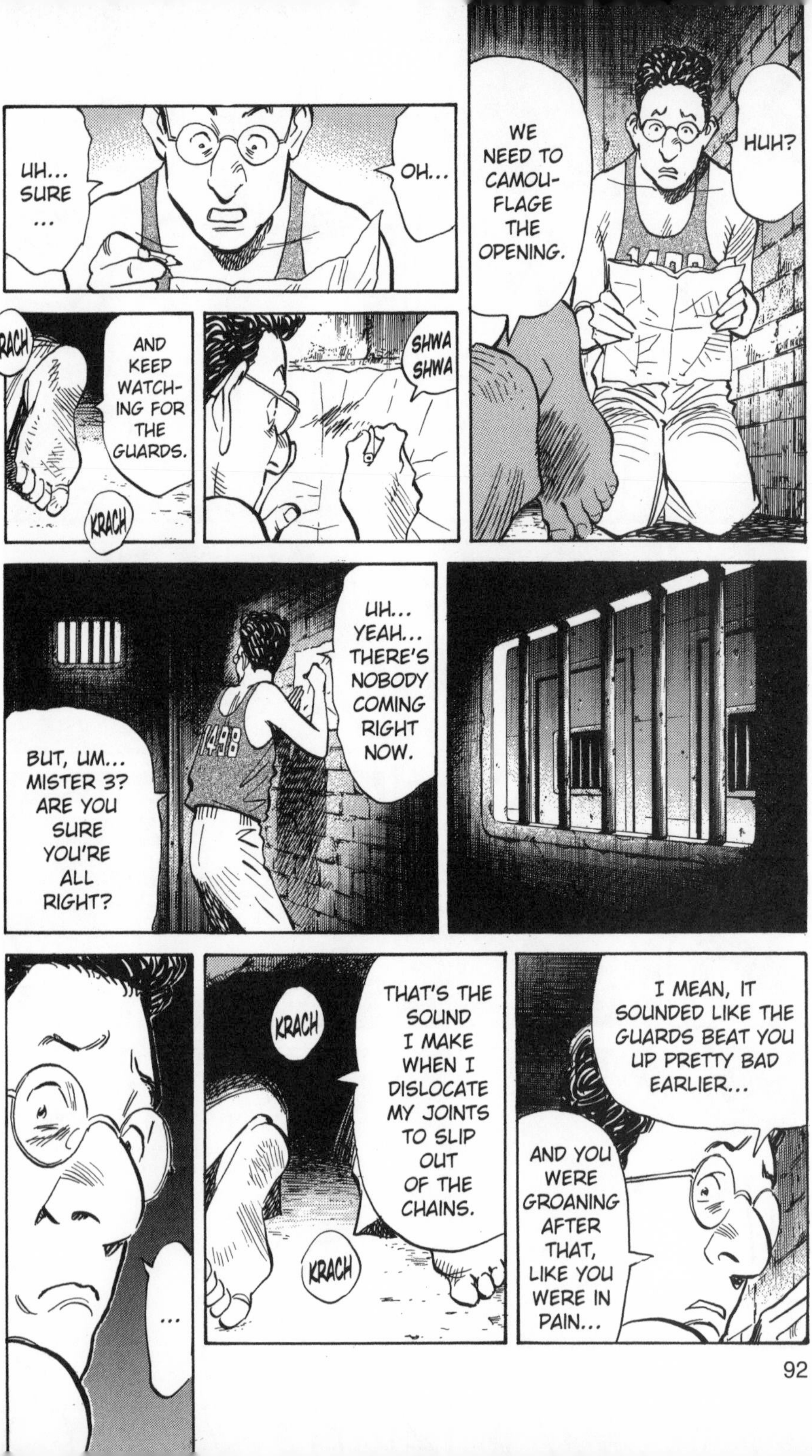
HUH?
WE NEED TO CAMOU-FLAGE THE OPENING.
OH...
UH... SURE ...
SHWA SHWA
KRACH
AND KEEP WATCH-ING FOR THE GUARDS.
KRACH
UH... YEAH... THERE'S NOBODY COMING RIGHT NOW.
BUT, UM... MISTER 3? ARE YOU SURE YOU'RE ALL RIGHT?
I MEAN, IT SOUNDED LIKE THE GUARDS BEAT YOU UP PRETTY BAD EARLIER...
AND YOU WERE GROANING AFTER THAT, LIKE YOU WERE IN PAIN...
KRACH
THAT'S THE SOUND I MAKE WHEN I DISLOCATE MY JOINTS TO SLIP OUT OF THE CHAINS.
KRACH
...

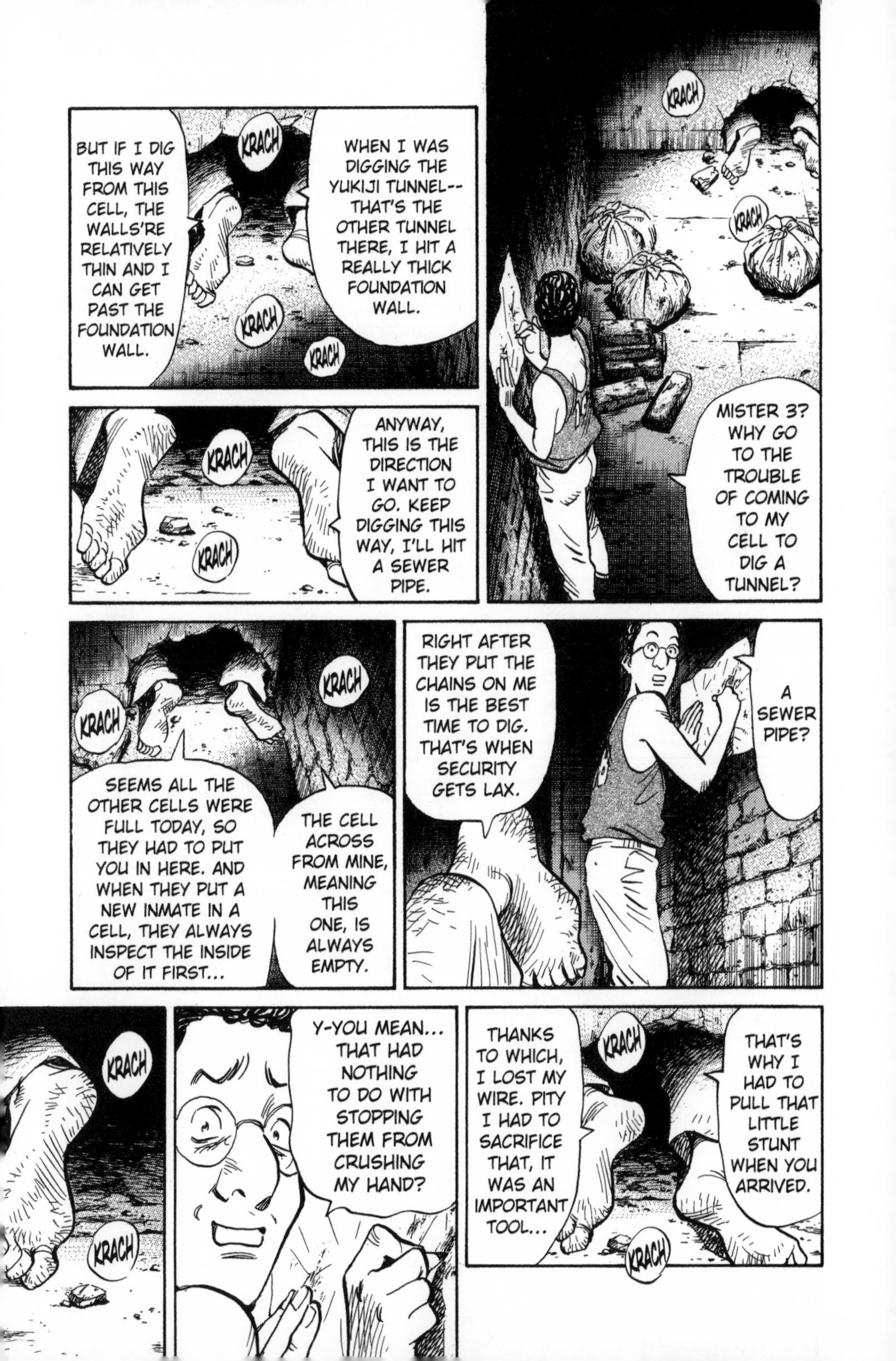
KRACH
KRACH
MISTER 3? WHY GO TO THE TROUBLE OF COMING TO MY CELL TO DIG A TUNNEL?
KRACH
WHEN I WAS DIGGING THE YUKIJI TUNNEL-- THAT'S THE OTHER TUNNEL THERE, I HIT A REALLY THICK FOUNDATION WALL.
BUT IF I DIG THIS WAY FROM THIS CELL, THE WALLS'RE RELATIVELY THIN AND I CAN GET PAST THE FOUNDATION WALL.
KRACH
KRACH
KRACH
ANYWAY, THIS IS THE DIRECTION I WANT TO GO. KEEP DIGGING THIS WAY, I'LL HIT A SEWER PIPE.
KRACH
A SEWER PIPE?
RIGHT AFTER THEY PUT THE CHAINS ON ME IS THE BEST TIME TO DIG. THAT'S WHEN SECURITY GETS LAX.
KRACH
KRACH
THE CELL ACROSS FROM MINE, MEANING THIS ONE, IS ALWAYS EMPTY.
SEEMS ALL THE OTHER CELLS WERE FULL TODAY, SO THEY HAD TO PUT YOU IN HERE. AND WHEN THEY PUT A NEW INMATE IN A CELL, THEY ALWAYS INSPECT THE INSIDE OF IT FIRST...
THAT'S WHY I HAD TO PULL THAT LITTLE STUNT WHEN YOU ARRIVED.
KRACH
THANKS TO WHICH, I LOST MY WIRE. PITY I HAD TO SACRIFICE THAT, IT WAS AN IMPORTANT TOOL...
KRACH
Y-YOU MEAN... THAT HAD NOTHING TO DO WITH STOPPING THEM FROM CRUSHING MY HAND?
KRACH
KRACH

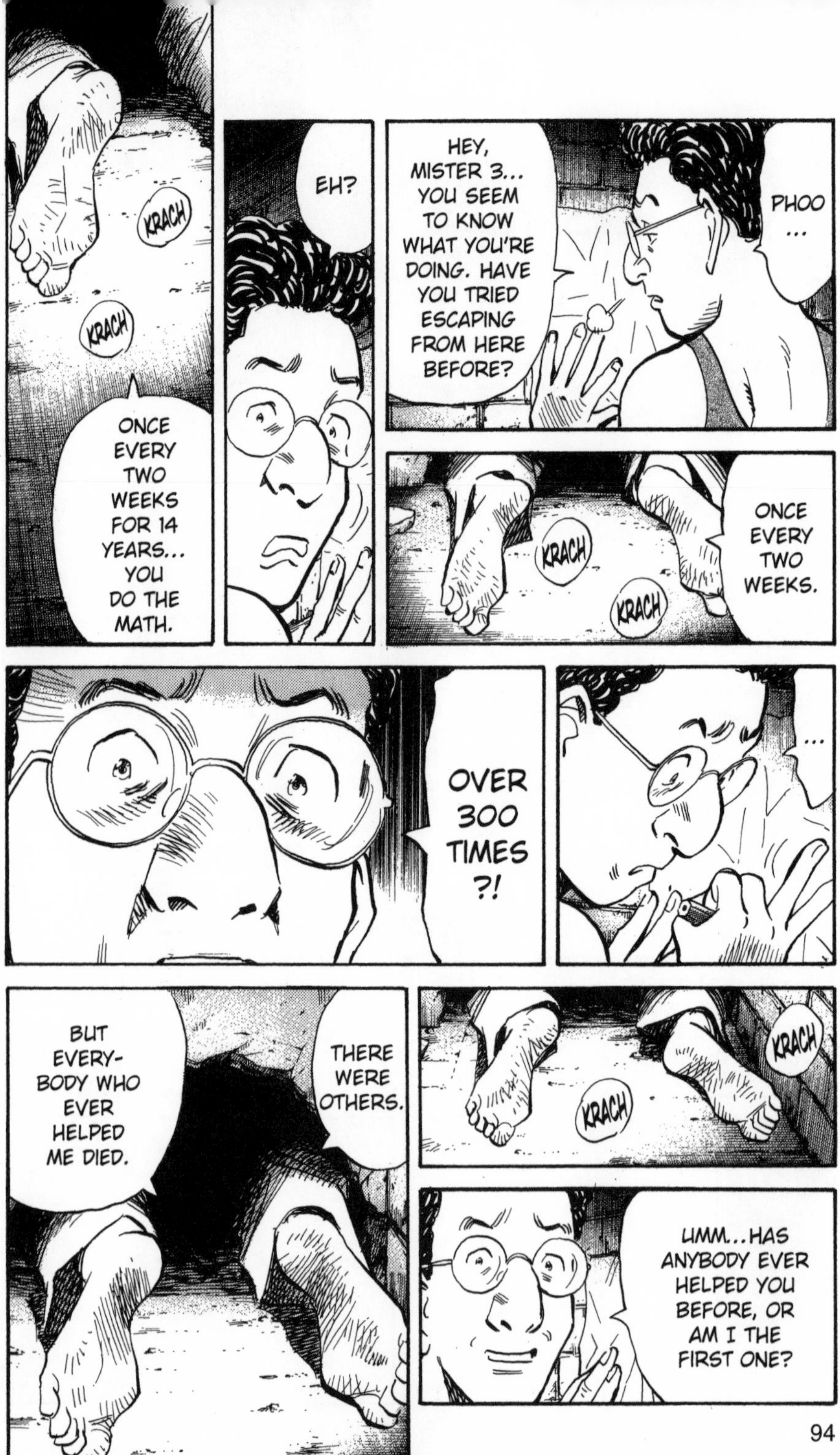
PHOO...
HEY, MISTER 3... YOU SEEM TO KNOW WHAT YOU'RE DOING. HAVE YOU TRIED ESCAPING FROM HERE BEFORE?
ONCE EVERY TWO WEEKS.
KRACH
KRACH
EH?
KRACH
KRACH
ONCE EVERY TWO WEEKS FOR 14 YEARS... YOU DO THE MATH.
...
OVER 300 TIMES ?!
KRACH
KRACH
UMM...HAS ANYBODY EVER HELPED YOU BEFORE, OR AM I THE FIRST ONE?
THERE WERE OTHERS.
BUT EVERY-BODY WHO EVER HELPED ME DIED.

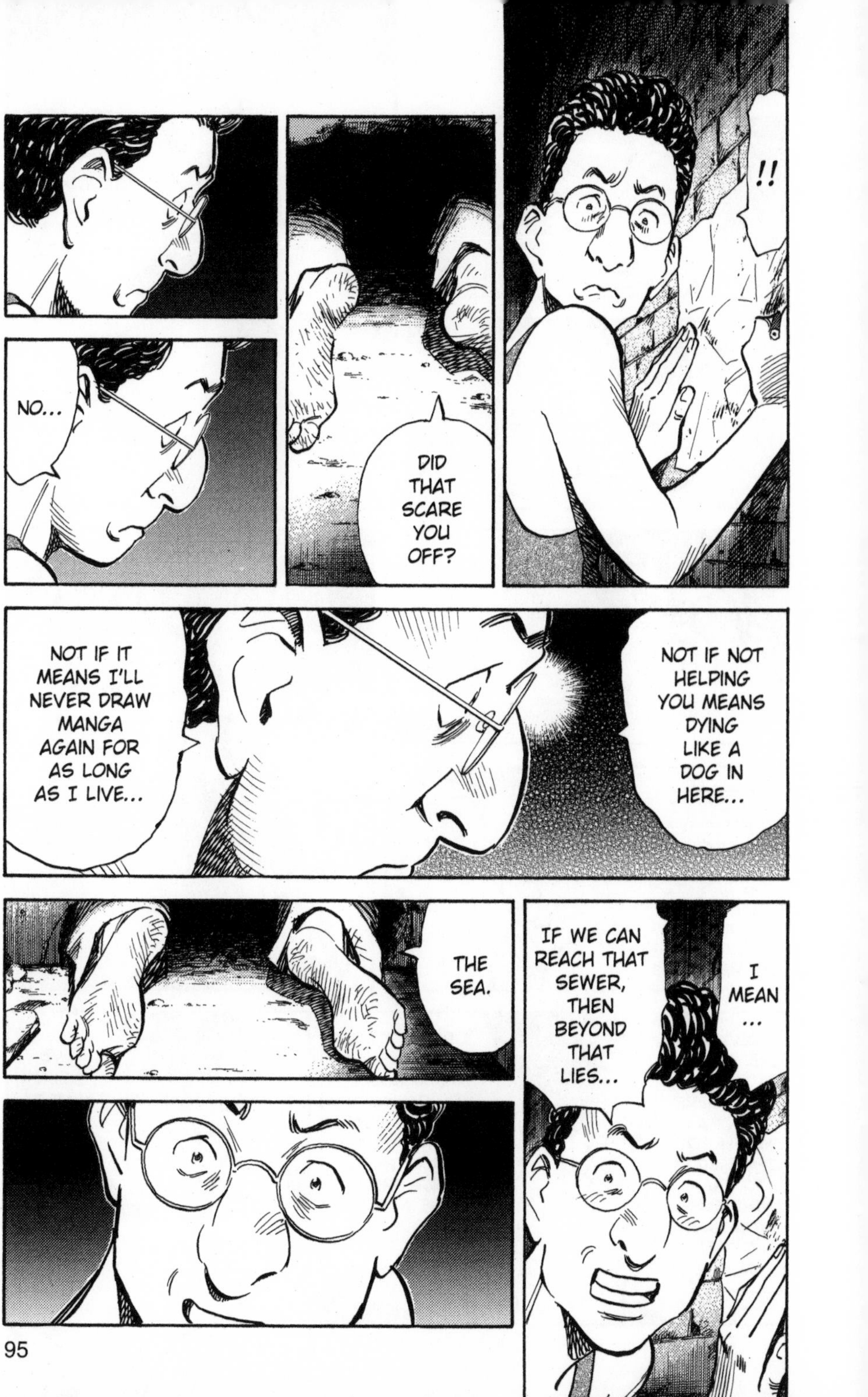
!!
DID THAT SCARE YOU OFF?
NO...
NOT IF NOT HELPING YOU MEANS DYING LIKE A DOG IN HERE...
NOT IF IT MEANS I'LL NEVER DRAW MANGA AGAIN FOR AS LONG AS I LIVE...
I MEAN ...
IF WE CAN REACH THAT SEWER, THEN BEYOND THAT LIES...
THE SEA.

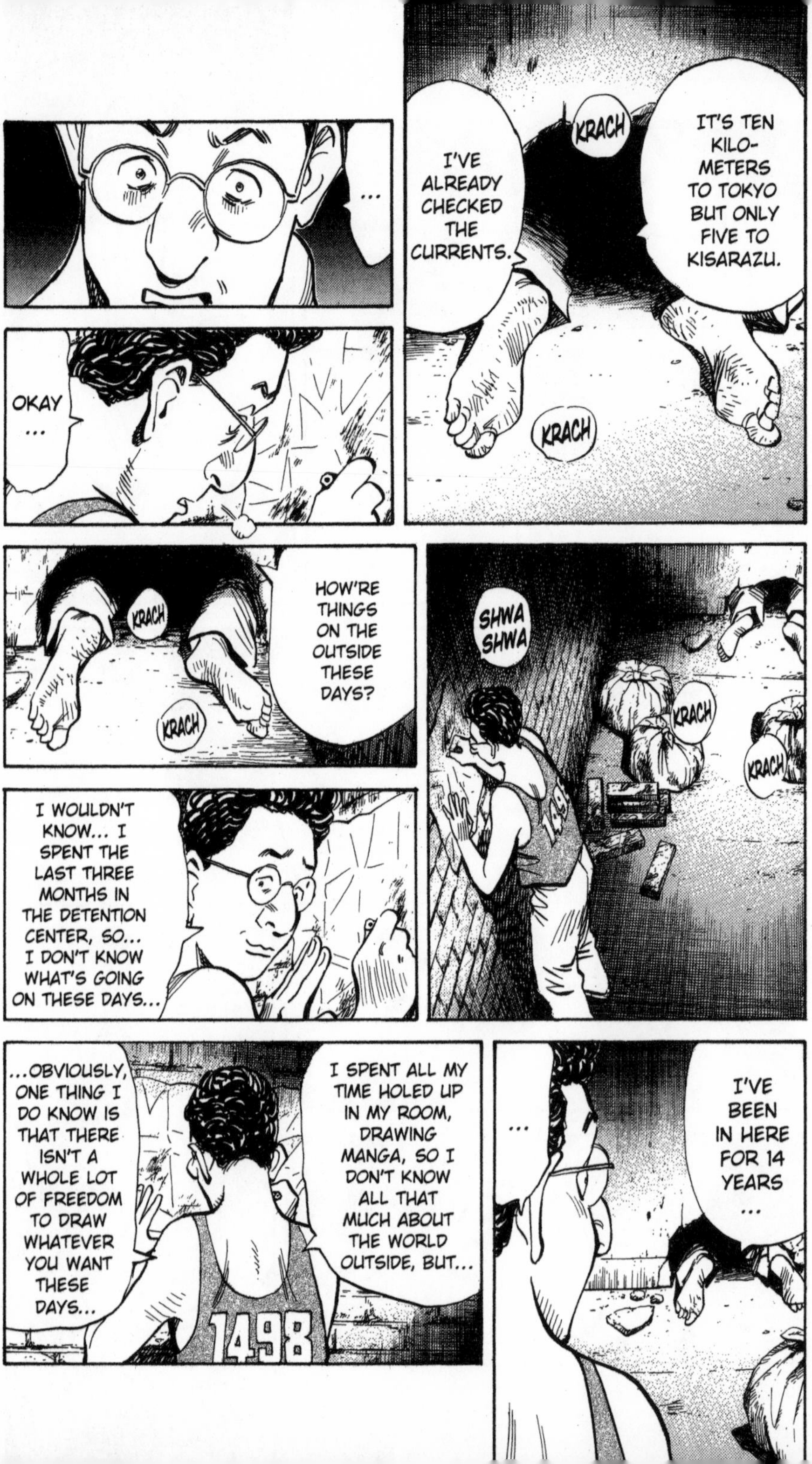

IT'S TEN KILO-METERS TO TOKYO BUT ONLY FIVE TO KISARAZU.
KRACH
I'VE ALREADY CHECKED THE CURRENTS.
KRACH
...
OKAY ...
SHWA SHWA
KRACH
KRACH
HOW'RE THINGS ON THE OUTSIDE THESE DAYS?
KRACH
KRACH
I WOULDN'T KNOW... I SPENT THE LAST THREE MONTHS IN THE DETENTION CENTER, SO... I DON'T KNOW WHAT'S GOING ON THESE DAYS...
I'VE BEEN IN HERE FOR 14 YEARS ...
...
I SPENT ALL MY TIME HOLED UP IN MY ROOM, DRAWING MANGA, SO I DON'T KNOW ALL THAT MUCH ABOUT THE WORLD OUTSIDE, BUT...
...OBVIOUSLY, ONE THING I DO KNOW IS THAT THERE ISN'T A WHOLE LOT OF FREEDOM TO DRAW WHATEVER YOU WANT THESE DAYS...
1498

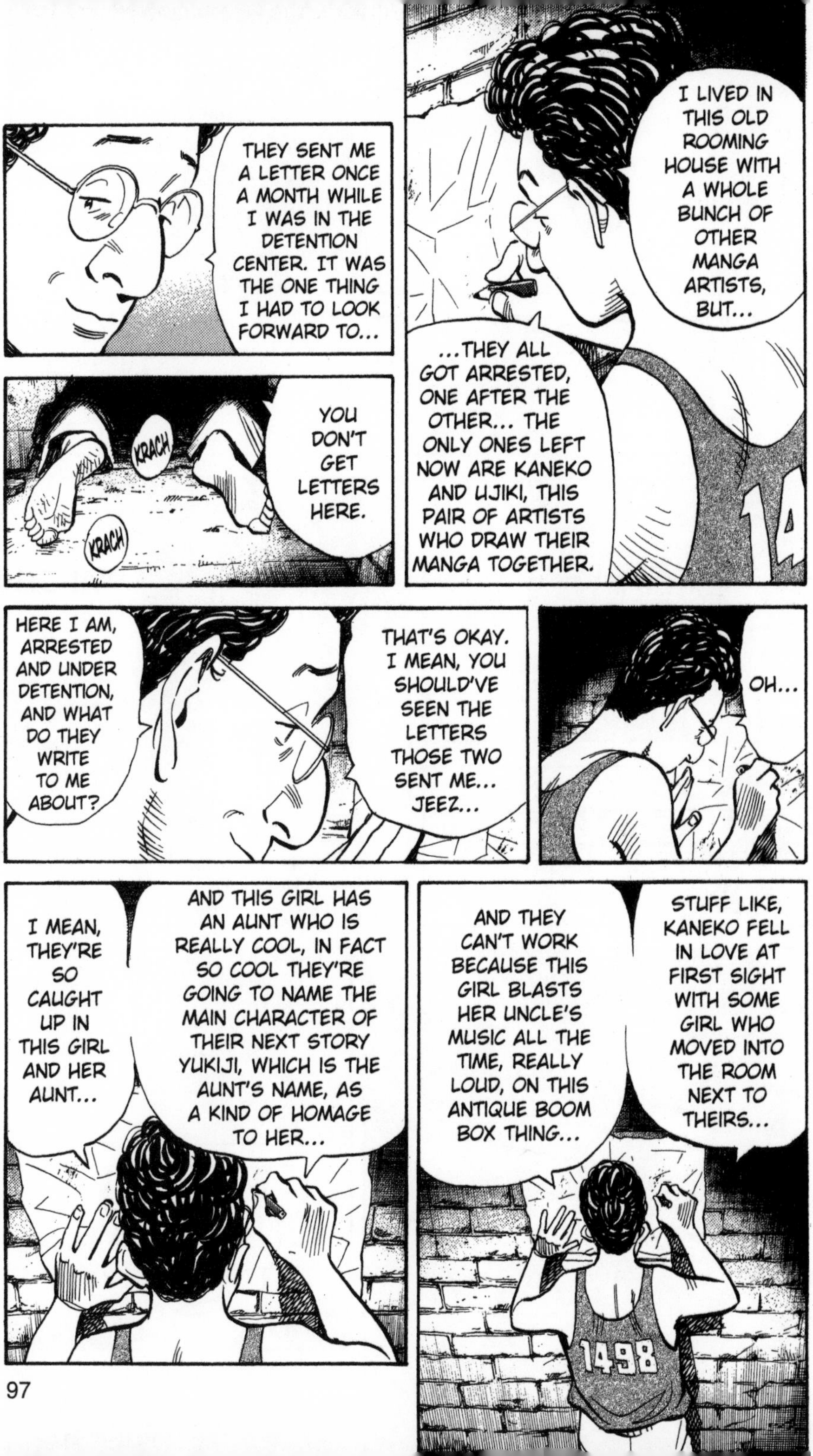
I LIVED IN THIS OLD ROOMING HOUSE WITH A WHOLE BUNCH OF OTHER MANGA ARTISTS, BUT...
...THEY ALL GOT ARRESTED, ONE AFTER THE OTHER... THE ONLY ONES LEFT NOW ARE KANEKO AND UJIKI, THIS PAIR OF ARTISTS WHO DRAW THEIR MANGA TOGETHER.
14
THEY SENT ME A LETTER ONCE A MONTH WHILE I WAS IN THE DETENTION CENTER. IT WAS THE ONE THING I HAD TO LOOK FORWARD TO...
YOU DON'T GET LETTERS HERE.
KRACH
KRACH
OH...
THAT'S OKAY. I MEAN, YOU SHOULD'VE SEEN THE LETTERS THOSE TWO SENT ME... JEEZ...
HERE I AM, ARRESTED AND UNDER DETENTION, AND WHAT DO THEY WRITE TO ME ABOUT?
STUFF LIKE, KANEKO FELL IN LOVE AT FIRST SIGHT WITH SOME GIRL WHO MOVED INTO THE ROOM NEXT TO THEIRS...
AND THEY CAN'T WORK BECAUSE THIS GIRL BLASTS HER UNCLE'S MUSIC ALL THE TIME, REALLY LOUD, ON THIS ANTIQUE BOOM BOX THING...
1498
AND THIS GIRL HAS AN AUNT WHO IS REALLY COOL, IN FACT SO COOL THEY'RE GOING TO NAME THE MAIN CHARACTER OF THEIR NEXT STORY YUKIJI, WHICH IS THE AUNT'S NAME, AS A KIND OF HOMAGE TO HER...
I MEAN, THEY'RE SO CAUGHT UP IN THIS GIRL AND HER AUNT...

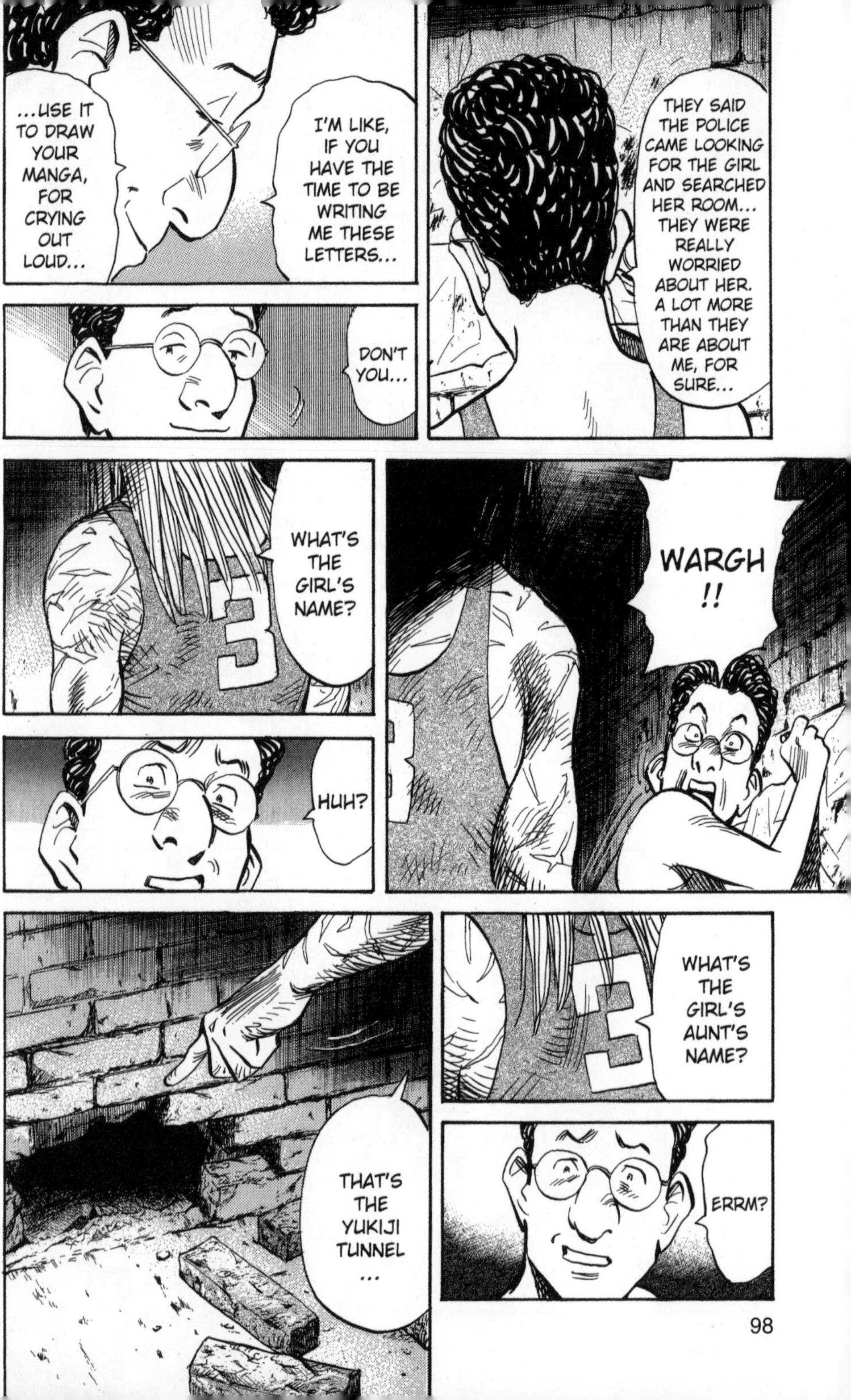
THEY SAID THE POLICE CAME LOOKING FOR THE GIRL AND SEARCHED HER ROOM... THEY WERE REALLY WORRIED ABOUT HER. A LOT MORE THAN THEY ARE ABOUT ME, FOR SURE...
I'M LIKE, IF YOU HAVE THE TIME TO BE WRITING ME THESE LETTERS...
...USE IT TO DRAW YOUR MANGA, FOR CRYING OUT LOUD...
DON'T YOU...
WARGH !!
WHAT'S THE GIRL'S NAME?
HUH?
WHAT'S THE GIRL'S AUNT'S NAME?
ERRM?
THAT'S THE YUKIJI TUNNEL ...

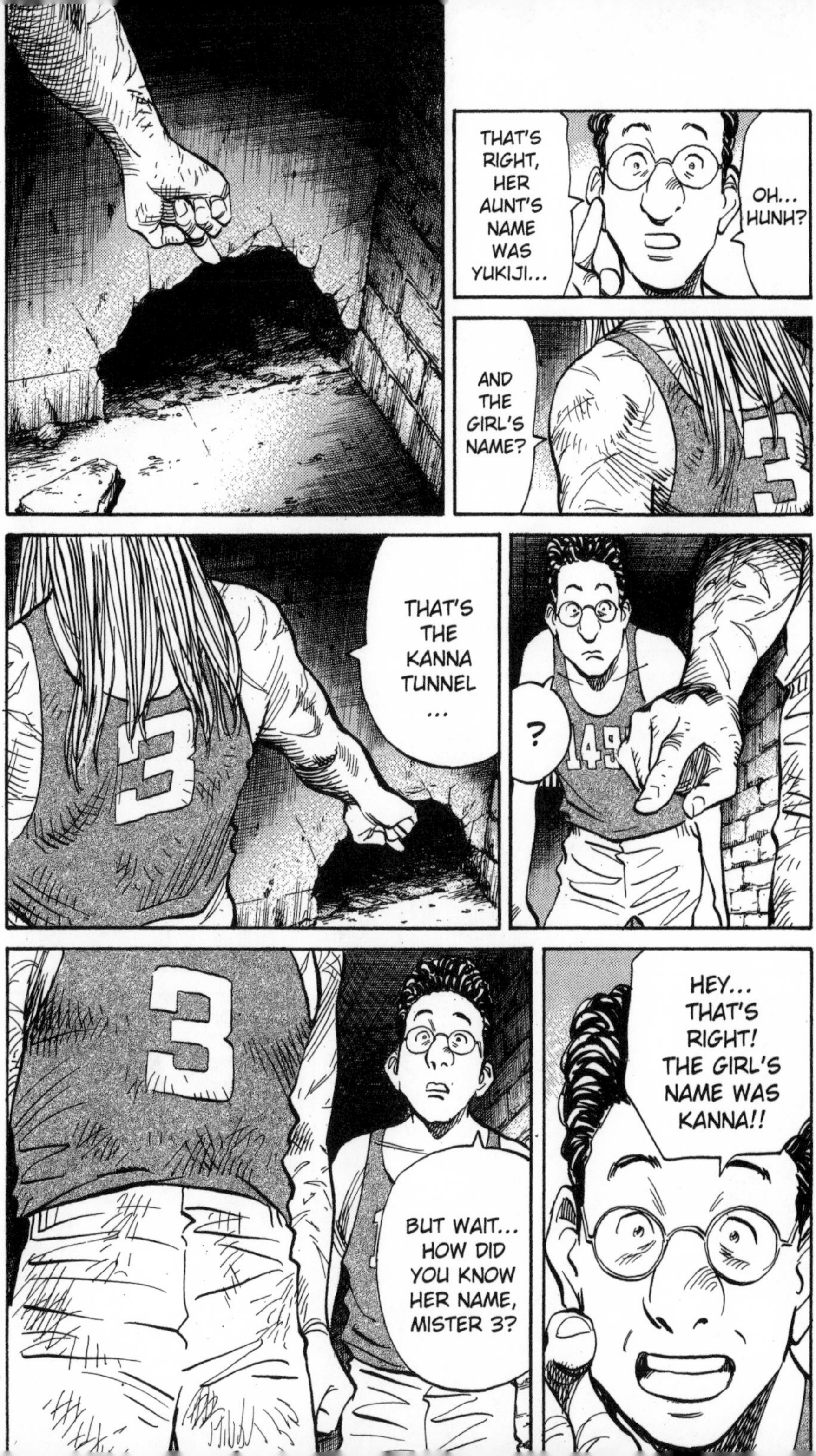
THAT'S RIGHT, HER AUNT'S NAME WAS YUKIJI...
OH... HUNH?
AND THE GIRL'S NAME?
?
THAT'S THE KANNA TUNNEL...
HEY... THAT'S RIGHT! THE GIRL'S NAME WAS KANNA!!
BUT WAIT... HOW DID YOU KNOW HER NAME, MISTER 3?

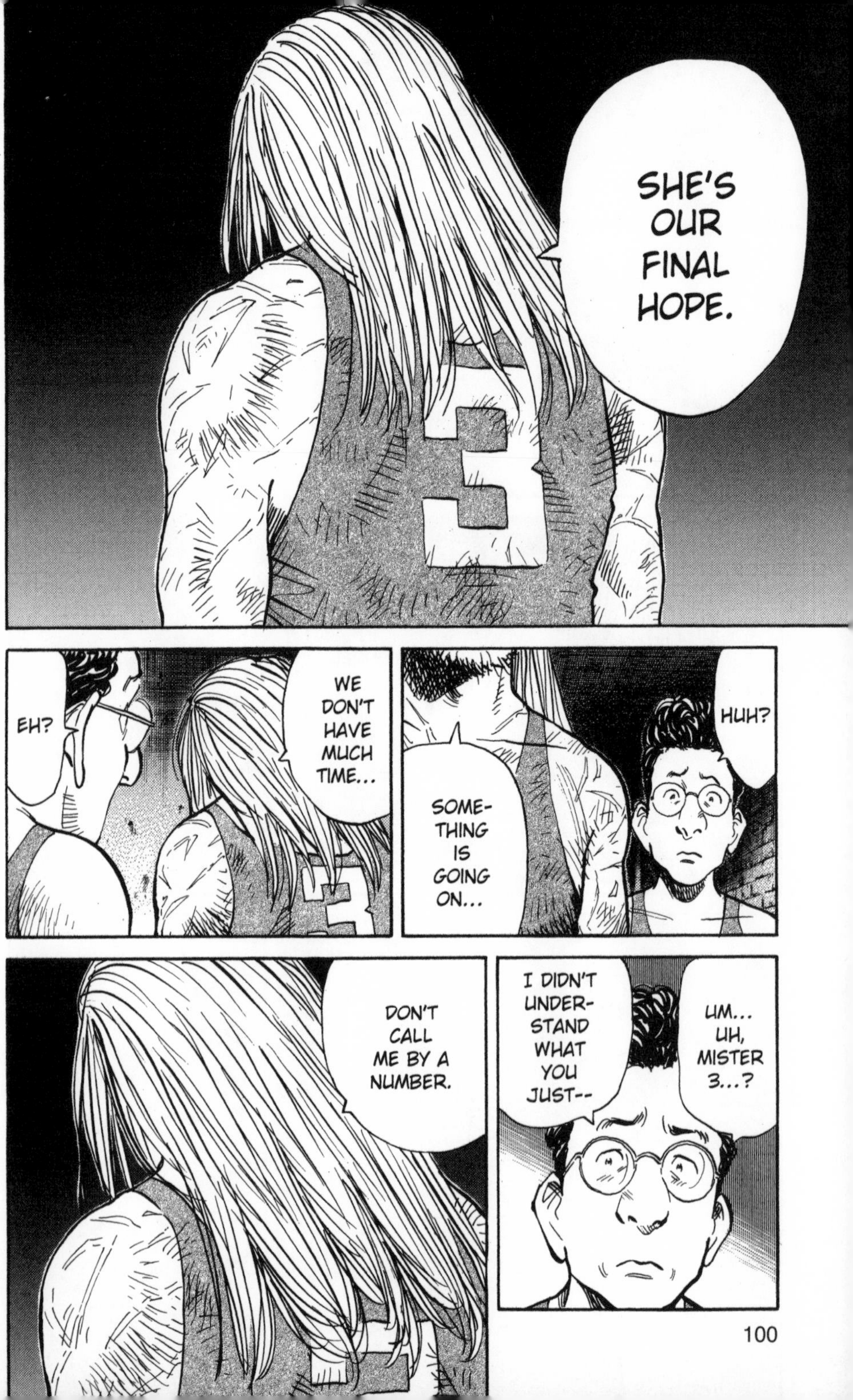
SHE'S OUR FINAL HOPE.
HUH?
SOMETHING IS GOING ON...
WE DON'T HAVE MUCH TIME...
EH?
UM... UH, MISTER 3...?
I DIDN'T UNDERSTAND WHAT YOU JUST--
DON'T CALL ME BY A NUMBER.

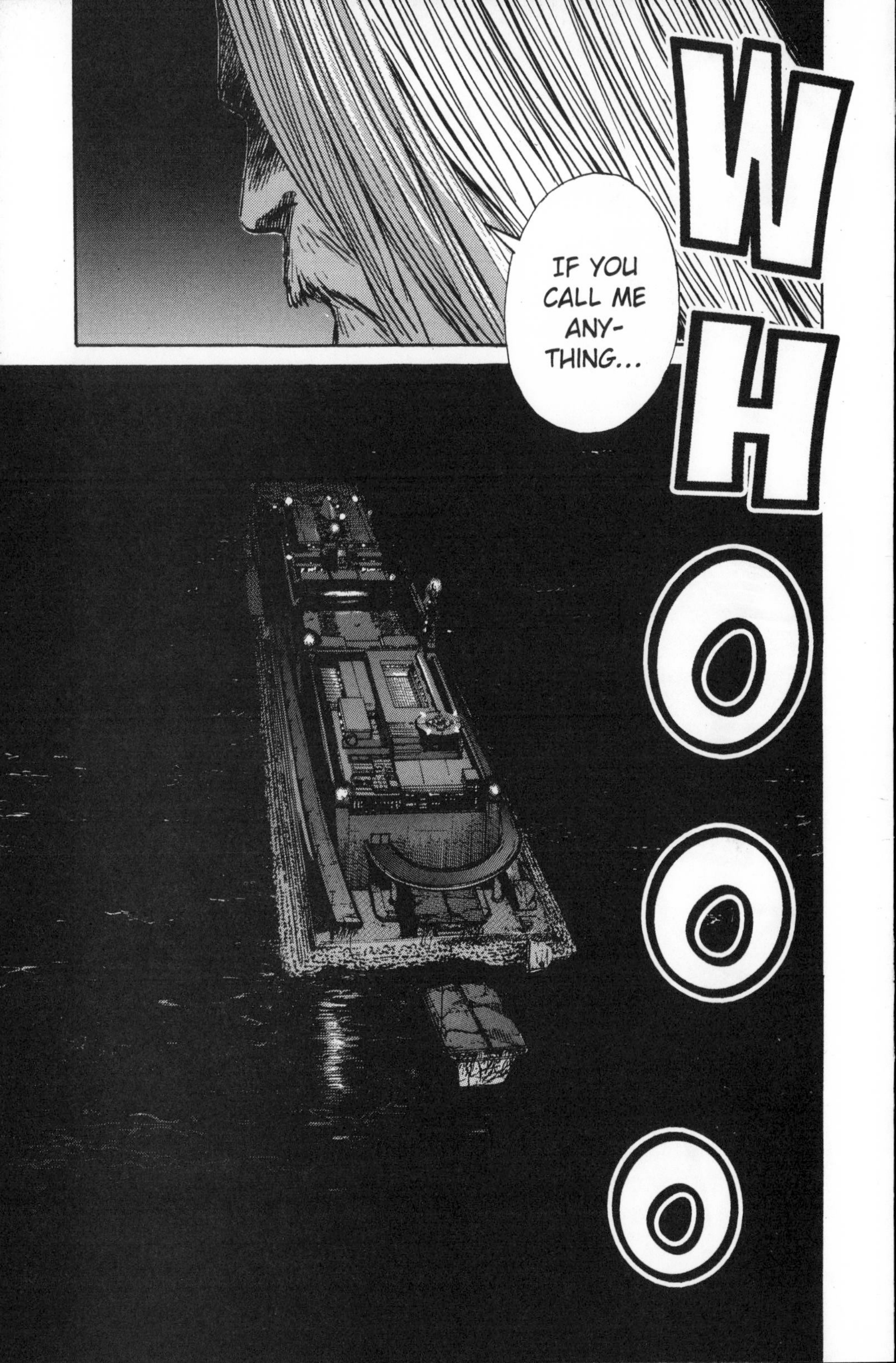
IF YOU CALL ME ANY-THING...
WHOOOO

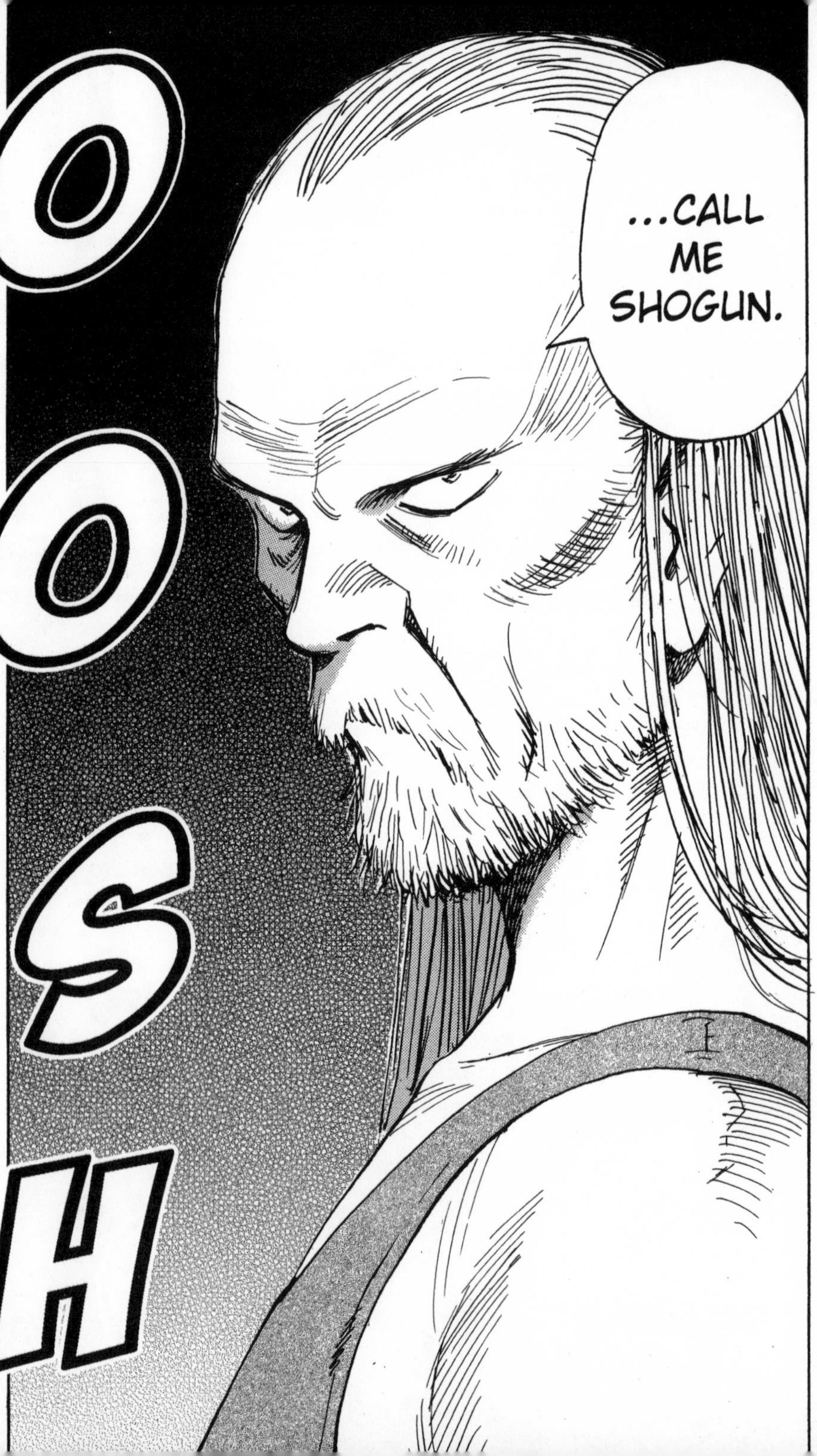
...CALL ME SHOGUN.
OOOSH

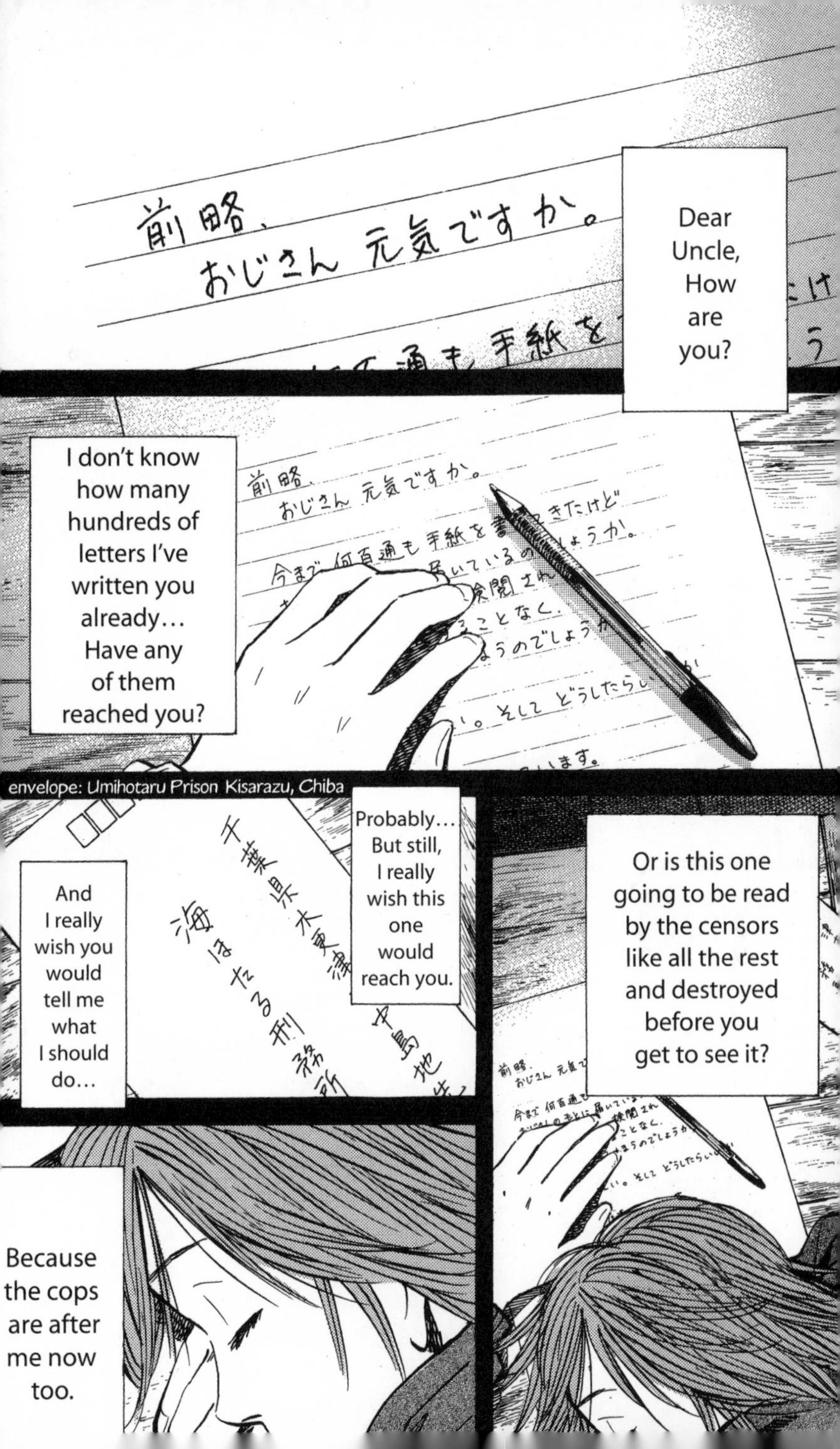

前略、
おじさん 元気ですか。
Dear Uncle, How are you?
I don't know how many hundreds of letters I've written you already… Have any of them reached you?
Or is this one going to be read by the censors like all the rest and destroyed before you get to see it?
envelope: Umihotaru Prison Kisarazu, Chiba
Probably… But still, I really wish this one would reach you.
And I really wish you would tell me what I should do…
Because the cops are after me now too.

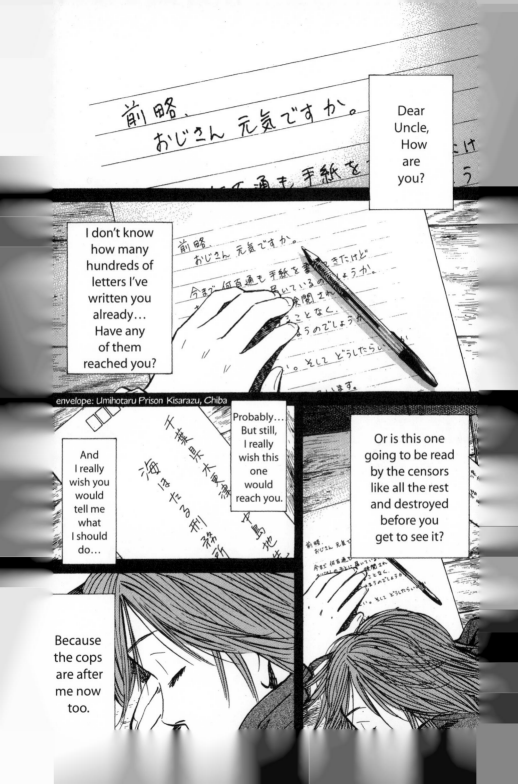

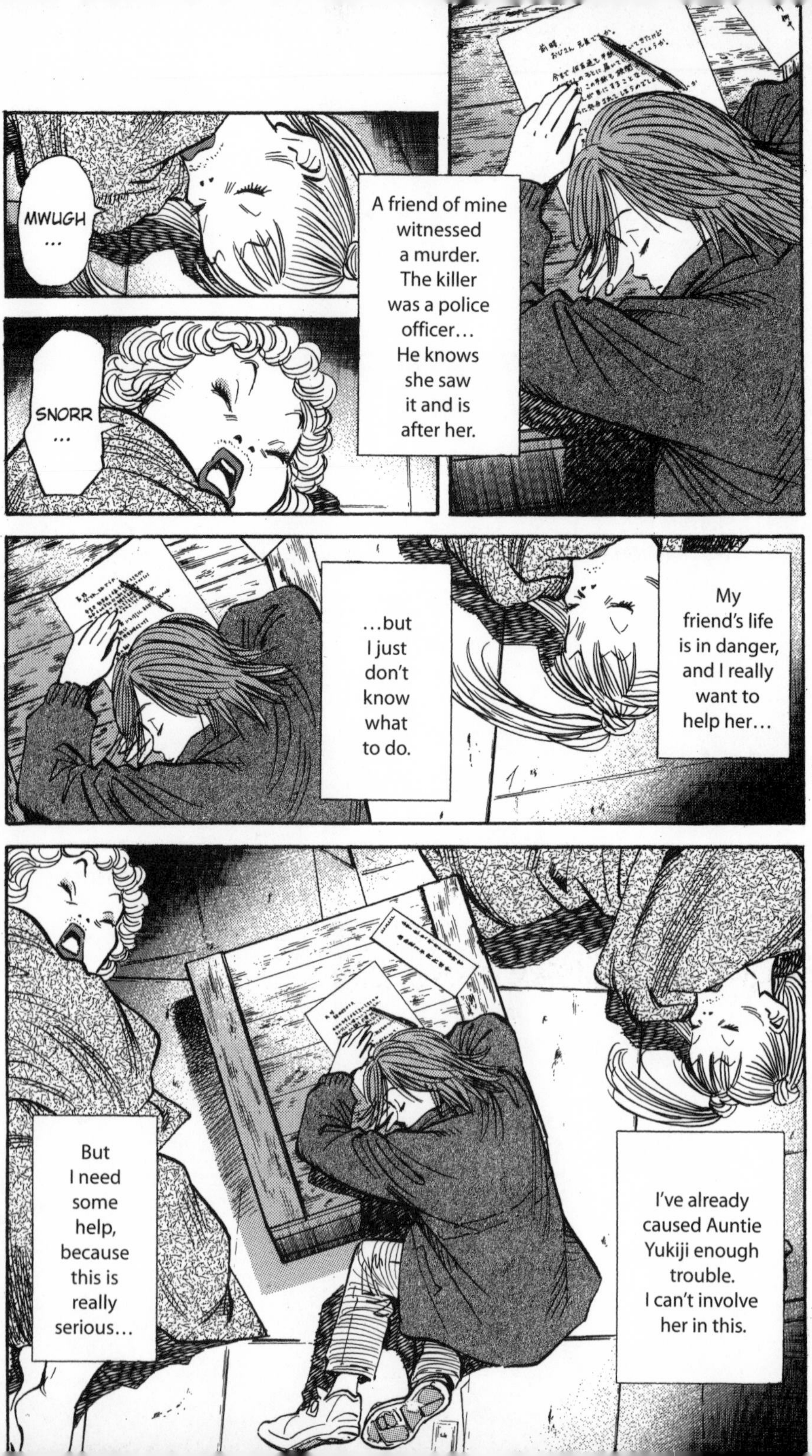
A friend of mine witnessed a murder. The killer was a police officer… He knows she saw it and is after her.
MWUGH …
SNORR …
My friend's life is in danger, and I really want to help her…
…but I just don't know what to do.
I've already caused Auntie Yukiji enough trouble. I can't involve her in this.
But I need some help, because this is really serious…

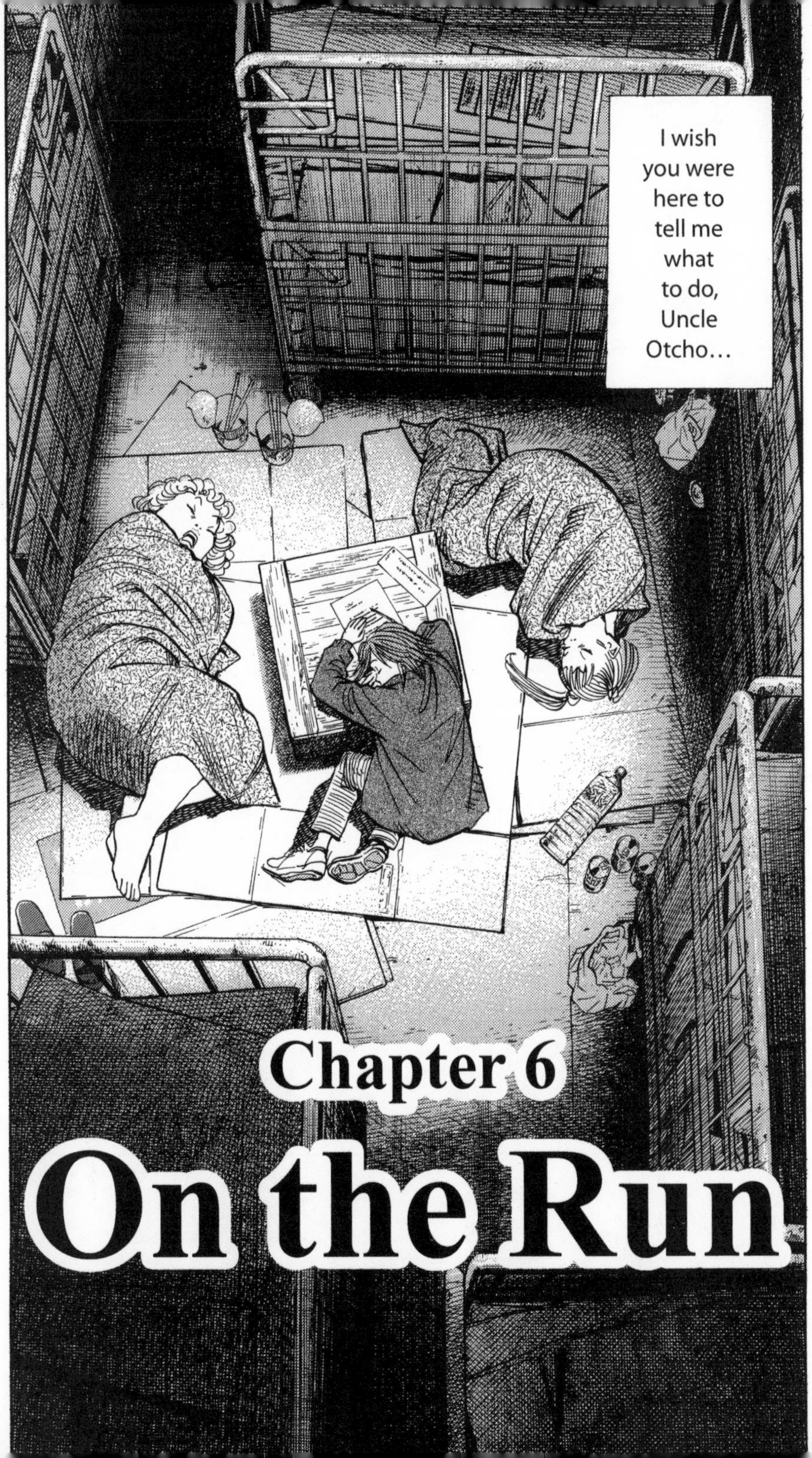
I wish you were here to tell me what to do, Uncle Otcho…
Chapter 6
On the Run

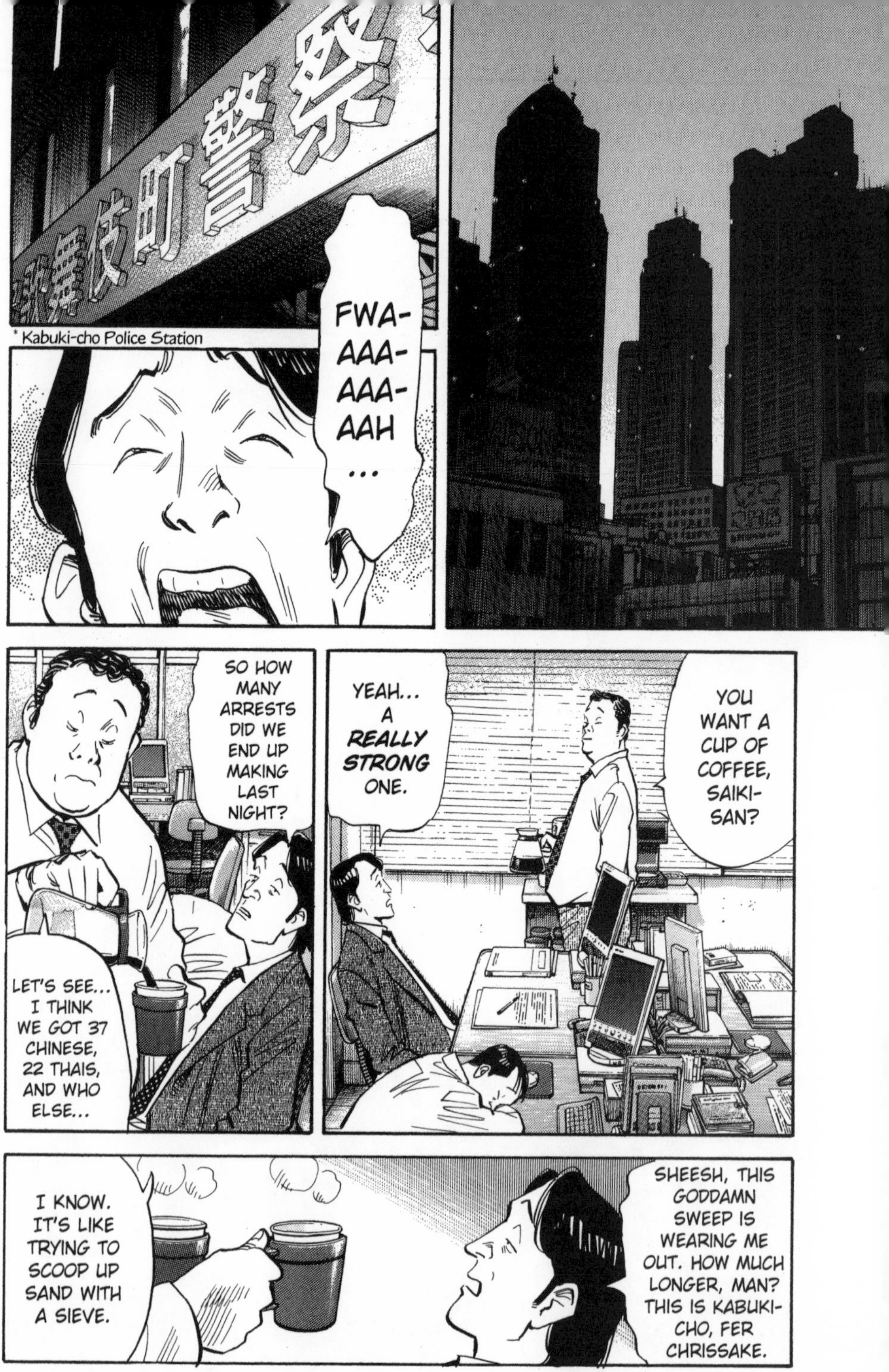
舞伎町警察
FWA-AAA-AAA-AAH...
* Kabuki-cho Police Station
YOU WANT A CUP OF COFFEE, SAIKI-SAN?
YEAH... A **REALLY STRONG** ONE.
SO HOW MANY ARRESTS DID WE END UP MAKING LAST NIGHT?
LET'S SEE... I THINK WE GOT 37 CHINESE, 22 THAIS, AND WHO ELSE...
SHEESH, THIS GODDAMN SWEEP IS WEARING ME OUT. HOW MUCH LONGER, MAN? THIS IS KABUKI-CHO, FER CHRISSAKE.
I KNOW. IT'S LIKE TRYING TO SCOOP UP SAND WITH A SIEVE.

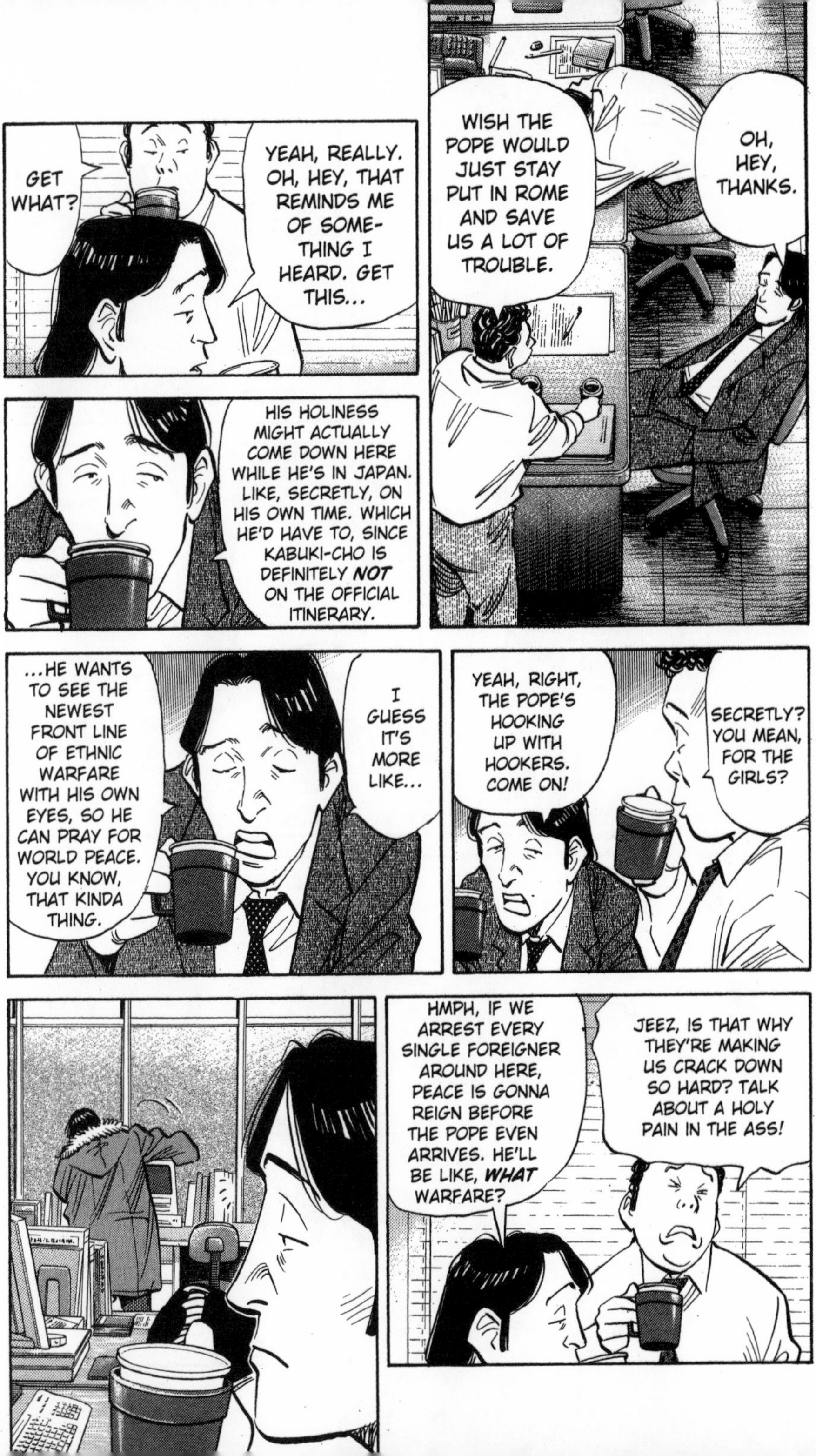
OH, HEY, THANKS.
WISH THE POPE WOULD JUST STAY PUT IN ROME AND SAVE US A LOT OF TROUBLE.
YEAH, REALLY. OH, HEY, THAT REMINDS ME OF SOME-THING I HEARD. GET THIS...
GET WHAT?
HIS HOLINESS MIGHT ACTUALLY COME DOWN HERE WHILE HE'S IN JAPAN. LIKE, SECRETLY, ON HIS OWN TIME. WHICH HE'D HAVE TO, SINCE KABUKI-CHO IS DEFINITELY ***NOT*** ON THE OFFICIAL ITINERARY.
SECRETLY? YOU MEAN, FOR THE GIRLS?
YEAH, RIGHT, THE POPE'S HOOKING UP WITH HOOKERS. COME ON!
I GUESS IT'S MORE LIKE...
...HE WANTS TO SEE THE NEWEST FRONT LINE OF ETHNIC WARFARE WITH HIS OWN EYES, SO HE CAN PRAY FOR WORLD PEACE. YOU KNOW, THAT KINDA THING.
JEEZ, IS THAT WHY THEY'RE MAKING US CRACK DOWN SO HARD? TALK ABOUT A HOLY PAIN IN THE ASS!
HMPH, IF WE ARREST EVERY SINGLE FOREIGNER AROUND HERE, PEACE IS GONNA REIGN BEFORE THE POPE EVEN ARRIVES. HE'LL BE LIKE, ***WHAT*** WARFARE?

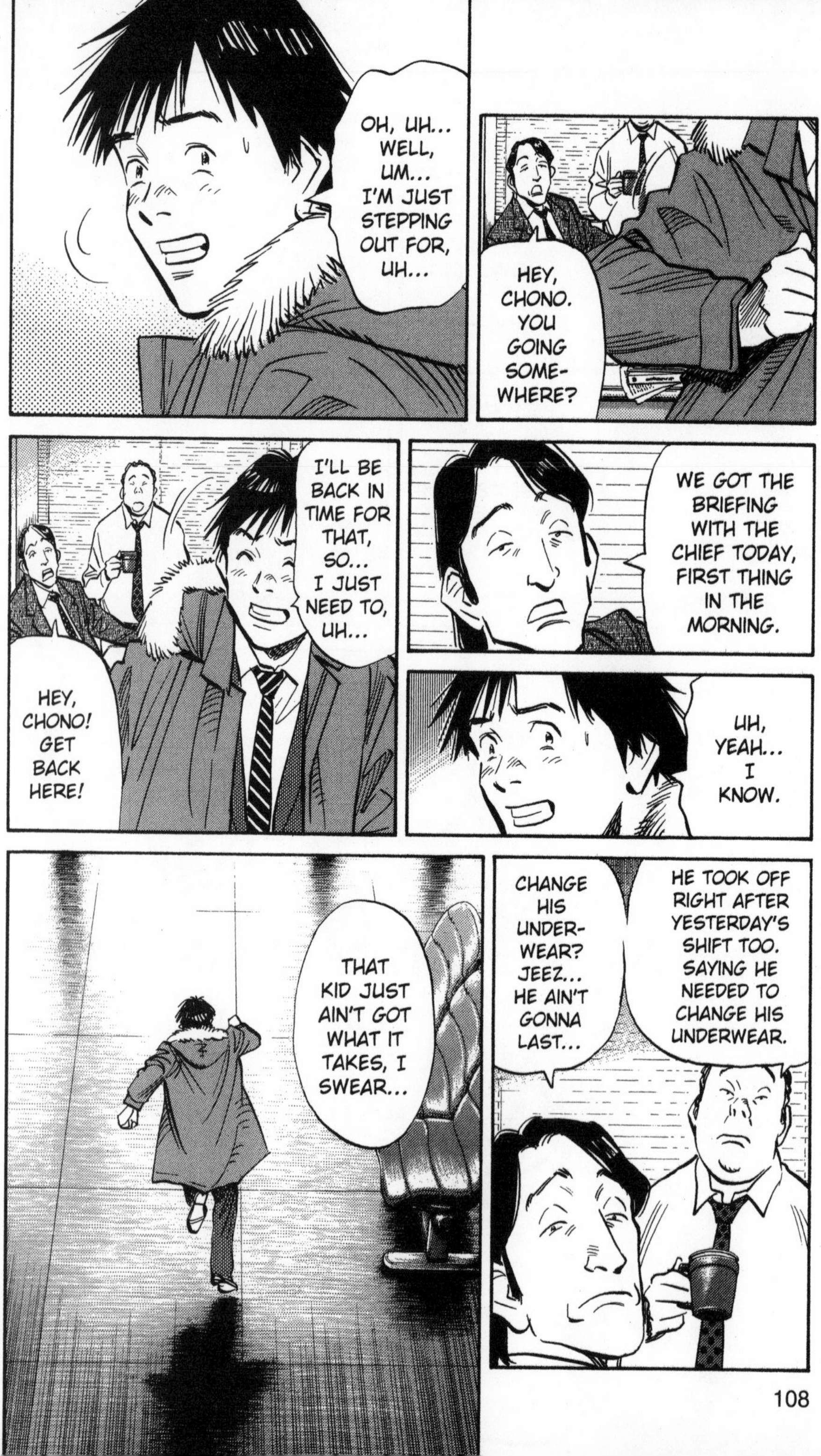
HEY, CHONO. YOU GOING SOMEWHERE?
OH, UH... WELL, UM... I'M JUST STEPPING OUT FOR, UH...
WE GOT THE BRIEFING WITH THE CHIEF TODAY, FIRST THING IN THE MORNING.
UH, YEAH... I KNOW.
I'LL BE BACK IN TIME FOR THAT, SO... I JUST NEED TO, UH...
HEY, CHONO! GET BACK HERE!
HE TOOK OFF RIGHT AFTER YESTERDAY'S SHIFT TOO. SAYING HE NEEDED TO CHANGE HIS UNDERWEAR.
CHANGE HIS UNDERWEAR? JEEZ... HE AIN'T GONNA LAST...
THAT KID JUST AIN'T GOT WHAT IT TAKES, I SWEAR...

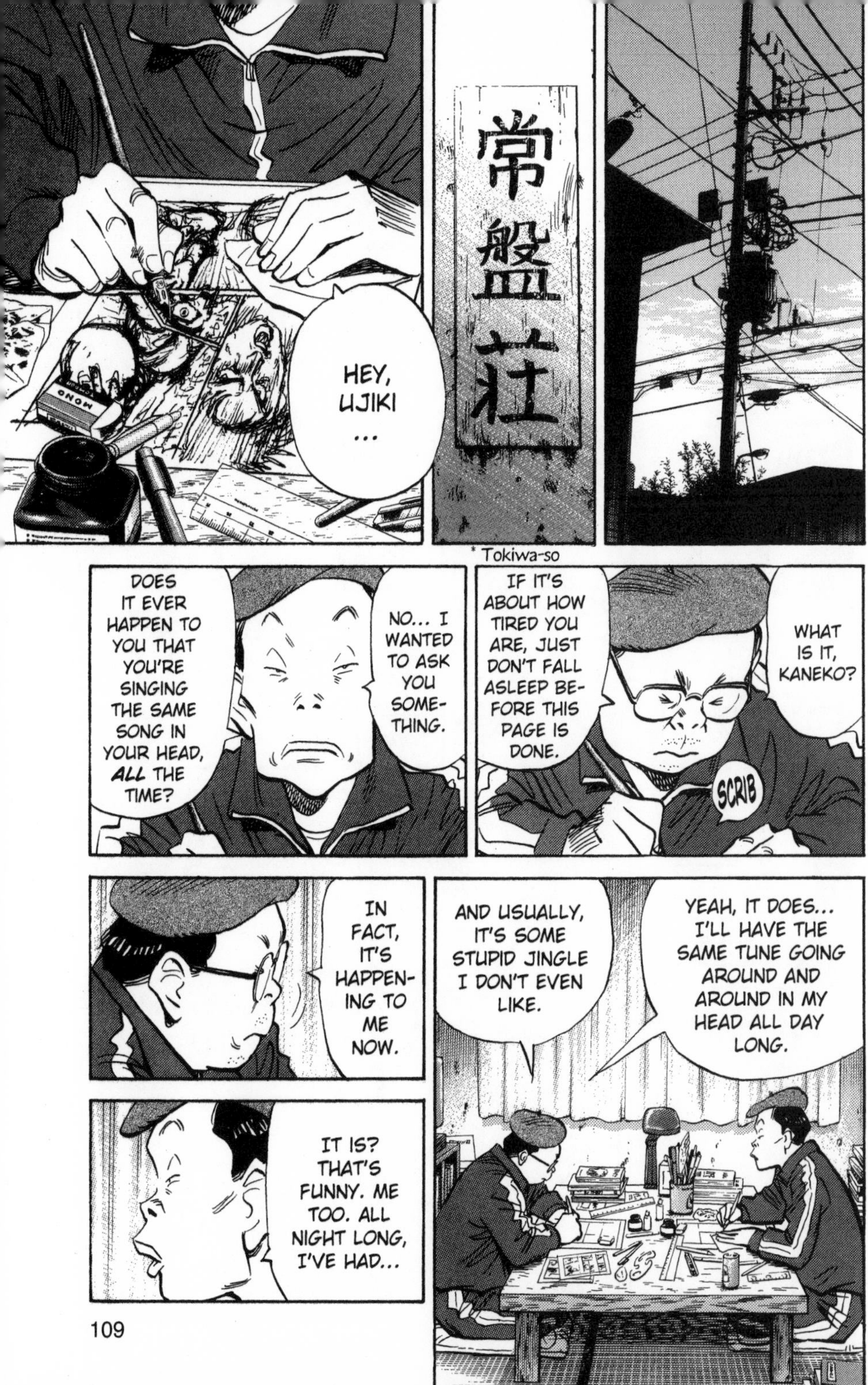
常盤荘
* Tokiwa-so
HEY, UJIKI ...
WHAT IS IT, KANEKO?
IF IT'S ABOUT HOW TIRED YOU ARE, JUST DON'T FALL ASLEEP BE-FORE THIS PAGE IS DONE.
SCRIB
NO... I WANTED TO ASK YOU SOME-THING.
DOES IT EVER HAPPEN TO YOU THAT YOU'RE SINGING THE SAME SONG IN YOUR HEAD, ***ALL*** THE TIME?
YEAH, IT DOES... I'LL HAVE THE SAME TUNE GOING AROUND AND AROUND IN MY HEAD ALL DAY LONG.
AND USUALLY, IT'S SOME STUPID JINGLE I DON'T EVEN LIKE.
IN FACT, IT'S HAPPEN-ING TO ME NOW.
IT IS? THAT'S FUNNY. ME TOO. ALL NIGHT LONG, I'VE HAD...

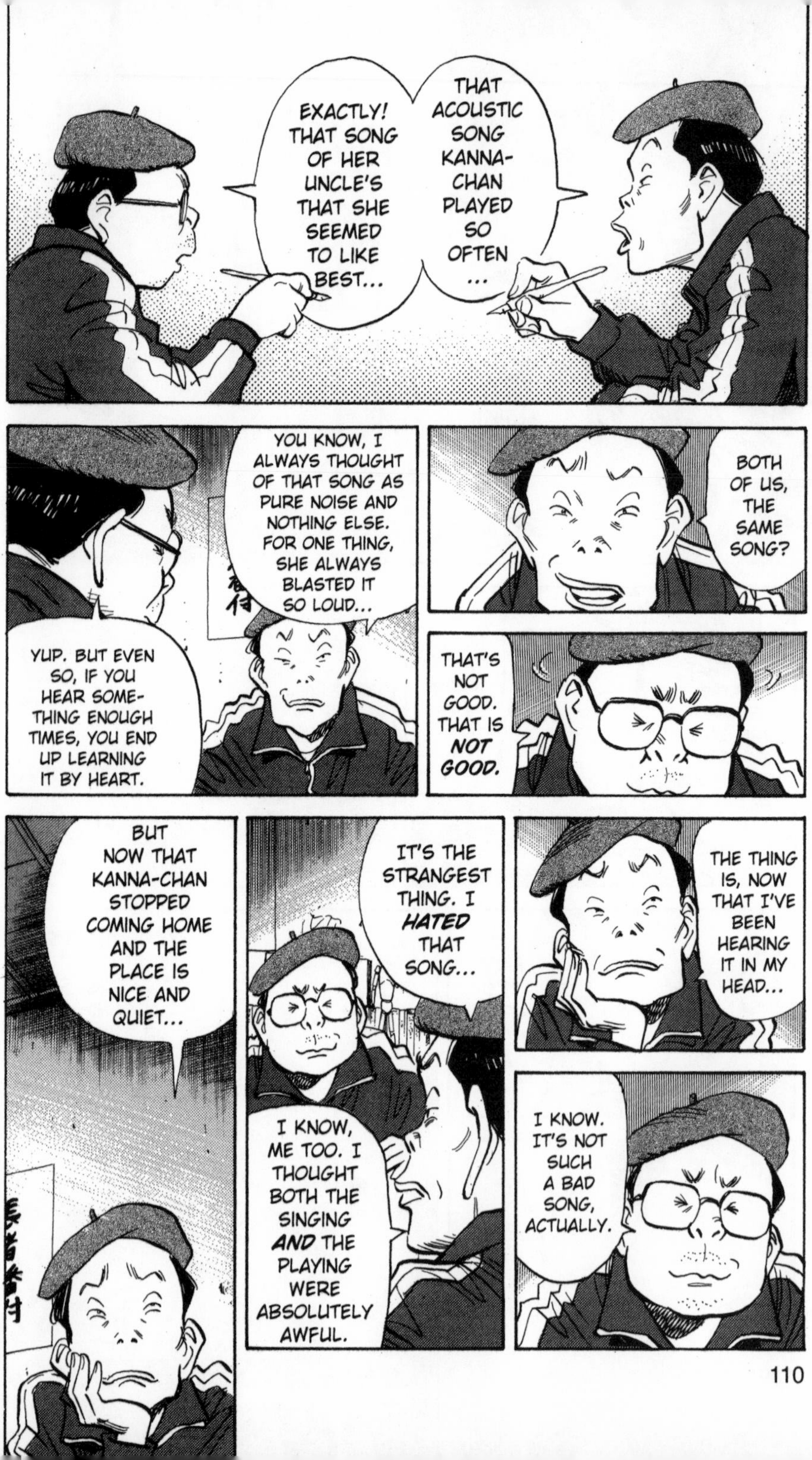
THAT ACOUSTIC SONG KANNA-CHAN PLAYED SO OFTEN ...
EXACTLY! THAT SONG OF HER UNCLE'S THAT SHE SEEMED TO LIKE BEST...
BOTH OF US, THE SAME SONG?
THAT'S NOT GOOD. THAT IS *NOT GOOD.*
YOU KNOW, I ALWAYS THOUGHT OF THAT SONG AS PURE NOISE AND NOTHING ELSE. FOR ONE THING, SHE ALWAYS BLASTED IT SO LOUD...
YUP. BUT EVEN SO, IF YOU HEAR SOME-THING ENOUGH TIMES, YOU END UP LEARNING IT BY HEART.
THE THING IS, NOW THAT I'VE BEEN HEARING IT IN MY HEAD...
I KNOW. IT'S NOT SUCH A BAD SONG, ACTUALLY.
IT'S THE STRANGEST THING. I *HATED* THAT SONG...
I KNOW, ME TOO. I THOUGHT BOTH THE SINGING *AND* THE PLAYING WERE ABSOLUTELY AWFUL.
BUT NOW THAT KANNA-CHAN STOPPED COMING HOME AND THE PLACE IS NICE AND QUIET...

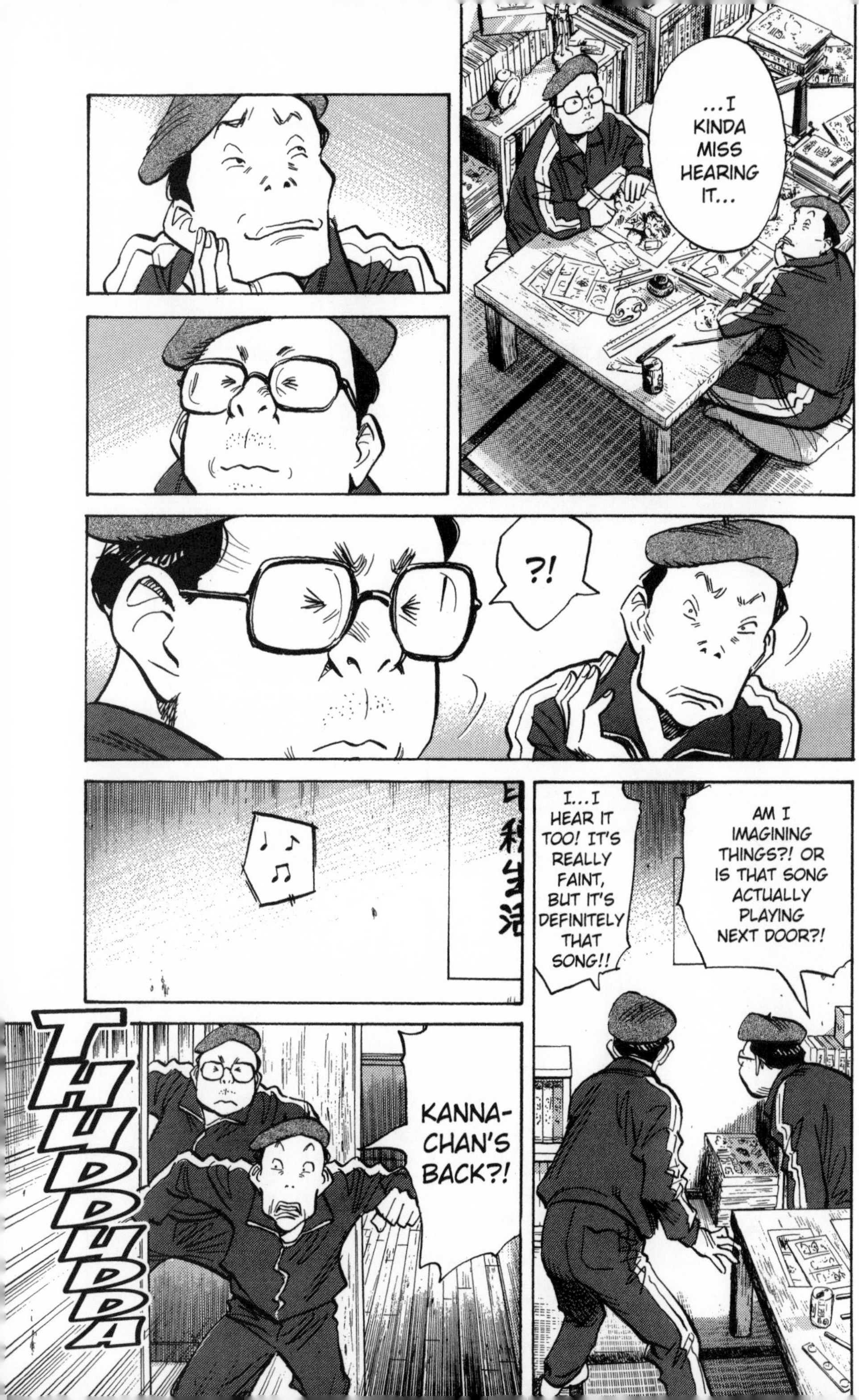
...I KINDA MISS HEARING IT...
?!
AM I IMAGINING THINGS?! OR IS THAT SONG ACTUALLY PLAYING NEXT DOOR?!
I...I HEAR IT TOO! IT'S REALLY FAINT, BUT IT'S DEFINITELY THAT SONG!!
♪ ♫
KANNA-CHAN'S BACK?!
THUDUDUDA

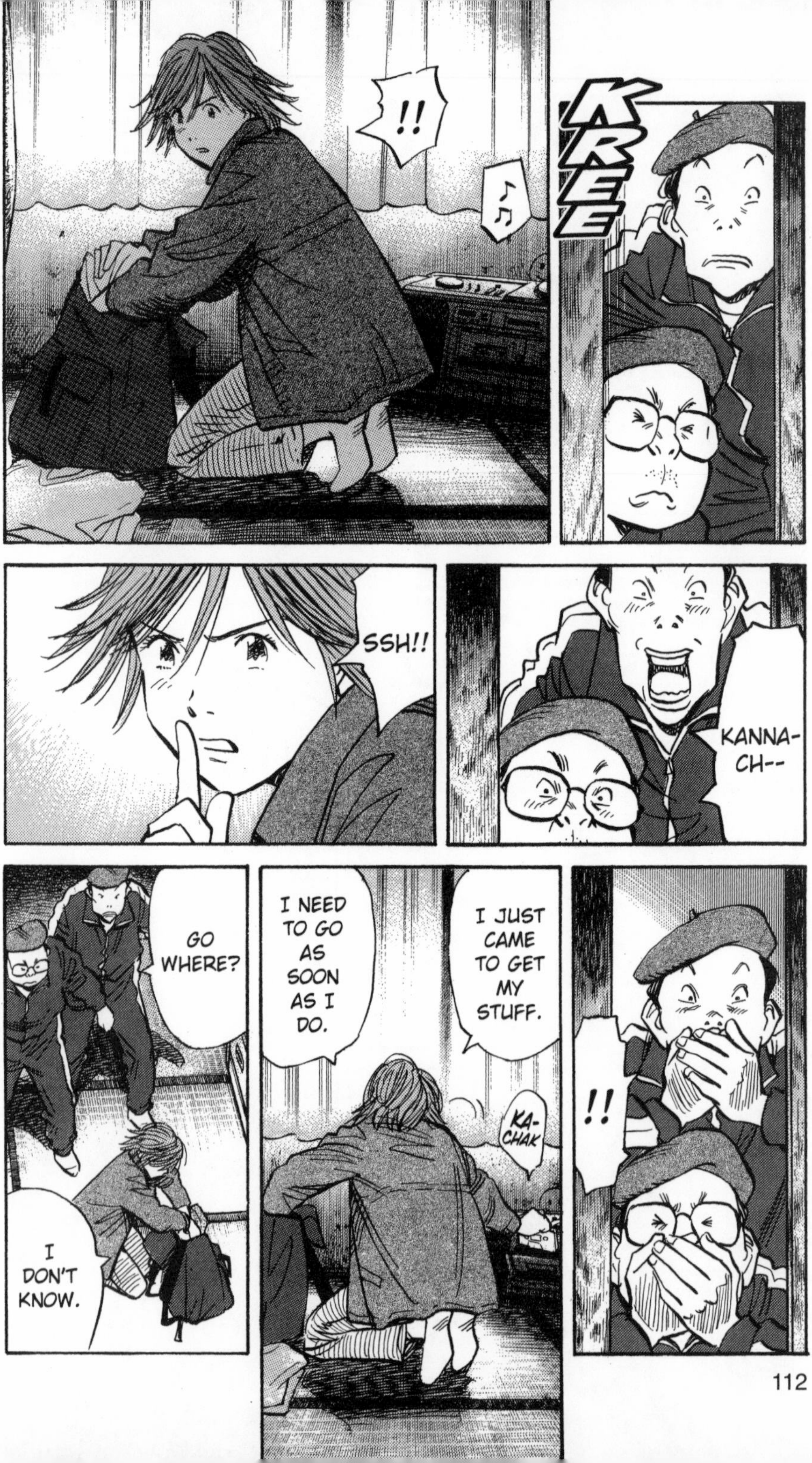
KREE
!!
♪♫
KANNA-CH--
SSH!!
!!
I JUST CAME TO GET MY STUFF.
KA-CHAK
I NEED TO GO AS SOON AS I DO.
GO WHERE?
I DON'T KNOW.

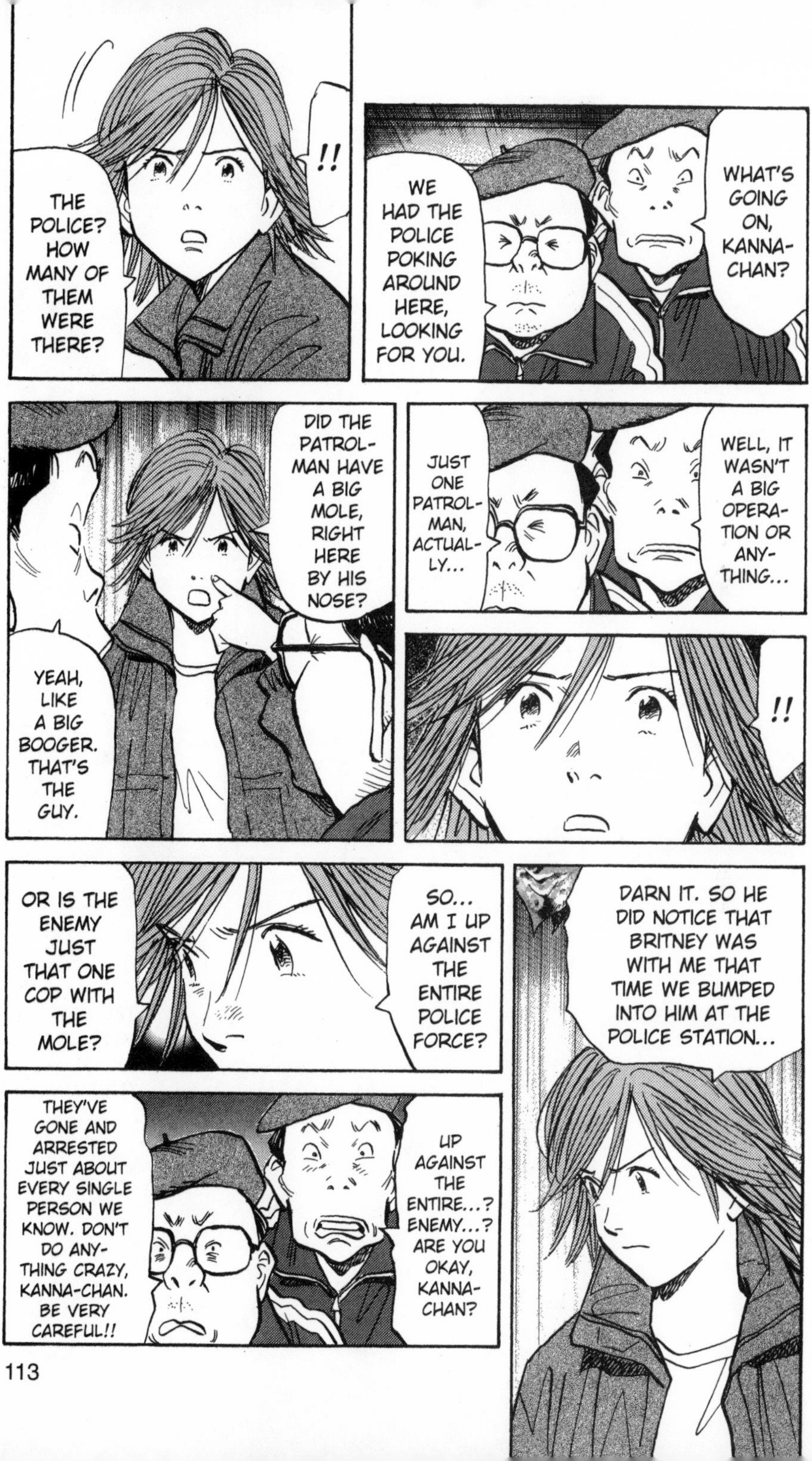
WHAT'S GOING ON, KANNA-CHAN?
WE HAD THE POLICE POKING AROUND HERE, LOOKING FOR YOU.
!!
THE POLICE? HOW MANY OF THEM WERE THERE?
WELL, IT WASN'T A BIG OPERATION OR ANYTHING...
JUST ONE PATROLMAN, ACTUALLY...
!!
DID THE PATROLMAN HAVE A BIG MOLE, RIGHT HERE BY HIS NOSE?
YEAH, LIKE A BIG BOOGER. THAT'S THE GUY.
DARN IT. SO HE DID NOTICE THAT BRITNEY WAS WITH ME THAT TIME WE BUMPED INTO HIM AT THE POLICE STATION...
SO... AM I UP AGAINST THE ENTIRE POLICE FORCE?
OR IS THE ENEMY JUST THAT ONE COP WITH THE MOLE?
UP AGAINST THE ENTIRE...? ENEMY...? ARE YOU OKAY, KANNA-CHAN?
THEY'VE GONE AND ARRESTED JUST ABOUT EVERY SINGLE PERSON WE KNOW. DON'T DO ANYTHING CRAZY, KANNA-CHAN. BE VERY CAREFUL!!

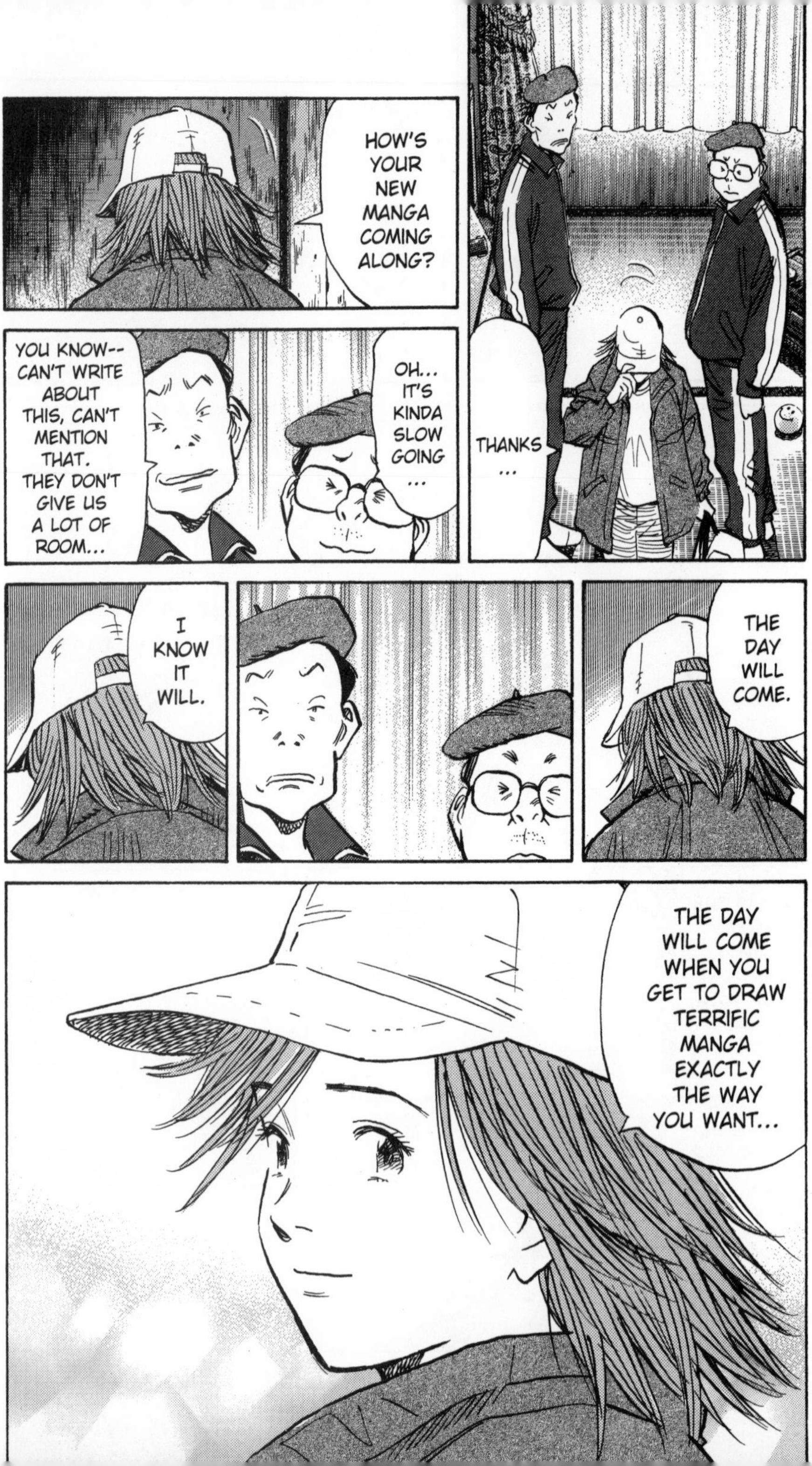
THANKS...
HOW'S YOUR NEW MANGA COMING ALONG?
OH... IT'S KINDA SLOW GOING...
YOU KNOW-- CAN'T WRITE ABOUT THIS, CAN'T MENTION THAT. THEY DON'T GIVE US A LOT OF ROOM...
THE DAY WILL COME.
I KNOW IT WILL.
THE DAY WILL COME WHEN YOU GET TO DRAW TERRIFIC MANGA EXACTLY THE WAY YOU WANT...

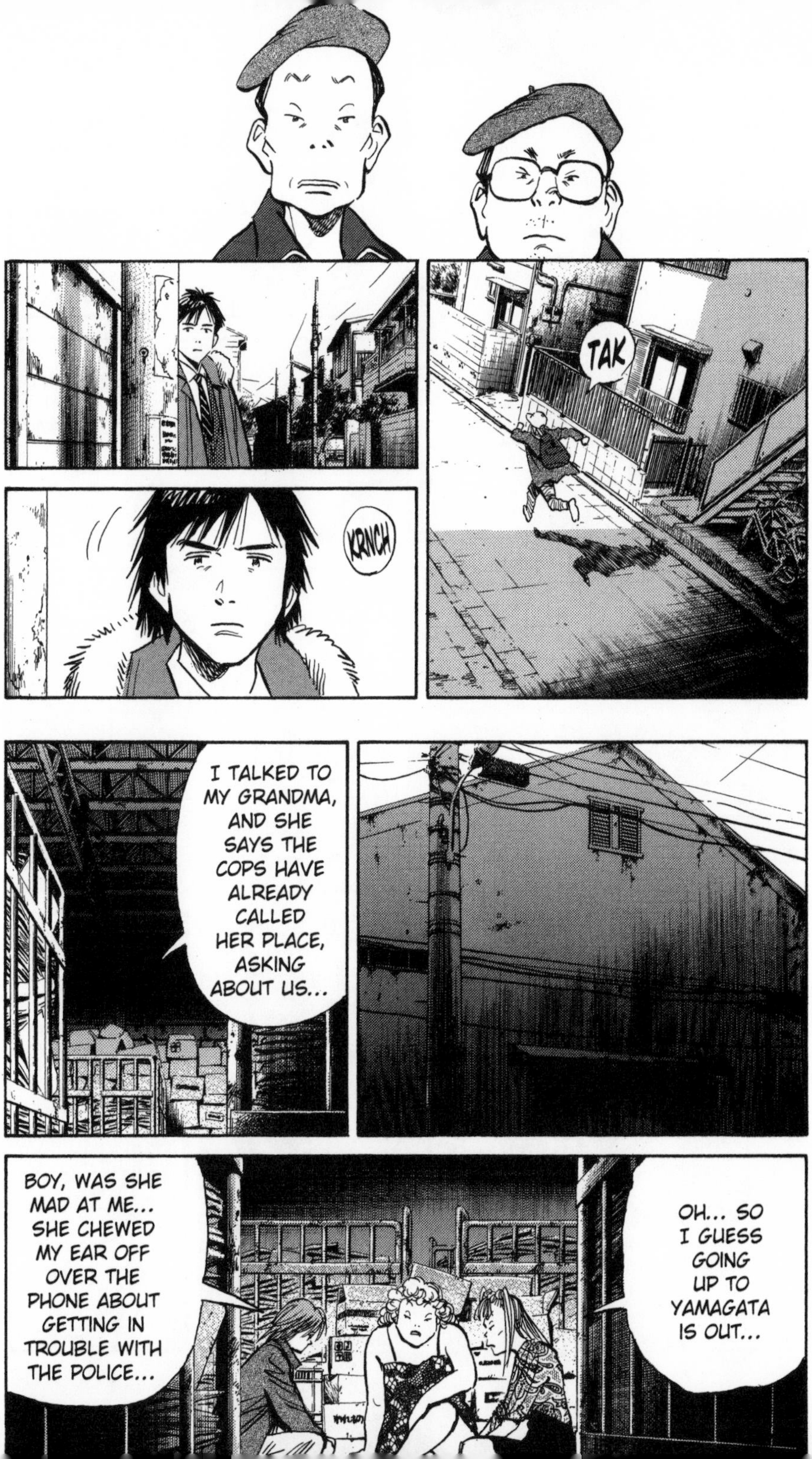
TAK
KRNCH
I TALKED TO MY GRANDMA, AND SHE SAYS THE COPS HAVE ALREADY CALLED HER PLACE, ASKING ABOUT US...
BOY, WAS SHE MAD AT ME... SHE CHEWED MY EAR OFF OVER THE PHONE ABOUT GETTING IN TROUBLE WITH THE POLICE...
OH... SO I GUESS GOING UP TO YAMAGATA IS OUT...

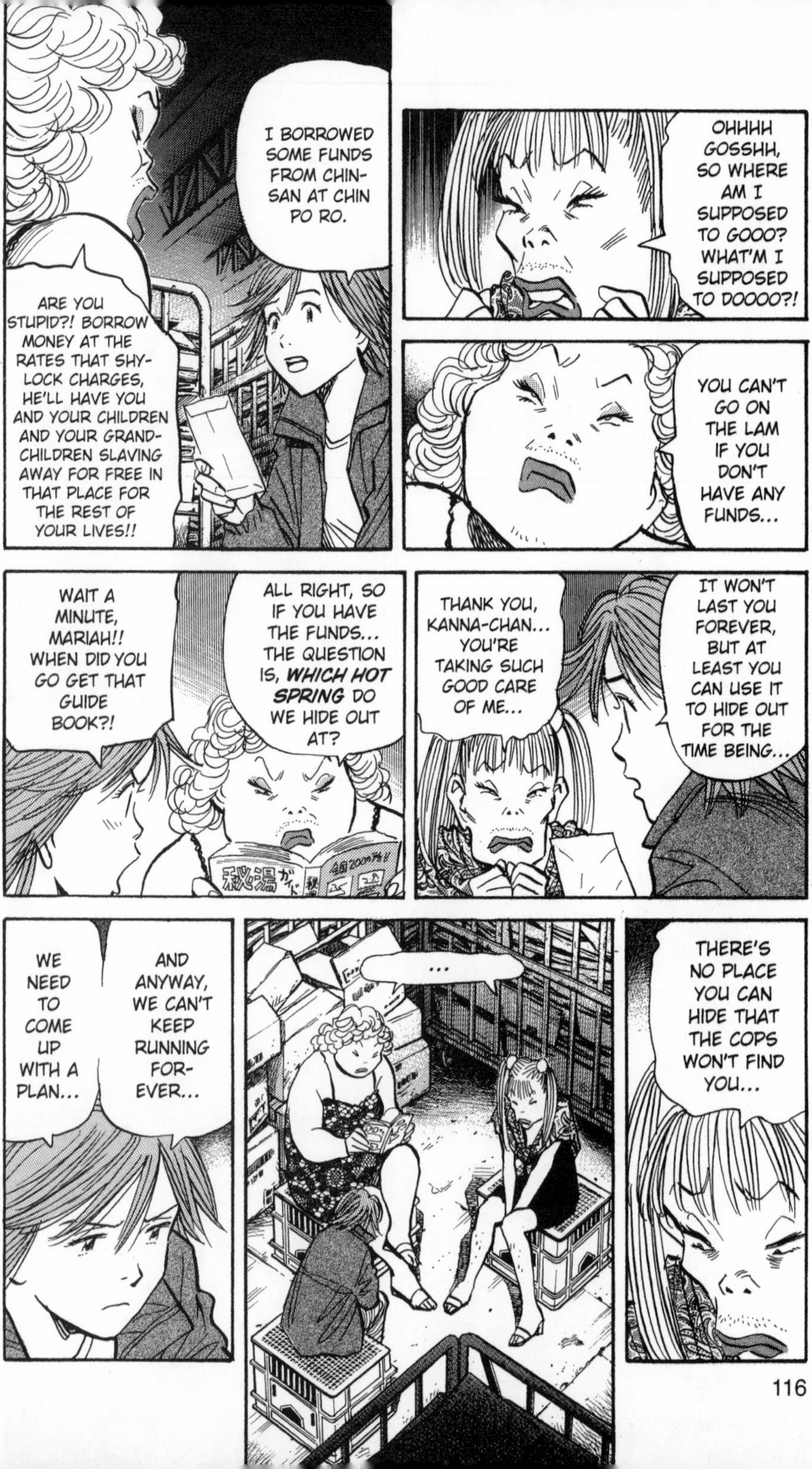
OHHHH GOSSHH, SO WHERE AM I SUPPOSED TO GOOO? WHAT'M I SUPPOSED TO DOOOO?!
YOU CAN'T GO ON THE LAM IF YOU DON'T HAVE ANY FUNDS...
I BORROWED SOME FUNDS FROM CHIN-SAN AT CHIN PO RO.
ARE YOU STUPID?! BORROW MONEY AT THE RATES THAT SHYLOCK CHARGES, HE'LL HAVE YOU AND YOUR CHILDREN AND YOUR GRANDCHILDREN SLAVING AWAY FOR FREE IN THAT PLACE FOR THE REST OF YOUR LIVES!!
IT WON'T LAST YOU FOREVER, BUT AT LEAST YOU CAN USE IT TO HIDE OUT FOR THE TIME BEING...
THANK YOU, KANNA-CHAN... YOU'RE TAKING SUCH GOOD CARE OF ME...
ALL RIGHT, SO IF YOU HAVE THE FUNDS... THE QUESTION IS, ***WHICH HOT SPRING*** DO WE HIDE OUT AT?
WAIT A MINUTE, MARIAH!! WHEN DID YOU GO GET THAT GUIDE BOOK?!
THERE'S NO PLACE YOU CAN HIDE THAT THE COPS WON'T FIND YOU...
...
AND ANYWAY, WE CAN'T KEEP RUNNING FOREVER...
WE NEED TO COME UP WITH A PLAN...

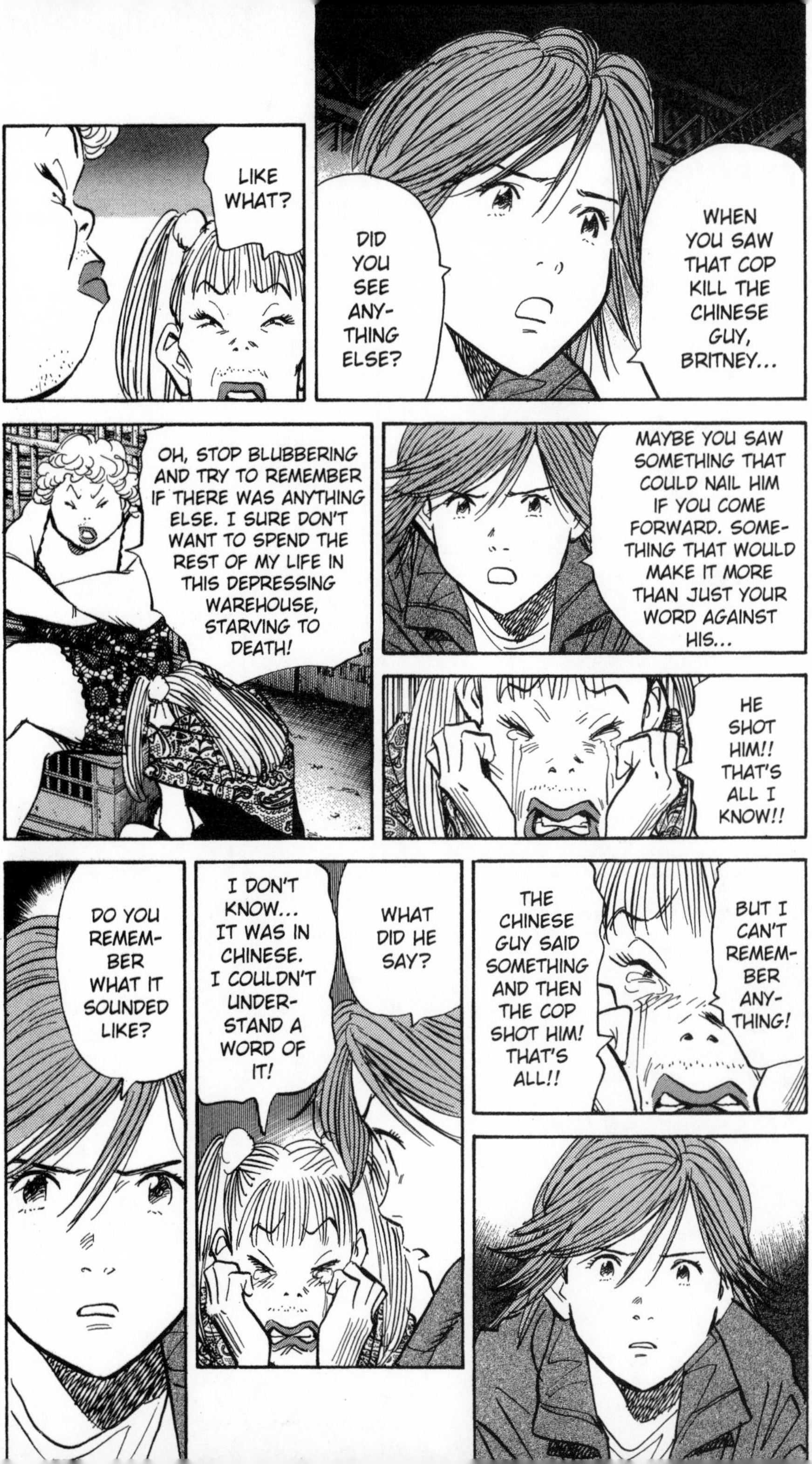
WHEN YOU SAW THAT COP KILL THE CHINESE GUY, BRITNEY...
DID YOU SEE ANYTHING ELSE?
LIKE WHAT?
MAYBE YOU SAW SOMETHING THAT COULD NAIL HIM IF YOU COME FORWARD. SOMETHING THAT WOULD MAKE IT MORE THAN JUST YOUR WORD AGAINST HIS...
HE SHOT HIM!! THAT'S ALL I KNOW!!
OH, STOP BLUBBERING AND TRY TO REMEMBER IF THERE WAS ANYTHING ELSE. I SURE DON'T WANT TO SPEND THE REST OF MY LIFE IN THIS DEPRESSING WAREHOUSE, STARVING TO DEATH!
THE CHINESE GUY SAID SOMETHING AND THEN THE COP SHOT HIM! THAT'S ALL!!
BUT I CAN'T REMEMBER ANYTHING!
WHAT DID HE SAY?
I DON'T KNOW... IT WAS IN CHINESE. I COULDN'T UNDERSTAND A WORD OF IT!
DO YOU REMEMBER WHAT IT SOUNDED LIKE?

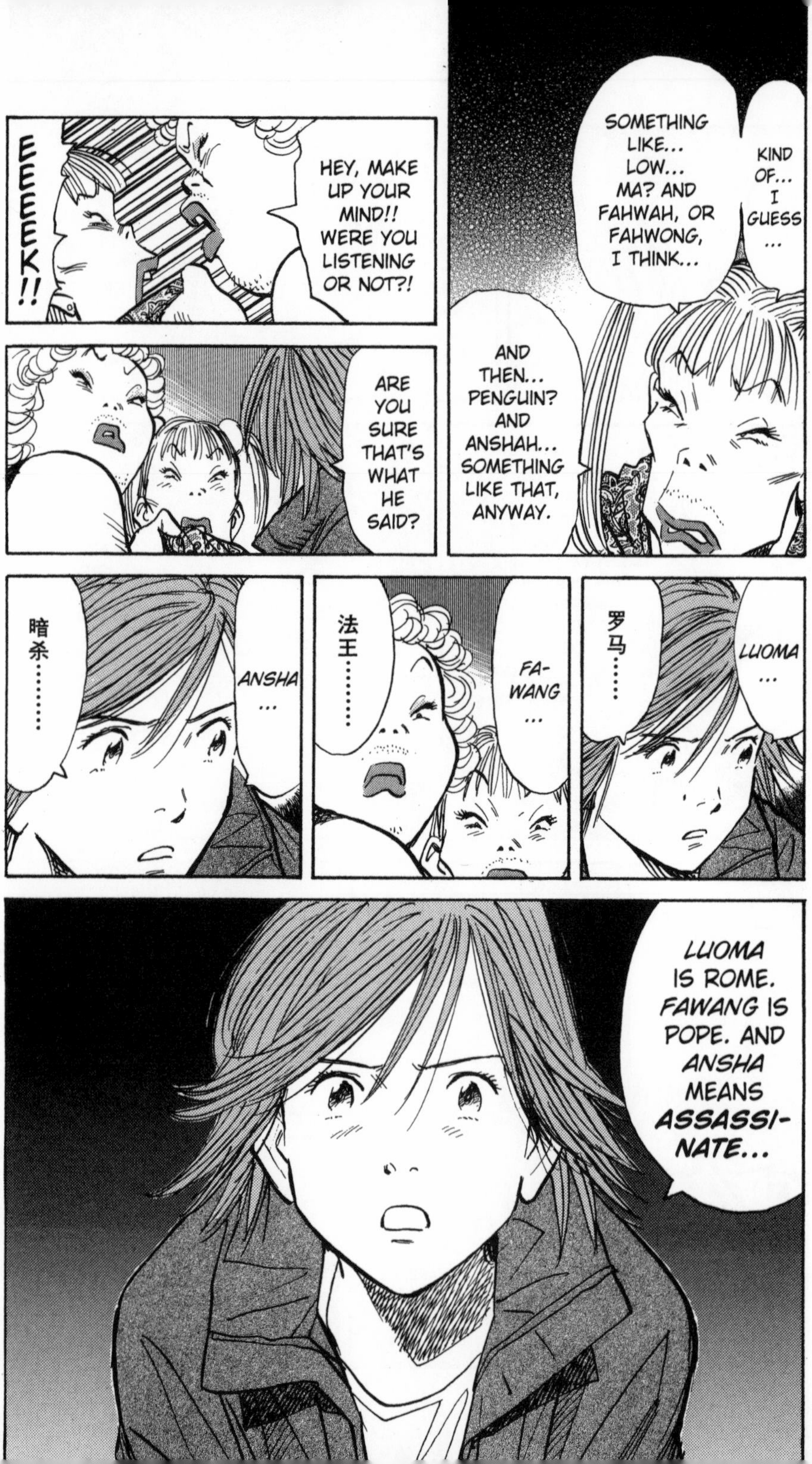

SOMETHING LIKE... LOW... MA? AND FAHWAH, OR FAHWONG, I THINK...
KIND OF... I GUESS...
AND THEN... PENGUIN? AND ANSHAH... SOMETHING LIKE THAT, ANYWAY.
HEY, MAKE UP YOUR MIND!! WERE YOU LISTENING OR NOT?!
EEEEEK!!
ARE YOU SURE THAT'S WHAT HE SAID?
罗马……
LUOMA...
法王……
FA-WANG...
暗杀……
ANSHA...
LUOMA IS ROME. FAWANG IS POPE. AND ANSHA MEANS ASSASSI-NATE...

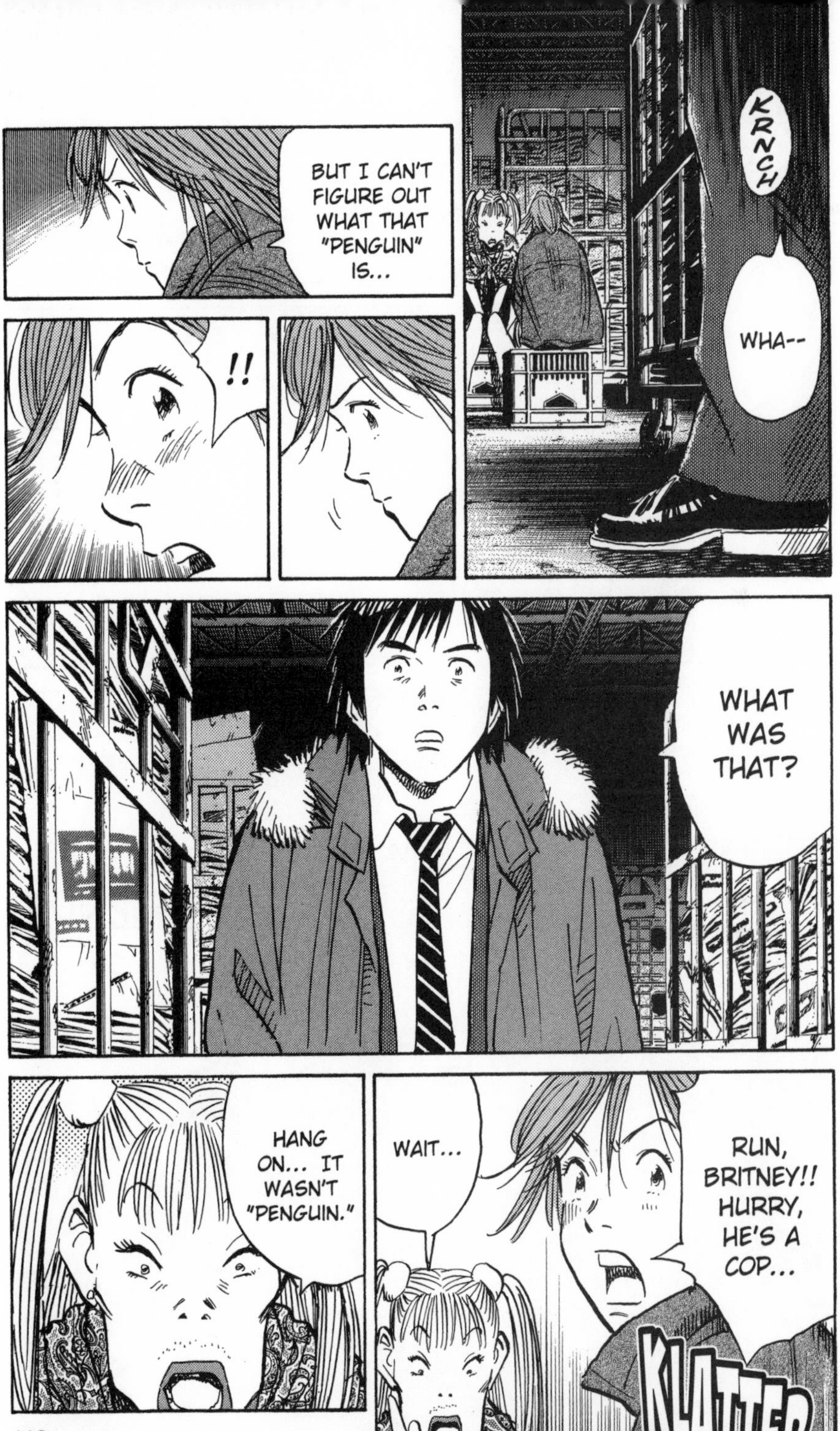
KRNCH
WHA--
BUT I CAN'T FIGURE OUT WHAT THAT "PENGUIN" IS...
!!
WHAT WAS THAT?
RUN, BRITNEY!! HURRY, HE'S A COP...
WAIT...
KLATTER
HANG ON... IT WASN'T "PENGUIN."

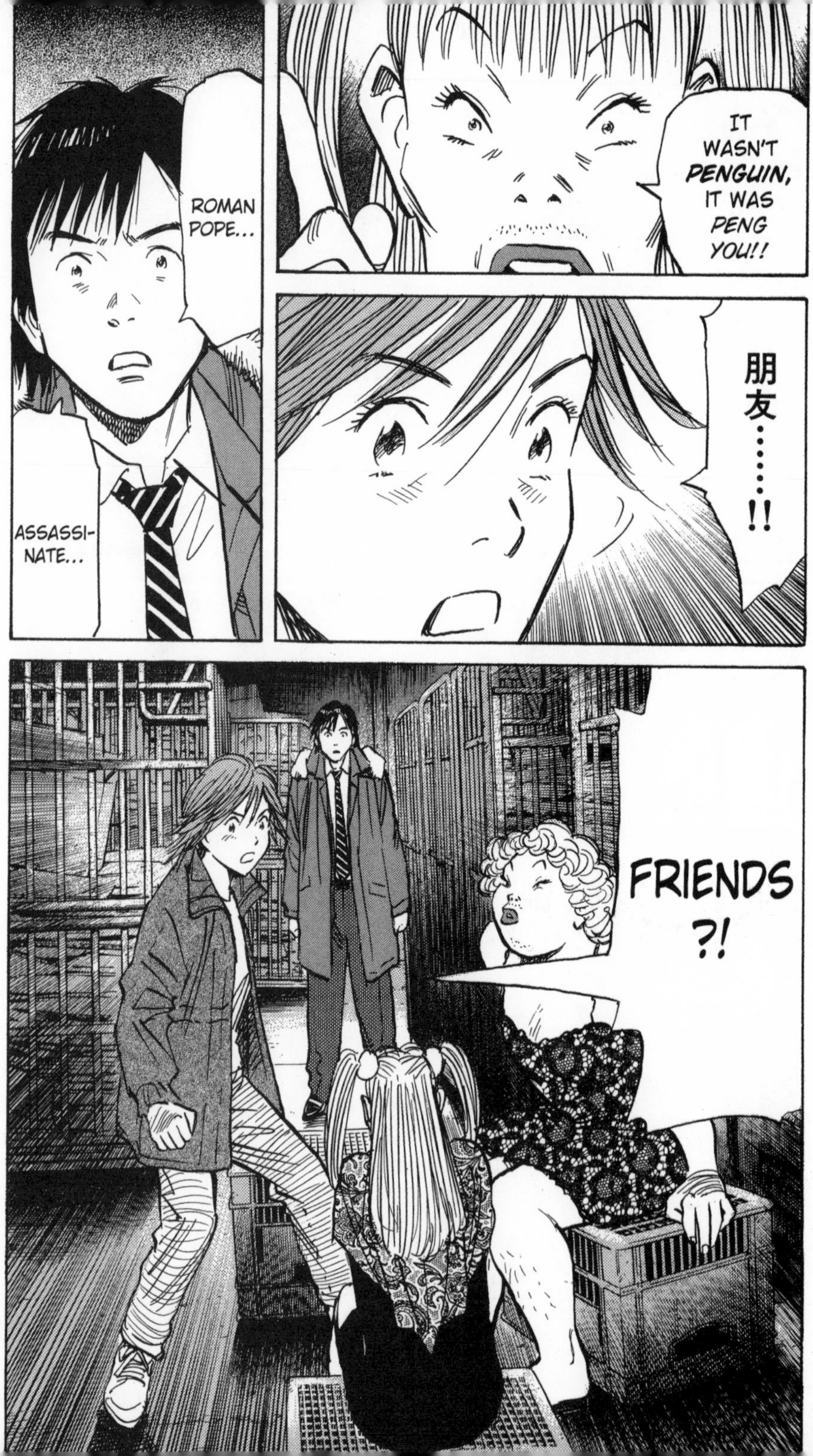
IT WASN'T PENGUIN, IT WAS PENG YOU!!
朋友……!!
ROMAN POPE…
ASSASSI-NATE…
FRIENDS ?!

Chapter 7 Big Shot

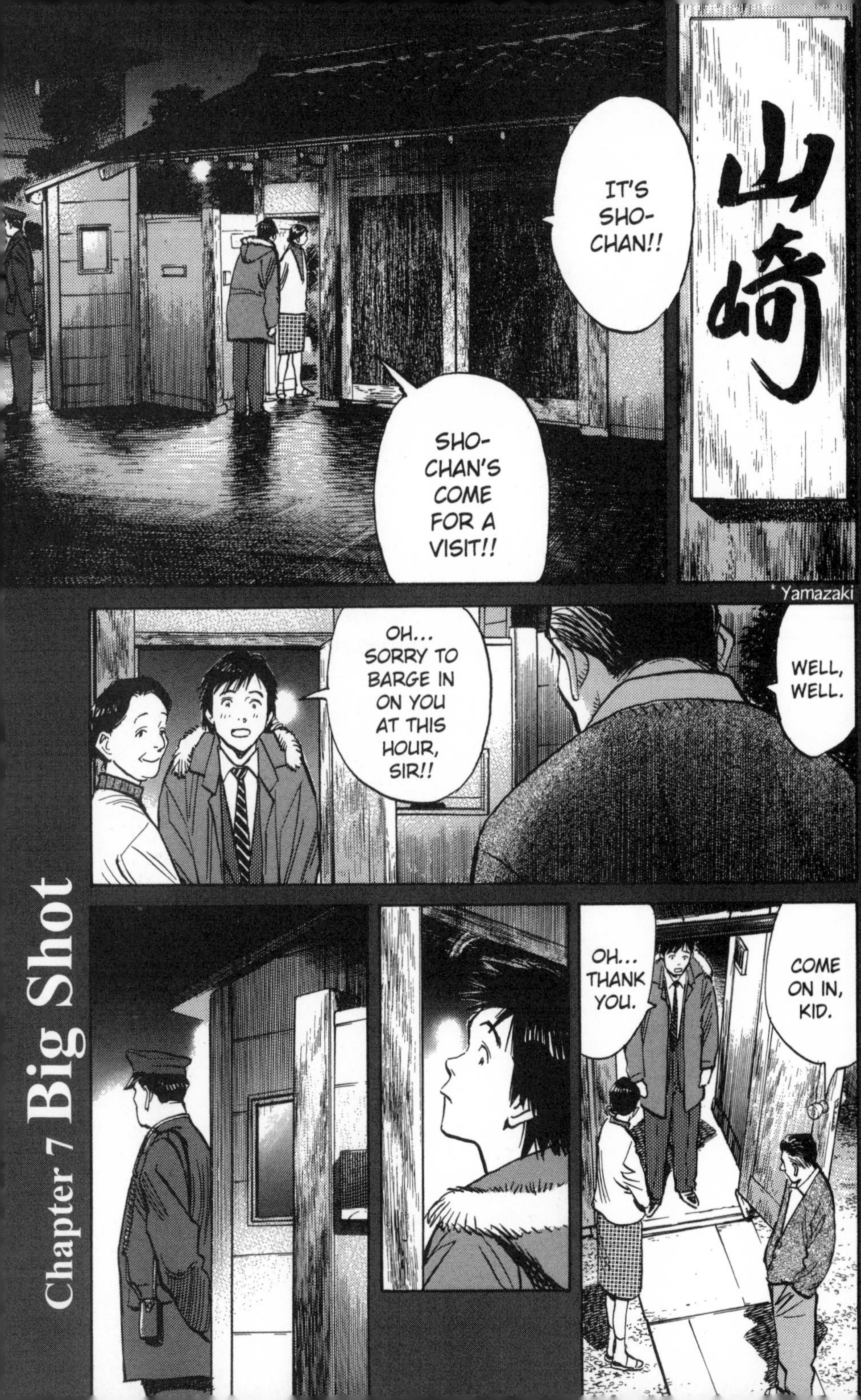
山崎
IT'S SHO-CHAN!!
SHO-CHAN'S COME FOR A VISIT!!
* Yamazaki
WELL, WELL.
OH... SORRY TO BARGE IN ON YOU AT THIS HOUR, SIR!!
COME ON IN, KID.
OH... THANK YOU.

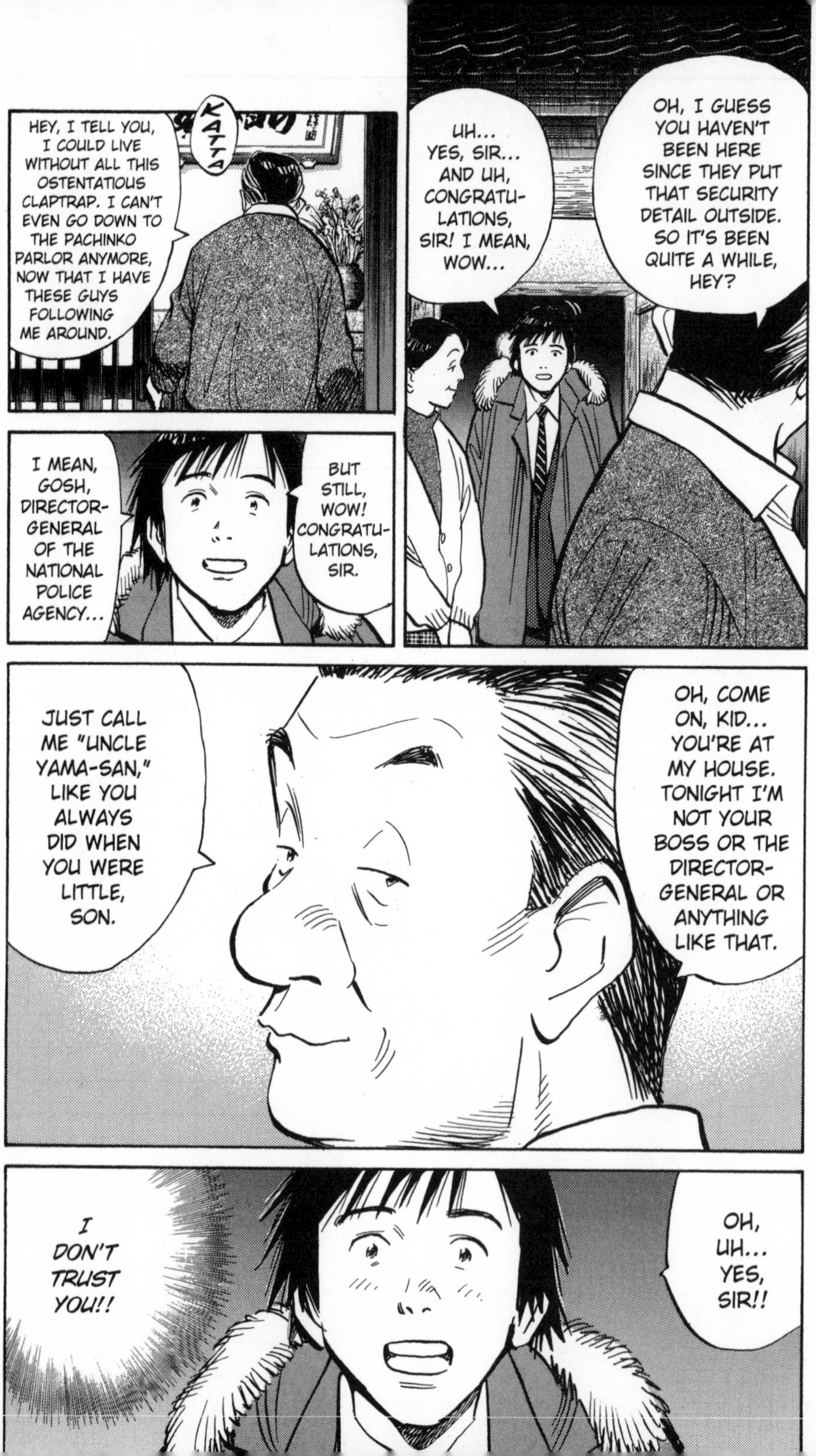
OH, I GUESS YOU HAVEN'T BEEN HERE SINCE THEY PUT THAT SECURITY DETAIL OUTSIDE. SO IT'S BEEN QUITE A WHILE, HEY?
UH... YES, SIR... AND UH, CONGRATULATIONS, SIR! I MEAN, WOW...
KATTA
HEY, I TELL YOU, I COULD LIVE WITHOUT ALL THIS OSTENTATIOUS CLAPTRAP. I CAN'T EVEN GO DOWN TO THE PACHINKO PARLOR ANYMORE, NOW THAT I HAVE THESE GUYS FOLLOWING ME AROUND.
BUT STILL, WOW! CONGRATULATIONS, SIR.
I MEAN, GOSH, DIRECTOR-GENERAL OF THE NATIONAL POLICE AGENCY...
OH, COME ON, KID... YOU'RE AT MY HOUSE. TONIGHT I'M NOT YOUR BOSS OR THE DIRECTOR-GENERAL OR ANYTHING LIKE THAT.
JUST CALL ME "UNCLE YAMA-SAN," LIKE YOU ALWAYS DID WHEN YOU WERE LITTLE, SON.
OH, UH... YES, SIR!!
I DON'T TRUST YOU!!

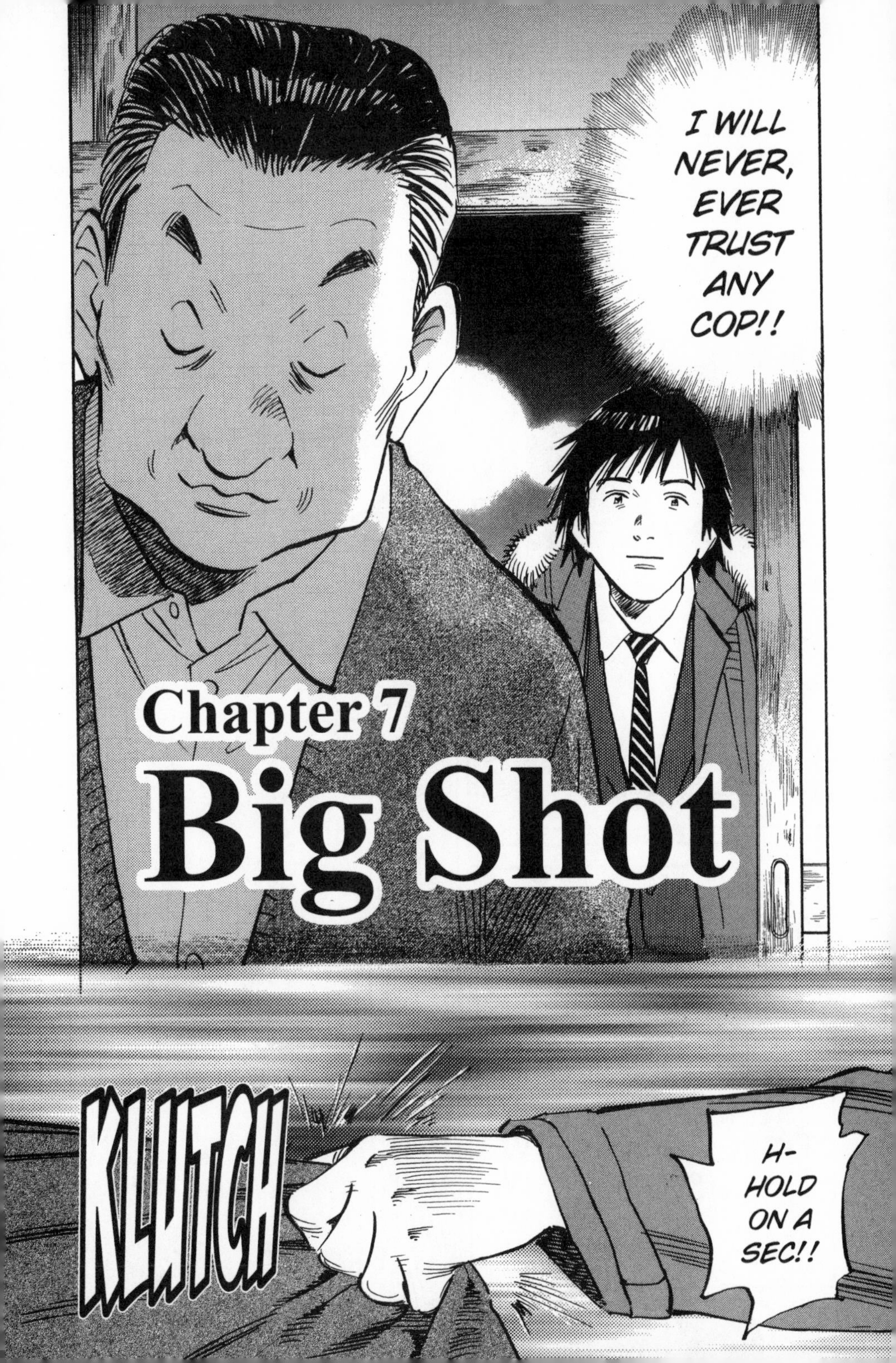
I WILL NEVER, EVER TRUST ANY COP!!
Chapter 7
Big Shot
H-HOLD ON A SEC!!
KLUTCH

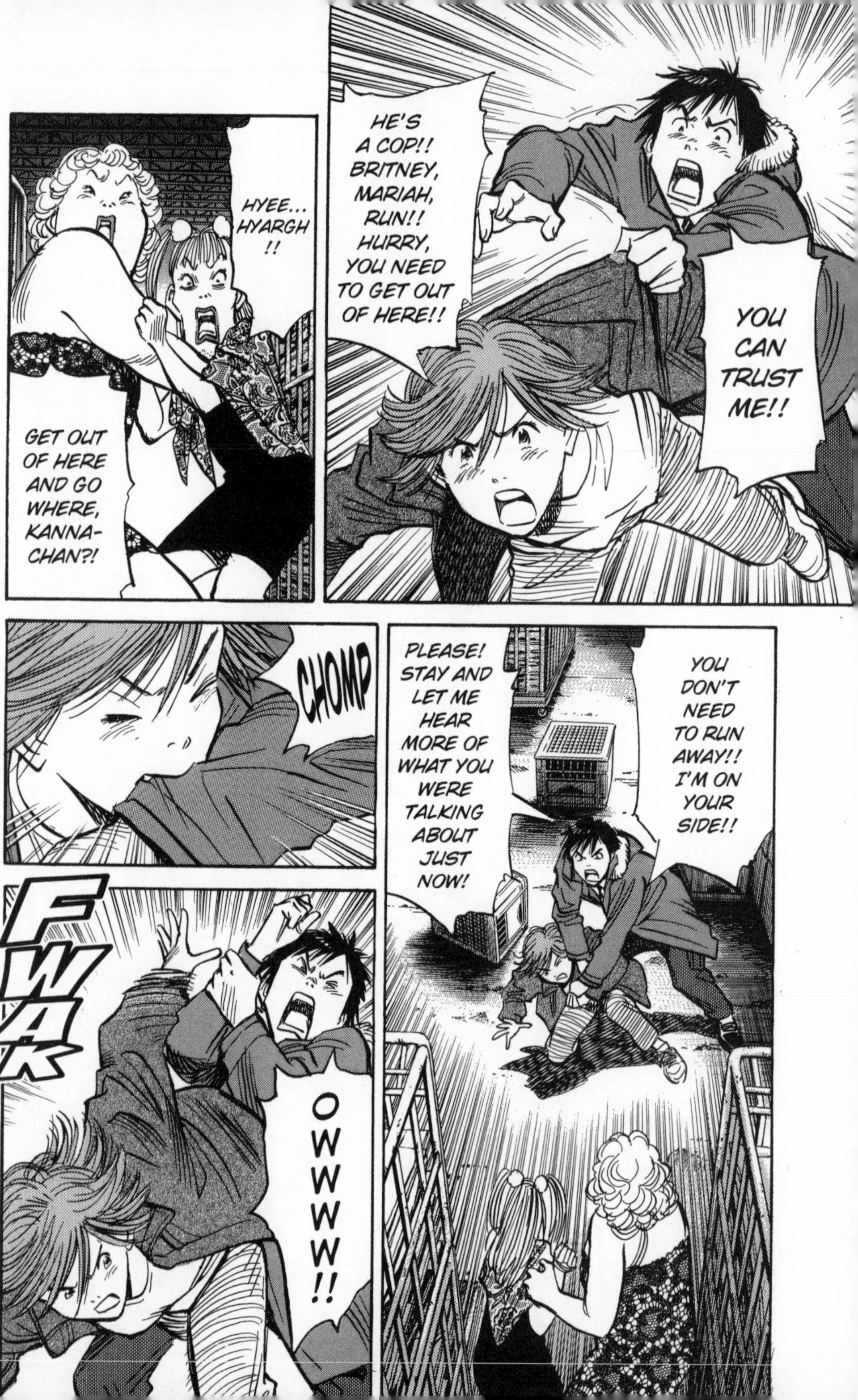
HE'S A COP!! BRITNEY, MARIAH, RUN!! HURRY, YOU NEED TO GET OUT OF HERE!!
YOU CAN TRUST ME!!
HYEE... HYARGH!!
GET OUT OF HERE AND GO WHERE, KANNA-CHAN?!
YOU DON'T NEED TO RUN AWAY!! I'M ON YOUR SIDE!!
PLEASE! STAY AND LET ME HEAR MORE OF WHAT YOU WERE TALKING ABOUT JUST NOW!
CHOMP
FWAK
OWWWWW!!

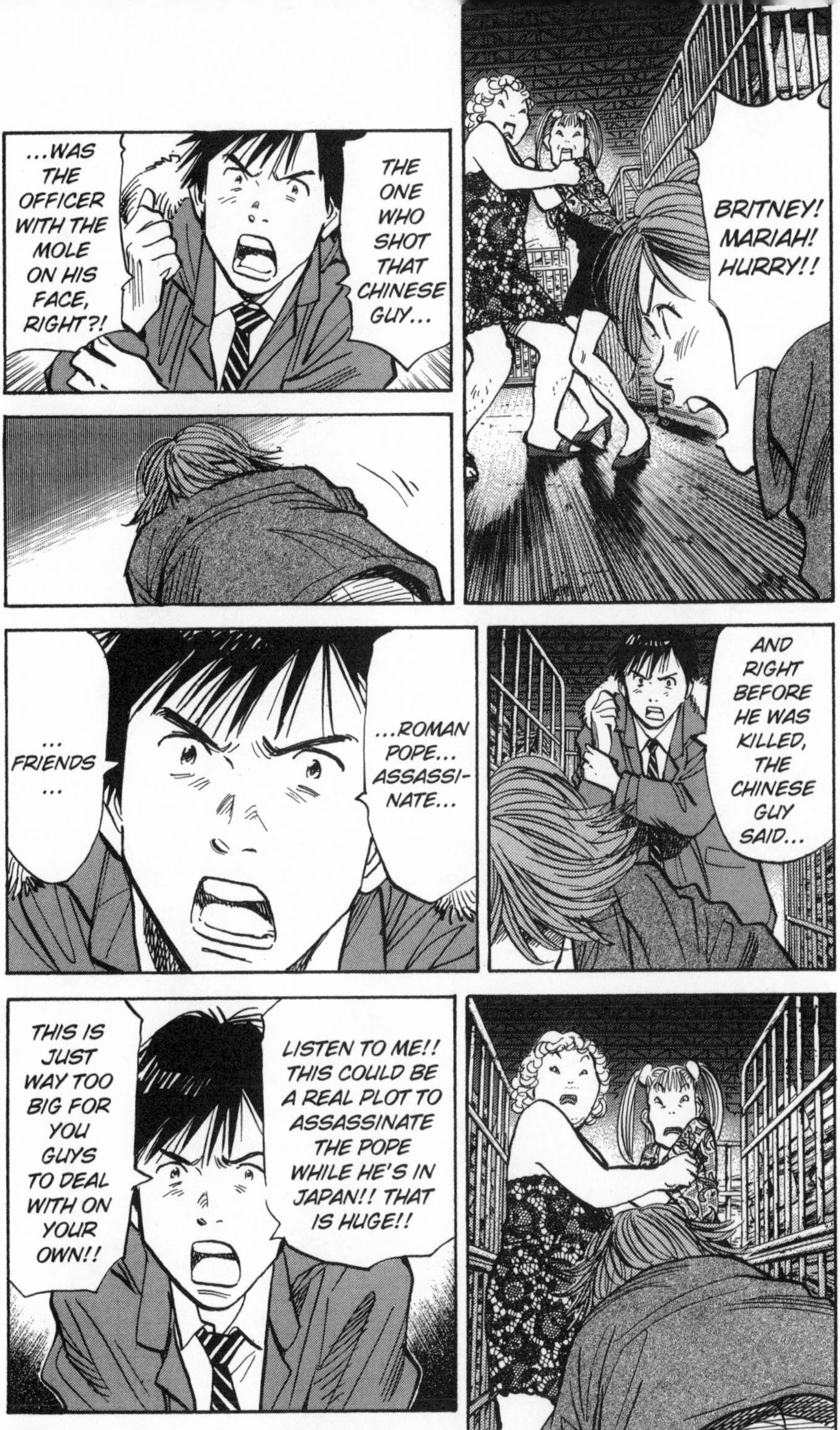
BRITNEY! MARIAH! HURRY!!
THE ONE WHO SHOT THAT CHINESE GUY...
...WAS THE OFFICER WITH THE MOLE ON HIS FACE, RIGHT?!
AND RIGHT BEFORE HE WAS KILLED, THE CHINESE GUY SAID...
...ROMAN POPE... ASSASSI-NATE...
...FRIENDS...
LISTEN TO ME!! THIS COULD BE A REAL PLOT TO ASSASSINATE THE POPE WHILE HE'S IN JAPAN!! THAT IS HUGE!!
THIS IS JUST WAY TOO BIG FOR YOU GUYS TO DEAL WITH ON YOUR OWN!!

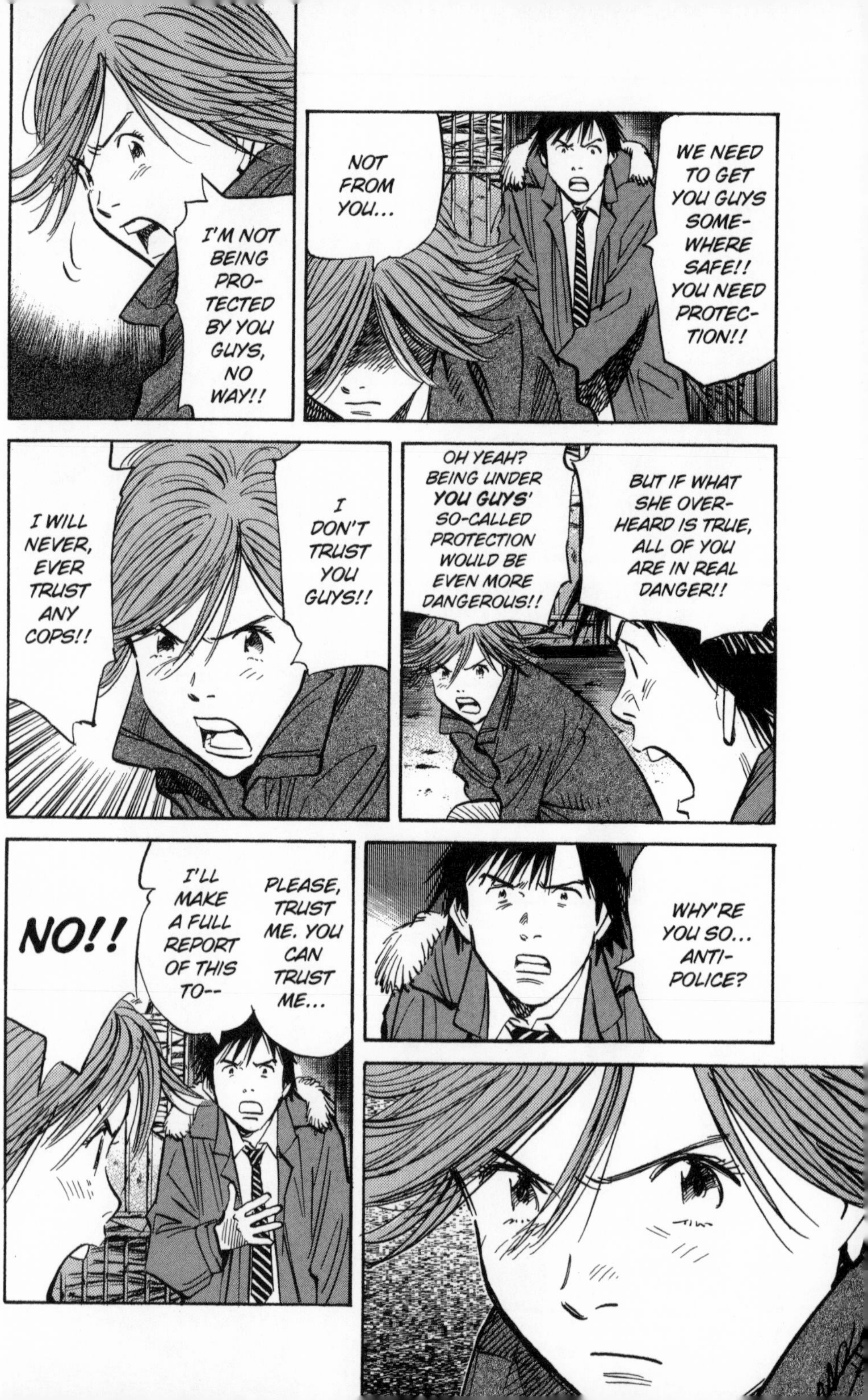
WE NEED TO GET YOU GUYS SOMEWHERE SAFE!! YOU NEED PROTECTION!!
NOT FROM YOU...
I'M NOT BEING PROTECTED BY YOU GUYS, NO WAY!!
BUT IF WHAT SHE OVERHEARD IS TRUE, ALL OF YOU ARE IN REAL DANGER!!
OH YEAH? BEING UNDER YOU GUYS' SO-CALLED PROTECTION WOULD BE EVEN MORE DANGEROUS!!
I DON'T TRUST YOU GUYS!!
I WILL NEVER, EVER TRUST ANY COPS!!
WHY'RE YOU SO... ANTI-POLICE?
PLEASE, TRUST ME. YOU CAN TRUST ME...
I'LL MAKE A FULL REPORT OF THIS TO--
NO!!

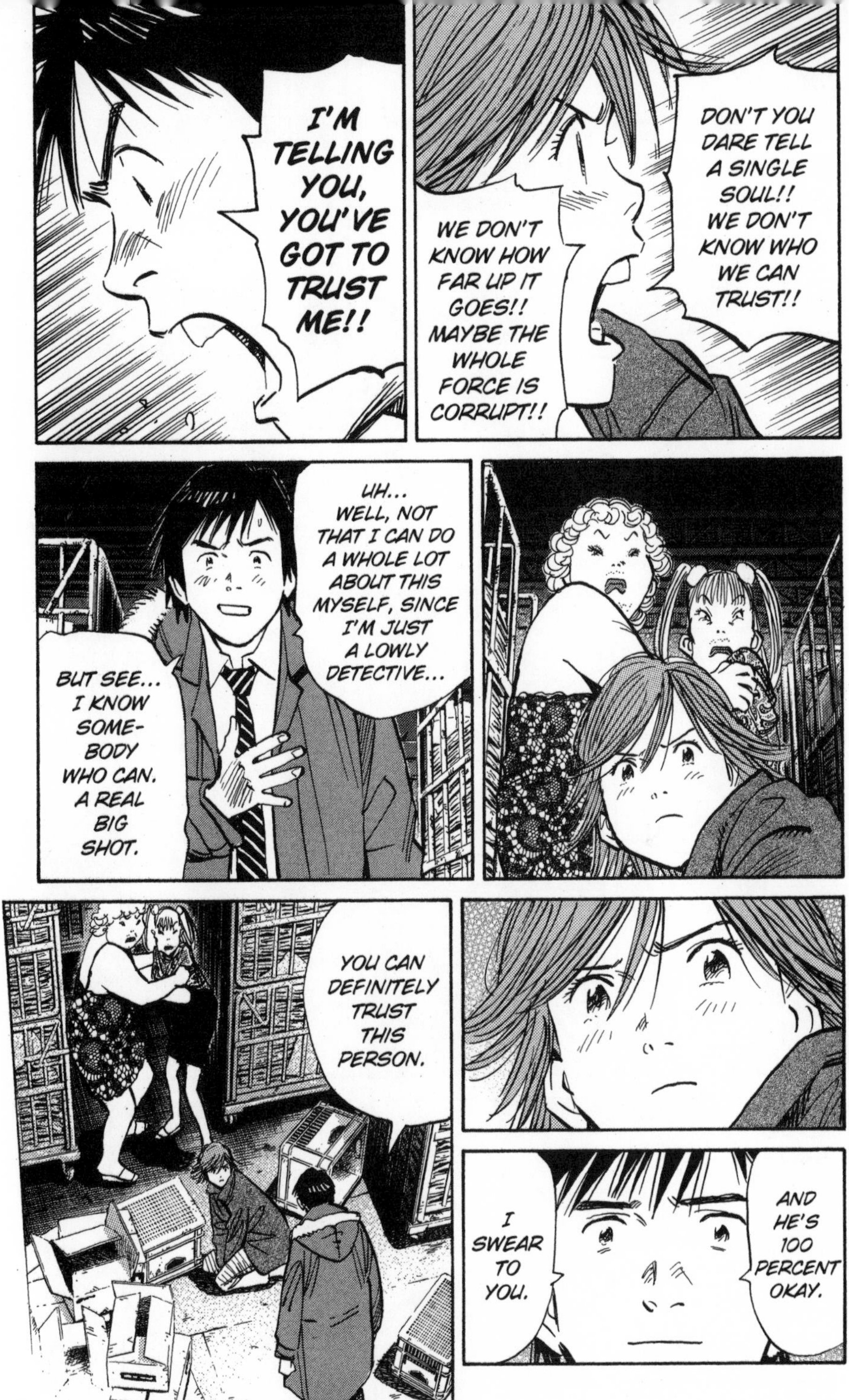
DON'T YOU DARE TELL A SINGLE SOUL!! WE DON'T KNOW WHO WE CAN TRUST!!
WE DON'T KNOW HOW FAR UP IT GOES!! MAYBE THE WHOLE FORCE IS CORRUPT!!
I'M TELLING YOU, YOU'VE GOT TO TRUST ME!!
UH... WELL, NOT THAT I CAN DO A WHOLE LOT ABOUT THIS MYSELF, SINCE I'M JUST A LOWLY DETECTIVE...
BUT SEE... I KNOW SOMEBODY WHO CAN. A REAL BIG SHOT.
AND HE'S 100 PERCENT OKAY.
I SWEAR TO YOU.
YOU CAN DEFINITELY TRUST THIS PERSON.

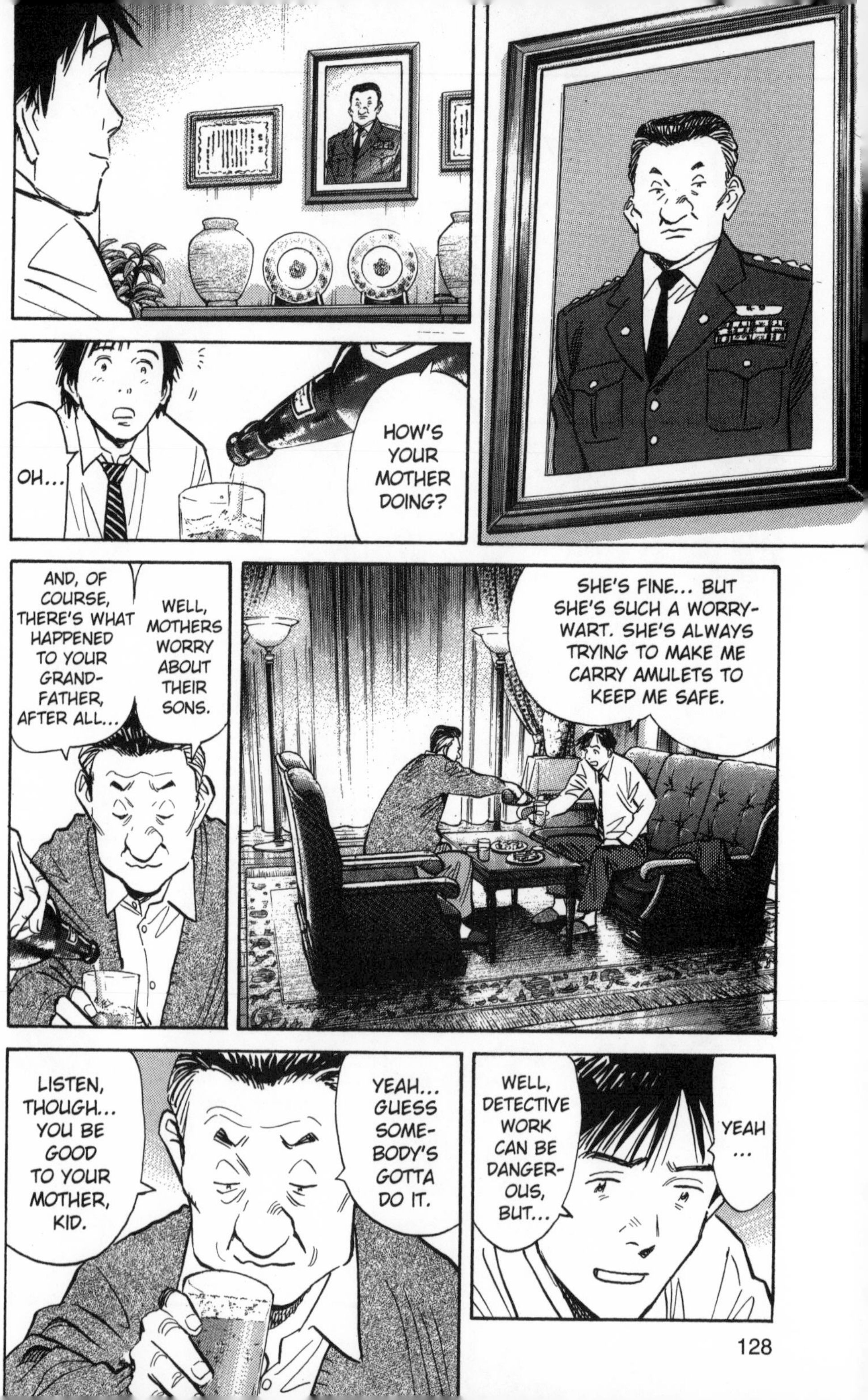
HOW'S YOUR MOTHER DOING?
OH...
SHE'S FINE... BUT SHE'S SUCH A WORRY-WART. SHE'S ALWAYS TRYING TO MAKE ME CARRY AMULETS TO KEEP ME SAFE.
WELL, MOTHERS WORRY ABOUT THEIR SONS.
AND, OF COURSE, THERE'S WHAT HAPPENED TO YOUR GRAND-FATHER, AFTER ALL...
YEAH...
WELL, DETECTIVE WORK CAN BE DANGER-OUS, BUT...
YEAH... GUESS SOME-BODY'S GOTTA DO IT.
LISTEN, THOUGH... YOU BE GOOD TO YOUR MOTHER, KID.

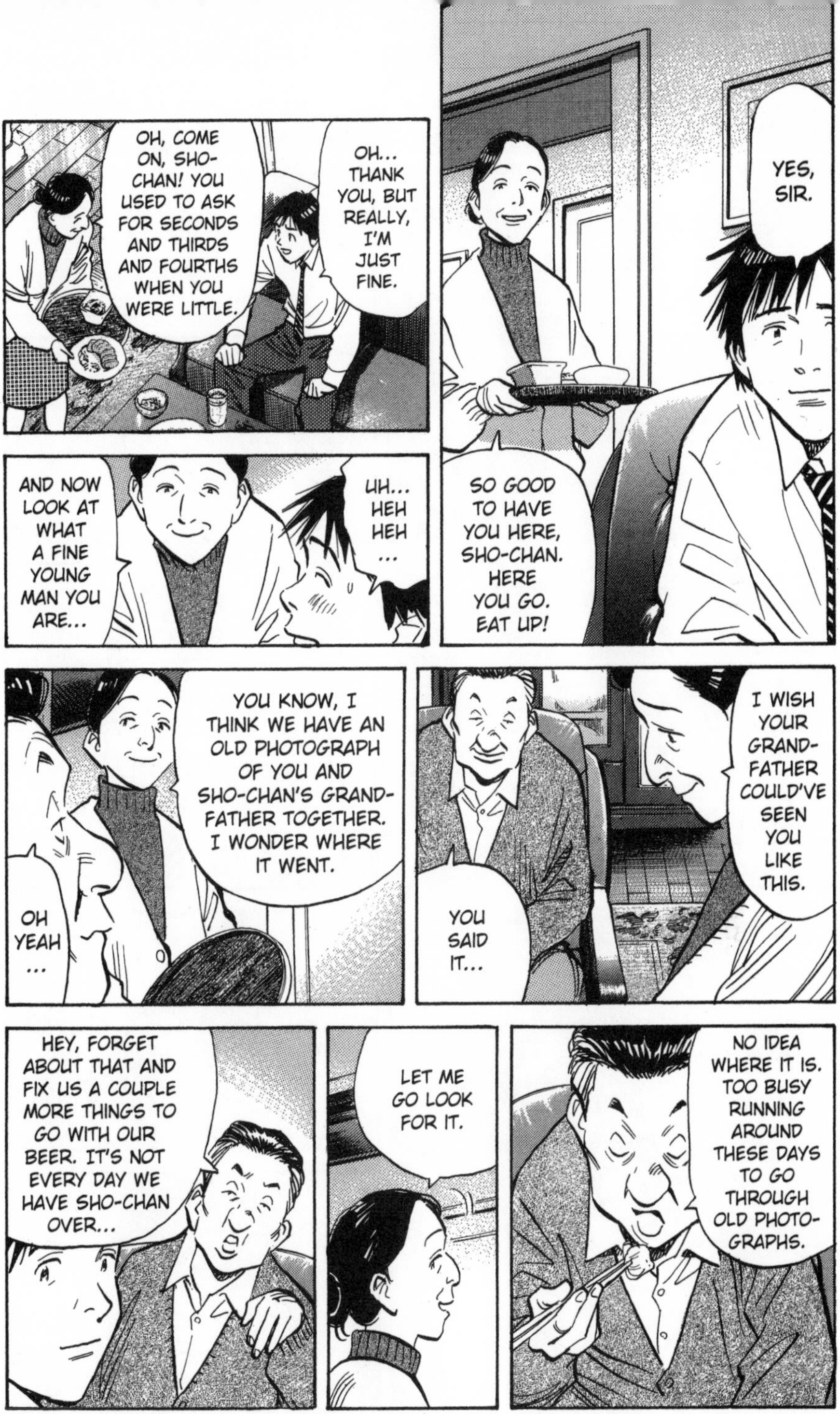
YES, SIR.
SO GOOD TO HAVE YOU HERE, SHO-CHAN. HERE YOU GO. EAT UP!
OH... THANK YOU, BUT REALLY, I'M JUST FINE.
OH, COME ON, SHO-CHAN! YOU USED TO ASK FOR SECONDS AND THIRDS AND FOURTHS WHEN YOU WERE LITTLE.
UH... HEH HEH ...
AND NOW LOOK AT WHAT A FINE YOUNG MAN YOU ARE...
I WISH YOUR GRAND-FATHER COULD'VE SEEN YOU LIKE THIS.
YOU SAID IT...
YOU KNOW, I THINK WE HAVE AN OLD PHOTOGRAPH OF YOU AND SHO-CHAN'S GRAND-FATHER TOGETHER. I WONDER WHERE IT WENT.
OH YEAH ...
NO IDEA WHERE IT IS. TOO BUSY RUNNING AROUND THESE DAYS TO GO THROUGH OLD PHOTO-GRAPHS.
LET ME GO LOOK FOR IT.
HEY, FORGET ABOUT THAT AND FIX US A COUPLE MORE THINGS TO GO WITH OUR BEER. IT'S NOT EVERY DAY WE HAVE SHO-CHAN OVER...

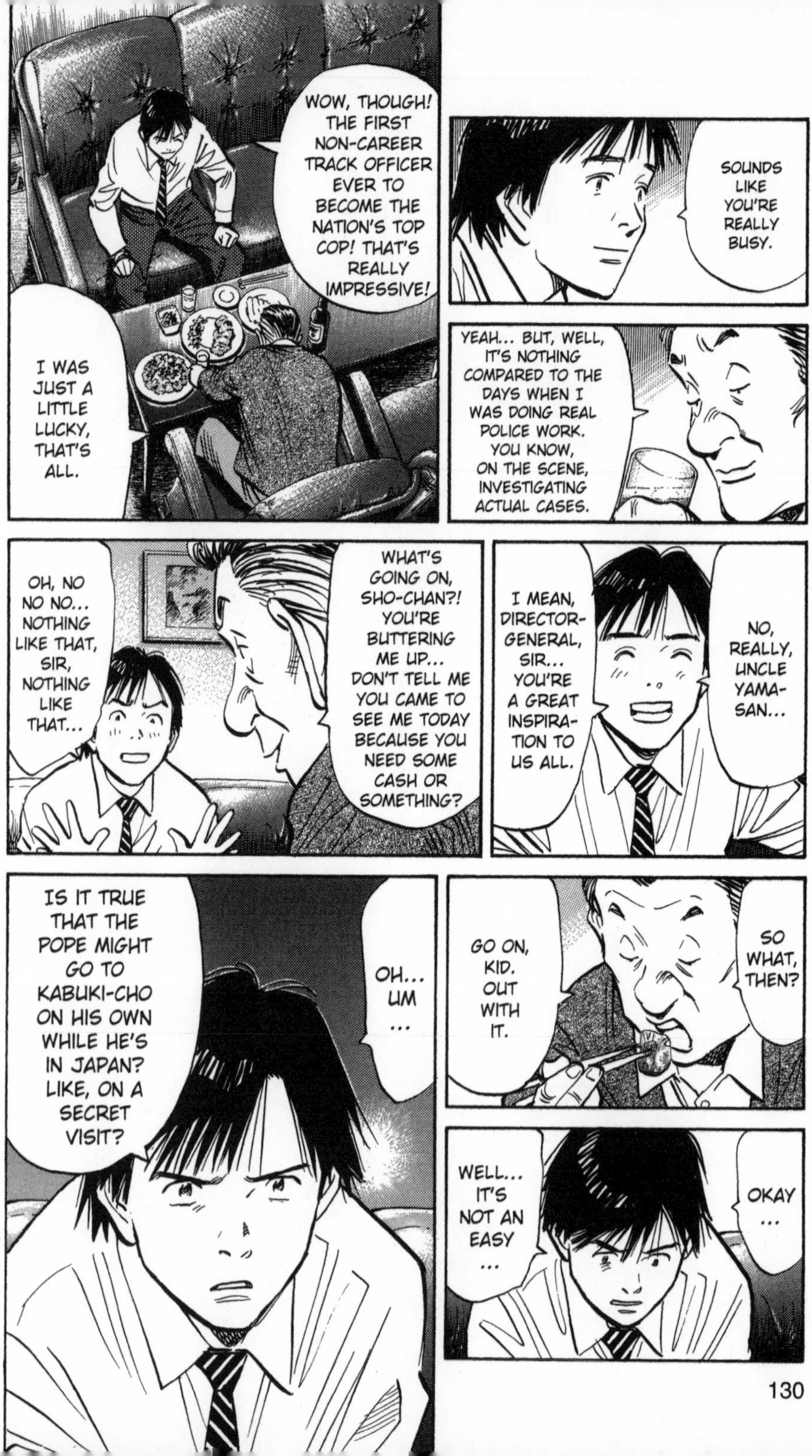
SOUNDS LIKE YOU'RE REALLY BUSY.
YEAH... BUT, WELL, IT'S NOTHING COMPARED TO THE DAYS WHEN I WAS DOING REAL POLICE WORK. YOU KNOW, ON THE SCENE, INVESTIGATING ACTUAL CASES.
WOW, THOUGH! THE FIRST NON-CAREER TRACK OFFICER EVER TO BECOME THE NATION'S TOP COP! THAT'S REALLY IMPRESSIVE!
I WAS JUST A LITTLE LUCKY, THAT'S ALL.
NO, REALLY, UNCLE YAMA-SAN...
I MEAN, DIRECTOR-GENERAL, SIR... YOU'RE A GREAT INSPIRATION TO US ALL.
WHAT'S GOING ON, SHO-CHAN?! YOU'RE BUTTERING ME UP... DON'T TELL ME YOU CAME TO SEE ME TODAY BECAUSE YOU NEED SOME CASH OR SOMETHING?
OH, NO NO NO... NOTHING LIKE THAT, SIR, NOTHING LIKE THAT...
SO WHAT, THEN?
GO ON, KID. OUT WITH IT.
OKAY ...
WELL... IT'S NOT AN EASY ...
OH... UM ...
IS IT TRUE THAT THE POPE MIGHT GO TO KABUKI-CHO ON HIS OWN WHILE HE'S IN JAPAN? LIKE, ON A SECRET VISIT?

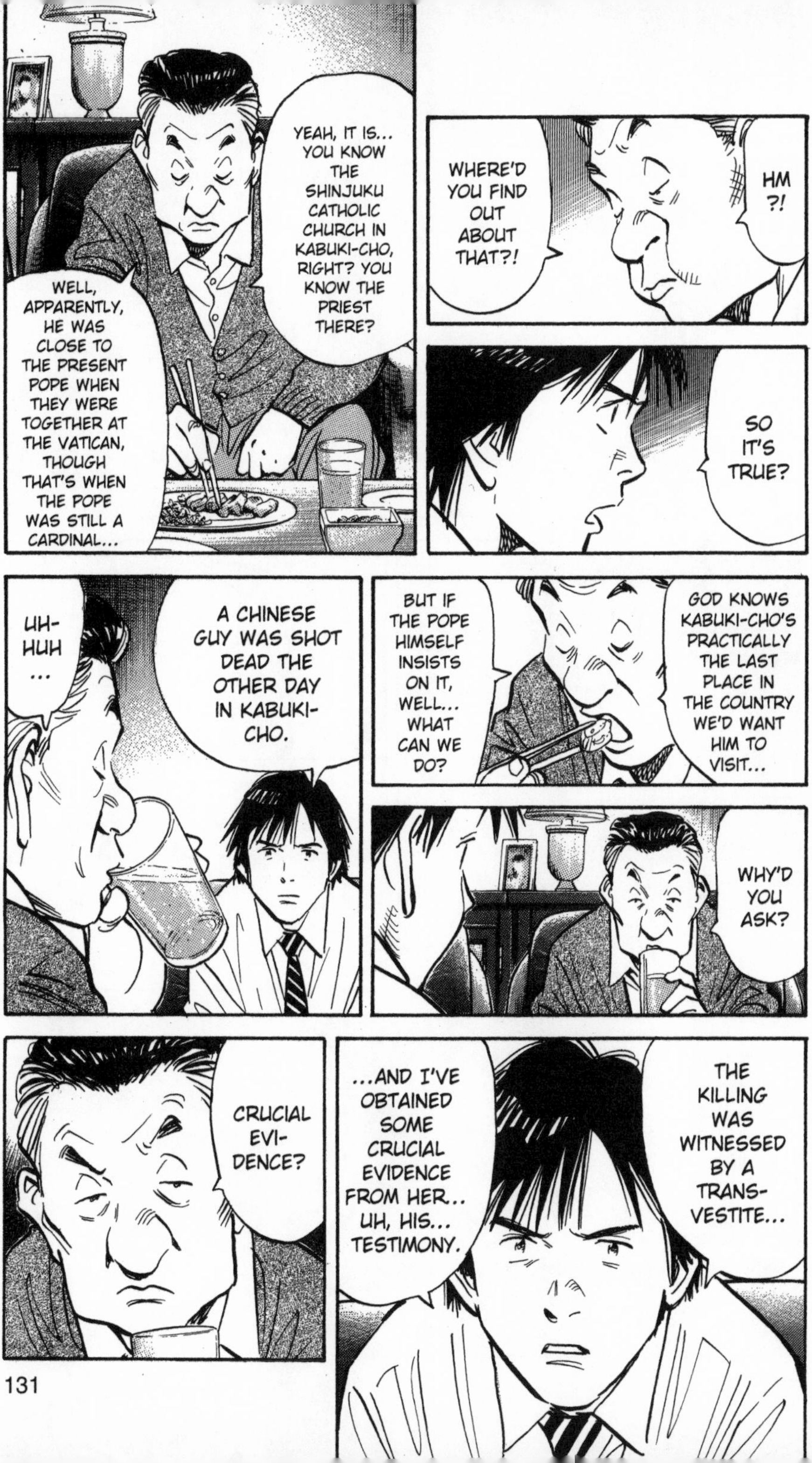
HM?!
WHERE'D YOU FIND OUT ABOUT THAT?!
SO IT'S TRUE?
YEAH, IT IS... YOU KNOW THE SHINJUKU CATHOLIC CHURCH IN KABUKI-CHO, RIGHT? YOU KNOW THE PRIEST THERE?
WELL, APPARENTLY, HE WAS CLOSE TO THE PRESENT POPE WHEN THEY WERE TOGETHER AT THE VATICAN, THOUGH THAT'S WHEN THE POPE WAS STILL A CARDINAL...
GOD KNOWS KABUKI-CHO'S PRACTICALLY THE LAST PLACE IN THE COUNTRY WE'D WANT HIM TO VISIT...
BUT IF THE POPE HIMSELF INSISTS ON IT, WELL... WHAT CAN WE DO?
WHY'D YOU ASK?
A CHINESE GUY WAS SHOT DEAD THE OTHER DAY IN KABUKI-CHO.
UH-HUH...
THE KILLING WAS WITNESSED BY A TRANS-VESTITE...
...AND I'VE OBTAINED SOME CRUCIAL EVIDENCE FROM HER... UH, HIS... TESTIMONY.
CRUCIAL EVI-DENCE?

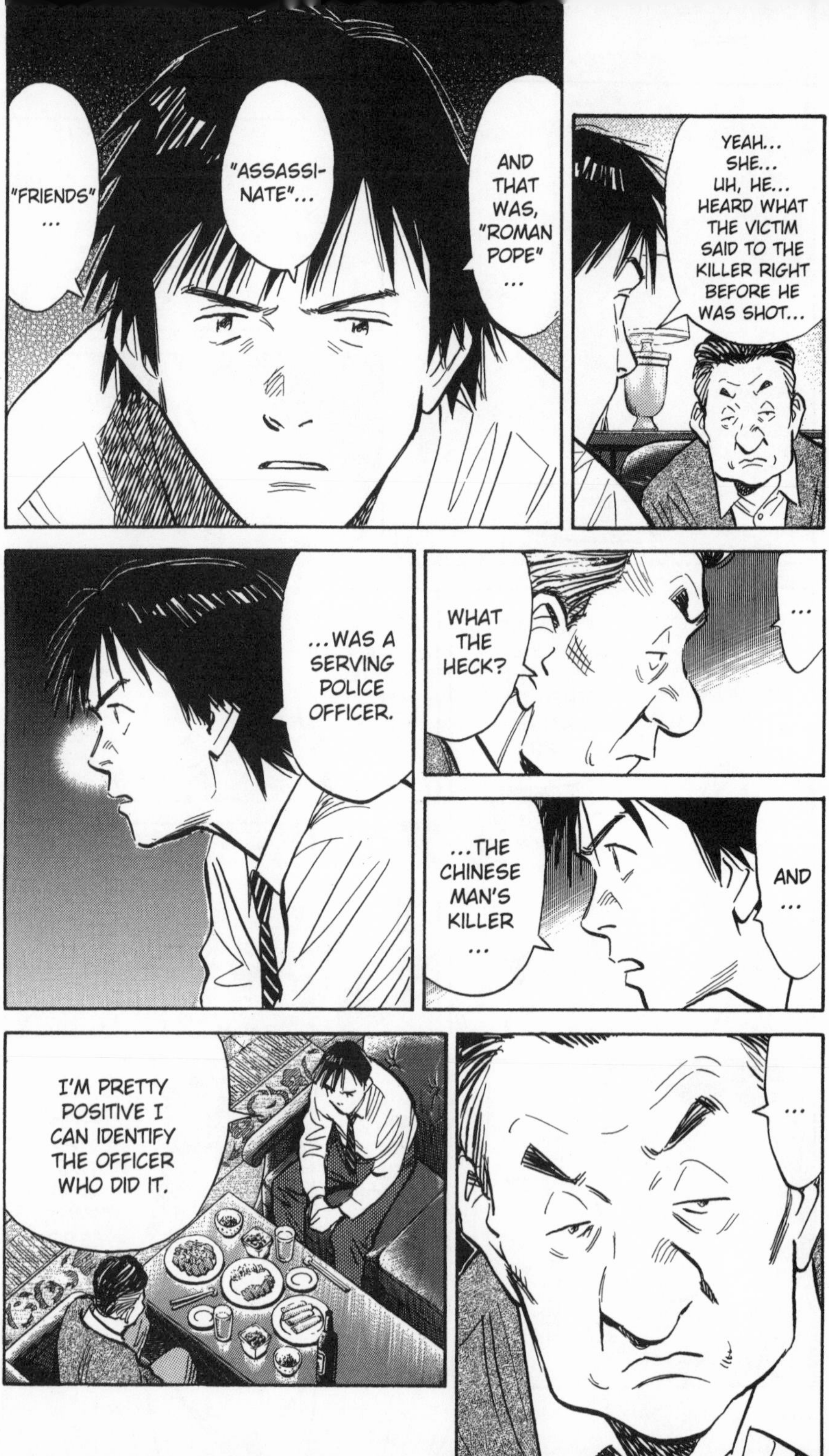
YEAH... SHE... UH, HE... HEARD WHAT THE VICTIM SAID TO THE KILLER RIGHT BEFORE HE WAS SHOT...
AND THAT WAS, "ROMAN POPE" ...
"ASSASSI-NATE"...
"FRIENDS" ...
...
WHAT THE HECK?
AND ...
...THE CHINESE MAN'S KILLER ...
...WAS A SERVING POLICE OFFICER.
...
I'M PRETTY POSITIVE I CAN IDENTIFY THE OFFICER WHO DID IT.

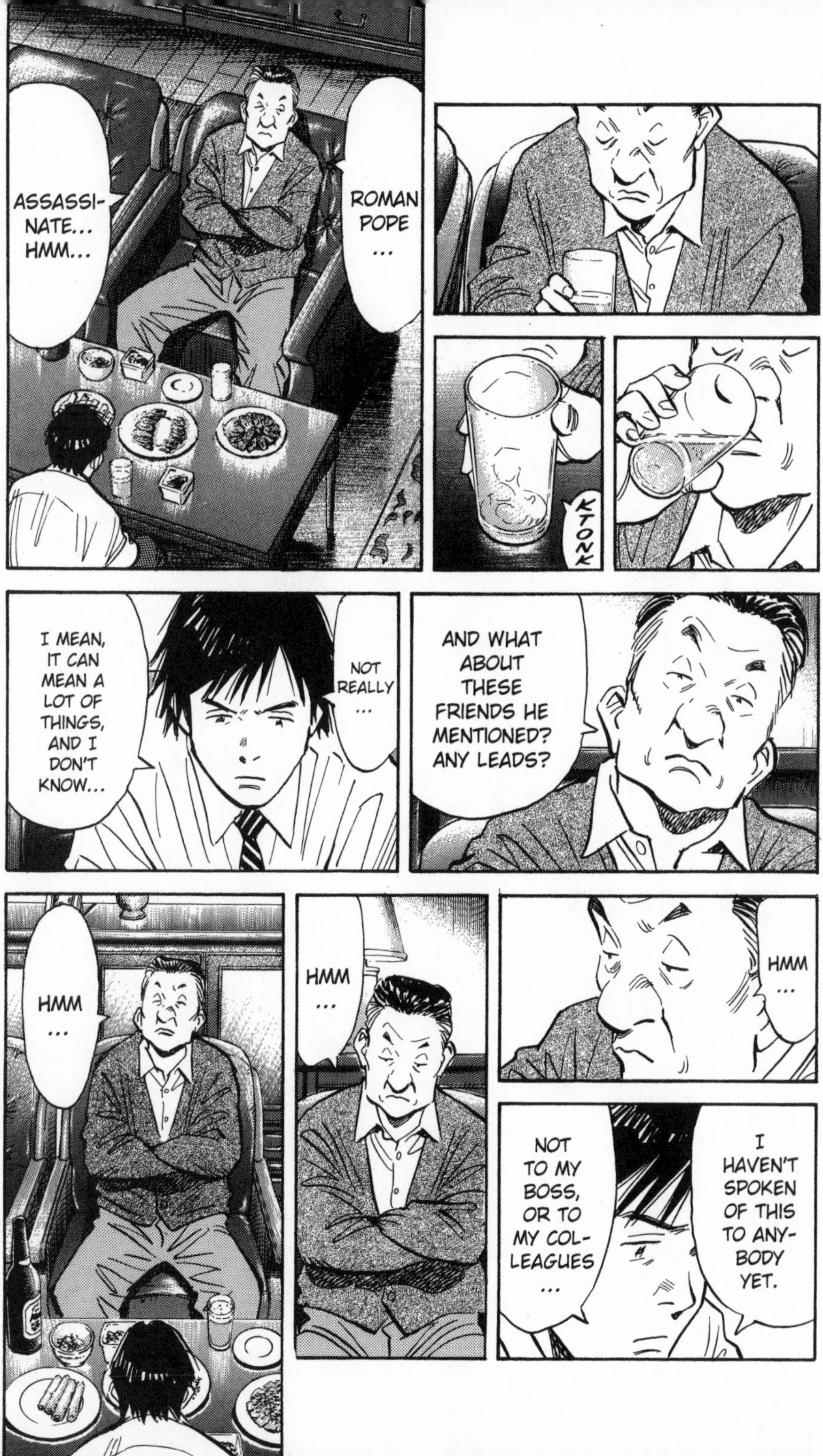
KTONK
ROMAN POPE ...
ASSASSI-NATE... HMM...
AND WHAT ABOUT THESE FRIENDS HE MENTIONED? ANY LEADS?
NOT REALLY ...
I MEAN, IT CAN MEAN A LOT OF THINGS, AND I DON'T KNOW...
HMM ...
I HAVEN'T SPOKEN OF THIS TO ANY-BODY YET.
NOT TO MY BOSS, OR TO MY COL-LEAGUES ...
HMM ...
HMM ...

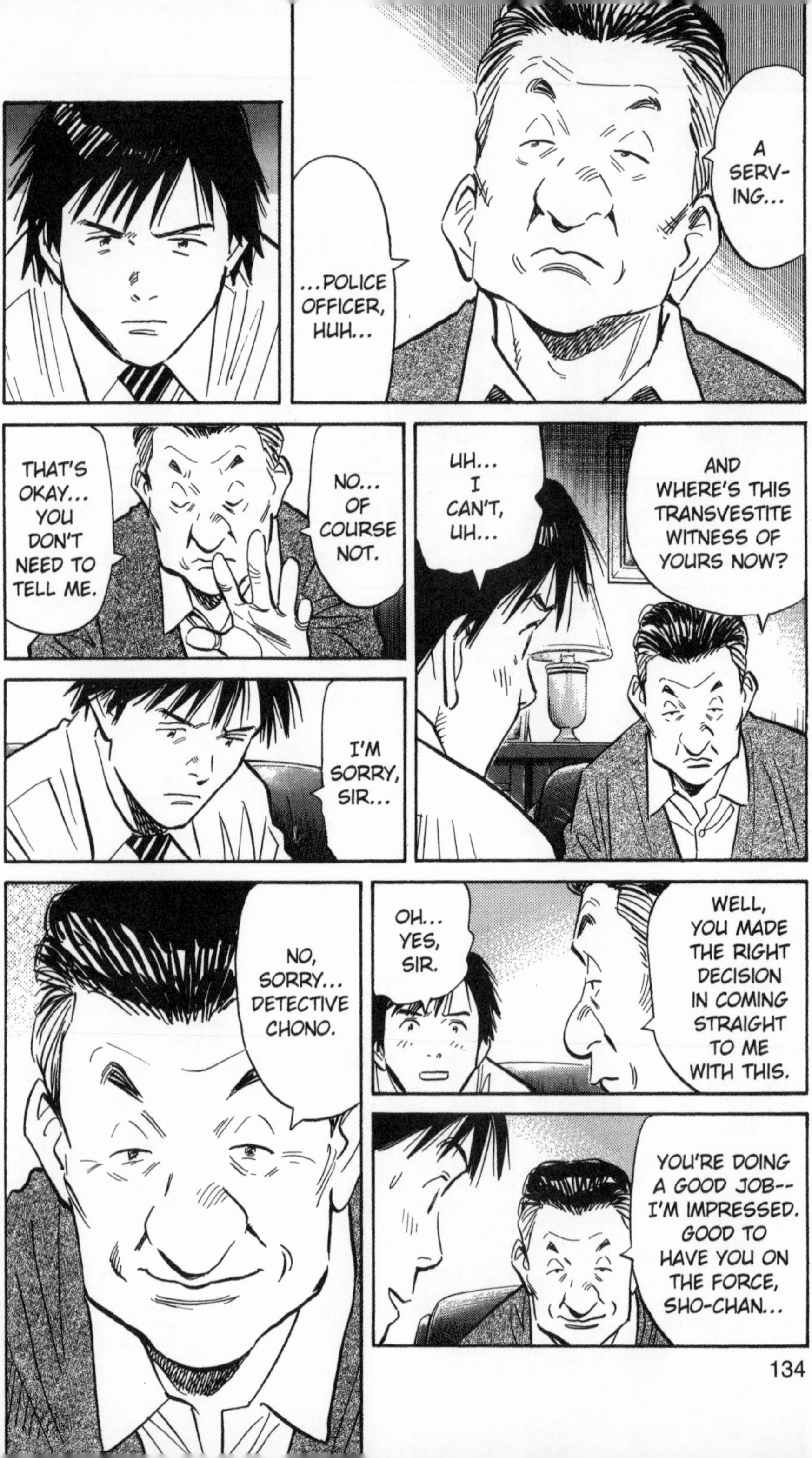
A SERV-ING...
...POLICE OFFICER, HUH...
AND WHERE'S THIS TRANSVESTITE WITNESS OF YOURS NOW?
UH... I CAN'T, UH...
NO... OF COURSE NOT.
THAT'S OKAY... YOU DON'T NEED TO TELL ME.
I'M SORRY, SIR...
WELL, YOU MADE THE RIGHT DECISION IN COMING STRAIGHT TO ME WITH THIS.
OH... YES, SIR.
YOU'RE DOING A GOOD JOB-- I'M IMPRESSED. GOOD TO HAVE YOU ON THE FORCE, SHO-CHAN...
NO, SORRY... DETECTIVE CHONO.

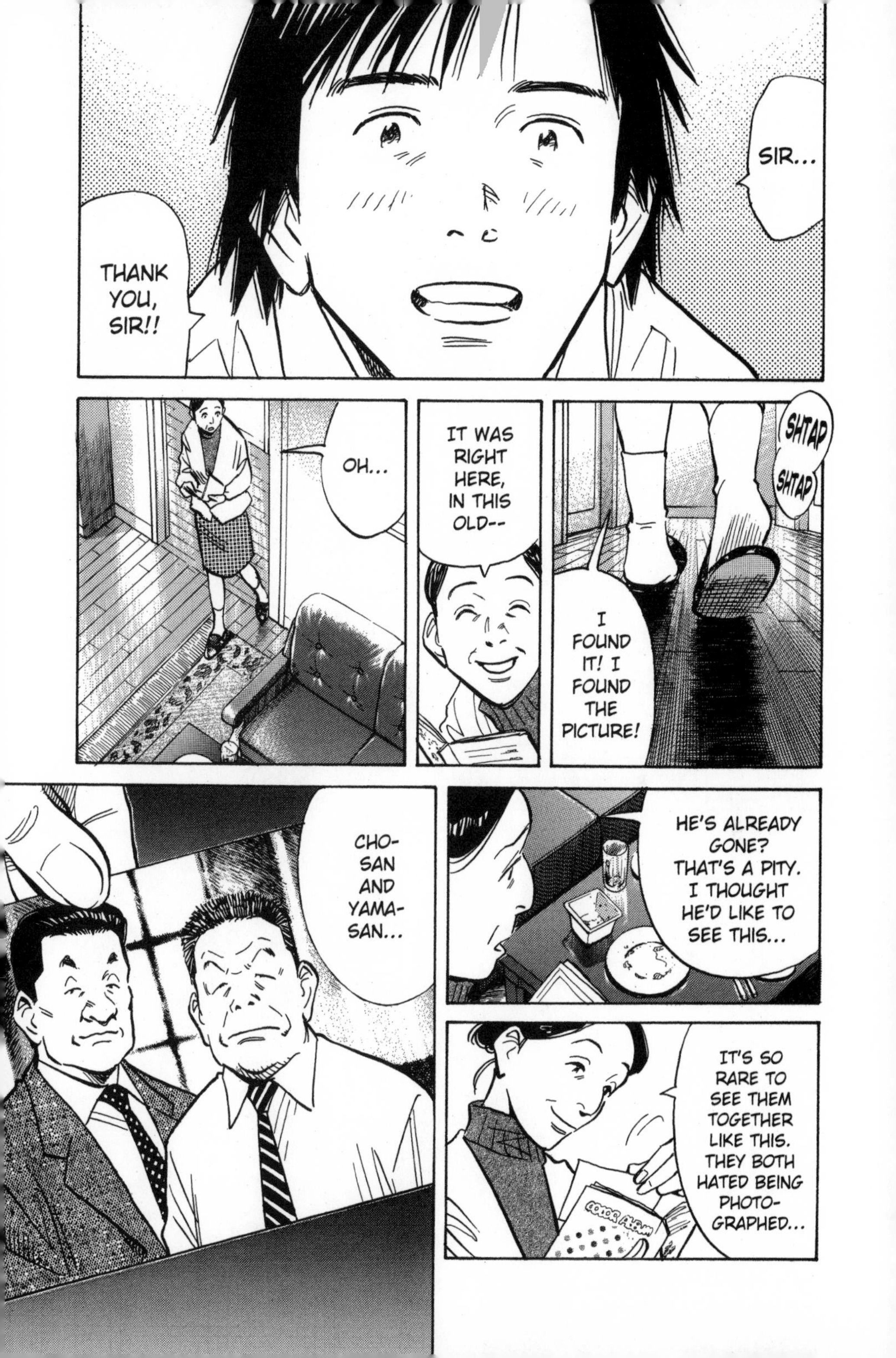
SIR...
THANK YOU, SIR!!
SHTAP
SHTAP
I FOUND IT! I FOUND THE PICTURE!
IT WAS RIGHT HERE, IN THIS OLD--
OH...
HE'S ALREADY GONE? THAT'S A PITY. I THOUGHT HE'D LIKE TO SEE THIS...
IT'S SO RARE TO SEE THEM TOGETHER LIKE THIS. THEY BOTH HATED BEING PHOTO-GRAPHED...
CHO-SAN AND YAMA-SAN...

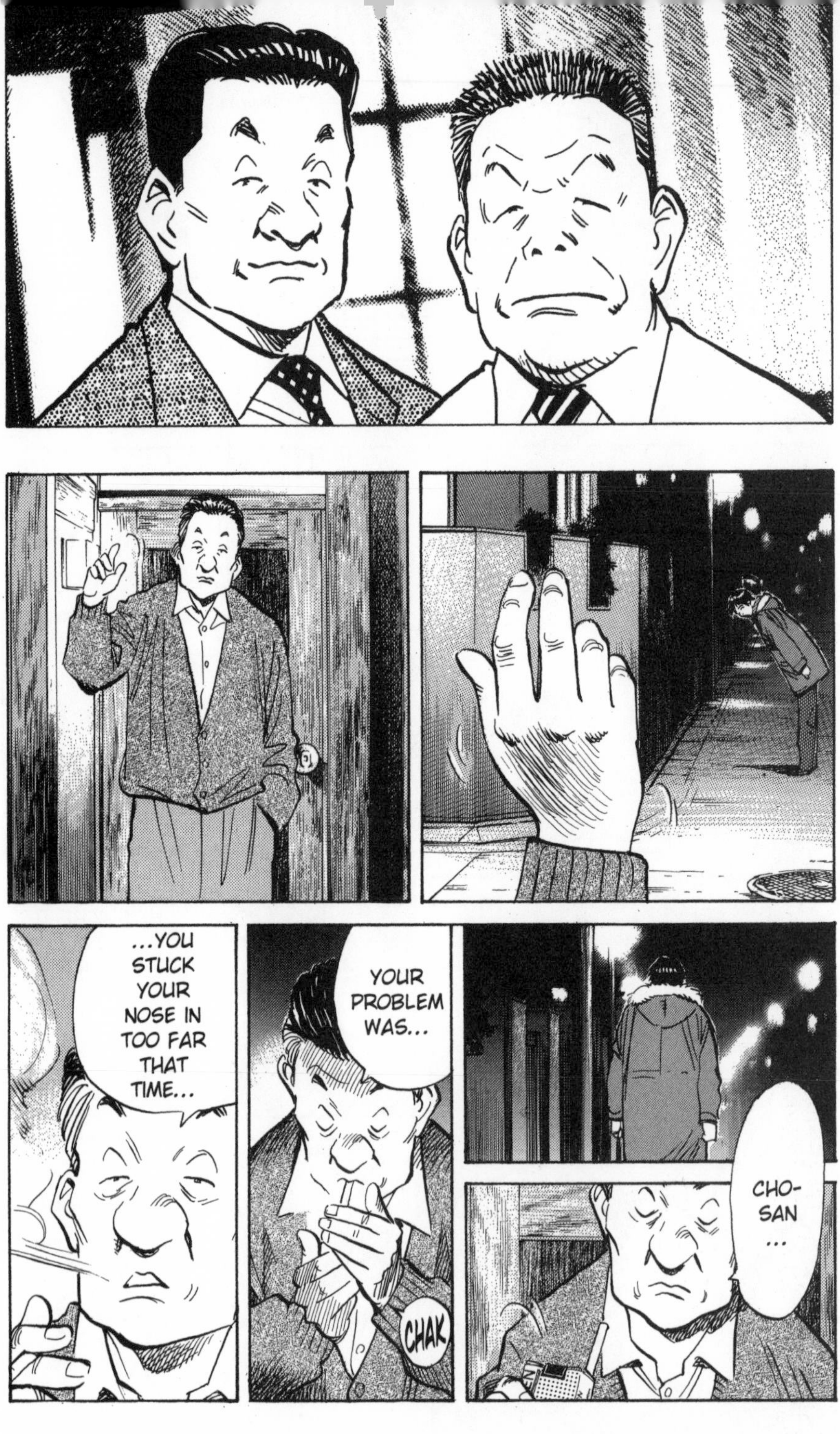
CHO-SAN ...
YOUR PROBLEM WAS...
CHAK
...YOU STUCK YOUR NOSE IN TOO FAR THAT TIME...

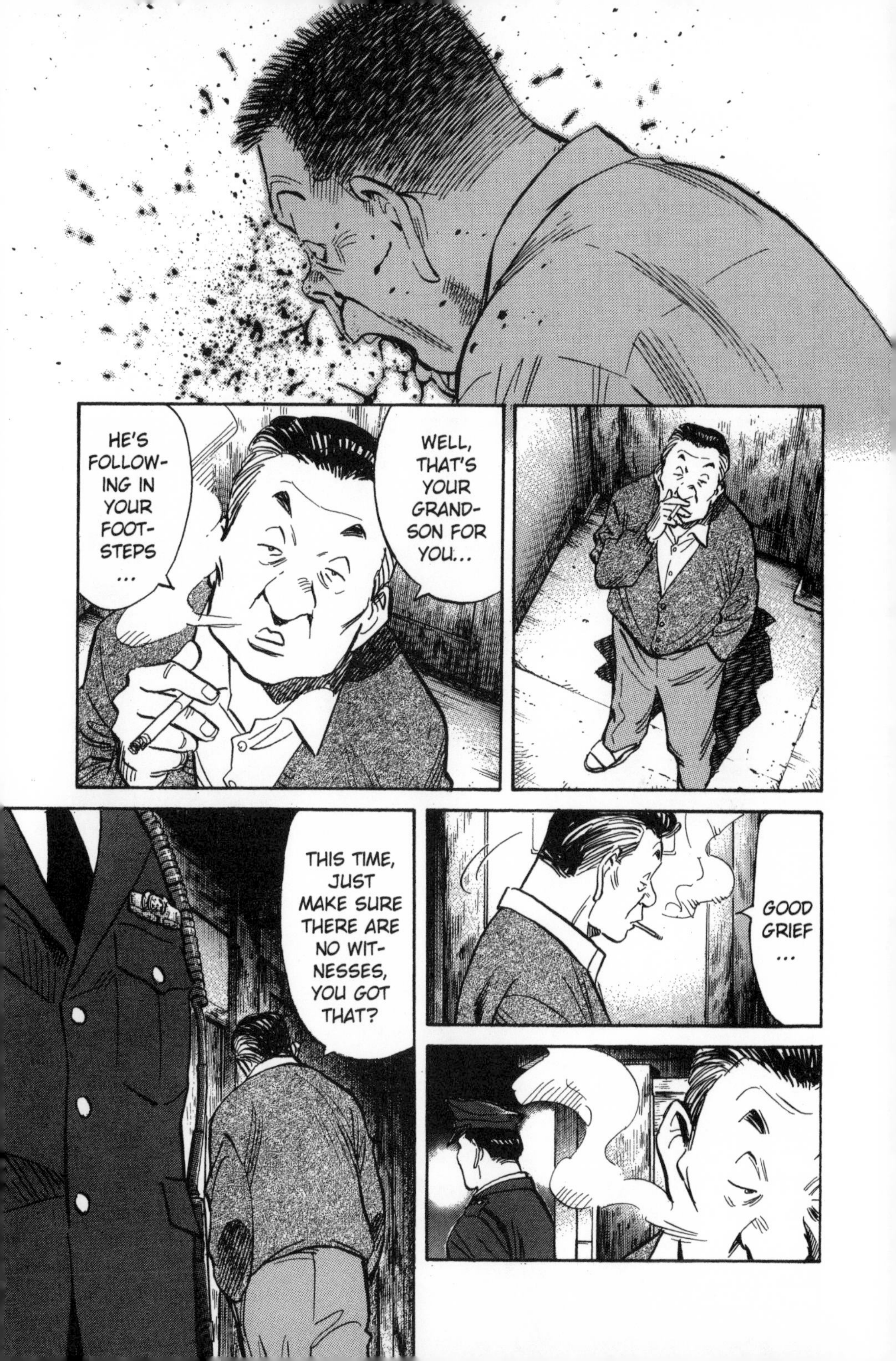
WELL, THAT'S YOUR GRANDSON FOR YOU...
HE'S FOLLOWING IN YOUR FOOTSTEPS...
GOOD GRIEF...
THIS TIME, JUST MAKE SURE THERE ARE NO WITNESSES, YOU GOT THAT?

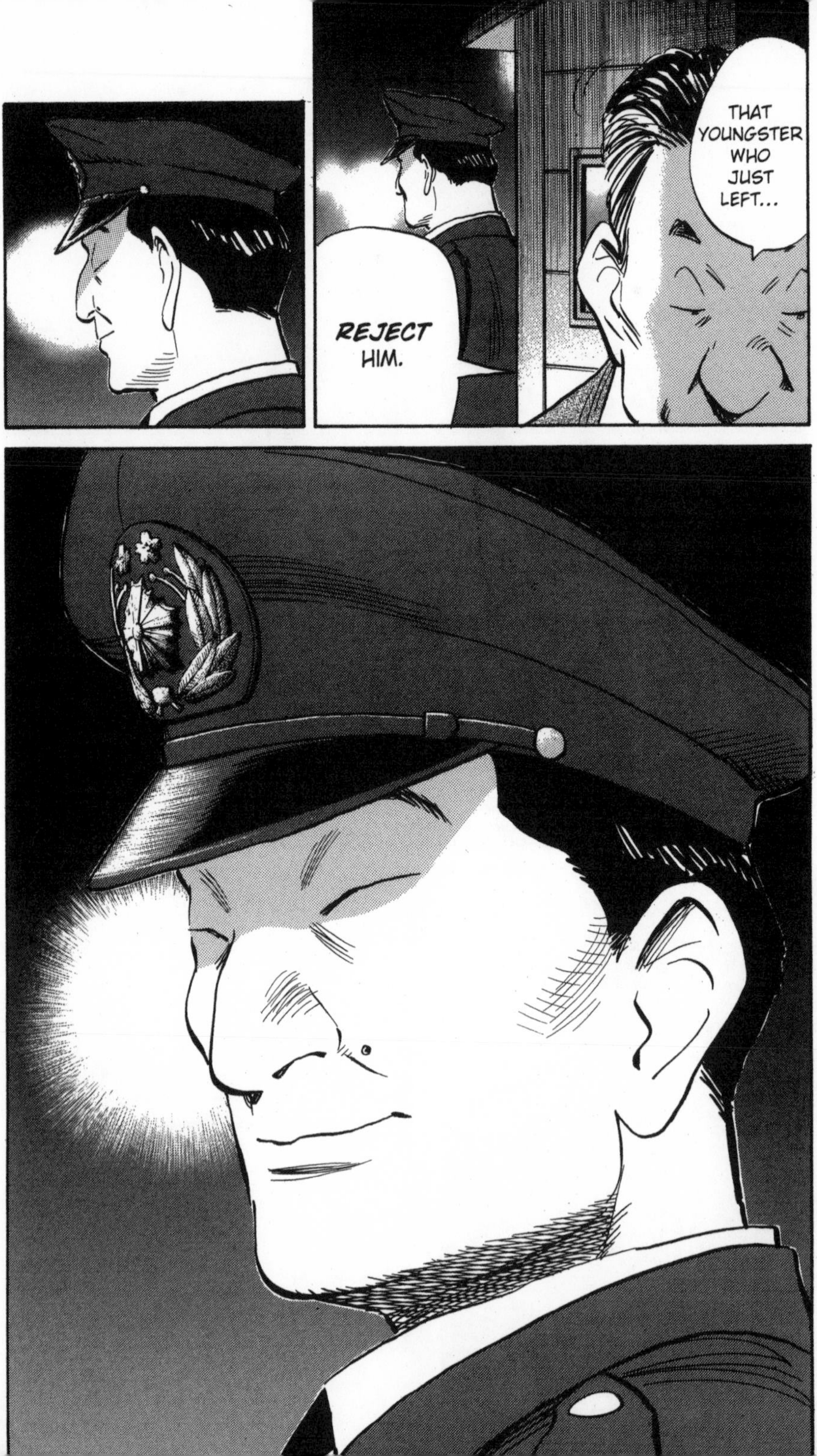
THAT YOUNGSTER WHO JUST LEFT...
REJECT HIM.

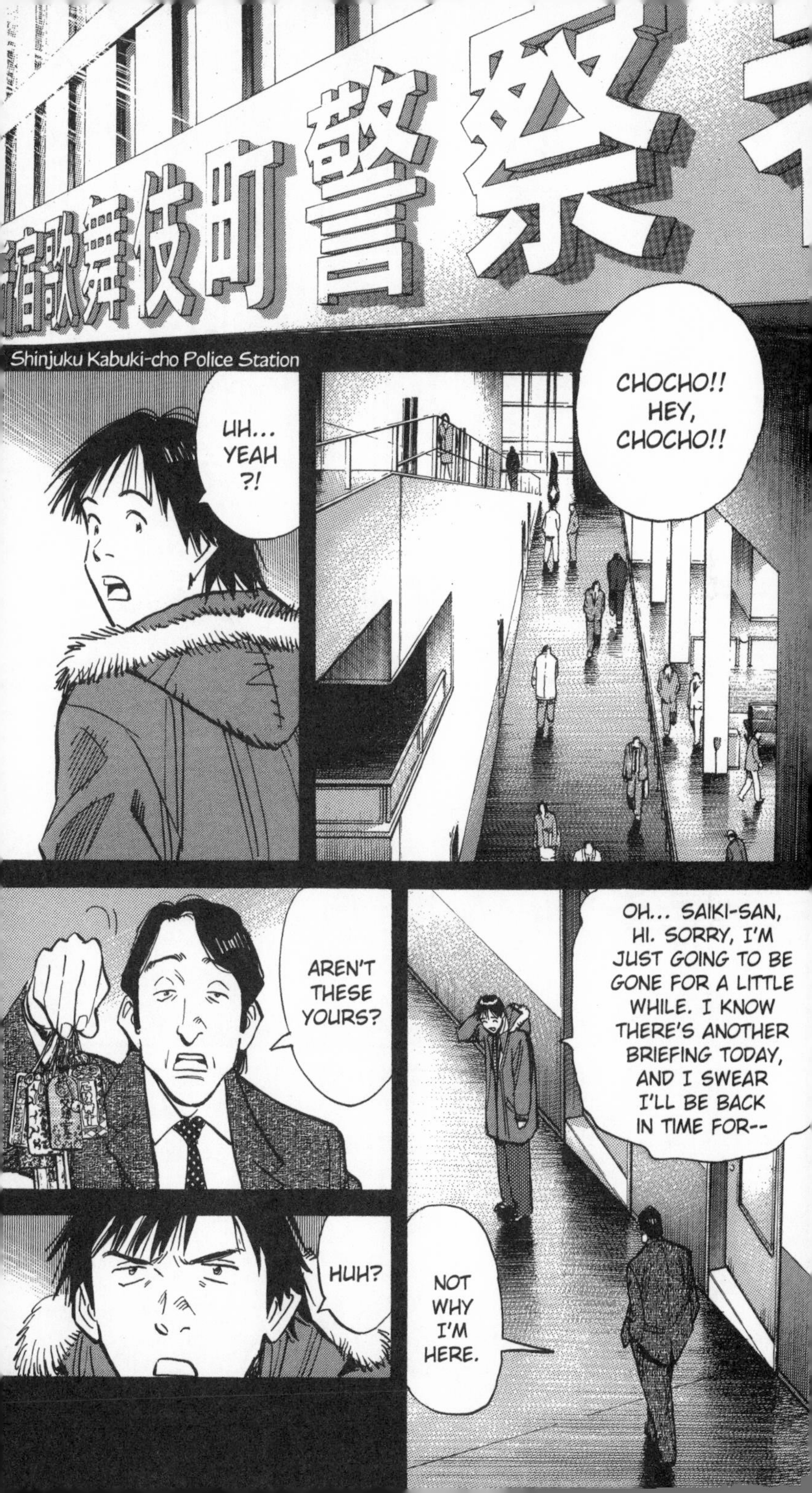
宿歌舞伎町警察
Shinjuku Kabuki-cho Police Station
CHOCHO!! HEY, CHOCHO!!
UH... YEAH ?!
OH... SAIKI-SAN, HI. SORRY, I'M JUST GOING TO BE GONE FOR A LITTLE WHILE. I KNOW THERE'S ANOTHER BRIEFING TODAY, AND I SWEAR I'LL BE BACK IN TIME FOR--
NOT WHY I'M HERE.
AREN'T THESE YOURS?
HUH?

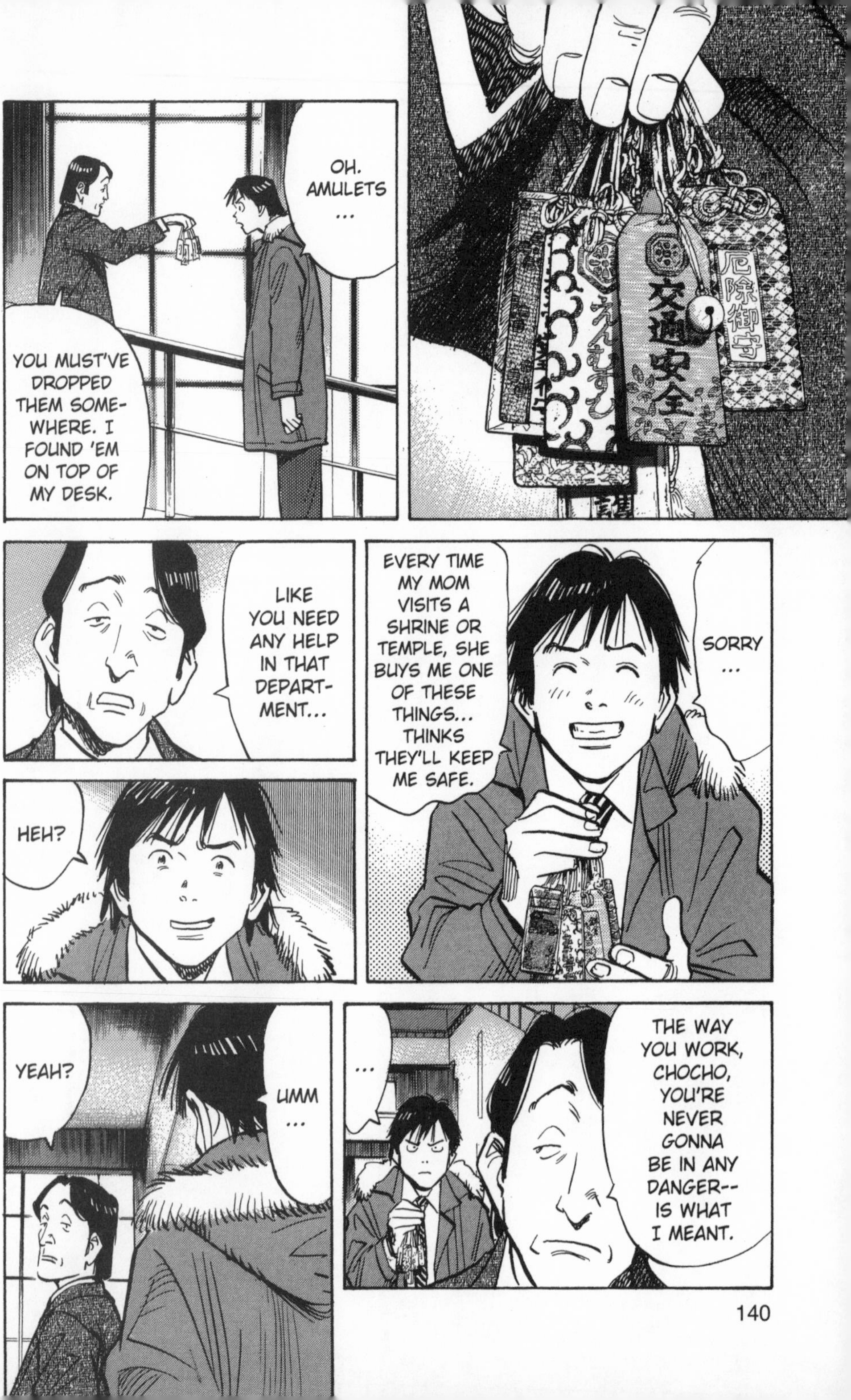
厄除御守
交通安全
えんむすび
OH. AMULETS ...
YOU MUST'VE DROPPED THEM SOMEWHERE. I FOUND 'EM ON TOP OF MY DESK.
SORRY ...
EVERY TIME MY MOM VISITS A SHRINE OR TEMPLE, SHE BUYS ME ONE OF THESE THINGS... THINKS THEY'LL KEEP ME SAFE.
LIKE YOU NEED ANY HELP IN THAT DEPARTMENT...
HEH?
THE WAY YOU WORK, CHOCHO, YOU'RE NEVER GONNA BE IN ANY DANGER-- IS WHAT I MEANT.
...
UMM ...
YEAH?

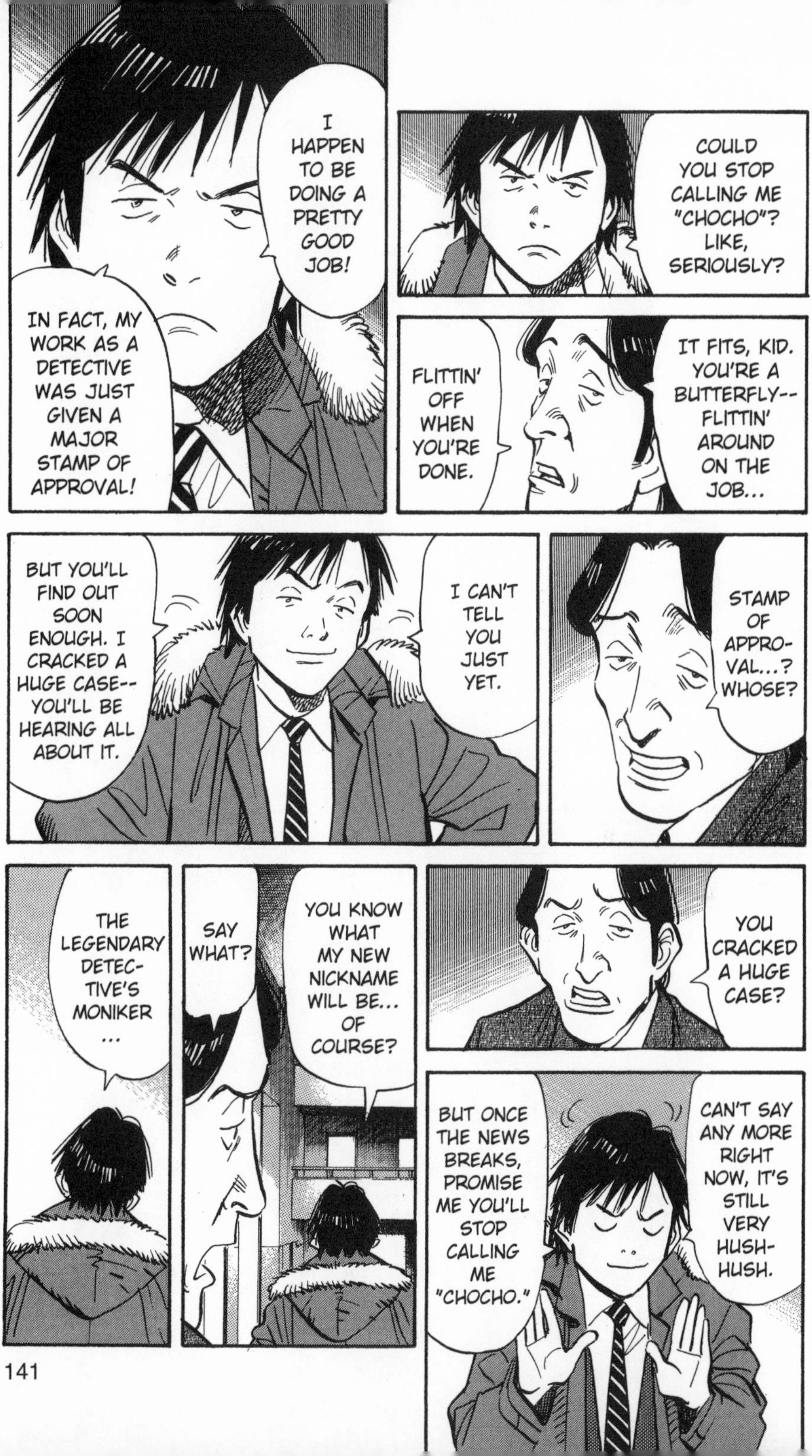
COULD YOU STOP CALLING ME "CHOCHO"? LIKE, SERIOUSLY?
IT FITS, KID. YOU'RE A BUTTERFLY-- FLITTIN' AROUND ON THE JOB...
FLITTIN' OFF WHEN YOU'RE DONE.
I HAPPEN TO BE DOING A PRETTY GOOD JOB!
IN FACT, MY WORK AS A DETECTIVE WAS JUST GIVEN A MAJOR STAMP OF APPROVAL!
STAMP OF APPRO-VAL...? WHOSE?
I CAN'T TELL YOU JUST YET.
BUT YOU'LL FIND OUT SOON ENOUGH. I CRACKED A HUGE CASE-- YOU'LL BE HEARING ALL ABOUT IT.
YOU CRACKED A HUGE CASE?
CAN'T SAY ANY MORE RIGHT NOW, IT'S STILL VERY HUSH-HUSH.
BUT ONCE THE NEWS BREAKS, PROMISE ME YOU'LL STOP CALLING ME "CHOCHO."
YOU KNOW WHAT MY NEW NICKNAME WILL BE... OF COURSE?
SAY WHAT?
THE LEGENDARY DETEC-TIVE'S MONIKER ...

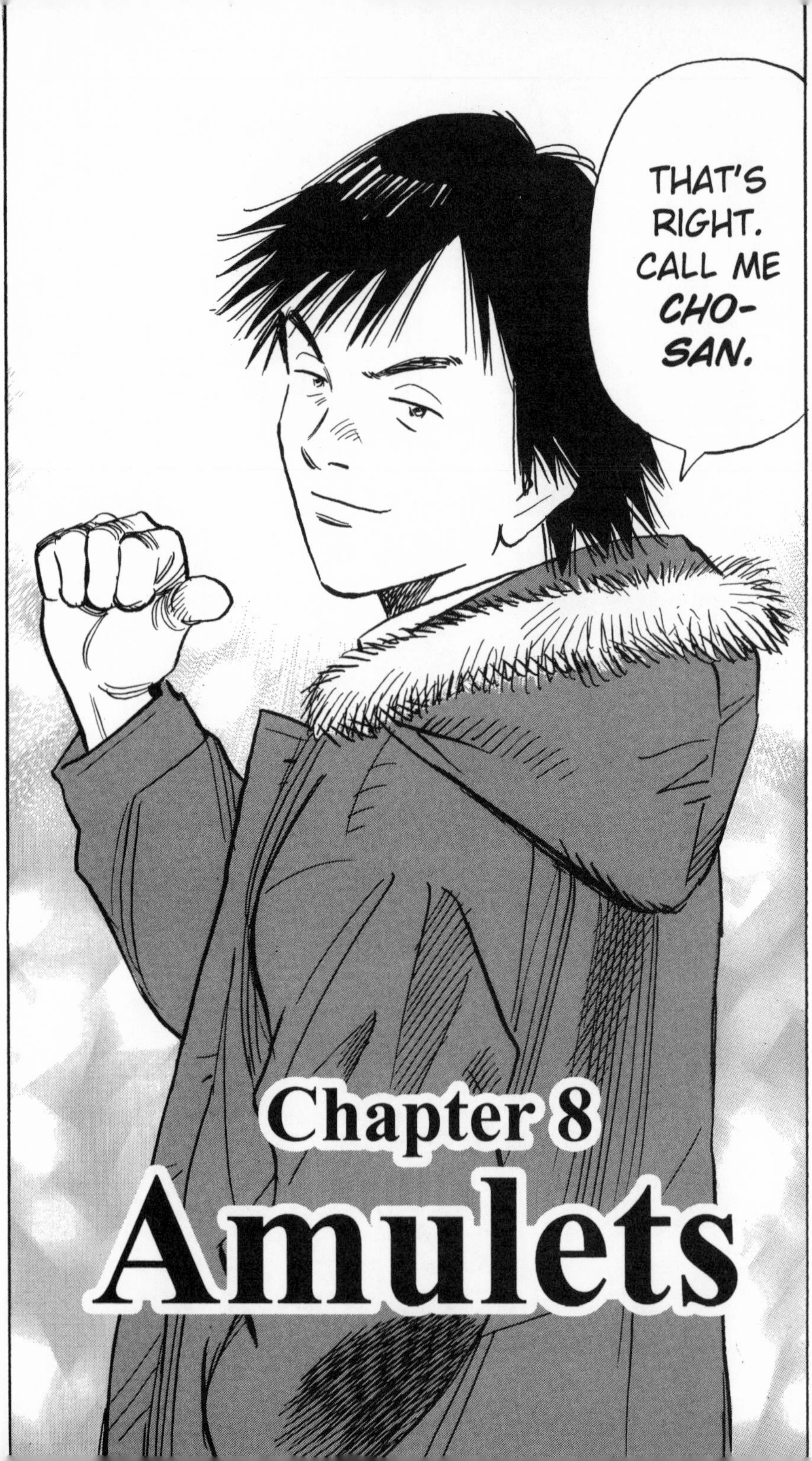
THAT'S RIGHT. CALL ME CHO-SAN.

Chapter 8
Amulets

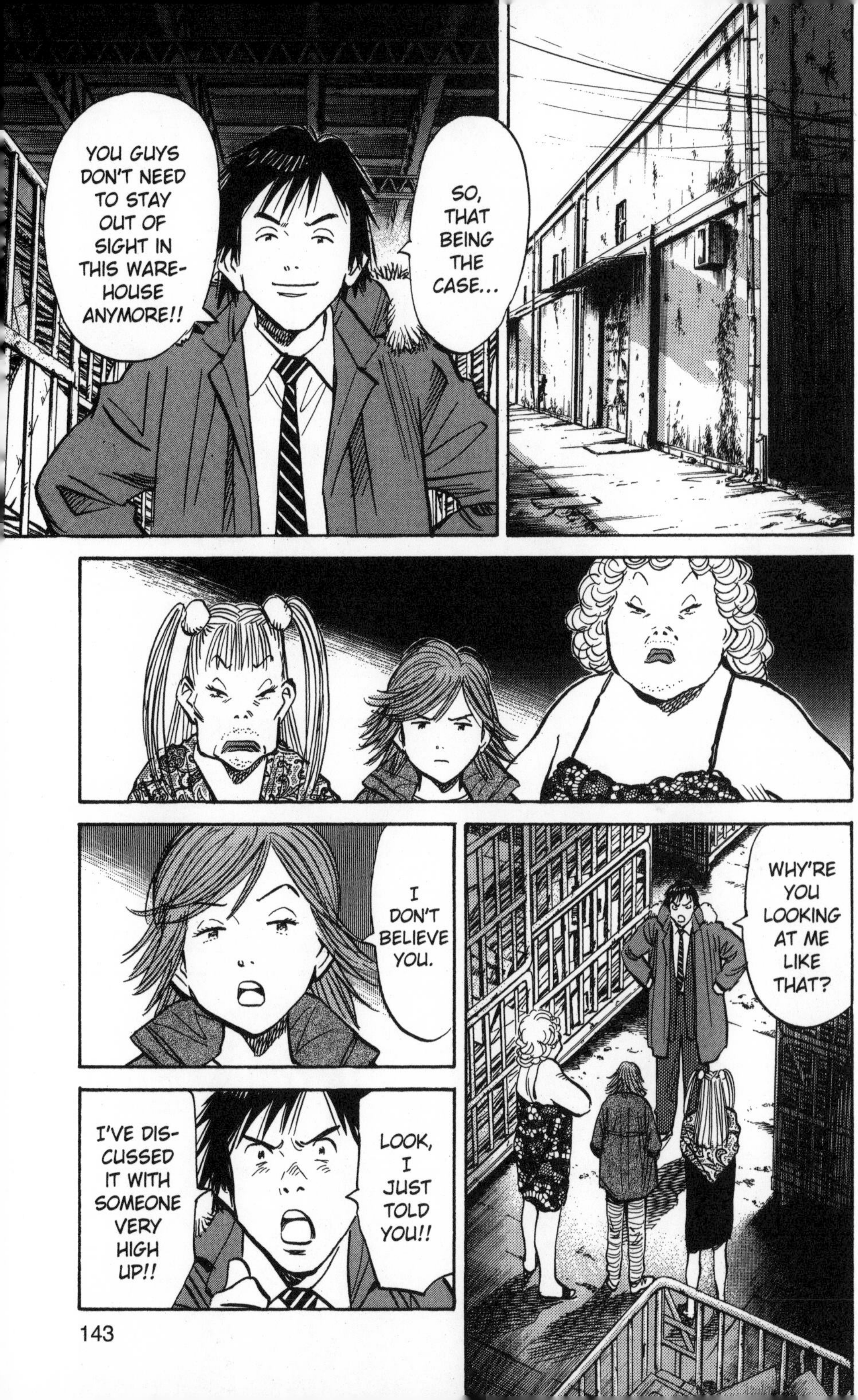
SO, THAT BEING THE CASE...
YOU GUYS DON'T NEED TO STAY OUT OF SIGHT IN THIS WAREHOUSE ANYMORE!!
WHY'RE YOU LOOKING AT ME LIKE THAT?
I DON'T BELIEVE YOU.
LOOK, I JUST TOLD YOU!!
I'VE DISCUSSED IT WITH SOMEONE VERY HIGH UP!!

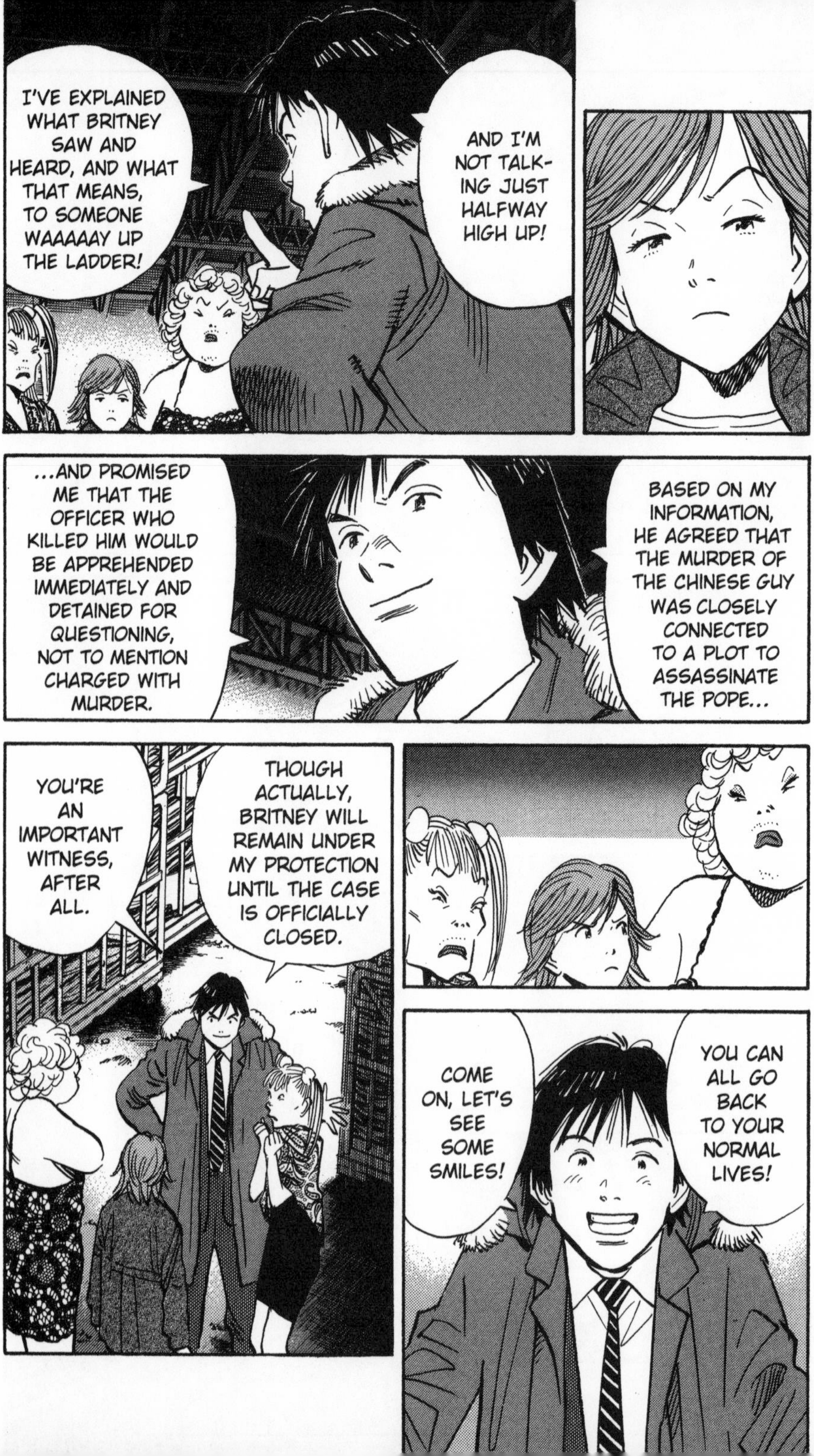
I'VE EXPLAINED WHAT BRITNEY SAW AND HEARD, AND WHAT THAT MEANS, TO SOMEONE WAAAAAY UP THE LADDER!
AND I'M NOT TALK-ING JUST HALFWAY HIGH UP!
BASED ON MY INFORMATION, HE AGREED THAT THE MURDER OF THE CHINESE GUY WAS CLOSELY CONNECTED TO A PLOT TO ASSASSINATE THE POPE...
...AND PROMISED ME THAT THE OFFICER WHO KILLED HIM WOULD BE APPREHENDED IMMEDIATELY AND DETAINED FOR QUESTIONING, NOT TO MENTION CHARGED WITH MURDER.
YOU CAN ALL GO BACK TO YOUR NORMAL LIVES!
COME ON, LET'S SEE SOME SMILES!
THOUGH ACTUALLY, BRITNEY WILL REMAIN UNDER MY PROTECTION UNTIL THE CASE IS OFFICIALLY CLOSED.
YOU'RE AN IMPORTANT WITNESS, AFTER ALL.

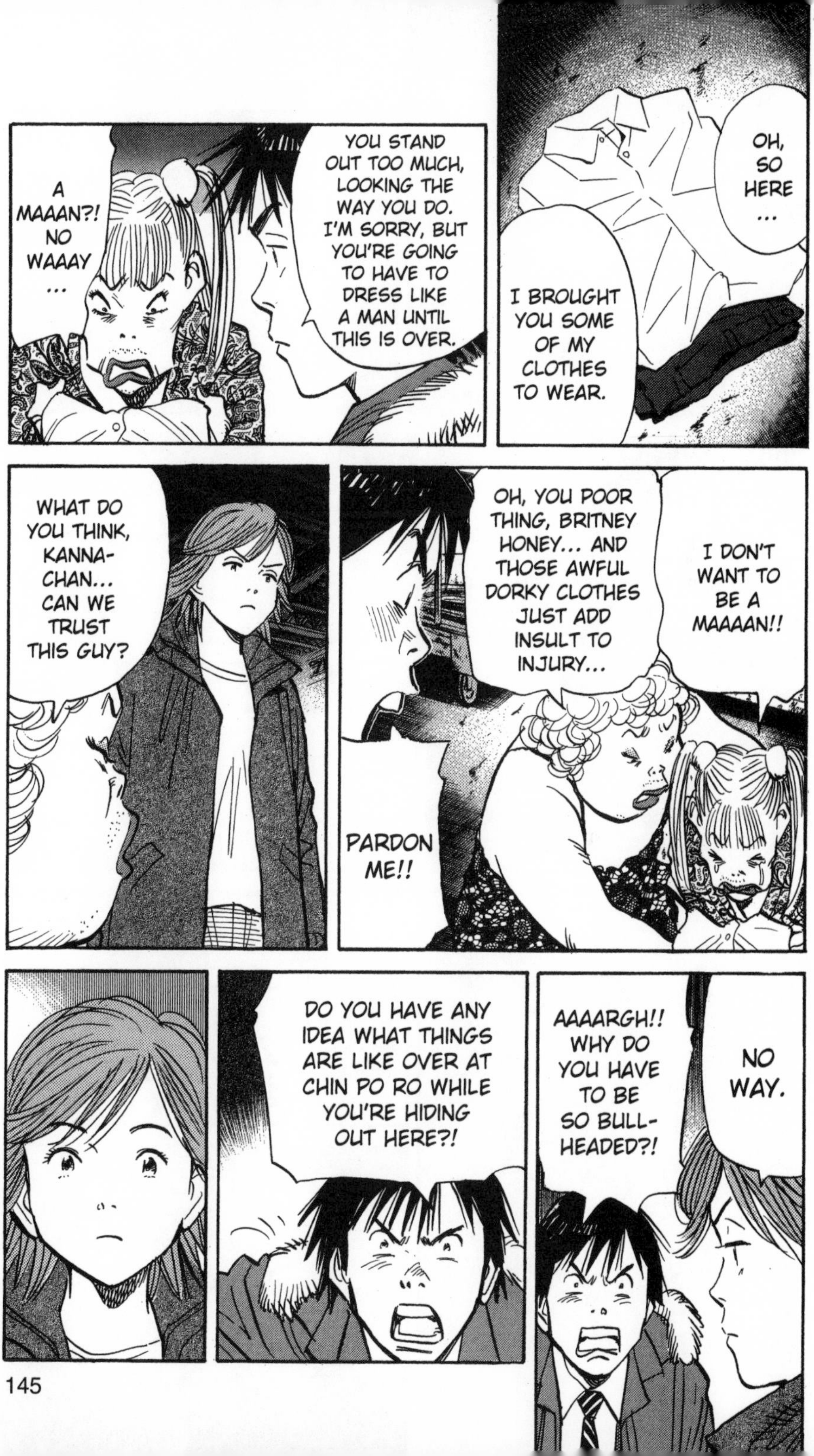
OH, SO HERE ...
I BROUGHT YOU SOME OF MY CLOTHES TO WEAR.
YOU STAND OUT TOO MUCH, LOOKING THE WAY YOU DO. I'M SORRY, BUT YOU'RE GOING TO HAVE TO DRESS LIKE A MAN UNTIL THIS IS OVER.
A MAAAN?! NO WAAAY ...
I DON'T WANT TO BE A MAAAAN!!
OH, YOU POOR THING, BRITNEY HONEY... AND THOSE AWFUL DORKY CLOTHES JUST ADD INSULT TO INJURY...
PARDON ME!!
WHAT DO YOU THINK, KANNA-CHAN... CAN WE TRUST THIS GUY?
NO WAY.
AAAARGH!! WHY DO YOU HAVE TO BE SO BULL-HEADED?!
DO YOU HAVE ANY IDEA WHAT THINGS ARE LIKE OVER AT CHIN PO RO WHILE YOU'RE HIDING OUT HERE?!

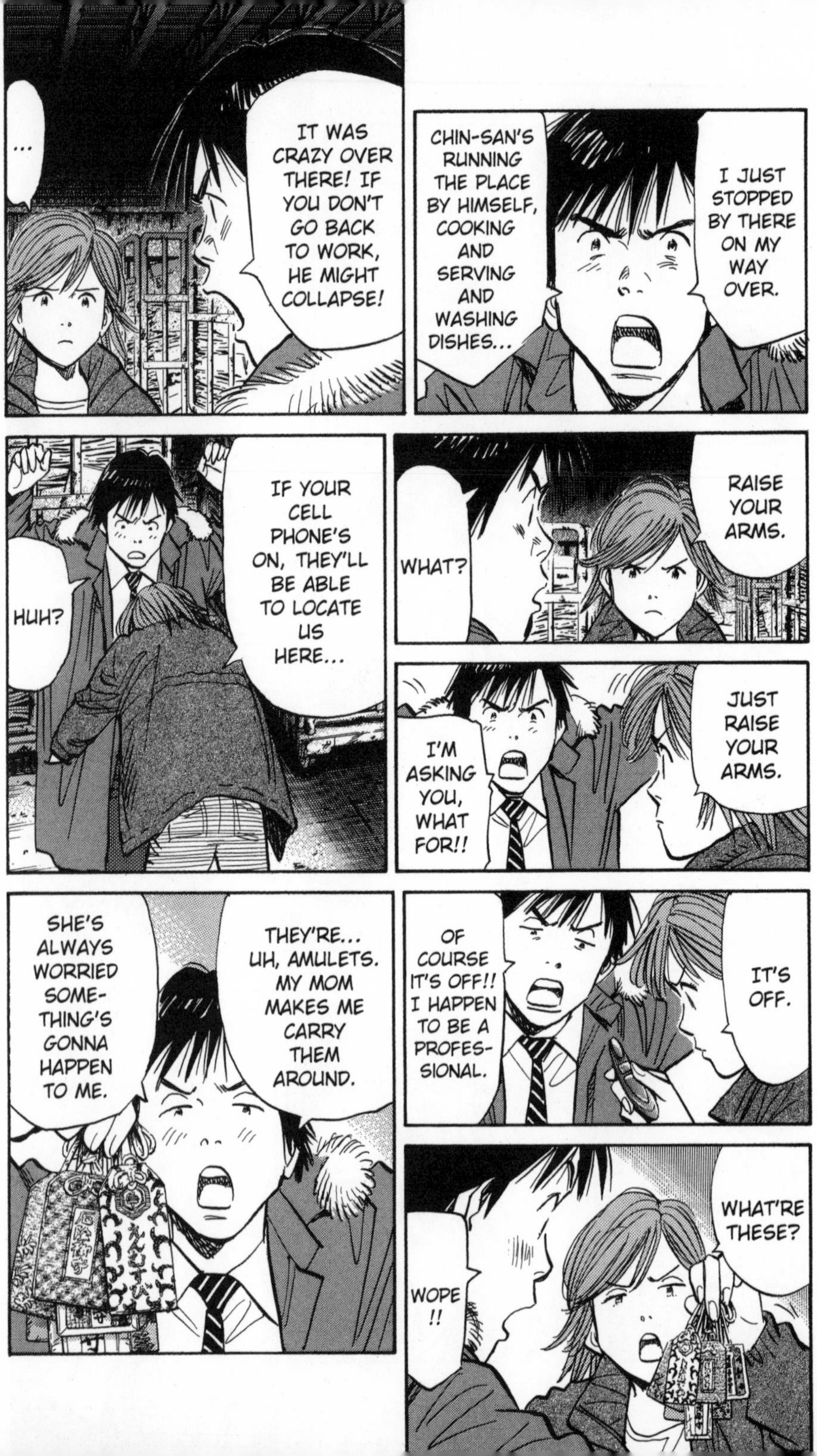
I JUST STOPPED BY THERE ON MY WAY OVER.
CHIN-SAN'S RUNNING THE PLACE BY HIMSELF, COOKING AND SERVING AND WASHING DISHES...
IT WAS CRAZY OVER THERE! IF YOU DON'T GO BACK TO WORK, HE MIGHT COLLAPSE!
...
RAISE YOUR ARMS.
WHAT?
JUST RAISE YOUR ARMS.
I'M ASKING YOU, WHAT FOR!!
IF YOUR CELL PHONE'S ON, THEY'LL BE ABLE TO LOCATE US HERE...
HUH?
IT'S OFF.
OF COURSE IT'S OFF!! I HAPPEN TO BE A PROFES-SIONAL.
WHAT'RE THESE?
WOPE !!
THEY'RE... UH, AMULETS. MY MOM MAKES ME CARRY THEM AROUND.
SHE'S ALWAYS WORRIED SOME-THING'S GONNA HAPPEN TO ME.

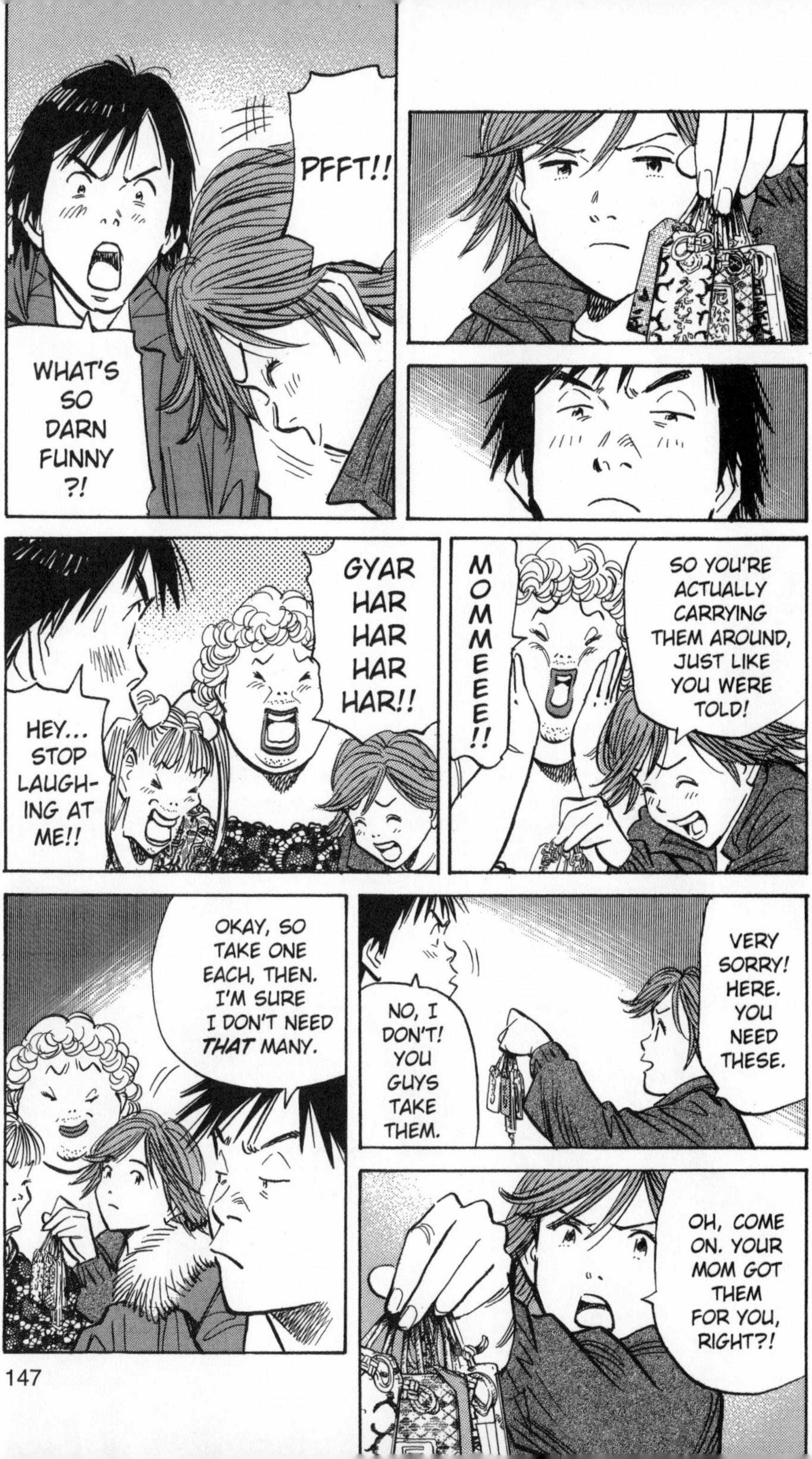
PFFT!!
WHAT'S SO DARN FUNNY ?!
SO YOU'RE ACTUALLY CARRYING THEM AROUND, JUST LIKE YOU WERE TOLD!
MOMMEEE!!
GYAR HAR HAR HAR HAR!!
HEY... STOP LAUGHING AT ME!!
VERY SORRY! HERE. YOU NEED THESE.
NO, I DON'T! YOU GUYS TAKE THEM.
OH, COME ON. YOUR MOM GOT THEM FOR YOU, RIGHT?!
OKAY, SO TAKE ONE EACH, THEN. I'M SURE I DON'T NEED *THAT* MANY.

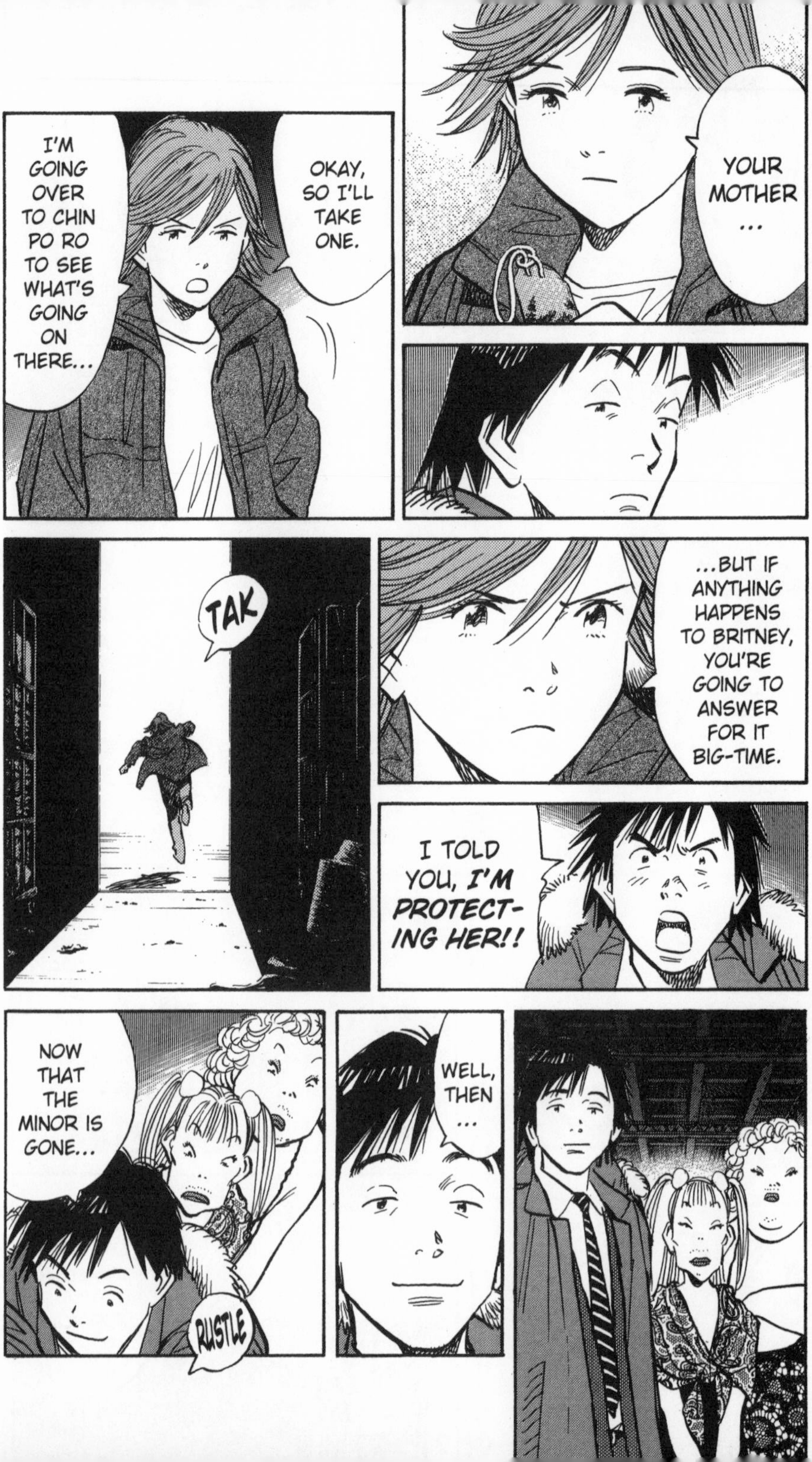
YOUR MOTHER ...
OKAY, SO I'LL TAKE ONE.
I'M GOING OVER TO CHIN PO RO TO SEE WHAT'S GOING ON THERE...
...BUT IF ANYTHING HAPPENS TO BRITNEY, YOU'RE GOING TO ANSWER FOR IT BIG-TIME.
I TOLD YOU, *I'M PROTECTING HER!!*
TAK
WELL, THEN ...
NOW THAT THE MINOR IS GONE...
RUSTLE

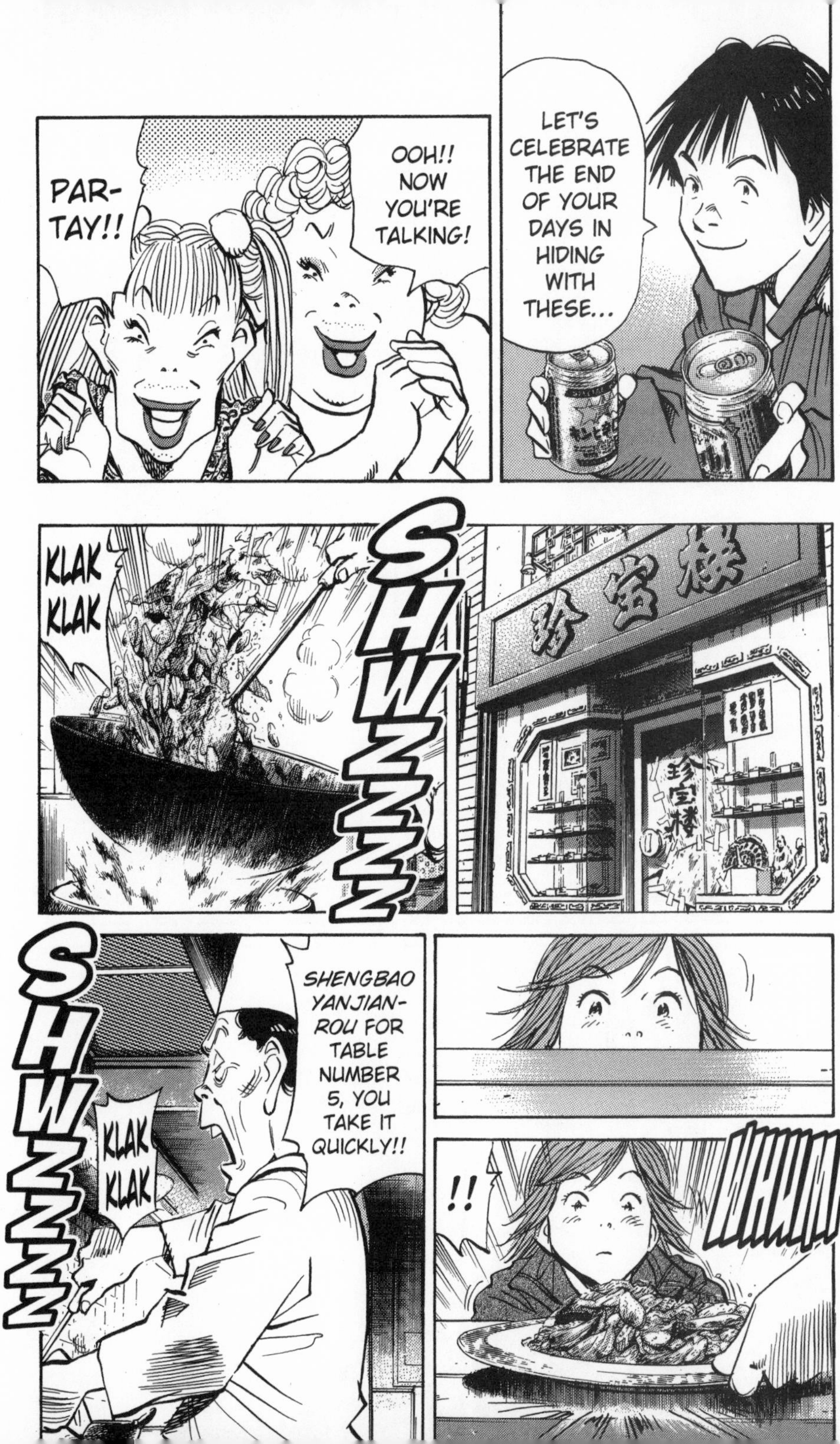
LET'S CELEBRATE THE END OF YOUR DAYS IN HIDING WITH THESE...
OOH!! NOW YOU'RE TALKING!
PAR-TAY!!
珍宝楼
KLAK KLAK
SHWZZZZZ
!!
SHWZZZZZ
SHENGBAO YANJIAN-ROU FOR TABLE NUMBER 5, YOU TAKE IT QUICKLY!!
KLAK KLAK

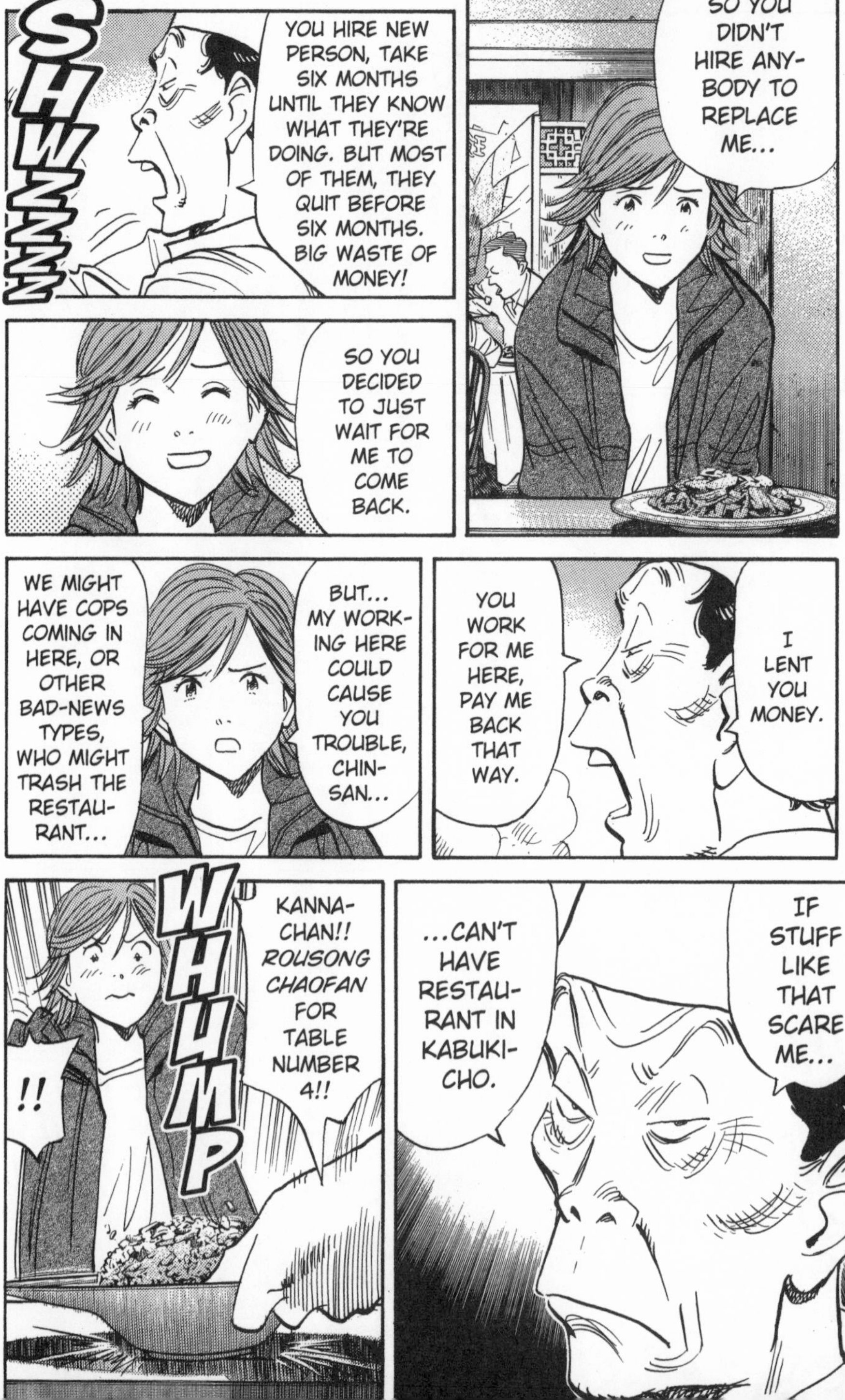
SO YOU DIDN'T HIRE ANYBODY TO REPLACE ME...
SHWZZZZ
YOU HIRE NEW PERSON, TAKE SIX MONTHS UNTIL THEY KNOW WHAT THEY'RE DOING. BUT MOST OF THEM, THEY QUIT BEFORE SIX MONTHS. BIG WASTE OF MONEY!
SO YOU DECIDED TO JUST WAIT FOR ME TO COME BACK.
I LENT YOU MONEY.
YOU WORK FOR ME HERE, PAY ME BACK THAT WAY.
BUT... MY WORKING HERE COULD CAUSE YOU TROUBLE, CHIN-SAN...
WE MIGHT HAVE COPS COMING IN HERE, OR OTHER BAD-NEWS TYPES, WHO MIGHT TRASH THE RESTAURANT...
IF STUFF LIKE THAT SCARE ME...
...CAN'T HAVE RESTAURANT IN KABUKICHO.
KANNA-CHAN!! *ROUSONG CHAOFAN* FOR TABLE NUMBER 4!!
WHUMP
!!

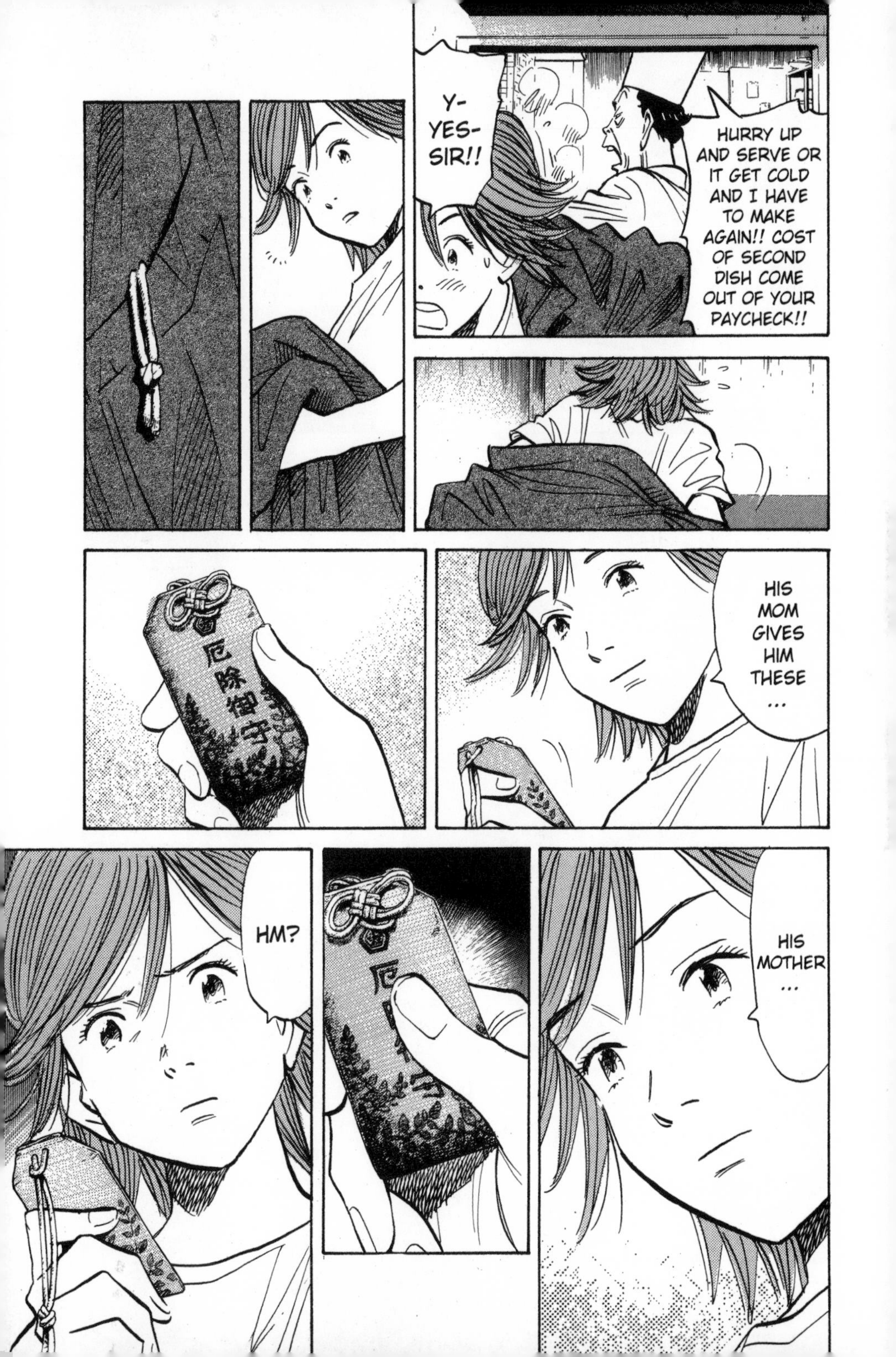
HURRY UP AND SERVE OR IT GET COLD AND I HAVE TO MAKE AGAIN!! COST OF SECOND DISH COME OUT OF YOUR PAYCHECK!!
Y-YES-SIR!!
HIS MOM GIVES HIM THESE ...
厄除御守
HIS MOTHER ...
HM?

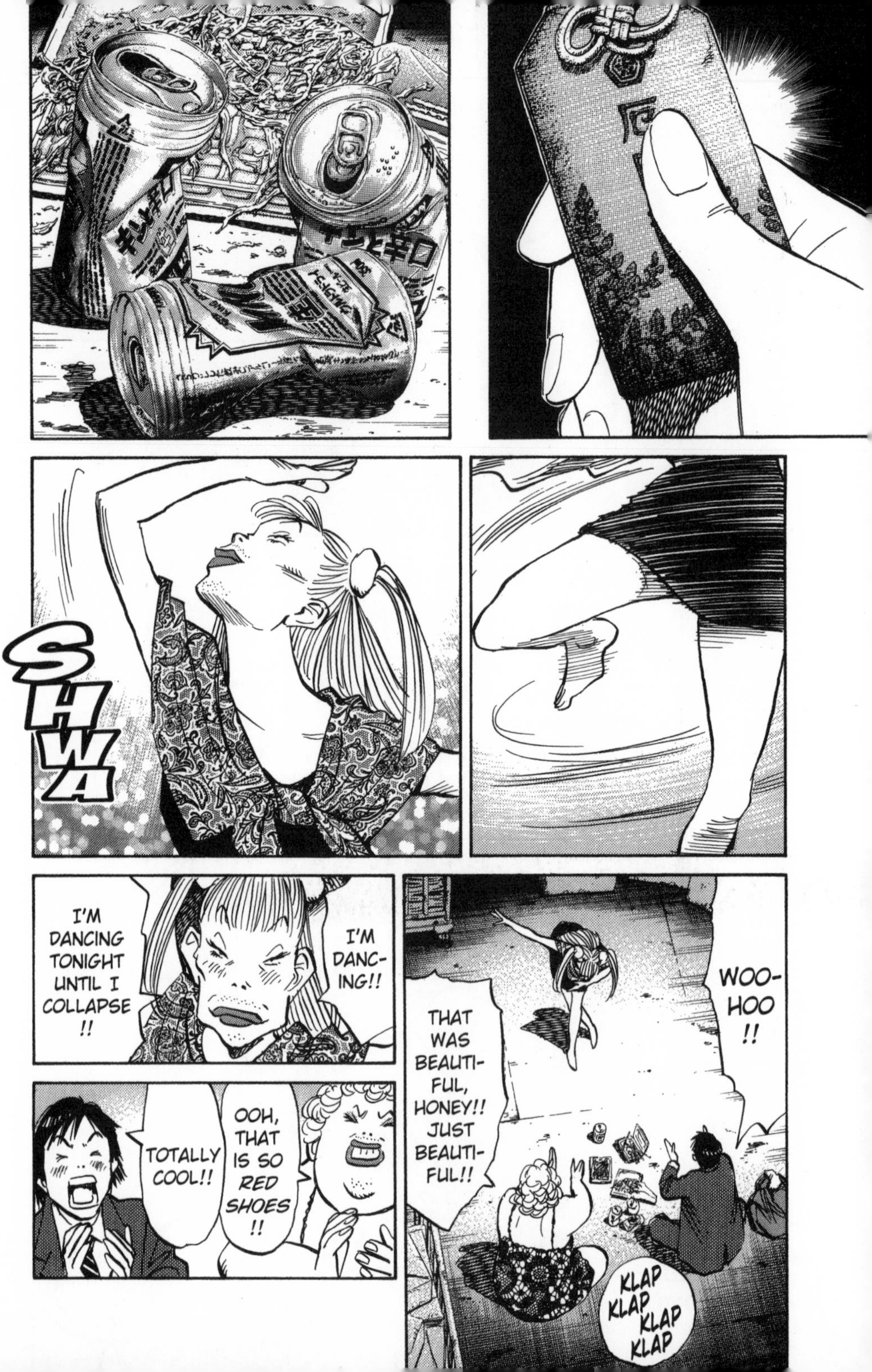
SHWA
WOO-HOO!!
THAT WAS BEAUTIFUL, HONEY!! JUST BEAUTIFUL!!
KLAP KLAP KLAP KLAP
I'M DANCING!!
I'M DANCING TONIGHT UNTIL I COLLAPSE!!
OOH, THAT IS SO RED SHOES!!
TOTALLY COOL!!

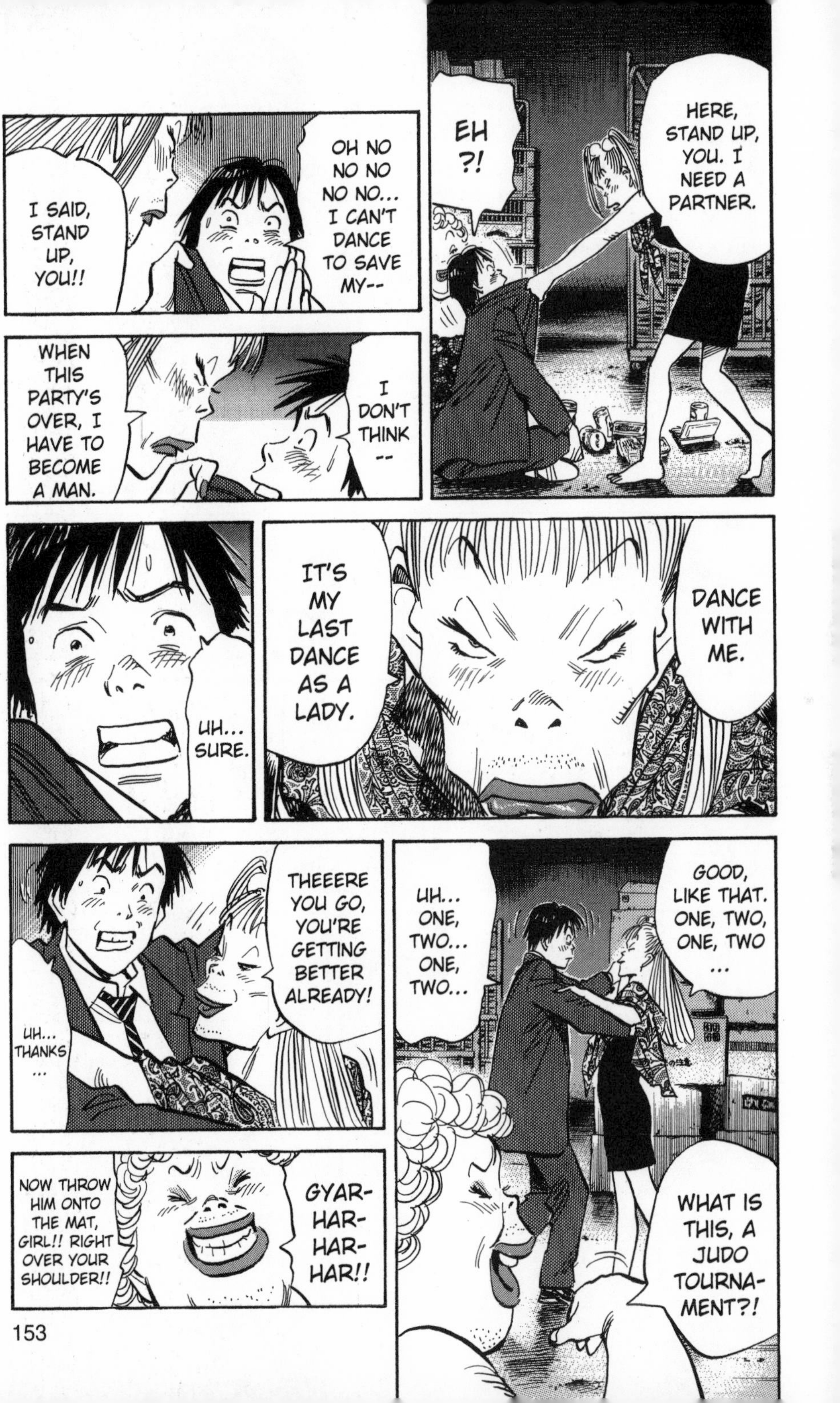
HERE, STAND UP, YOU. I NEED A PARTNER.
EH ?!
OH NO NO NO NO NO... I CAN'T DANCE TO SAVE MY--
I SAID, STAND UP, YOU!!
I DON'T THINK --
WHEN THIS PARTY'S OVER, I HAVE TO BECOME A MAN.
DANCE WITH ME.
IT'S MY LAST DANCE AS A LADY.
UH... SURE.
GOOD, LIKE THAT. ONE, TWO, ONE, TWO ...
UH... ONE, TWO... ONE, TWO...
WHAT IS THIS, A JUDO TOURNAMENT?!
THEEERE YOU GO, YOU'RE GETTING BETTER ALREADY!
UH... THANKS ...
GYAR-HAR-HAR-HAR!!
NOW THROW HIM ONTO THE MAT, GIRL!! RIGHT OVER YOUR SHOULDER!!

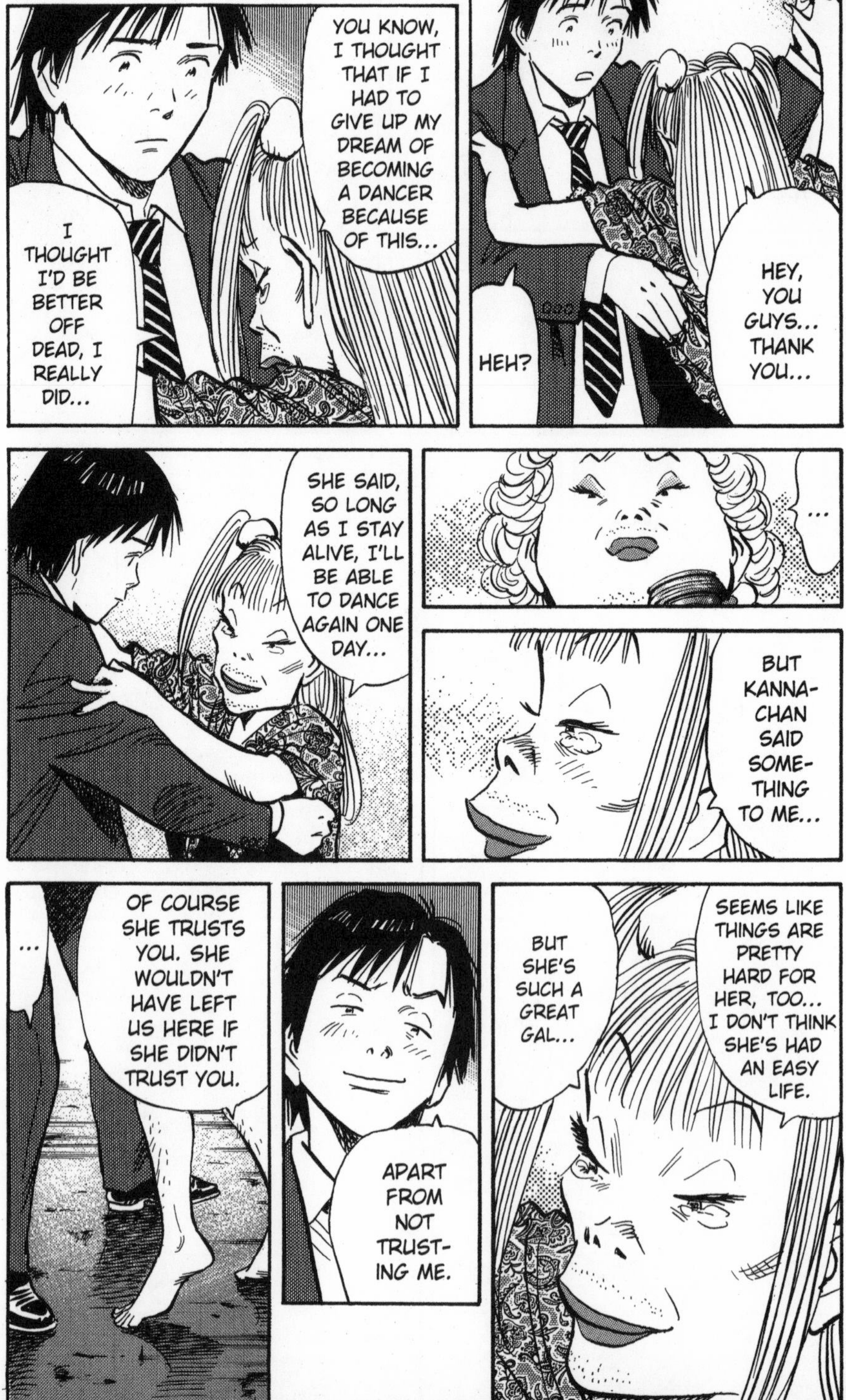
HEY, YOU GUYS... THANK YOU...
HEH?
YOU KNOW, I THOUGHT THAT IF I HAD TO GIVE UP MY DREAM OF BECOMING A DANCER BECAUSE OF THIS...
I THOUGHT I'D BE BETTER OFF DEAD, I REALLY DID...
...
BUT KANNA-CHAN SAID SOME-THING TO ME...
SHE SAID, SO LONG AS I STAY ALIVE, I'LL BE ABLE TO DANCE AGAIN ONE DAY...
SEEMS LIKE THINGS ARE PRETTY HARD FOR HER, TOO... I DON'T THINK SHE'S HAD AN EASY LIFE.
BUT SHE'S SUCH A GREAT GAL...
APART FROM NOT TRUST-ING ME.
OF COURSE SHE TRUSTS YOU. SHE WOULDN'T HAVE LEFT US HERE IF SHE DIDN'T TRUST YOU.
...

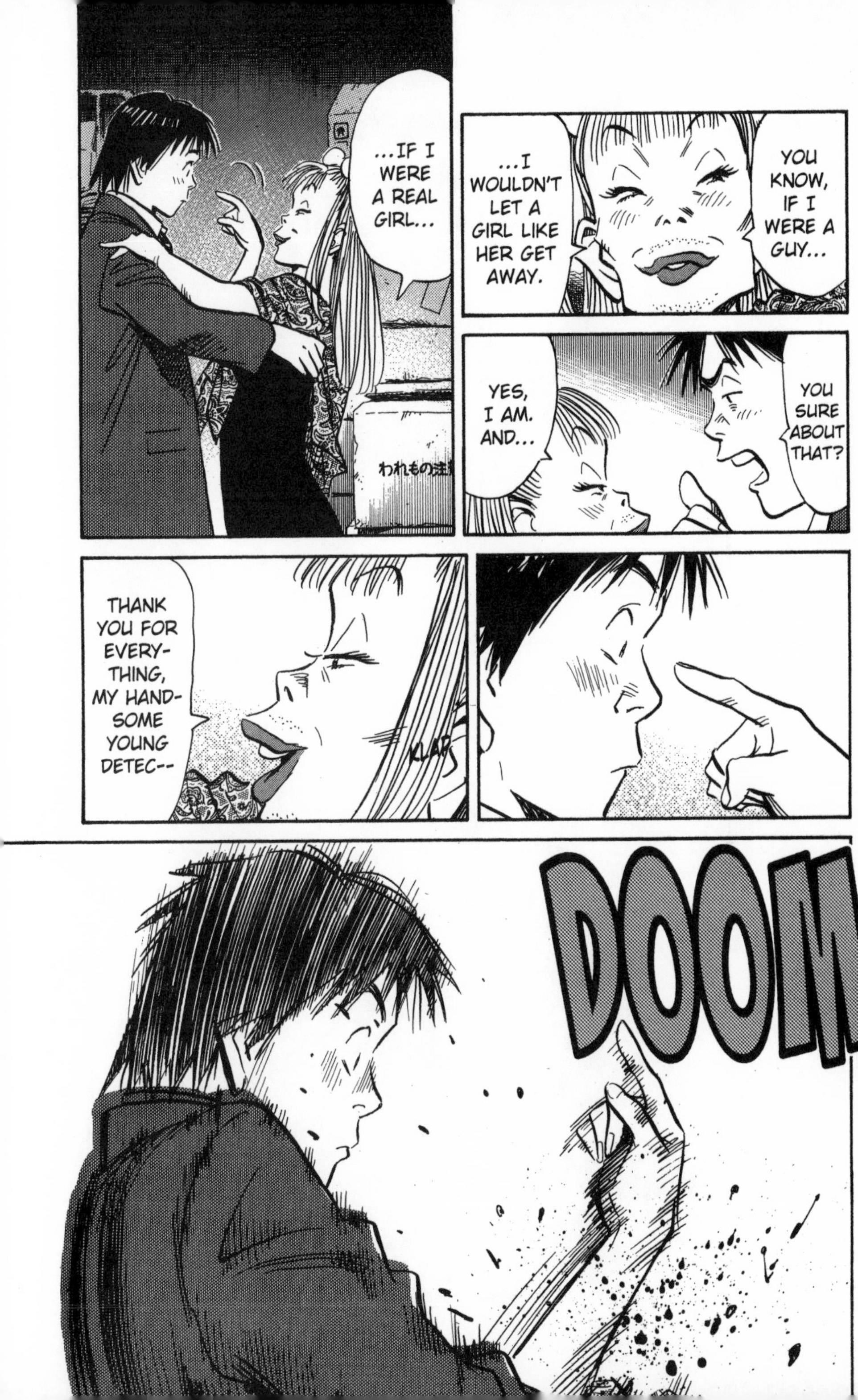
YOU KNOW, IF I WERE A GUY...
...I WOULDN'T LET A GIRL LIKE HER GET AWAY.
YOU SURE ABOUT THAT?
YES, I AM. AND...
...IF I WERE A REAL GIRL...
われもの注
THANK YOU FOR EVERY-THING, MY HAND-SOME YOUNG DETEC--
KLAP
DOOM

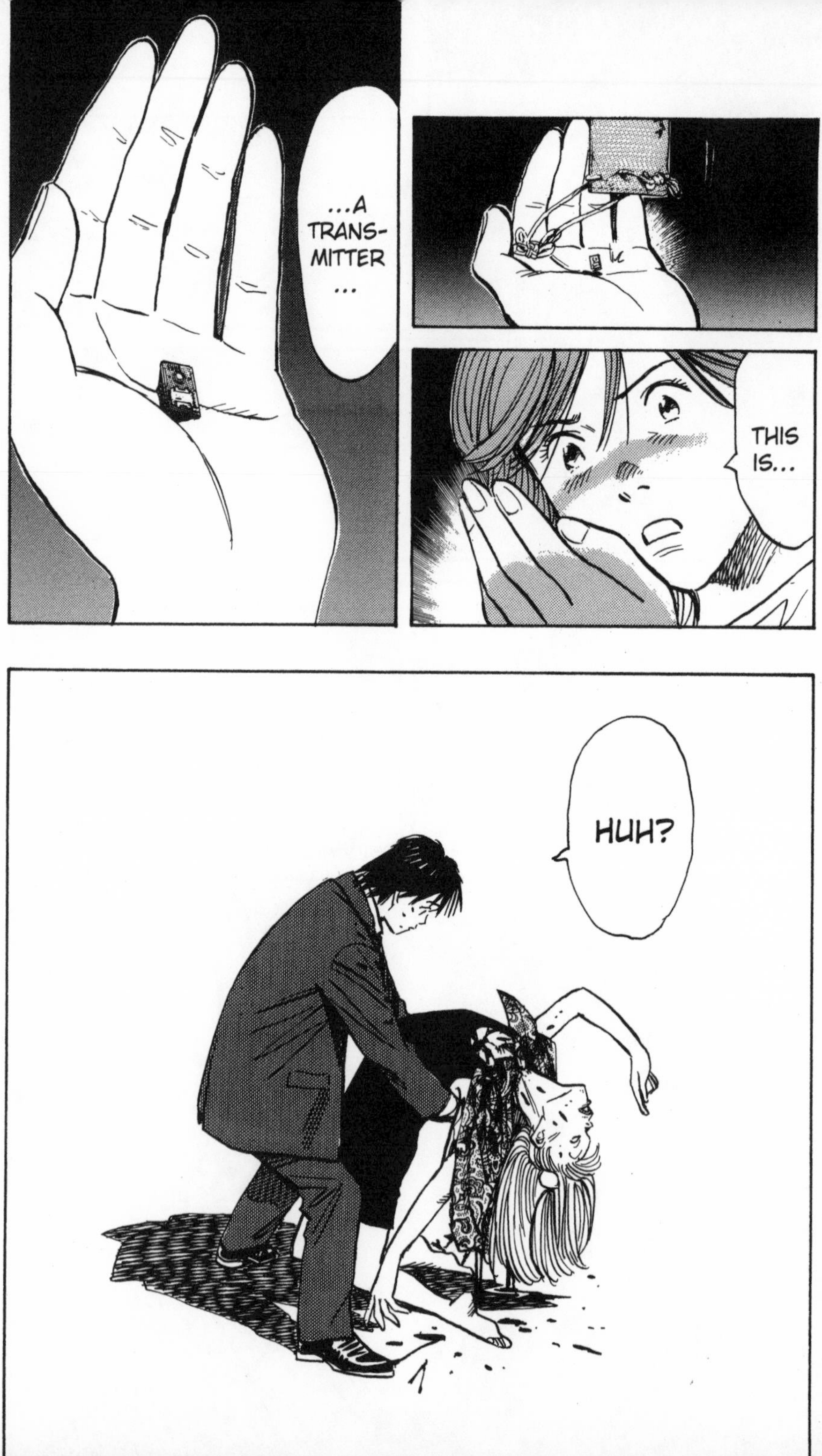
THIS IS...
...A TRANSMITTER...
HUH?

Chapter 9 Final Hope

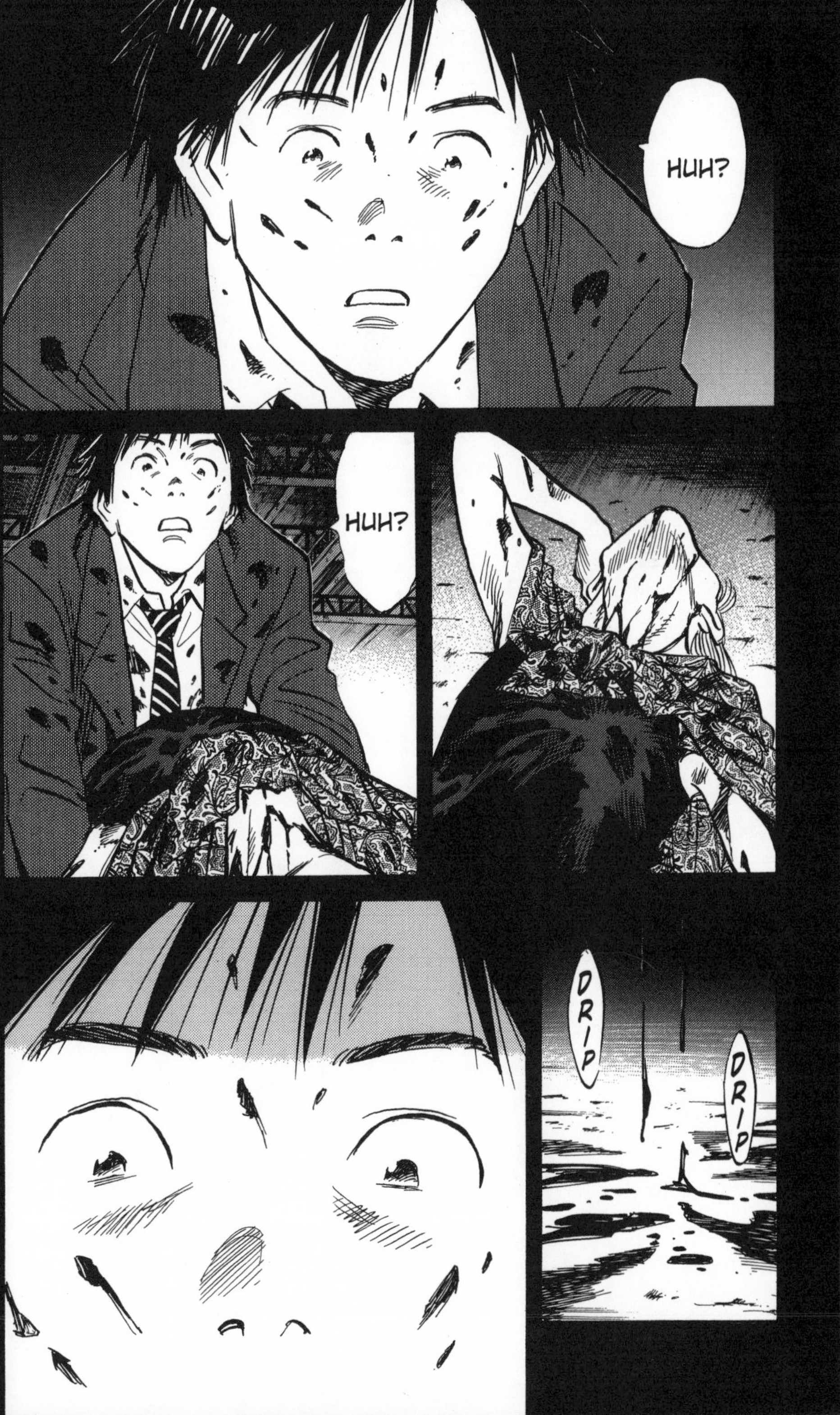
HUH?
HUH?
DRIP
DRIP

Chapter 9
Final Hope

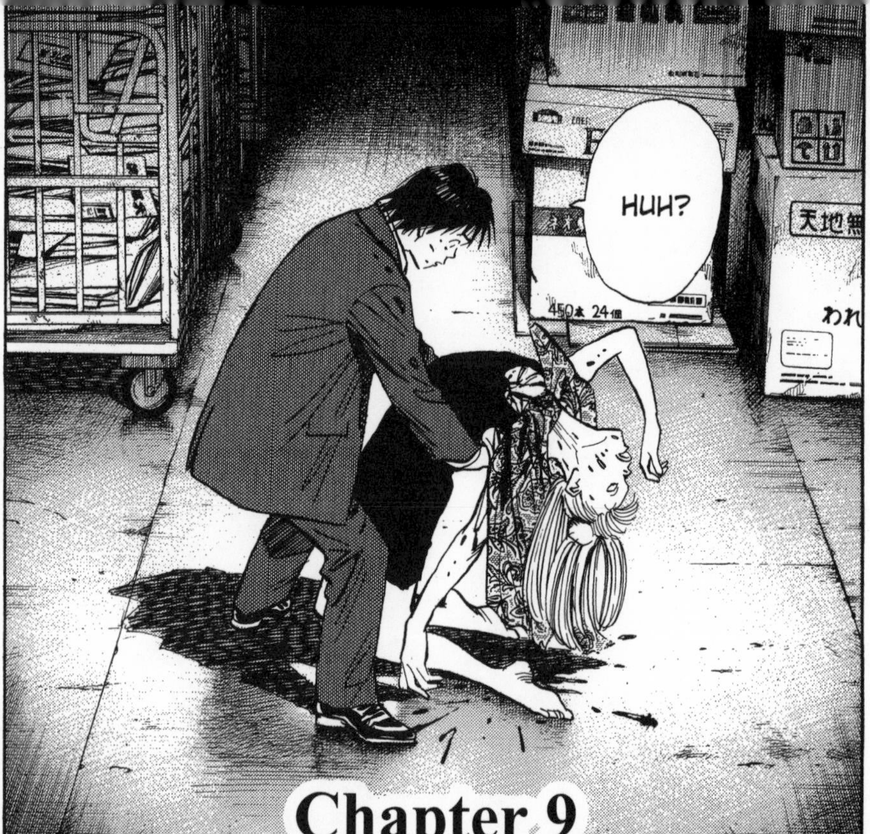
HUH?

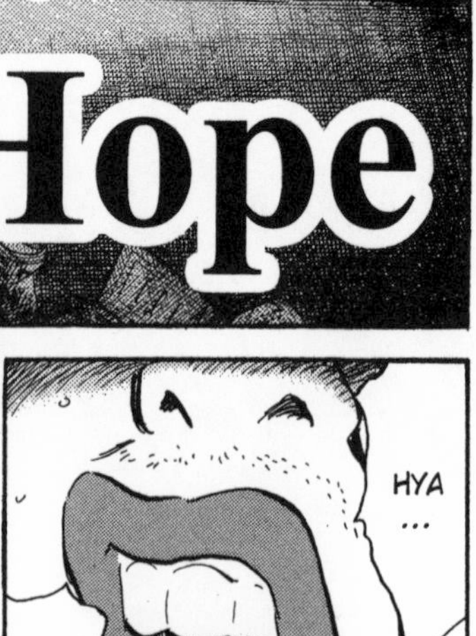
HYA ...
HYAGH ...

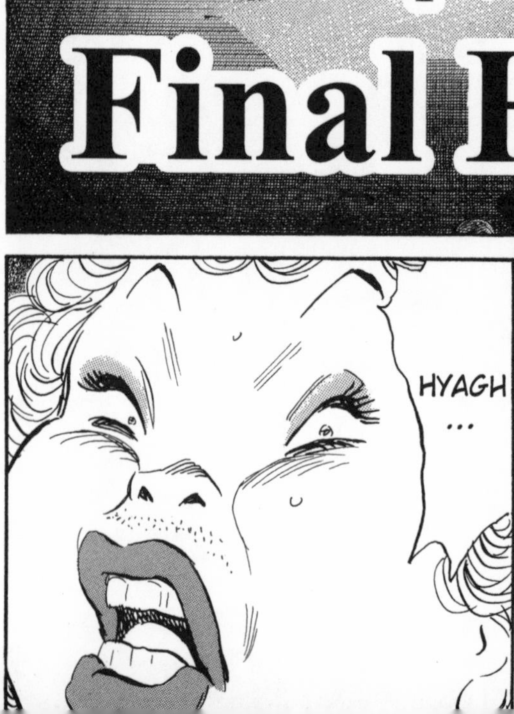
HYAGH ...

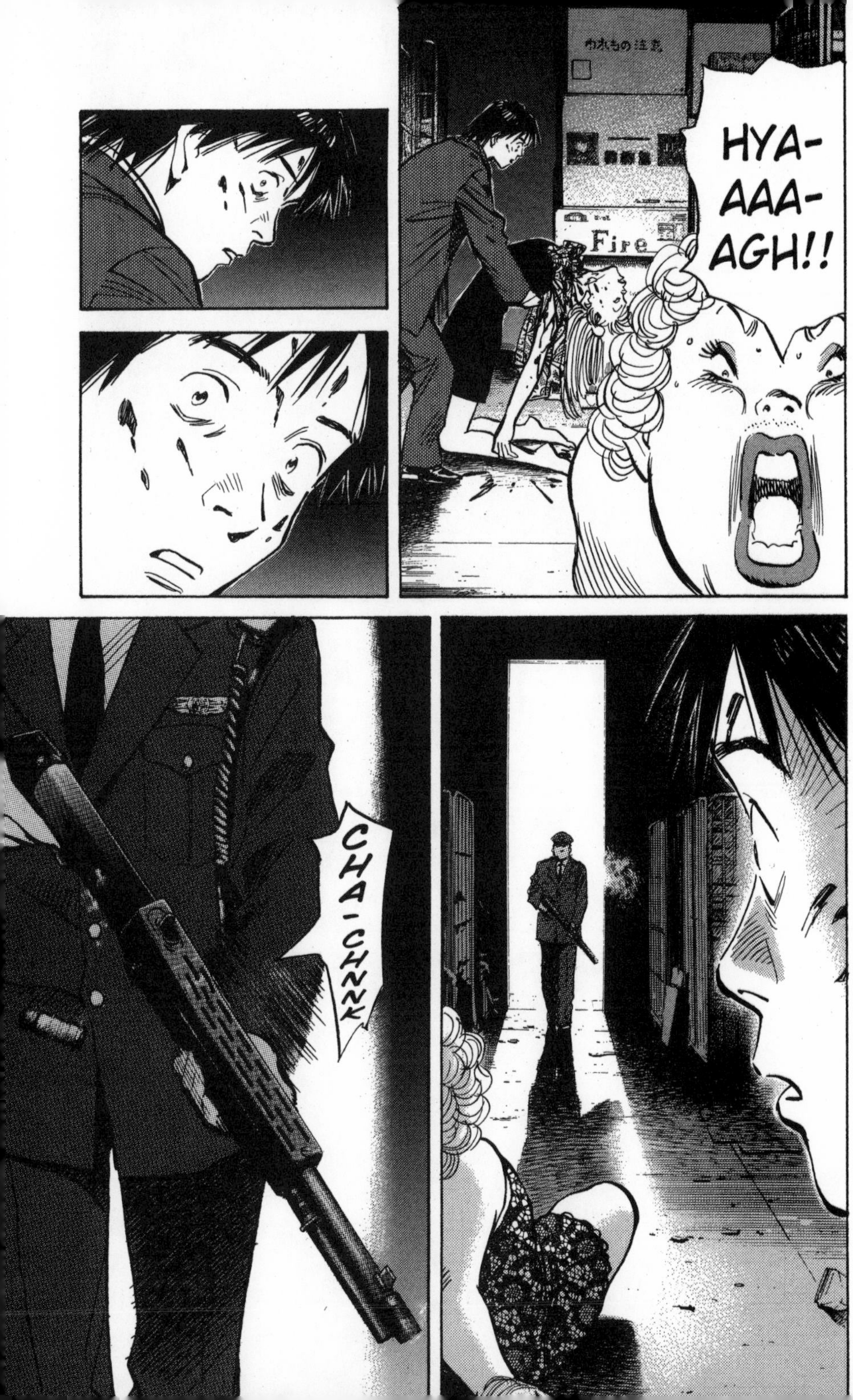

Fire
HYA-AAAA-AGH!!
CHA-CHNNK

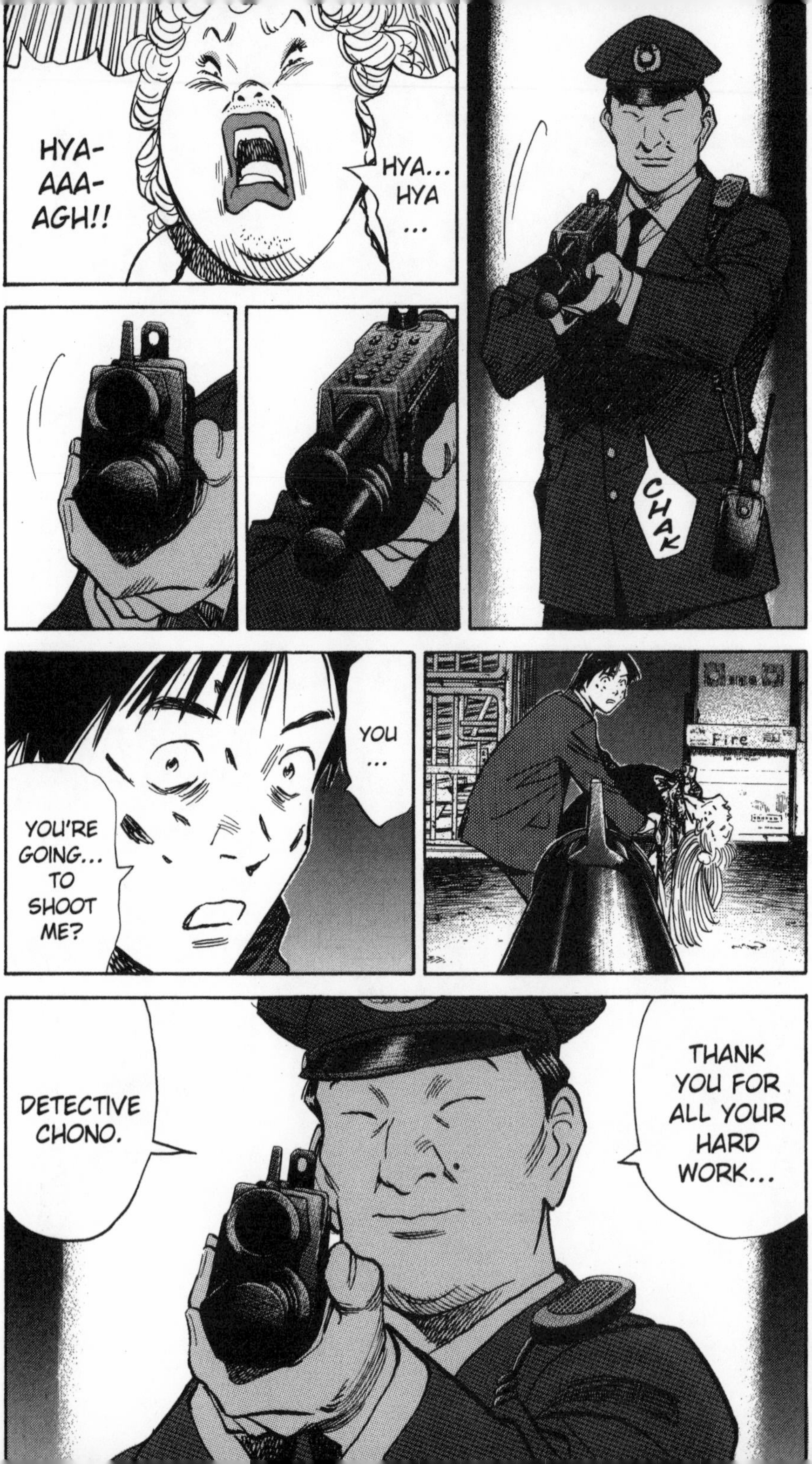
CHAK
HYA... HYA ...
HYA-AAA-AGH!!
Fire
YOU ...
YOU'RE GOING... TO SHOOT ME?
THANK YOU FOR ALL YOUR HARD WORK...
DETECTIVE CHONO.

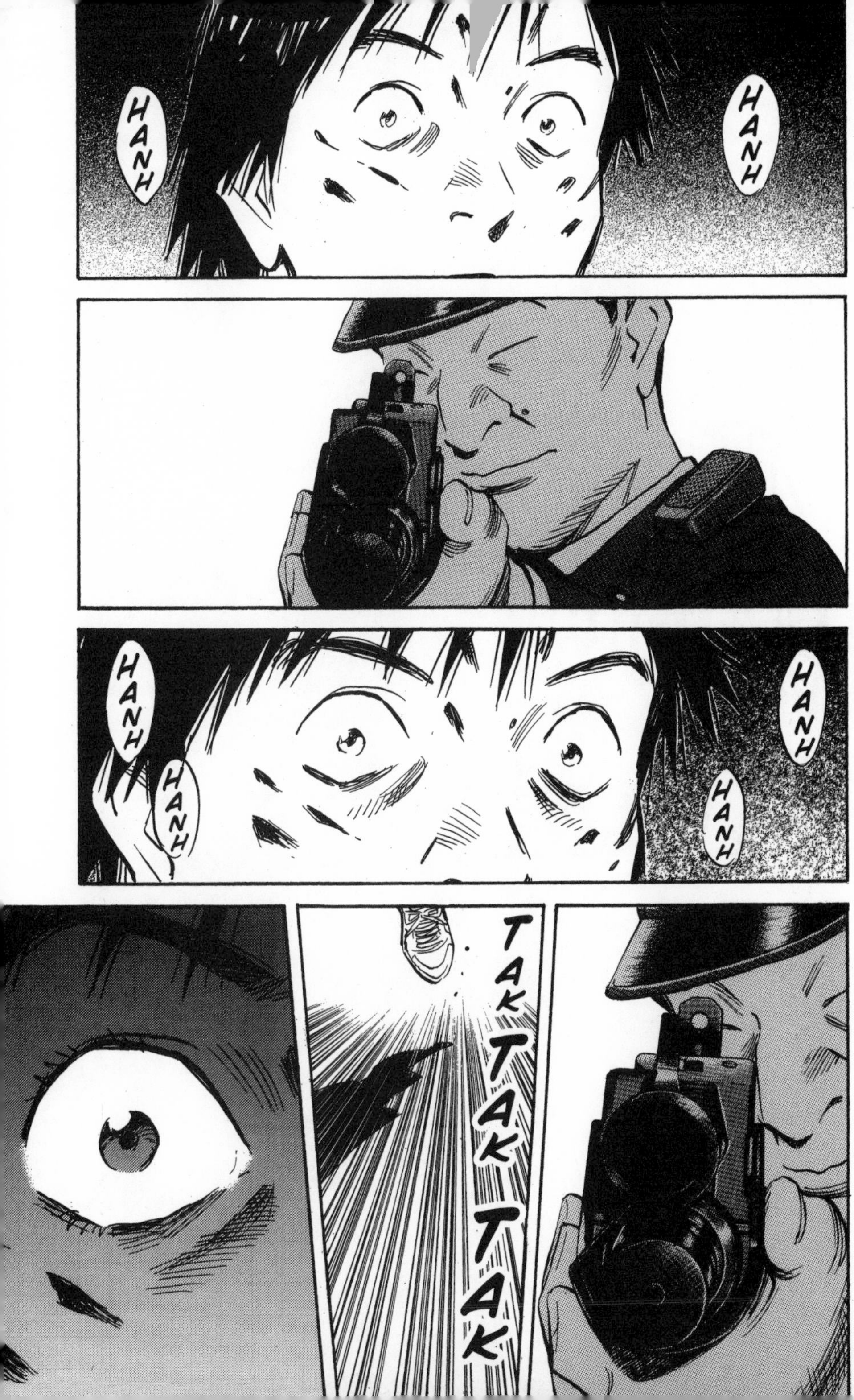
HANH
HANH
HANH
HANH
HANH
HANH
TAK
TAK
TAK
TAK

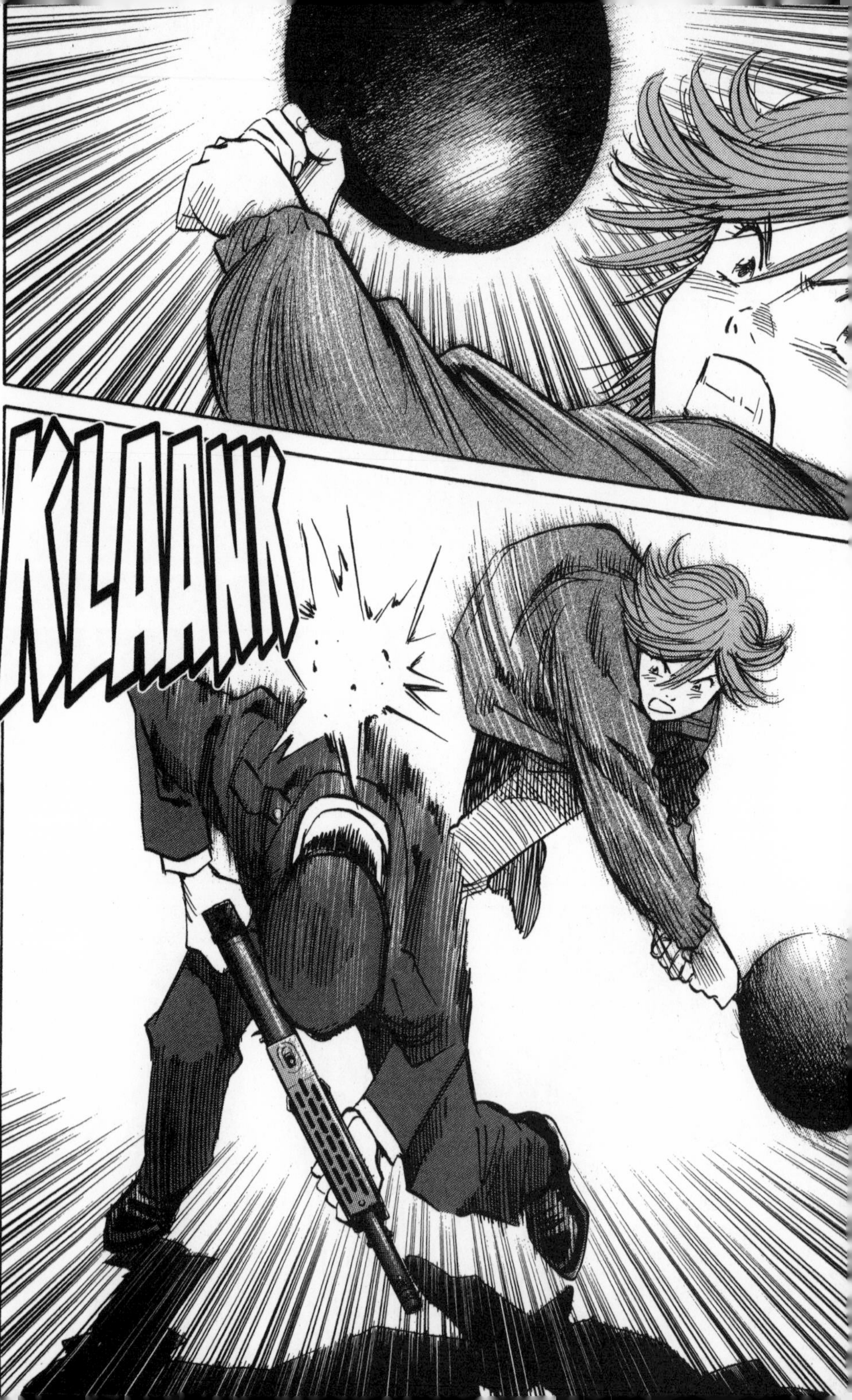
KLAANK

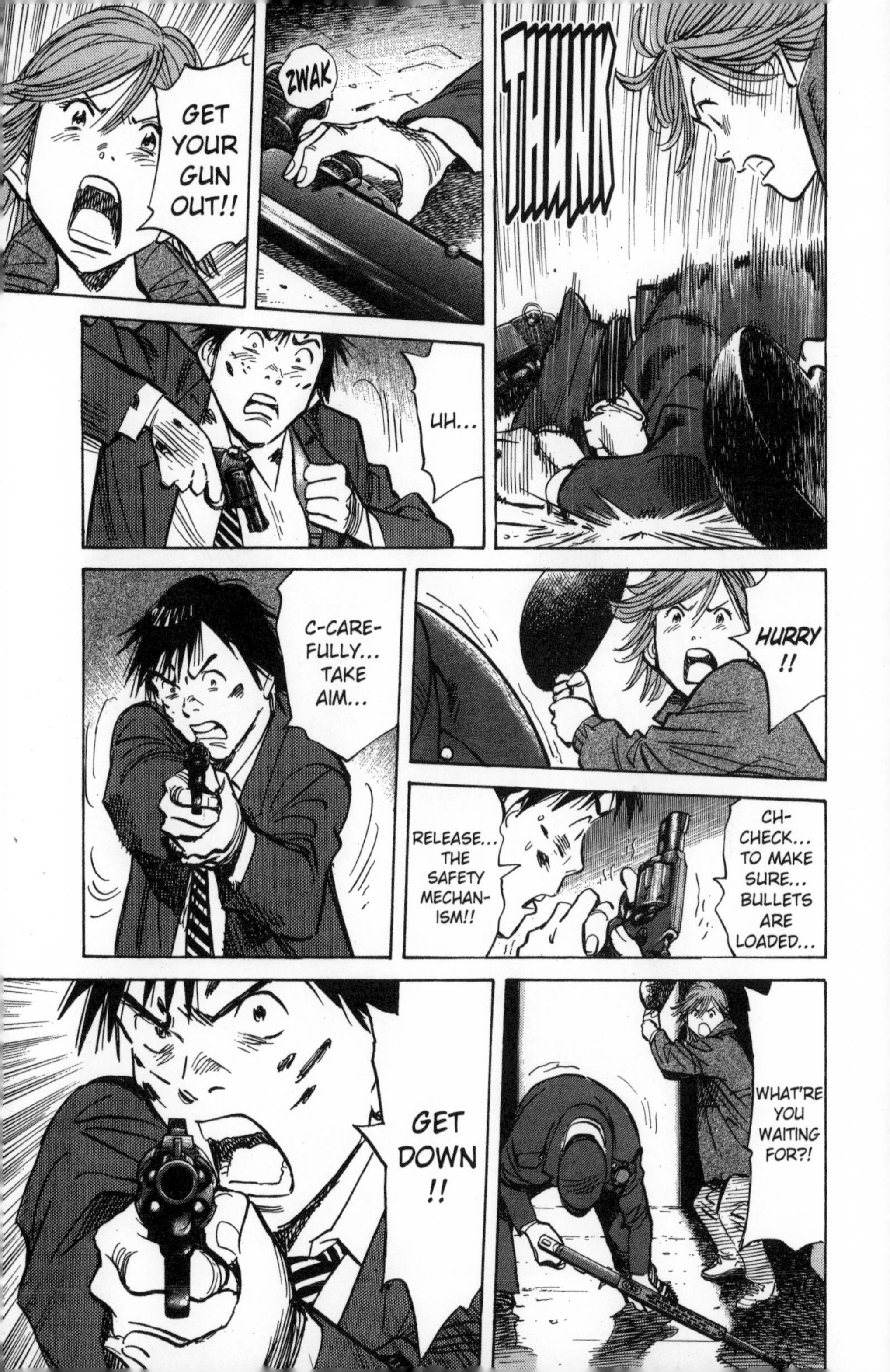
THUNK
ZWAK
GET YOUR GUN OUT!!
UH...
HURRY!!
CH-CHECK... TO MAKE SURE... BULLETS ARE LOADED...
RELEASE... THE SAFETY MECHANISM!!
C-CAREFULLY... TAKE AIM...
WHAT'RE YOU WAITING FOR?!
GET DOWN!!

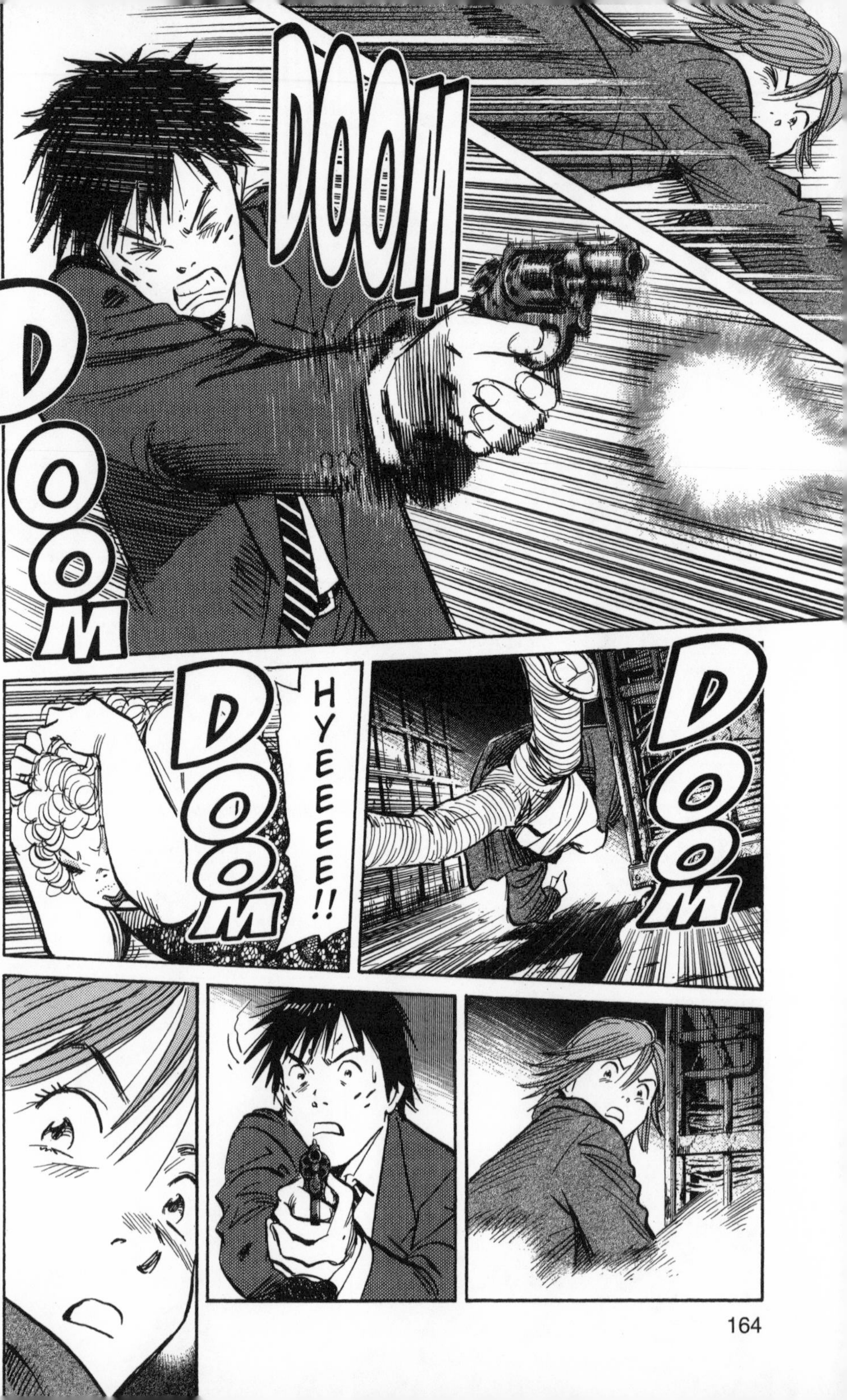
DOOM
DOOM
DOOM
HYEEEE!!
DOOM

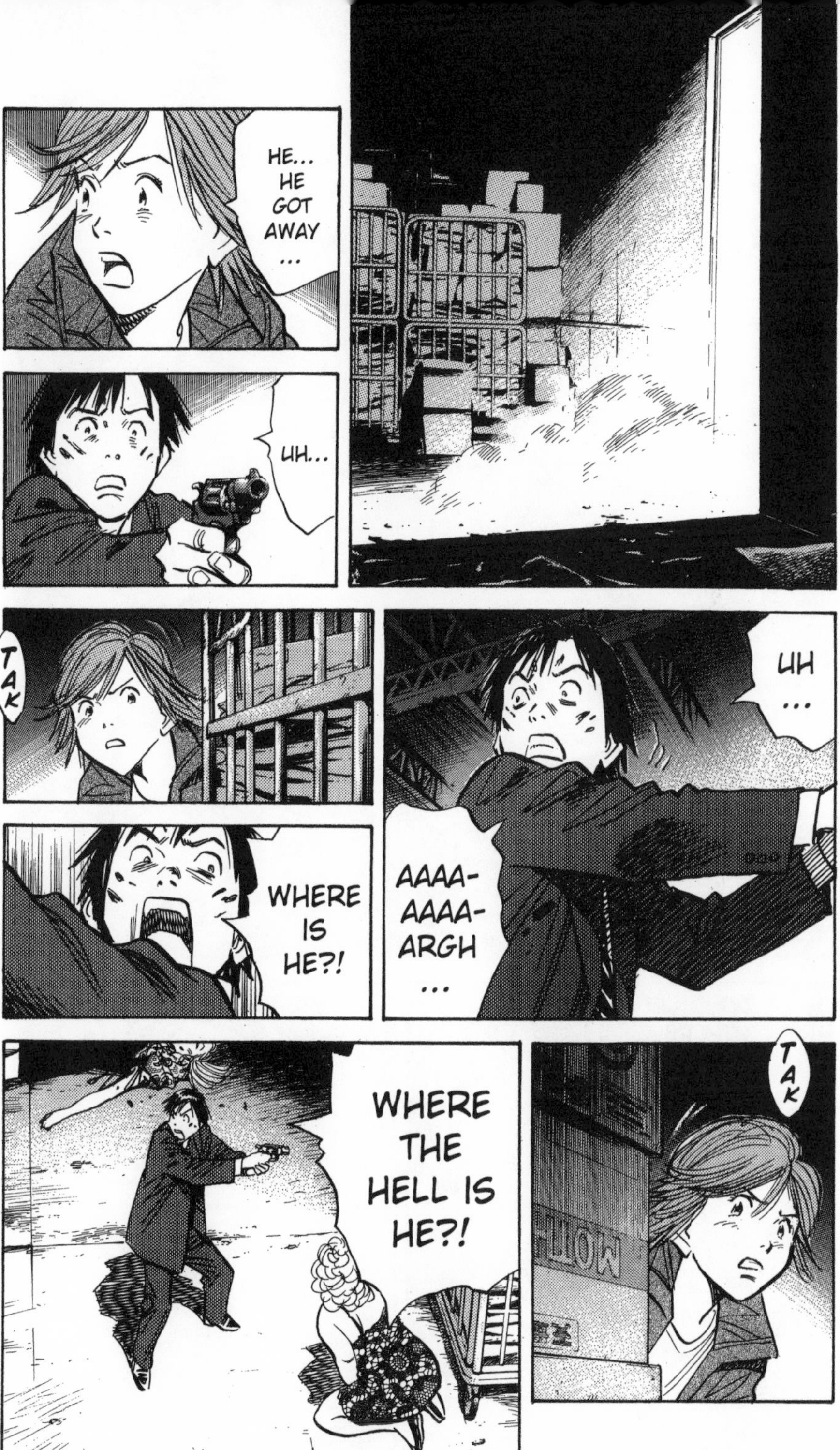
HE... HE GOT AWAY...
UH...
UH ...
AAAA-AAAA-ARGH ...
TAK
WHERE IS HE?!
TAK
WHERE THE HELL IS HE?!

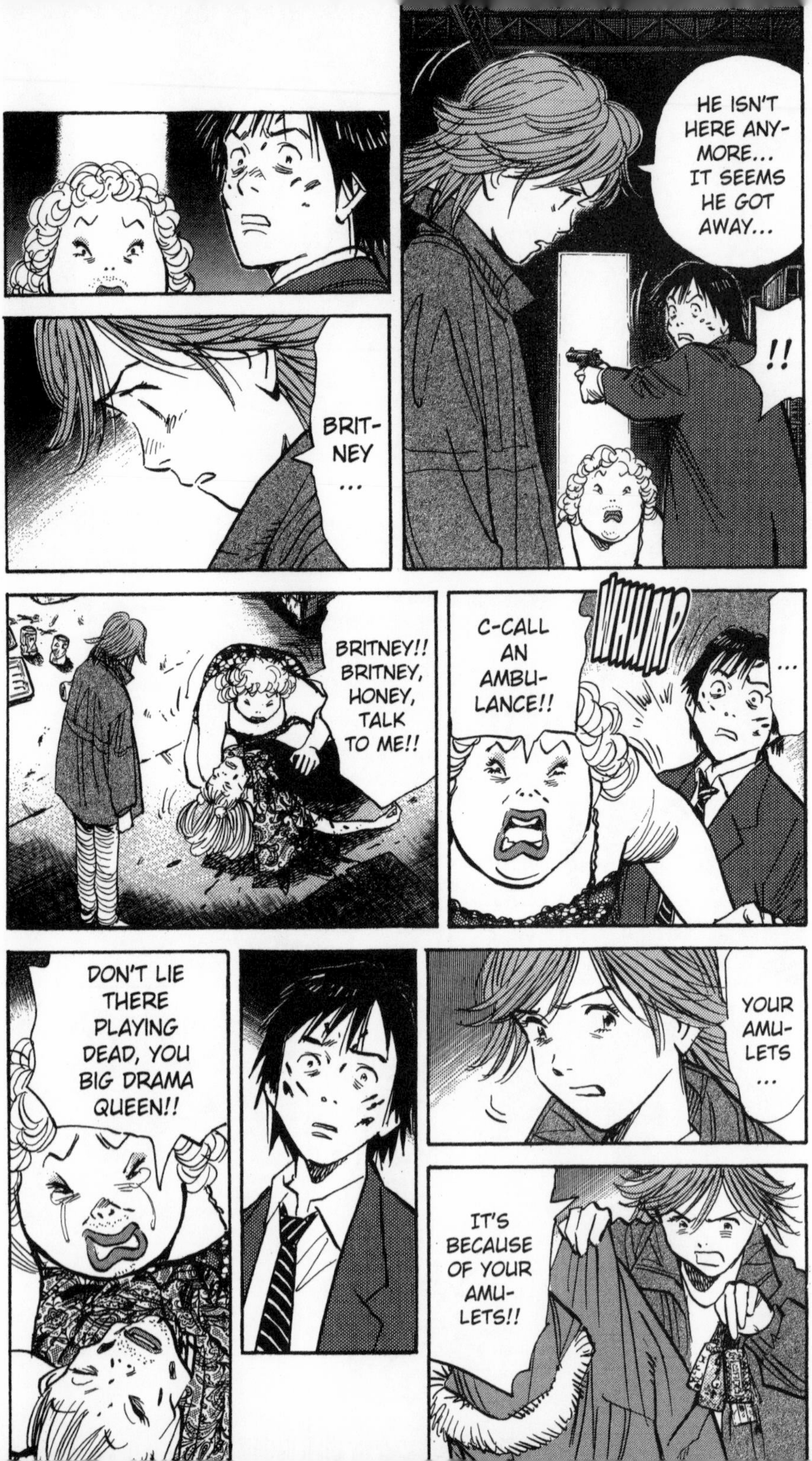
HE ISN'T HERE ANY-MORE... IT SEEMS HE GOT AWAY...
!!
BRIT-NEY ...
...
C-CALL AN AMBU-LANCE!!
BRITNEY!! BRITNEY, HONEY, TALK TO ME!!
YOUR AMU-LETS ...
IT'S BECAUSE OF YOUR AMU-LETS!!
DON'T LIE THERE PLAYING DEAD, YOU BIG DRAMA QUEEN!!

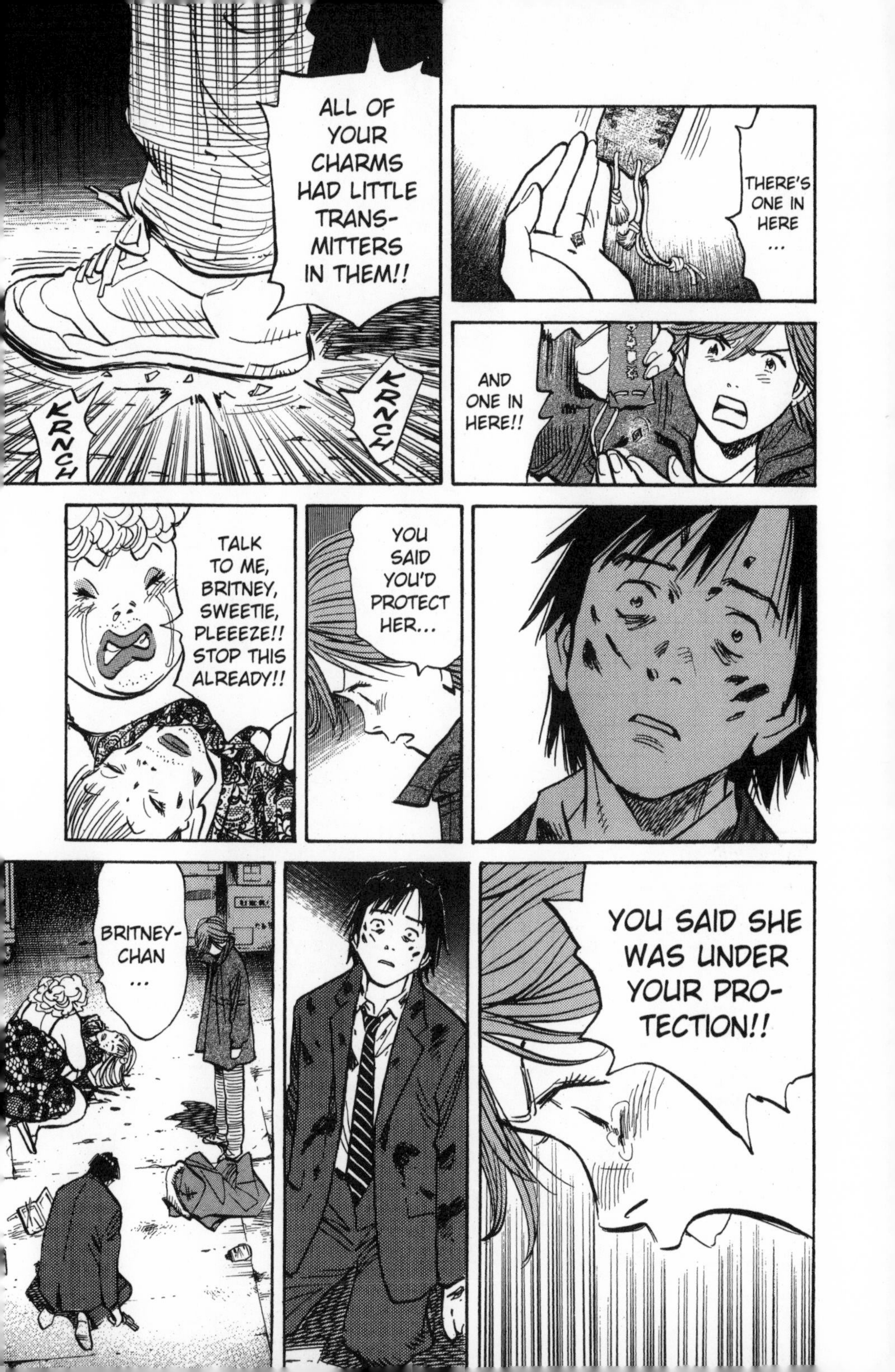
THERE'S ONE IN HERE ...
AND ONE IN HERE!!
ALL OF YOUR CHARMS HAD LITTLE TRANS-MITTERS IN THEM!!
KRNCH
KRNCH
YOU SAID YOU'D PROTECT HER...
TALK TO ME, BRITNEY, SWEETIE, PLEEEZE!! STOP THIS ALREADY!!
YOU SAID SHE WAS UNDER YOUR PRO-TECTION!!
BRITNEY-CHAN ...

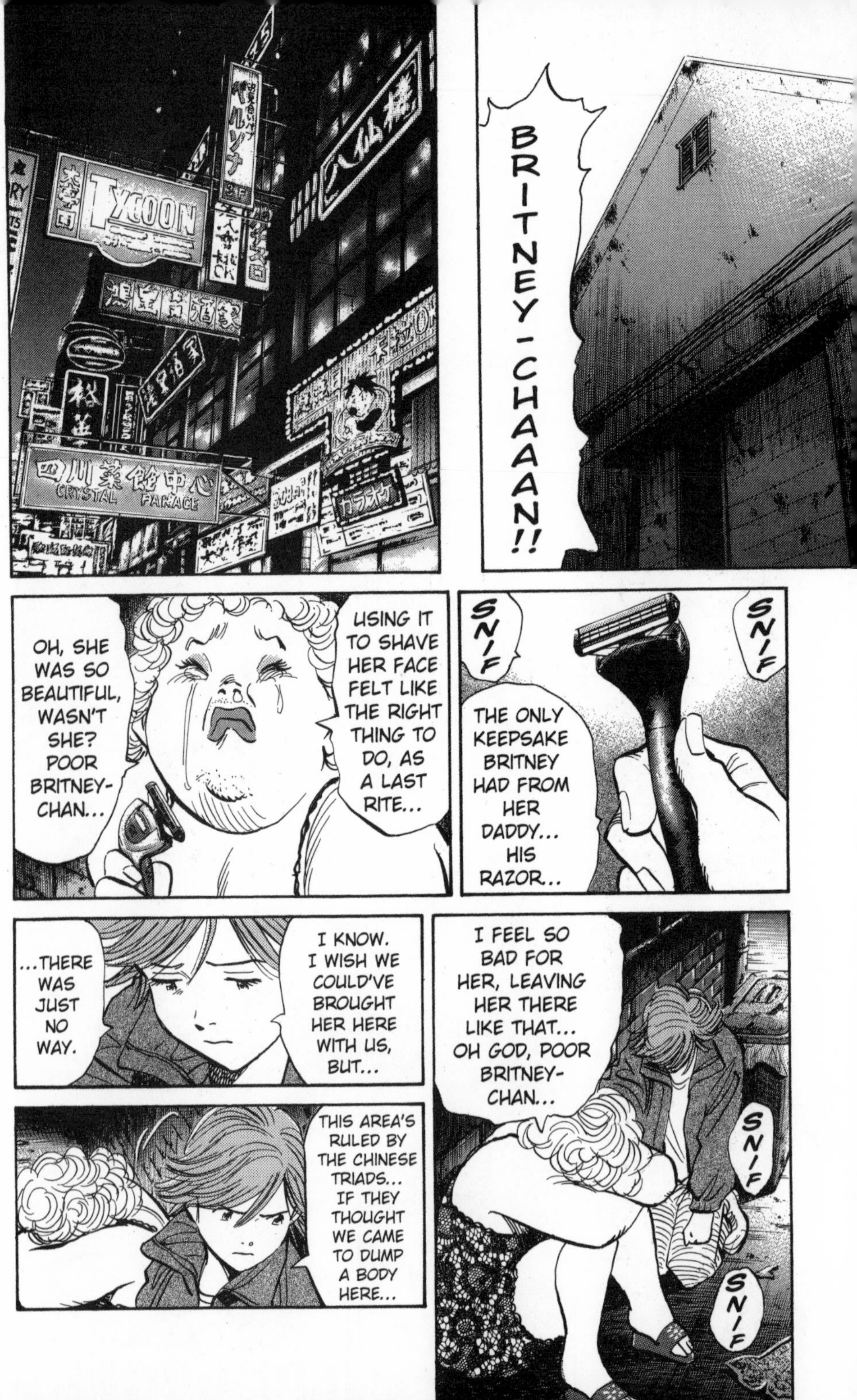
BRITNEY-CHAAAAN!!
TYCOON
四川菜館中心
カラオケ
SNIF
SNIF
THE ONLY KEEPSAKE BRITNEY HAD FROM HER DADDY... HIS RAZOR...
USING IT TO SHAVE HER FACE FELT LIKE THE RIGHT THING TO DO, AS A LAST RITE...
OH, SHE WAS SO BEAUTIFUL, WASN'T SHE? POOR BRITNEY-CHAN...
I FEEL SO BAD FOR HER, LEAVING HER THERE LIKE THAT... OH GOD, POOR BRITNEY-CHAN...
SNIF
SNIF
I KNOW. I WISH WE COULD'VE BROUGHT HER HERE WITH US, BUT...
...THERE WAS JUST NO WAY.
THIS AREA'S RULED BY THE CHINESE TRIADS... IF THEY THOUGHT WE CAME TO DUMP A BODY HERE...

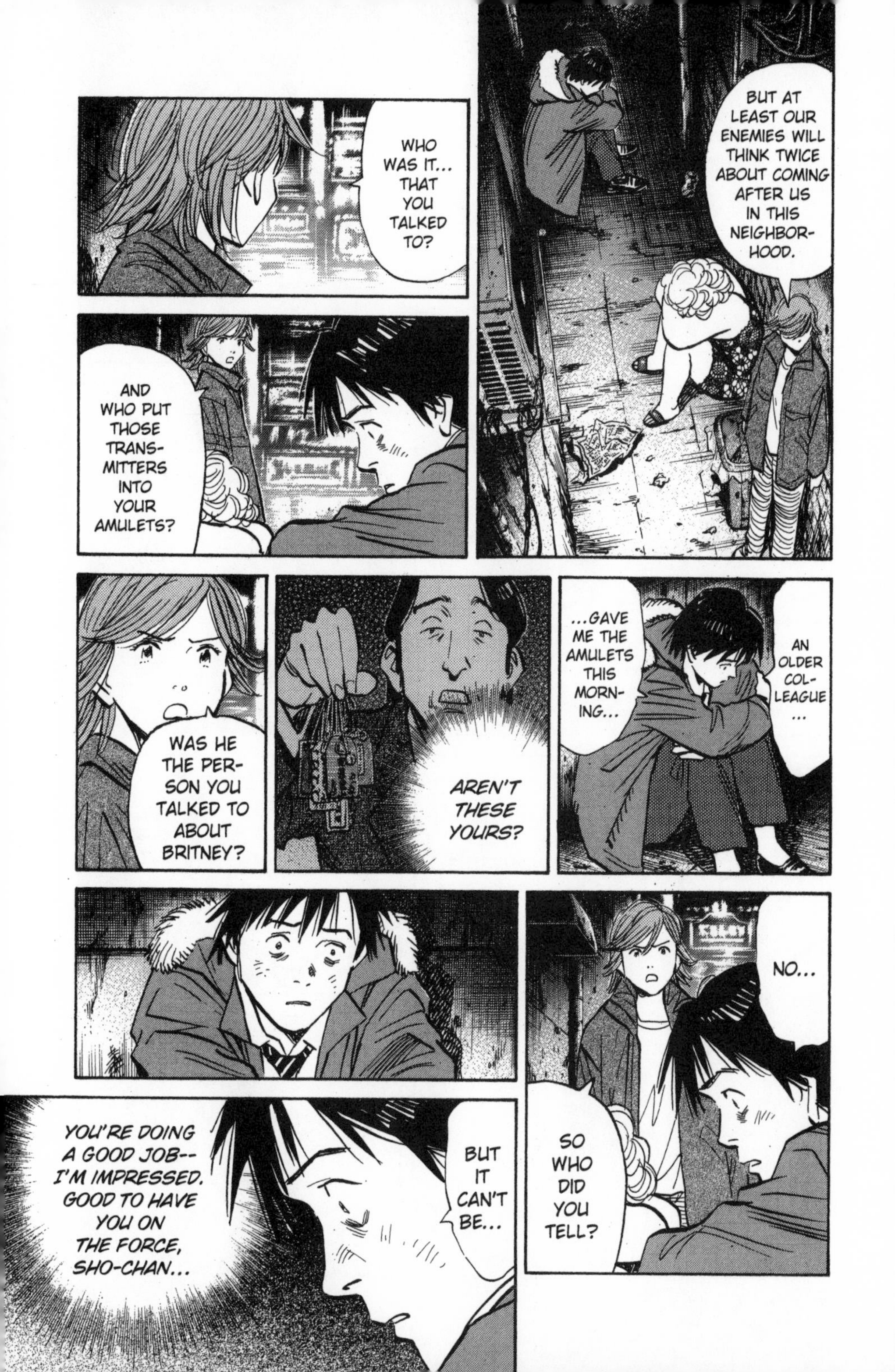
BUT AT LEAST OUR ENEMIES WILL THINK TWICE ABOUT COMING AFTER US IN THIS NEIGHBOR-HOOD.
WHO WAS IT... THAT YOU TALKED TO?
AND WHO PUT THOSE TRANS-MITTERS INTO YOUR AMULETS?
AN OLDER COL-LEAGUE...
...GAVE ME THE AMULETS THIS MORN-ING...
AREN'T THESE YOURS?
WAS HE THE PER-SON YOU TALKED TO ABOUT BRITNEY?
NO...
SO WHO DID YOU TELL?
BUT IT CAN'T BE...
YOU'RE DOING A GOOD JOB-- I'M IMPRESSED. GOOD TO HAVE YOU ON THE FORCE, SHO-CHAN...

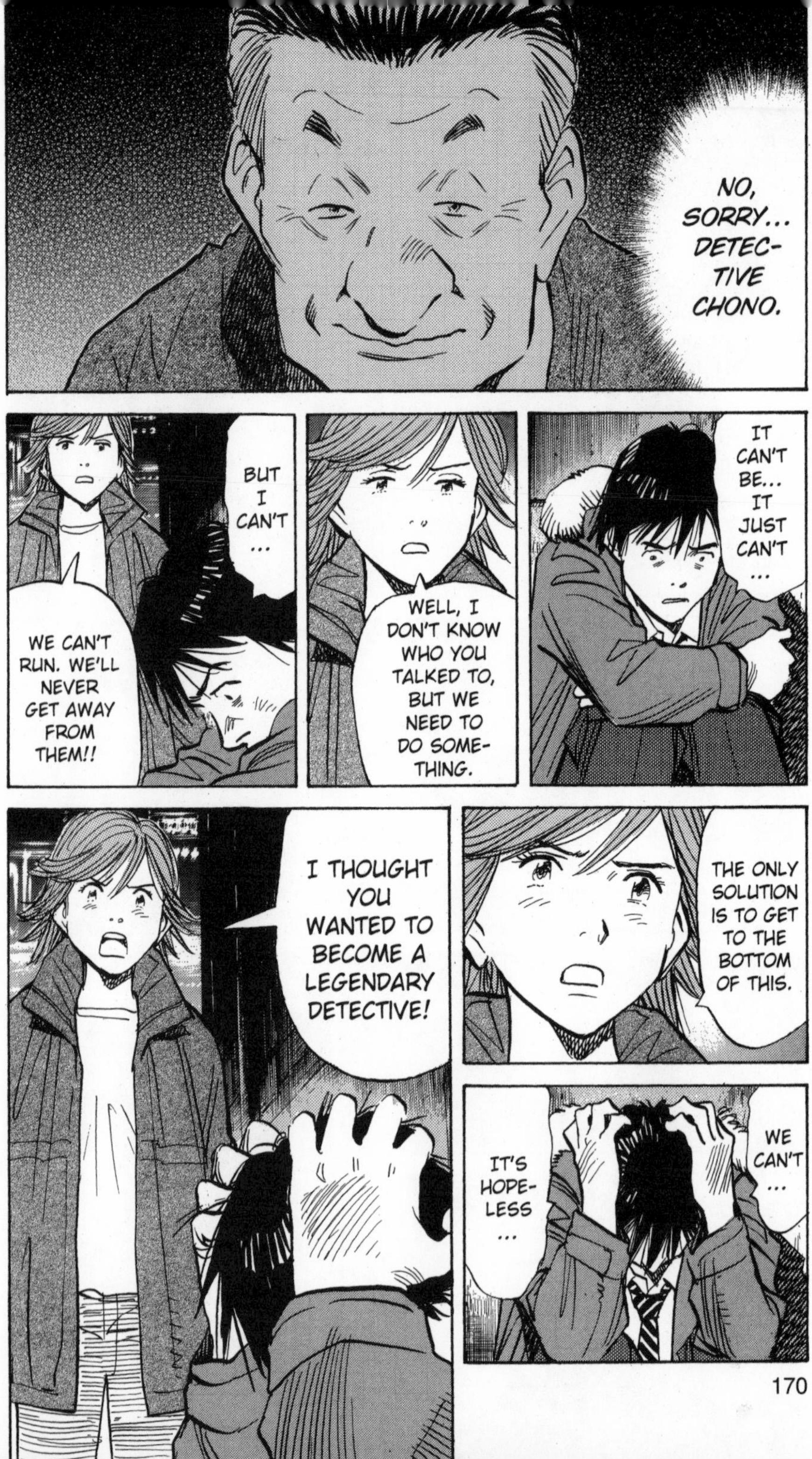
NO, SORRY... DETECTIVE CHONO.
IT CAN'T BE... IT JUST CAN'T ...
WELL, I DON'T KNOW WHO YOU TALKED TO, BUT WE NEED TO DO SOMETHING.
BUT I CAN'T ...
WE CAN'T RUN. WE'LL NEVER GET AWAY FROM THEM!!
THE ONLY SOLUTION IS TO GET TO THE BOTTOM OF THIS.
WE CAN'T ...
IT'S HOPELESS ...
I THOUGHT YOU WANTED TO BECOME A LEGENDARY DETECTIVE!

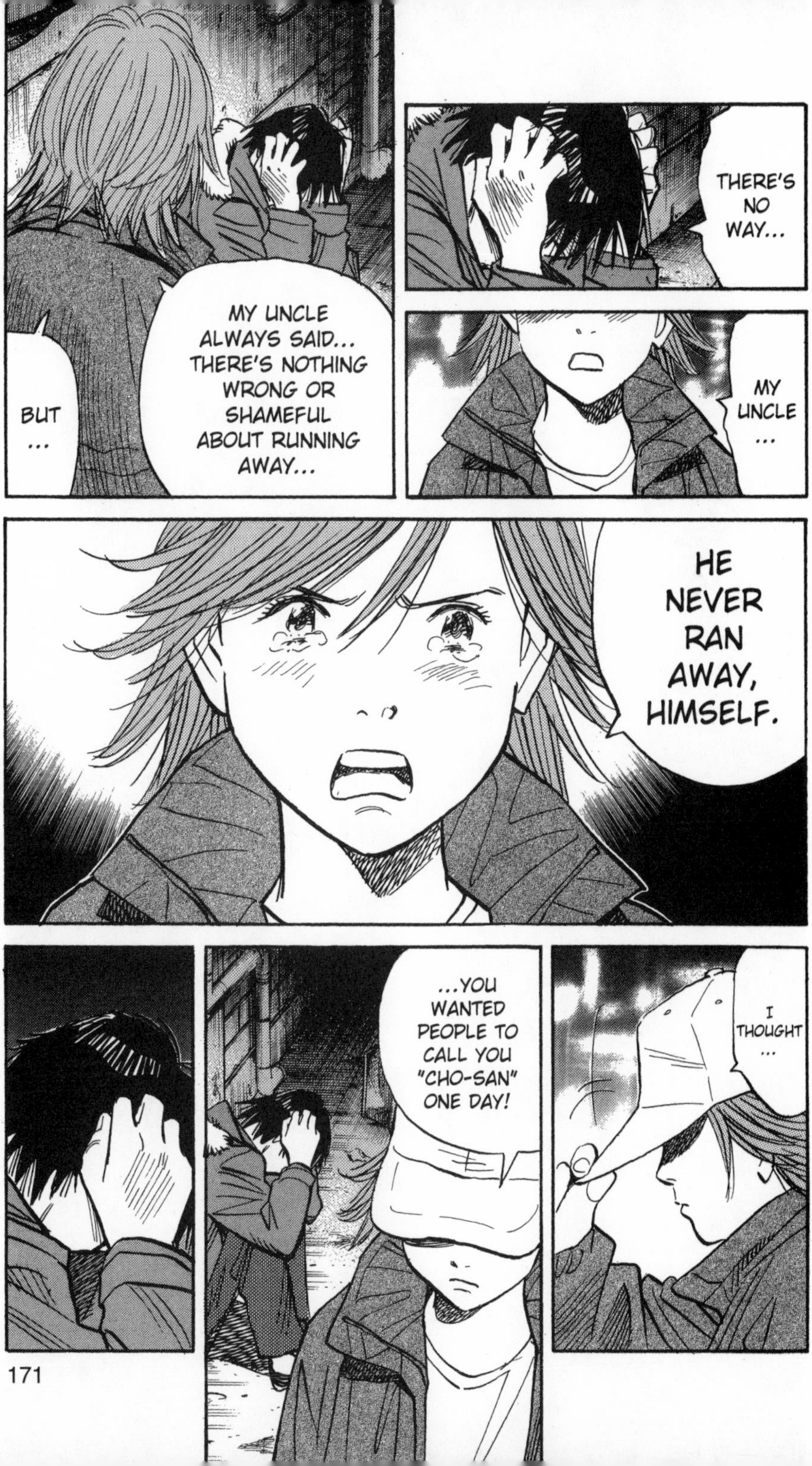
THERE'S NO WAY...
MY UNCLE...
MY UNCLE ALWAYS SAID... THERE'S NOTHING WRONG OR SHAMEFUL ABOUT RUNNING AWAY...
BUT...
HE NEVER RAN AWAY, HIMSELF.
I THOUGHT...
...YOU WANTED PEOPLE TO CALL YOU "CHO-SAN" ONE DAY!

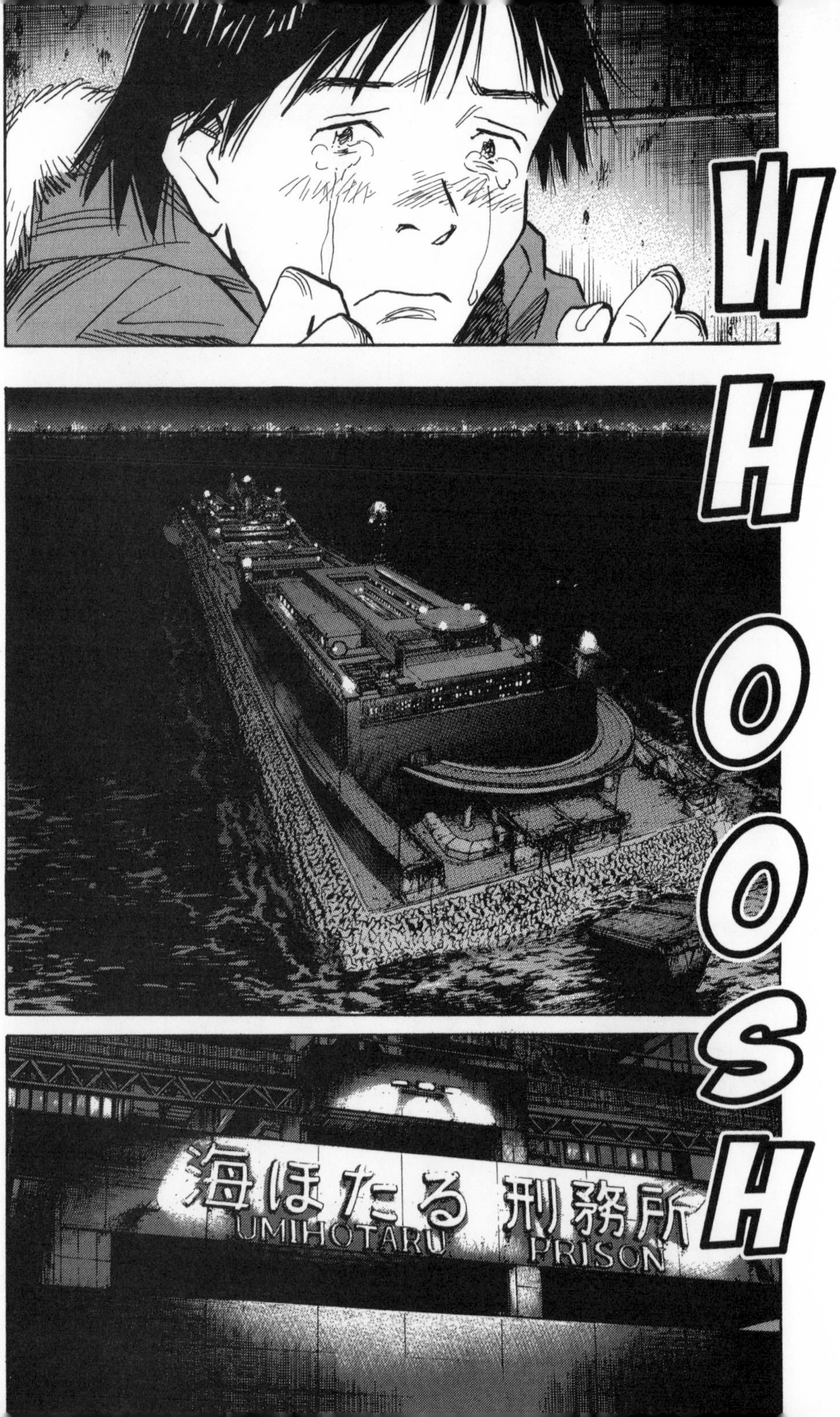
WHOOSH
海ほたる 刑務所
UMIHOTARU PRISON

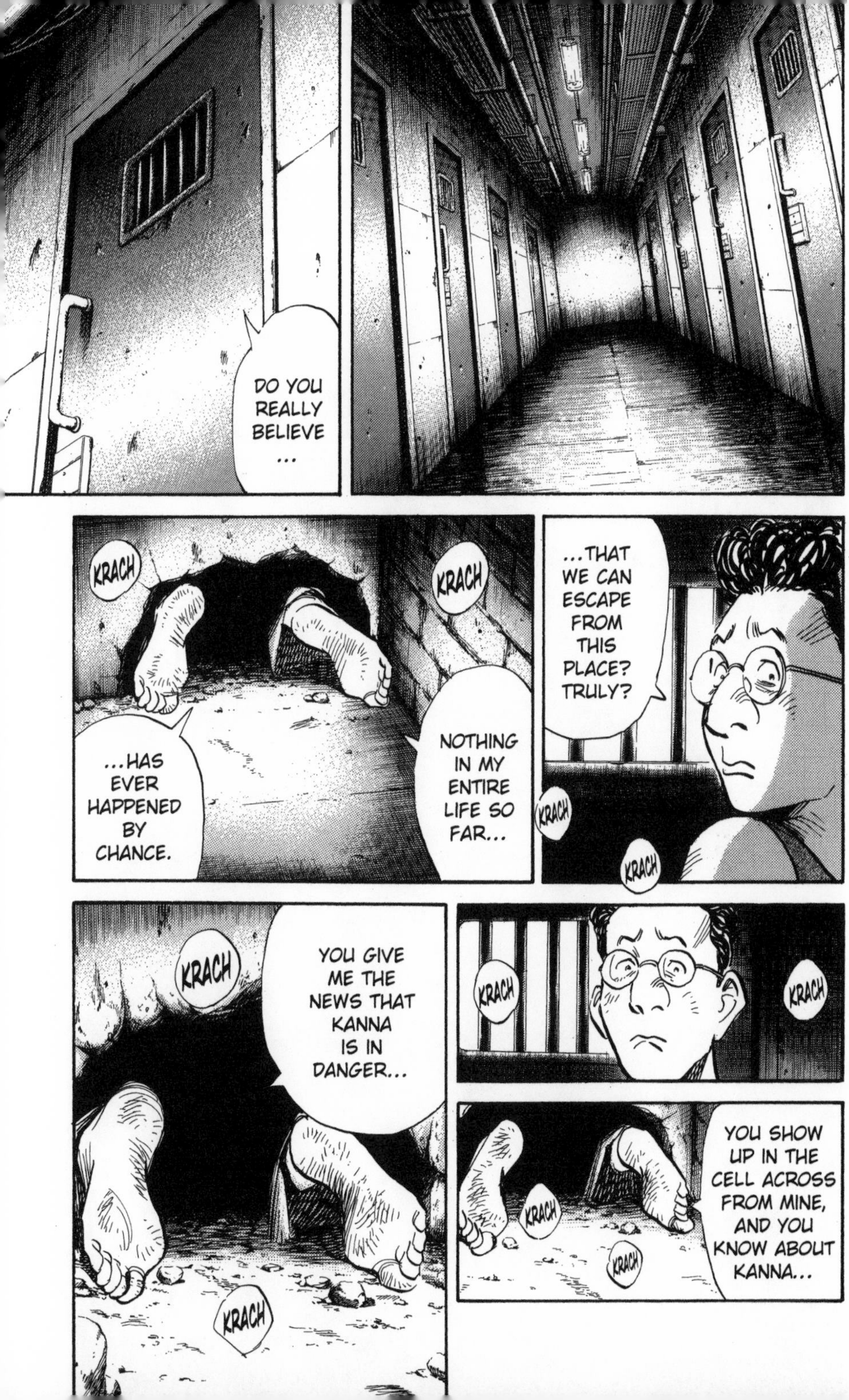
DO YOU REALLY BELIEVE ...
...THAT WE CAN ESCAPE FROM THIS PLACE? TRULY?
KRACH
KRACH
KRACH
KRACH
NOTHING IN MY ENTIRE LIFE SO FAR...
...HAS EVER HAPPENED BY CHANCE.
KRACH
KRACH
YOU SHOW UP IN THE CELL ACROSS FROM MINE, AND YOU KNOW ABOUT KANNA...
KRACH
KRACH
KRACH
YOU GIVE ME THE NEWS THAT KANNA IS IN DANGER...
KRACH

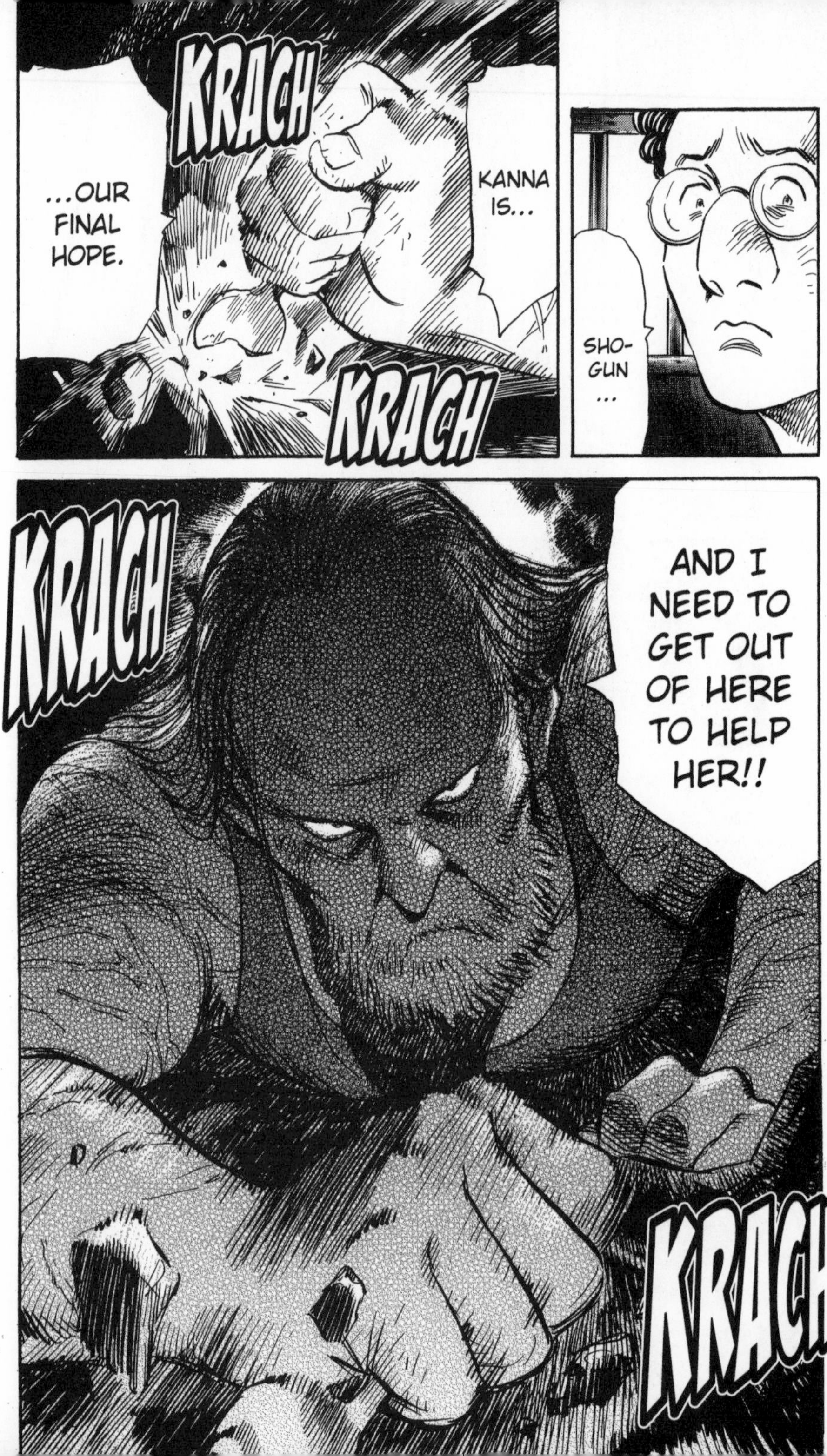
SHO-
GUN
...
KANNA
IS...
KRACH
...OUR
FINAL
HOPE.
KRACH
AND I
NEED TO
GET OUT
OF HERE
TO HELP
HER!!
KRACH
KRACH

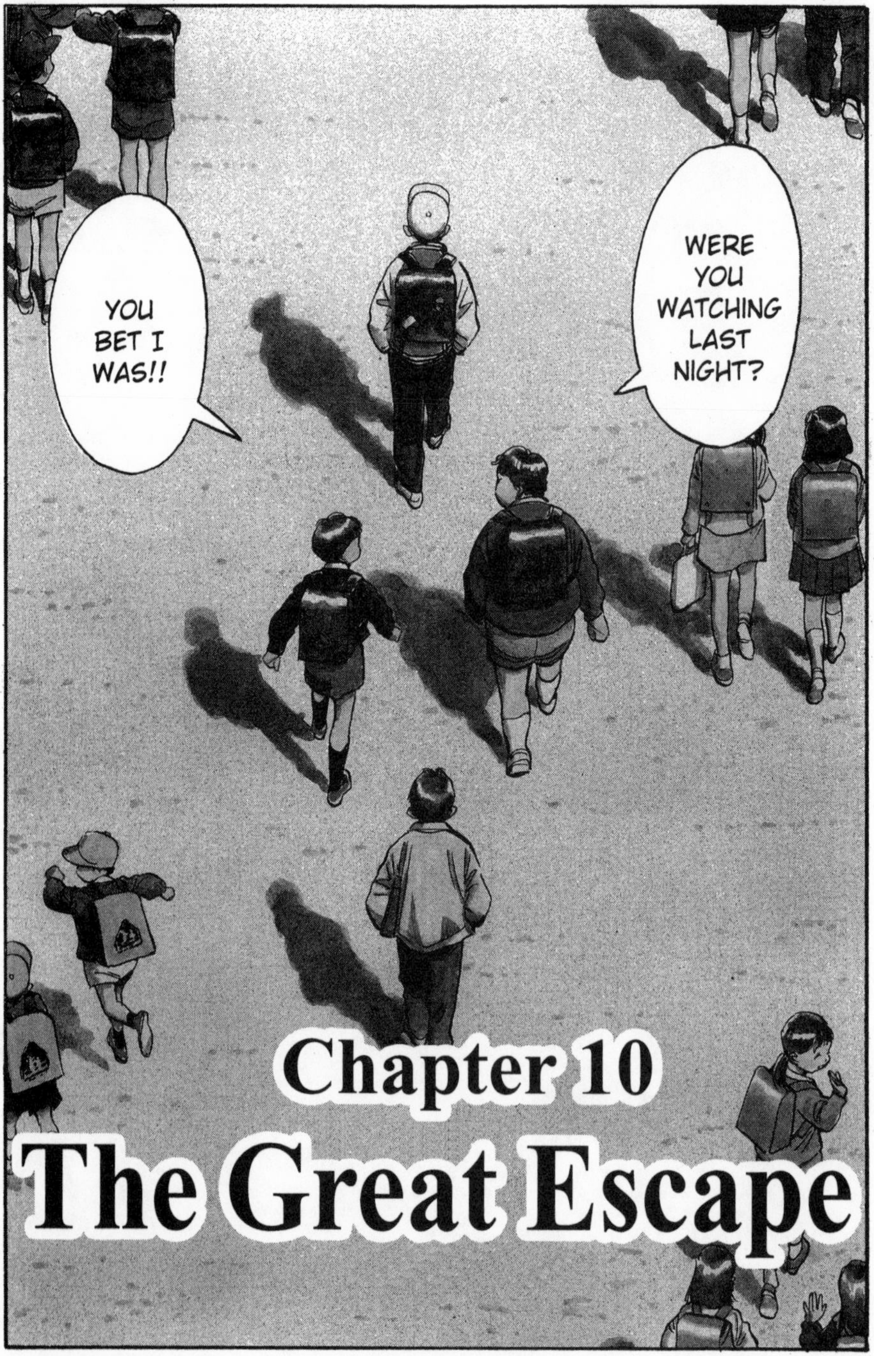
WERE YOU WATCHING LAST NIGHT?
YOU BET I WAS!!
Chapter 10
The Great Escape

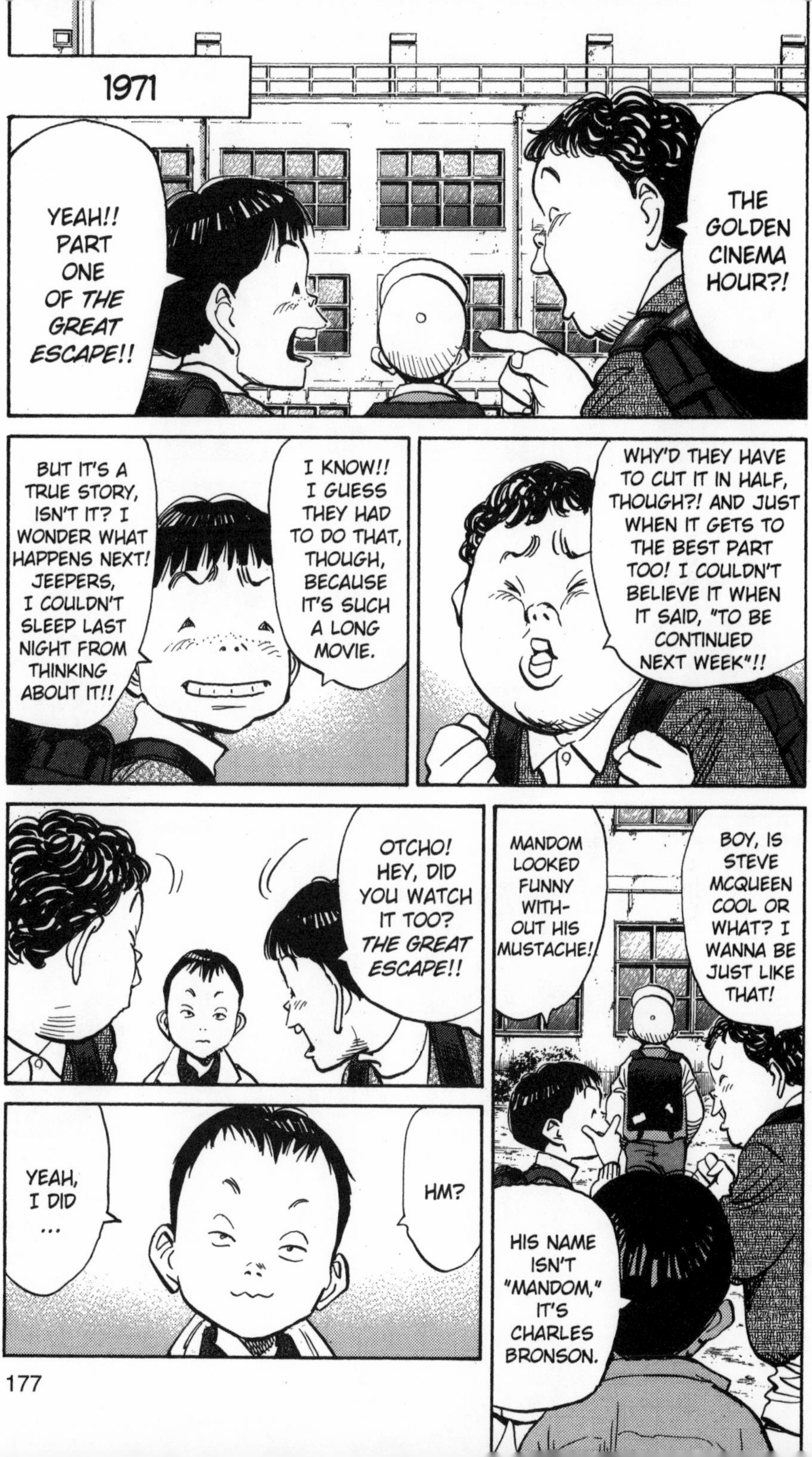
1971
THE GOLDEN CINEMA HOUR?!
YEAH!! PART ONE OF *THE GREAT ESCAPE*!!
WHY'D THEY HAVE TO CUT IT IN HALF, THOUGH?! AND JUST WHEN IT GETS TO THE BEST PART TOO! I COULDN'T BELIEVE IT WHEN IT SAID, "TO BE CONTINUED NEXT WEEK"!!
I KNOW!! I GUESS THEY HAD TO DO THAT, THOUGH, BECAUSE IT'S SUCH A LONG MOVIE.
BUT IT'S A TRUE STORY, ISN'T IT? I WONDER WHAT HAPPENS NEXT! JEEPERS, I COULDN'T SLEEP LAST NIGHT FROM THINKING ABOUT IT!!
BOY, IS STEVE MCQUEEN COOL OR WHAT? I WANNA BE JUST LIKE THAT!
MANDOM LOOKED FUNNY WITH-OUT HIS MUSTACHE!
HIS NAME ISN'T "MANDOM," IT'S CHARLES BRONSON.
OTCHO! HEY, DID YOU WATCH IT TOO? *THE GREAT ESCAPE*!!
HM?
YEAH, I DID ...

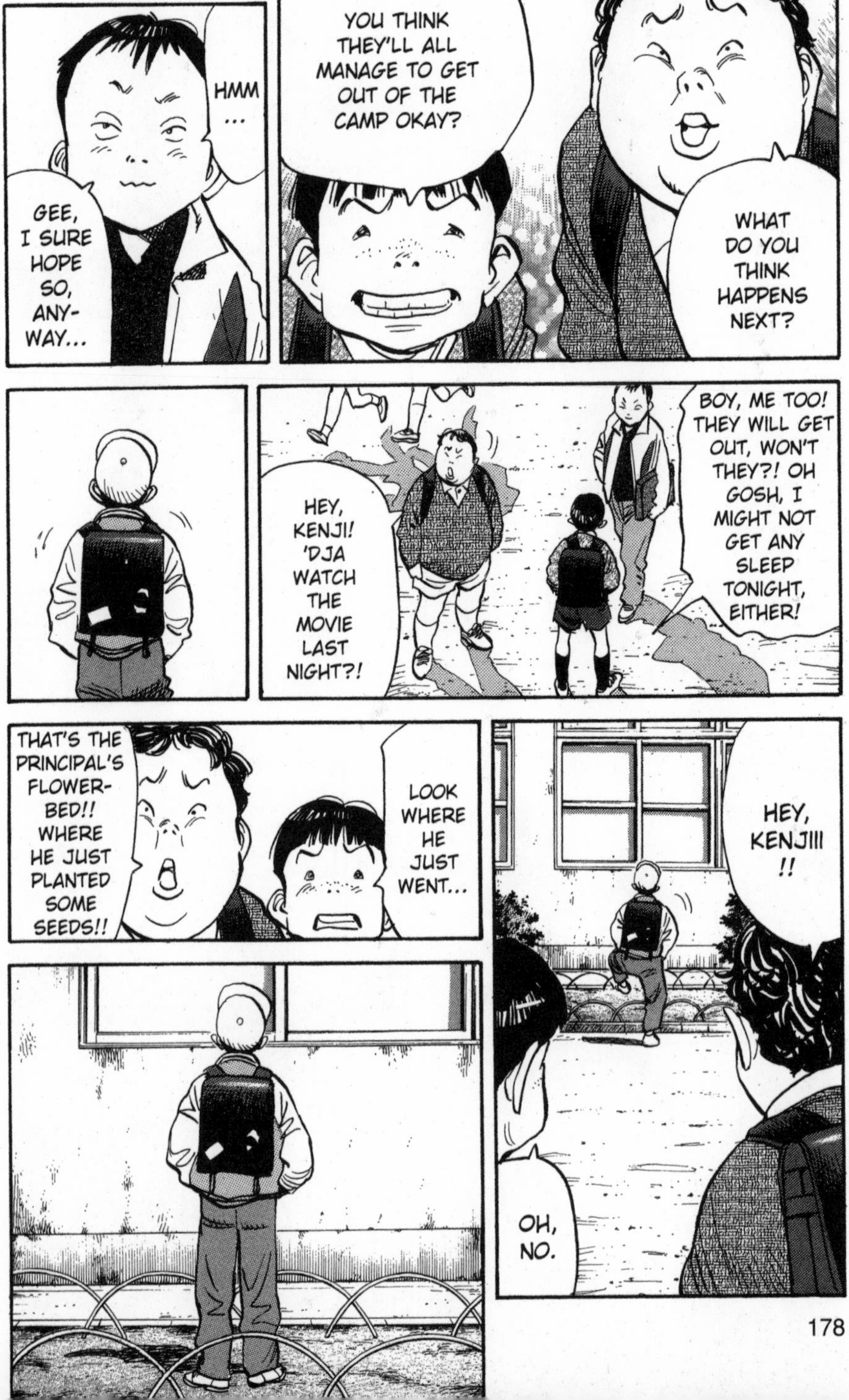
WHAT DO YOU THINK HAPPENS NEXT?
YOU THINK THEY'LL ALL MANAGE TO GET OUT OF THE CAMP OKAY?
HMM ...
GEE, I SURE HOPE SO, ANY-WAY...
BOY, ME TOO! THEY WILL GET OUT, WON'T THEY?! OH GOSH, I MIGHT NOT GET ANY SLEEP TONIGHT, EITHER!
HEY, KENJI! 'DJA WATCH THE MOVIE LAST NIGHT?!
HEY, KENJIII !!
OH, NO.
LOOK WHERE HE JUST WENT...
THAT'S THE PRINCIPAL'S FLOWER-BED!! WHERE HE JUST PLANTED SOME SEEDS!!

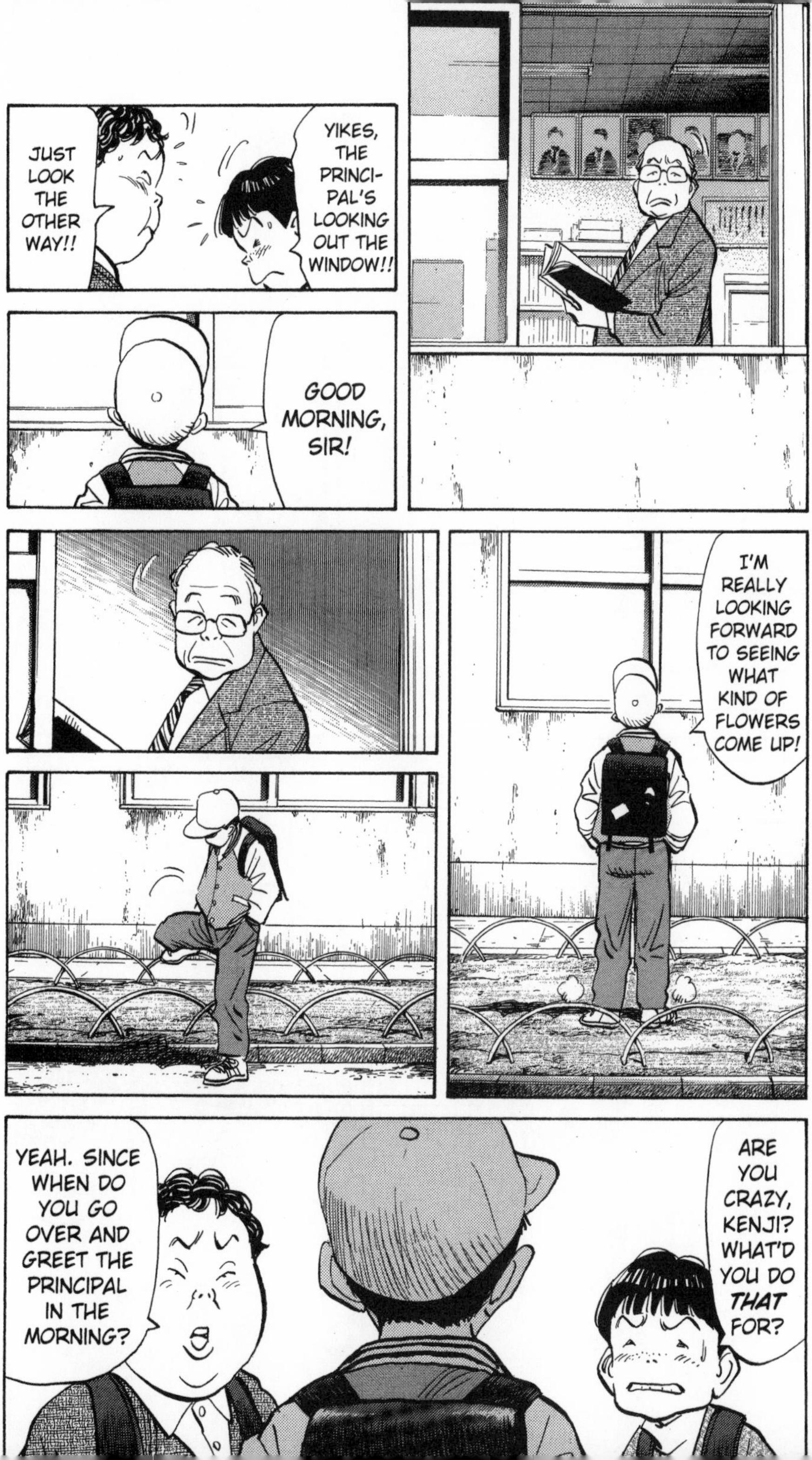
YIKES, THE PRINCI-PAL'S LOOKING OUT THE WINDOW!!
JUST LOOK THE OTHER WAY!!
GOOD MORNING, SIR!
I'M REALLY LOOKING FORWARD TO SEEING WHAT KIND OF FLOWERS COME UP!
ARE YOU CRAZY, KENJI? WHAT'D YOU DO *THAT* FOR?
YEAH. SINCE WHEN DO YOU GO OVER AND GREET THE PRINCIPAL IN THE MORNING?

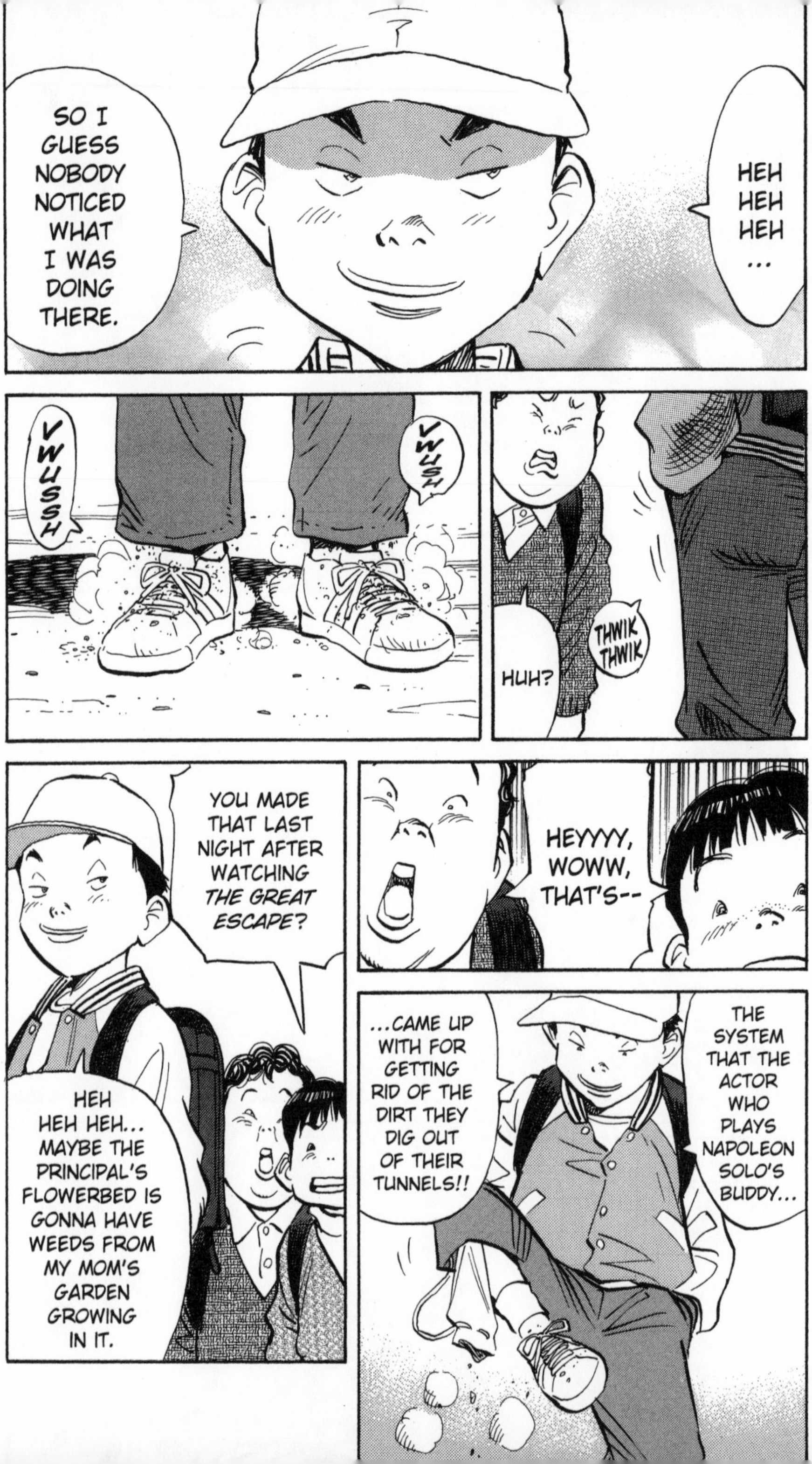
HEH HEH HEH ...
SO I GUESS NOBODY NOTICED WHAT I WAS DOING THERE.
THWIK THWIK
HUH?
VWUSH
VWUSSH
HEYYYY, WOWW, THAT'S--
THE SYSTEM THAT THE ACTOR WHO PLAYS NAPOLEON SOLO'S BUDDY...
...CAME UP WITH FOR GETTING RID OF THE DIRT THEY DIG OUT OF THEIR TUNNELS!!
YOU MADE THAT LAST NIGHT AFTER WATCHING *THE GREAT ESCAPE*?
HEH HEH HEH... MAYBE THE PRINCIPAL'S FLOWERBED IS GONNA HAVE WEEDS FROM MY MOM'S GARDEN GROWING IN IT.

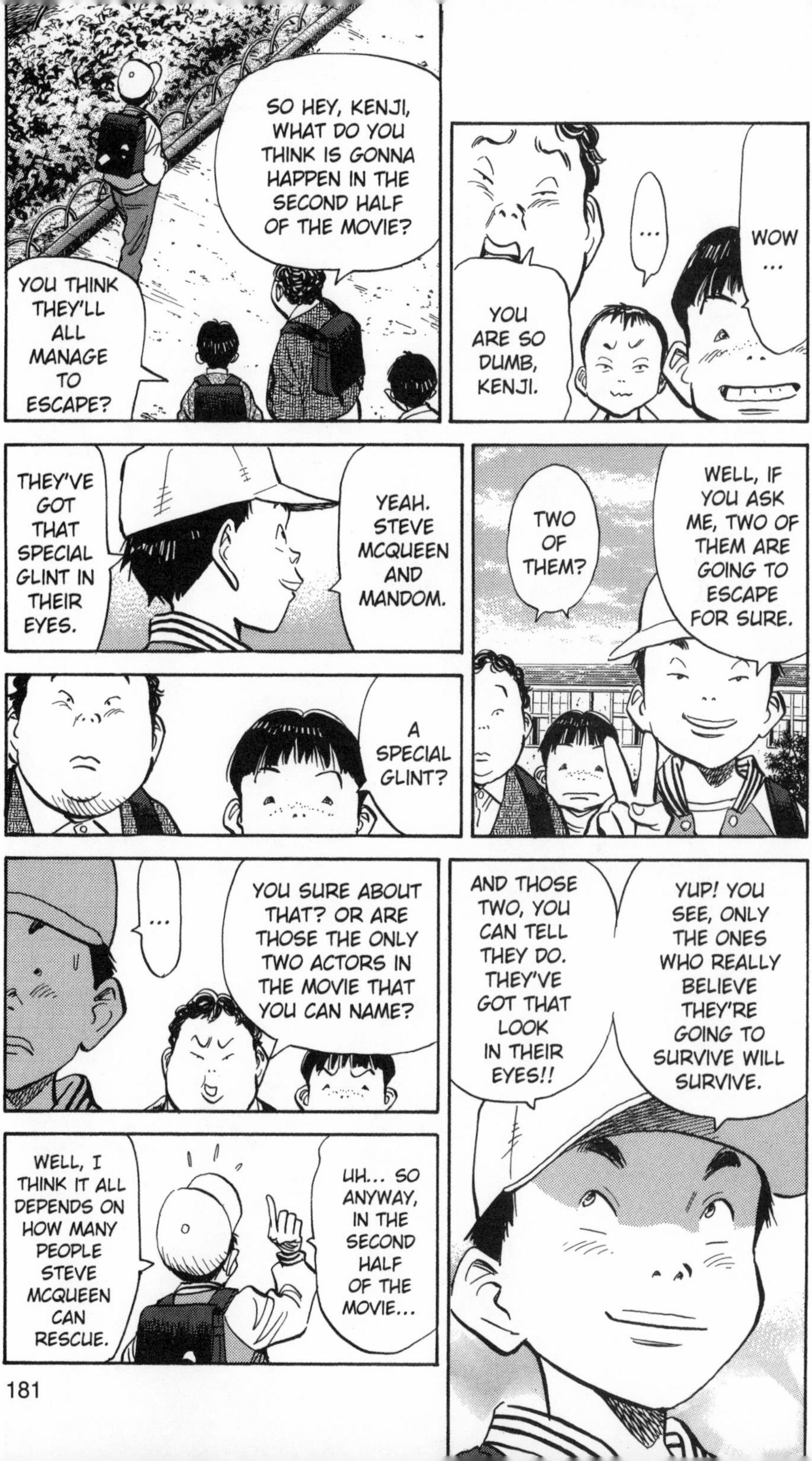
WOW...
...
YOU ARE SO DUMB, KENJI.
SO HEY, KENJI, WHAT DO YOU THINK IS GONNA HAPPEN IN THE SECOND HALF OF THE MOVIE?
YOU THINK THEY'LL ALL MANAGE TO ESCAPE?
WELL, IF YOU ASK ME, TWO OF THEM ARE GOING TO ESCAPE FOR SURE.
TWO OF THEM?
YEAH. STEVE MCQUEEN AND MANDOM.
THEY'VE GOT THAT SPECIAL GLINT IN THEIR EYES.
A SPECIAL GLINT?
YUP! YOU SEE, ONLY THE ONES WHO REALLY BELIEVE THEY'RE GOING TO SURVIVE WILL SURVIVE.
AND THOSE TWO, YOU CAN TELL THEY DO. THEY'VE GOT THAT LOOK IN THEIR EYES!!
YOU SURE ABOUT THAT? OR ARE THOSE THE ONLY TWO ACTORS IN THE MOVIE THAT YOU CAN NAME?
...
UH... SO ANYWAY, IN THE SECOND HALF OF THE MOVIE...
WELL, I THINK IT ALL DEPENDS ON HOW MANY PEOPLE STEVE MCQUEEN CAN RESCUE.

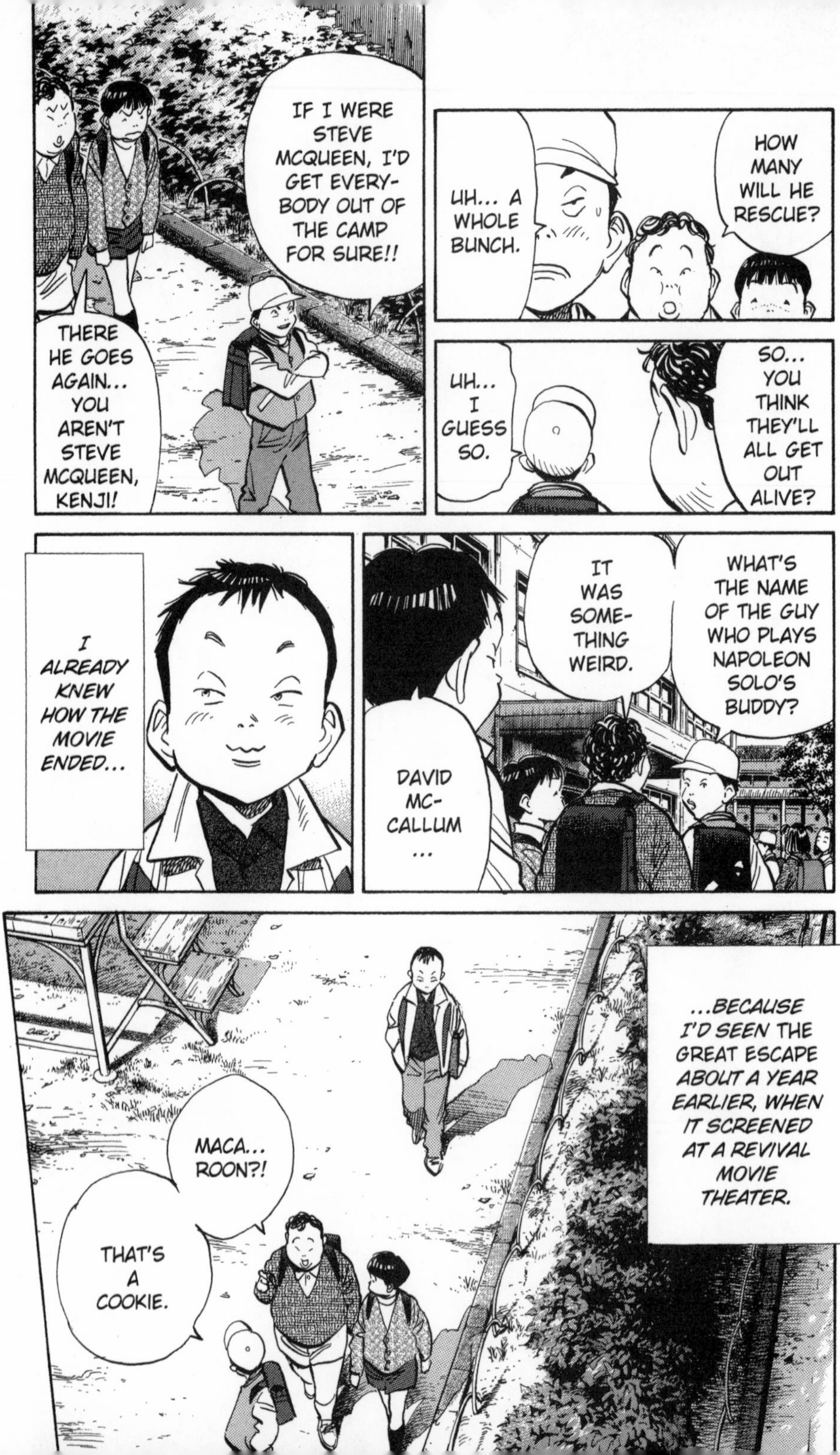
HOW MANY WILL HE RESCUE?
UH... A WHOLE BUNCH.
SO... YOU THINK THEY'LL ALL GET OUT ALIVE?
UH... I GUESS SO.
IF I WERE STEVE MCQUEEN, I'D GET EVERY-BODY OUT OF THE CAMP FOR SURE!!
THERE HE GOES AGAIN... YOU AREN'T STEVE MCQUEEN, KENJI!
WHAT'S THE NAME OF THE GUY WHO PLAYS NAPOLEON SOLO'S BUDDY?
IT WAS SOME-THING WEIRD.
DAVID MC-CALLUM ...
I ALREADY KNEW HOW THE MOVIE ENDED...
...BECAUSE I'D SEEN THE GREAT ESCAPE ABOUT A YEAR EARLIER, WHEN IT SCREENED AT A REVIVAL MOVIE THEATER.
MACA... ROON?!
THAT'S A COOKIE.

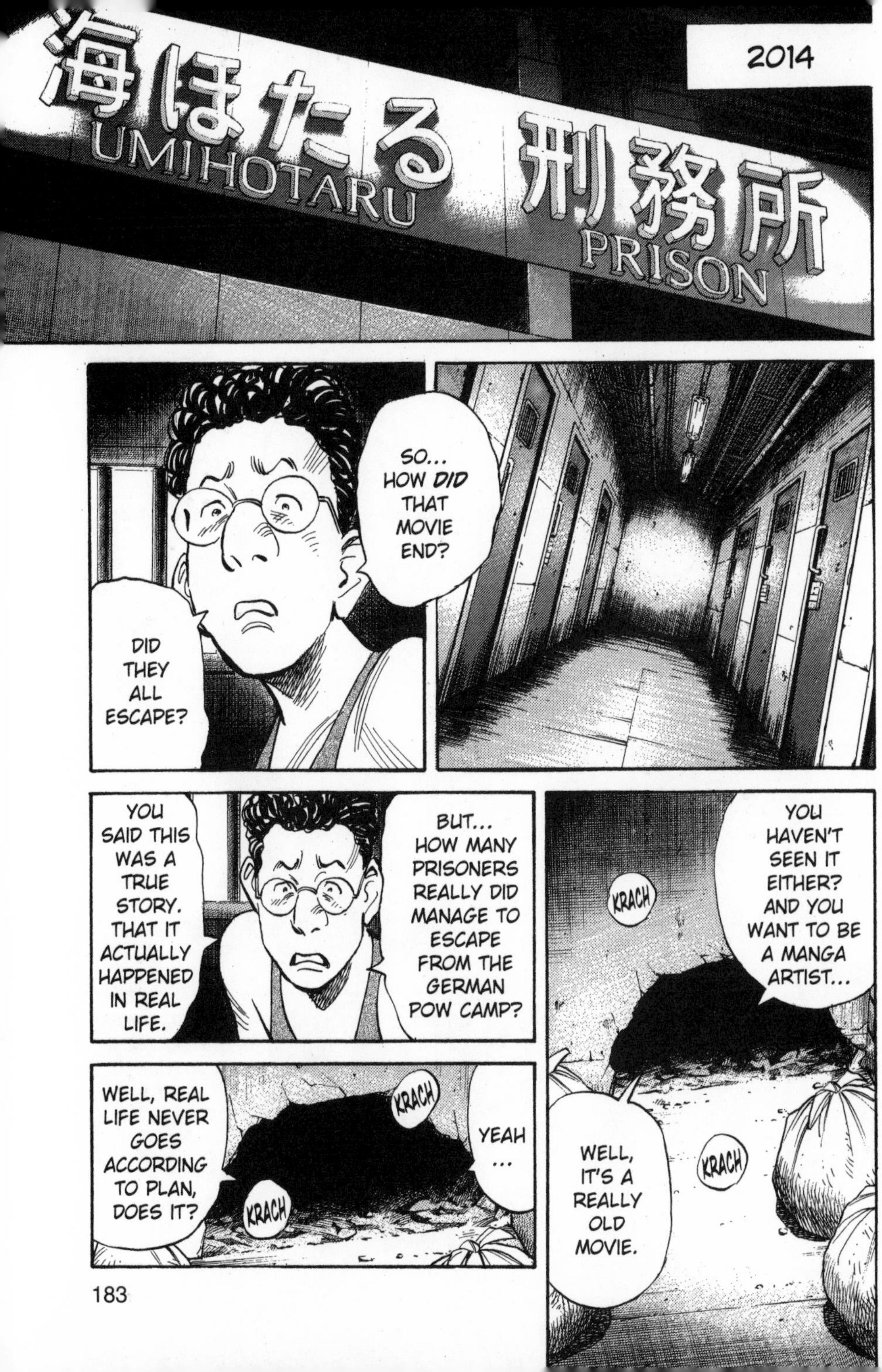
2014
海ほたる 刑務所
UMIHOTARU PRISON
SO... HOW *DID* THAT MOVIE END?
DID THEY ALL ESCAPE?
YOU HAVEN'T SEEN IT EITHER? AND YOU WANT TO BE A MANGA ARTIST...
KRACH
WELL, IT'S A REALLY OLD MOVIE.
KRACH
BUT... HOW MANY PRISONERS REALLY DID MANAGE TO ESCAPE FROM THE GERMAN POW CAMP?
YOU SAID THIS WAS A TRUE STORY. THAT IT ACTUALLY HAPPENED IN REAL LIFE.
YEAH...
KRACH
WELL, REAL LIFE NEVER GOES ACCORDING TO PLAN, DOES IT?
KRACH

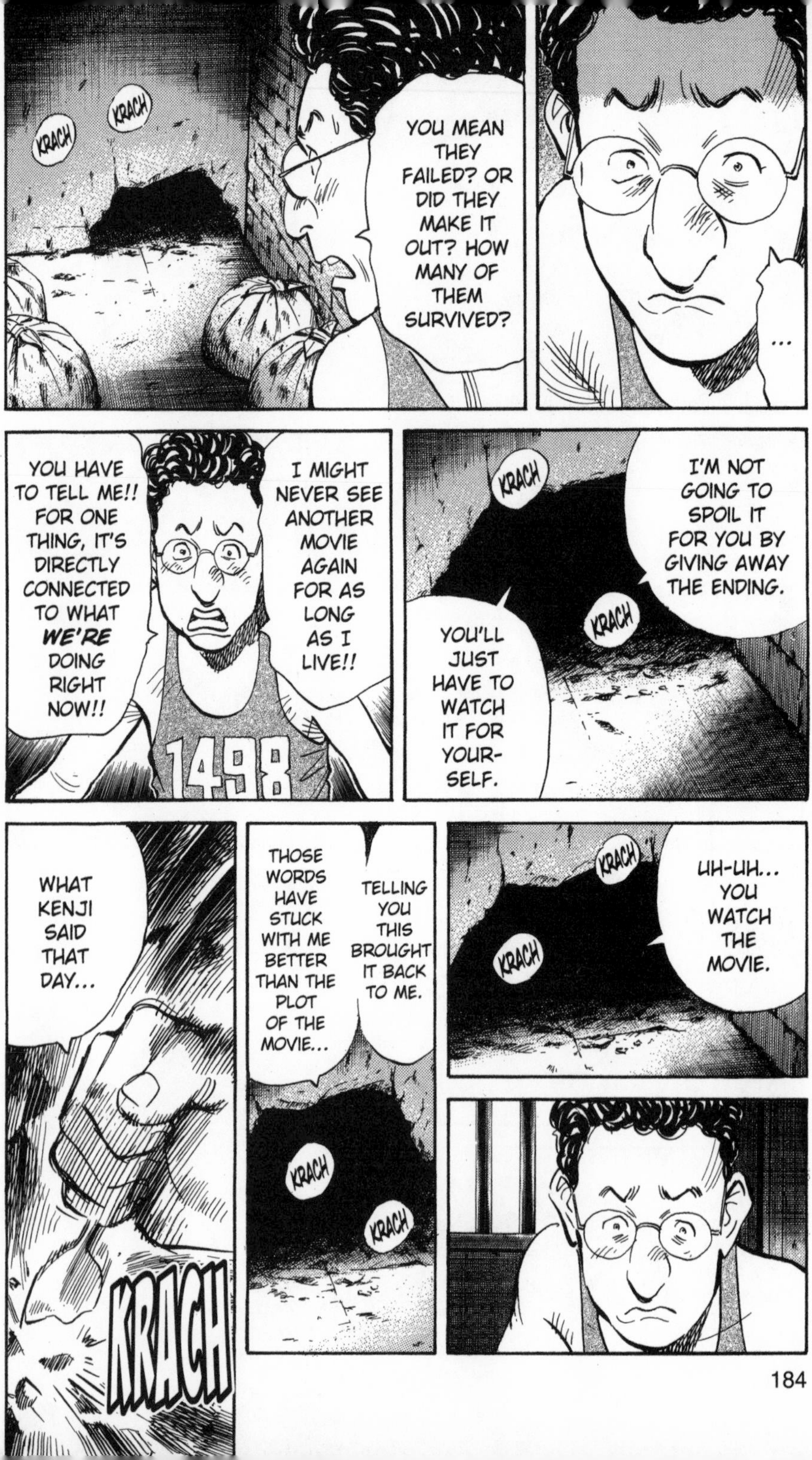
...
KRACH
KRACH
YOU MEAN THEY FAILED? OR DID THEY MAKE IT OUT? HOW MANY OF THEM SURVIVED?
I'M NOT GOING TO SPOIL IT FOR YOU BY GIVING AWAY THE ENDING.
KRACH
KRACH
YOU'LL JUST HAVE TO WATCH IT FOR YOUR-SELF.
I MIGHT NEVER SEE ANOTHER MOVIE AGAIN FOR AS LONG AS I LIVE!!
YOU HAVE TO TELL ME!! FOR ONE THING, IT'S DIRECTLY CONNECTED TO WHAT ***WE'RE*** DOING RIGHT NOW!!
1498
UH-UH... YOU WATCH THE MOVIE.
KRACH
KRACH
TELLING YOU THIS BROUGHT IT BACK TO ME.
THOSE WORDS HAVE STUCK WITH ME BETTER THAN THE PLOT OF THE MOVIE...
KRACH
KRACH
WHAT KENJI SAID THAT DAY...
KRACH

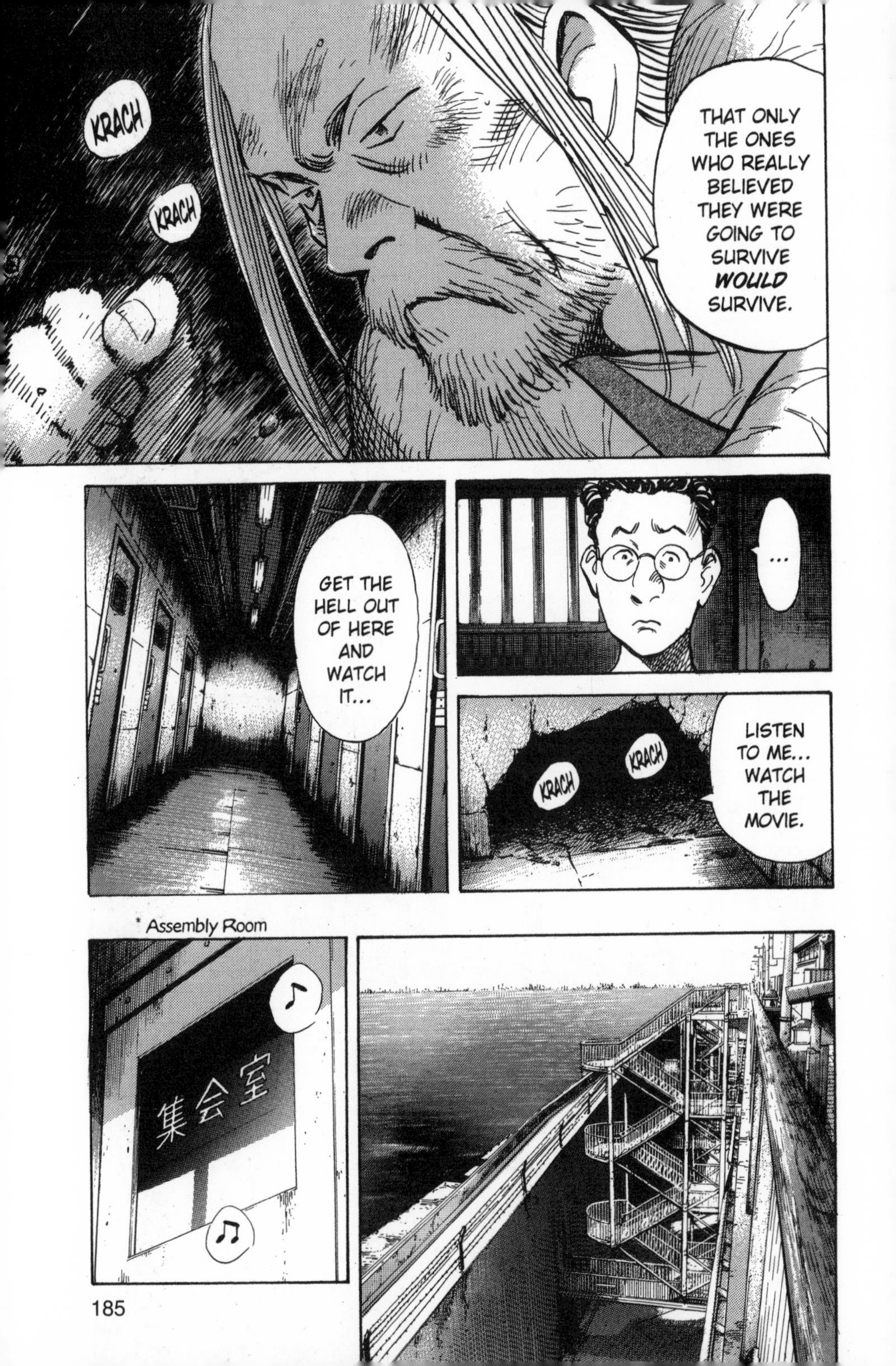
THAT ONLY THE ONES WHO REALLY BELIEVED THEY WERE GOING TO SURVIVE **WOULD** SURVIVE.
KRACH
KRACH
...
LISTEN TO ME... WATCH THE MOVIE.
KRACH
KRACH
GET THE HELL OUT OF HERE AND WATCH IT...
集会室
* Assembly Room

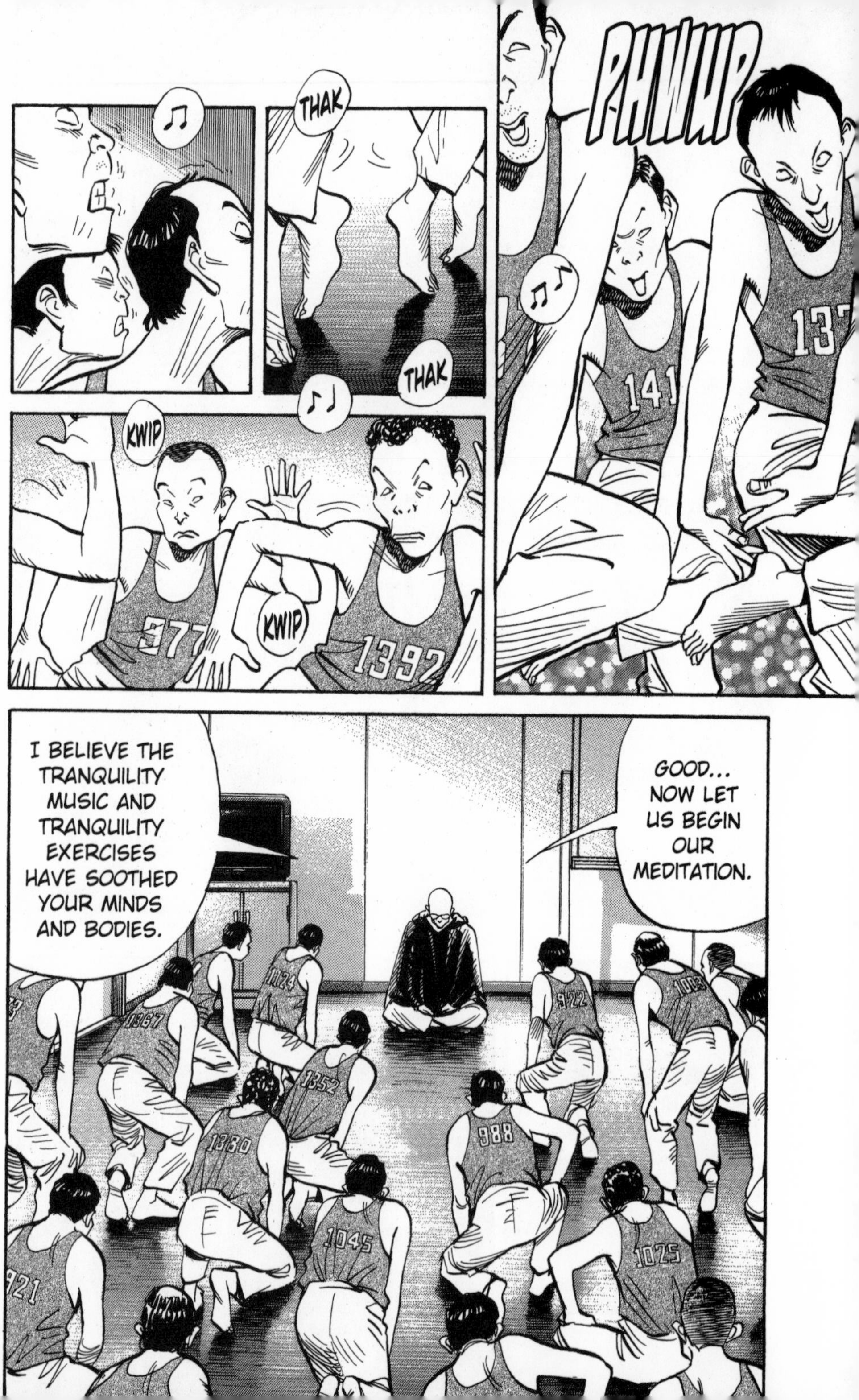
PHWUP
♫♪
THAK
THAK
♫
♪♩
KWIP
KWIP
GOOD... NOW LET US BEGIN OUR MEDITATION.
I BELIEVE THE TRANQUILITY MUSIC AND TRANQUILITY EXERCISES HAVE SOOTHED YOUR MINDS AND BODIES.

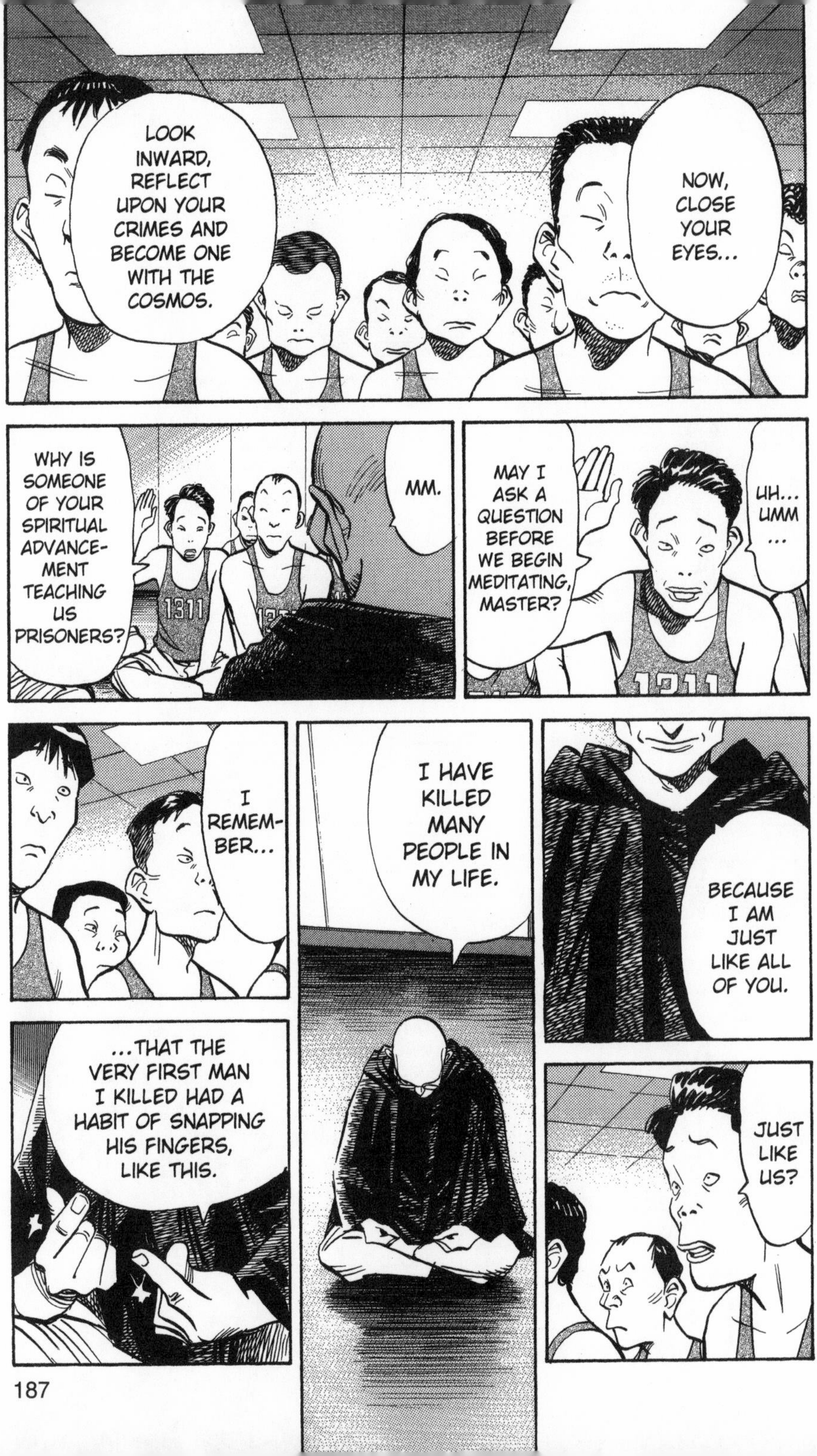
NOW, CLOSE YOUR EYES...
LOOK INWARD, REFLECT UPON YOUR CRIMES AND BECOME ONE WITH THE COSMOS.
UH... UMM ...
MAY I ASK A QUESTION BEFORE WE BEGIN MEDITATING, MASTER?
MM.
WHY IS SOMEONE OF YOUR SPIRITUAL ADVANCEMENT TEACHING US PRISONERS?
1311
BECAUSE I AM JUST LIKE ALL OF YOU.
JUST LIKE US?
I HAVE KILLED MANY PEOPLE IN MY LIFE.
I REMEMBER...
...THAT THE VERY FIRST MAN I KILLED HAD A HABIT OF SNAPPING HIS FINGERS, LIKE THIS.

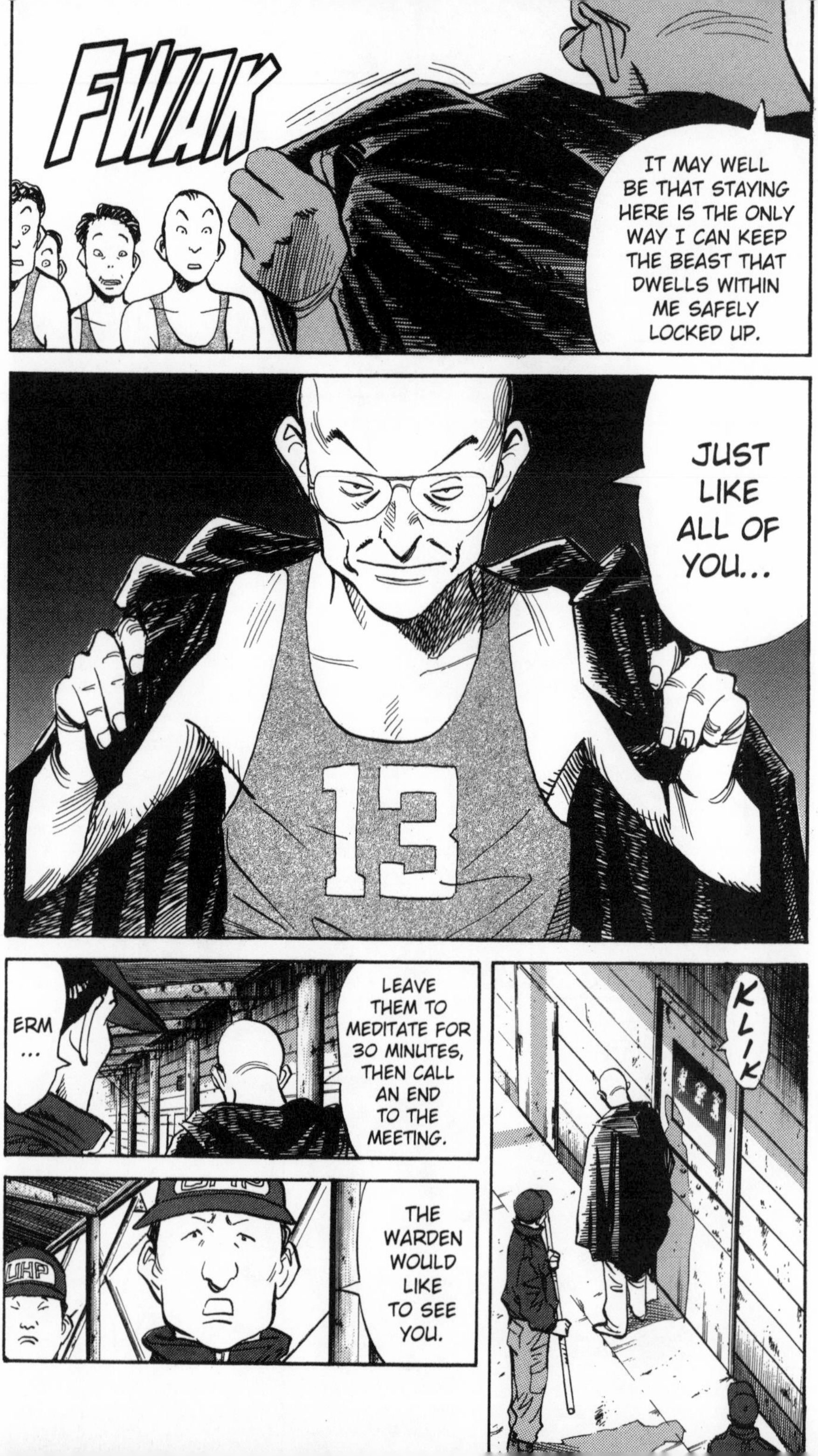
FWAK
IT MAY WELL BE THAT STAYING HERE IS THE ONLY WAY I CAN KEEP THE BEAST THAT DWELLS WITHIN ME SAFELY LOCKED UP.
JUST LIKE ALL OF YOU...
KLIK
LEAVE THEM TO MEDITATE FOR 30 MINUTES, THEN CALL AN END TO THE MEETING.
ERM ...
THE WARDEN WOULD LIKE TO SEE YOU.

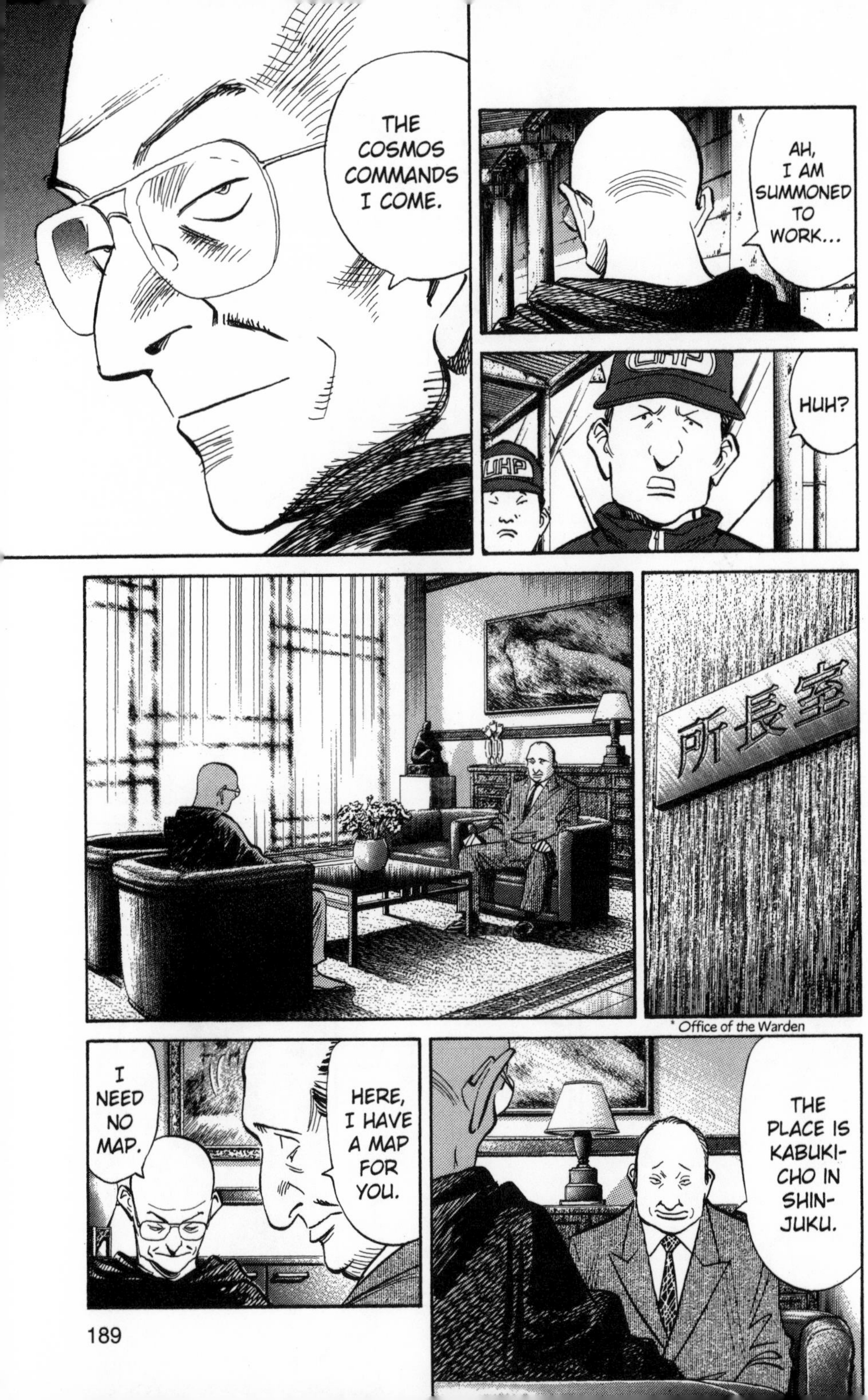
AH, I AM SUMMONED TO WORK...
HUH?
THE COSMOS COMMANDS I COME.
所長室
* Office of the Warden
THE PLACE IS KABUKICHO IN SHINJUKU.
HERE, I HAVE A MAP FOR YOU.
I NEED NO MAP.

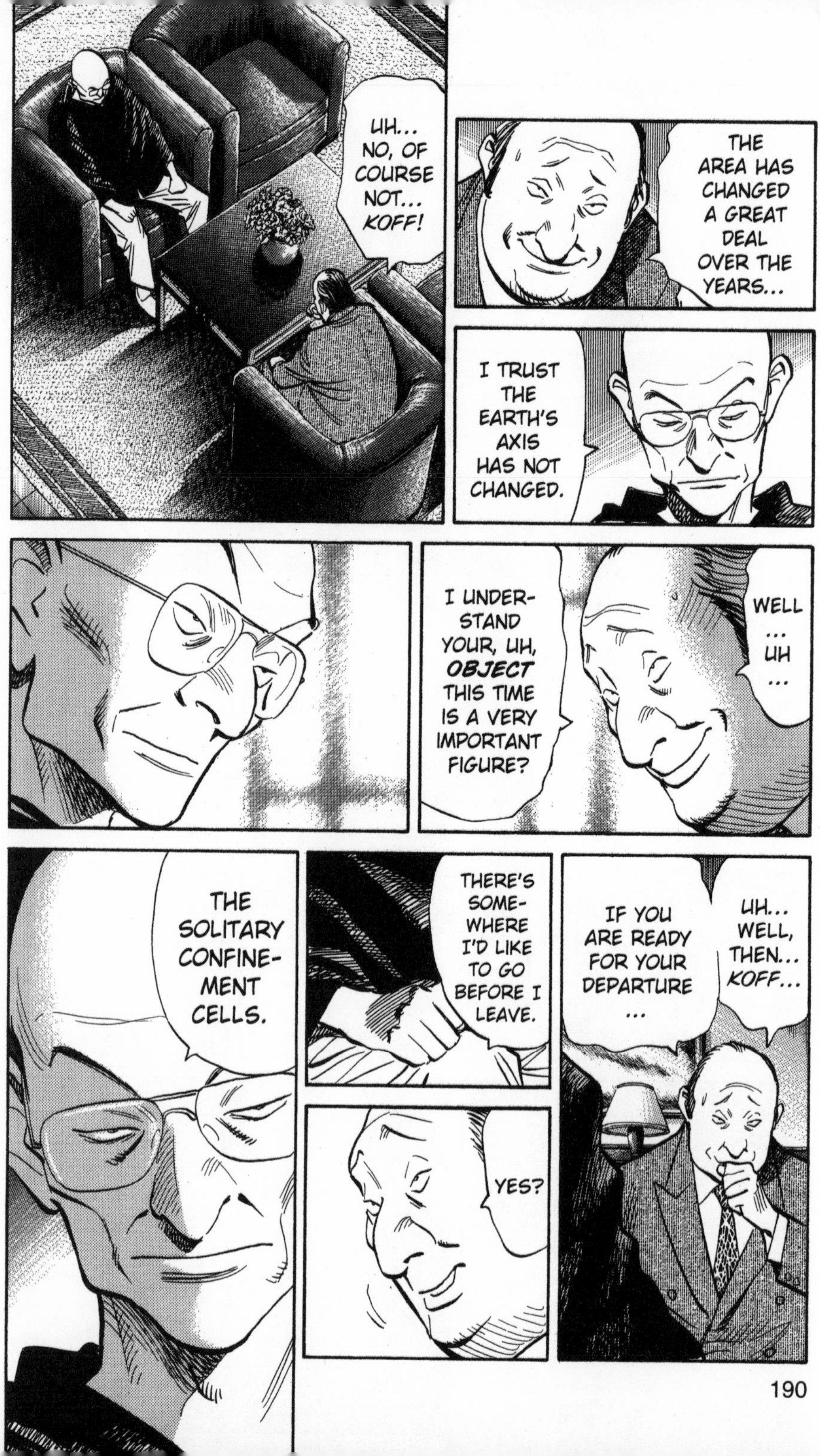
THE AREA HAS CHANGED A GREAT DEAL OVER THE YEARS...
I TRUST THE EARTH'S AXIS HAS NOT CHANGED.
UH... NO, OF COURSE NOT... *KOFF!*
WELL... UH...
I UNDER-STAND YOUR, UH, ***OBJECT*** THIS TIME IS A VERY IMPORTANT FIGURE?
UH... WELL, THEN... *KOFF*...
IF YOU ARE READY FOR YOUR DEPARTURE...
THERE'S SOME-WHERE I'D LIKE TO GO BEFORE I LEAVE.
YES?
THE SOLITARY CONFINE-MENT CELLS.

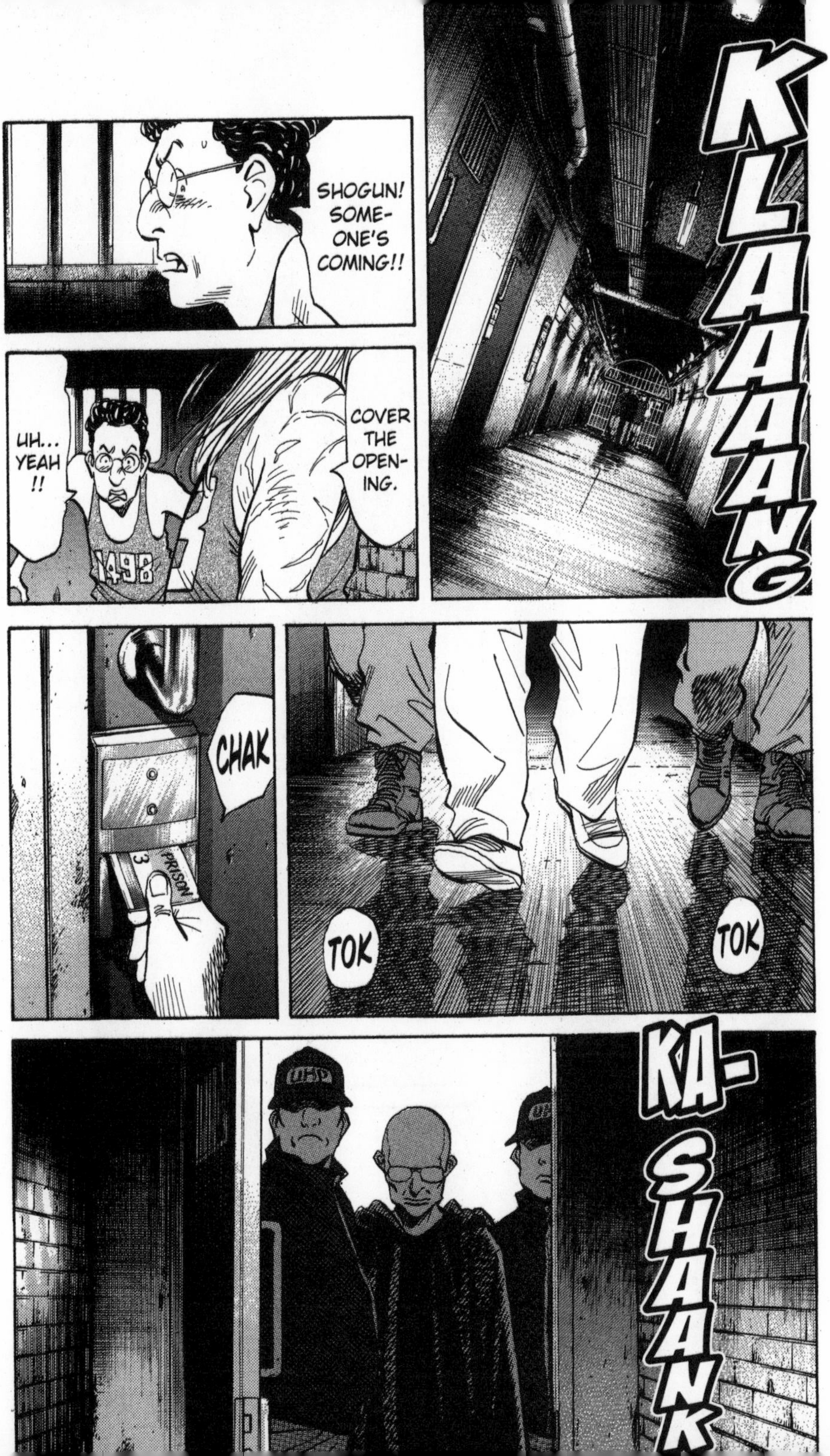
KLAAAANG
SHOGUN! SOME-ONE'S COMING!!
COVER THE OPEN-ING.
UH... YEAH !!
1498
TOK
TOK
CHAK
PRISON
3
KA-SHAANK
UHP

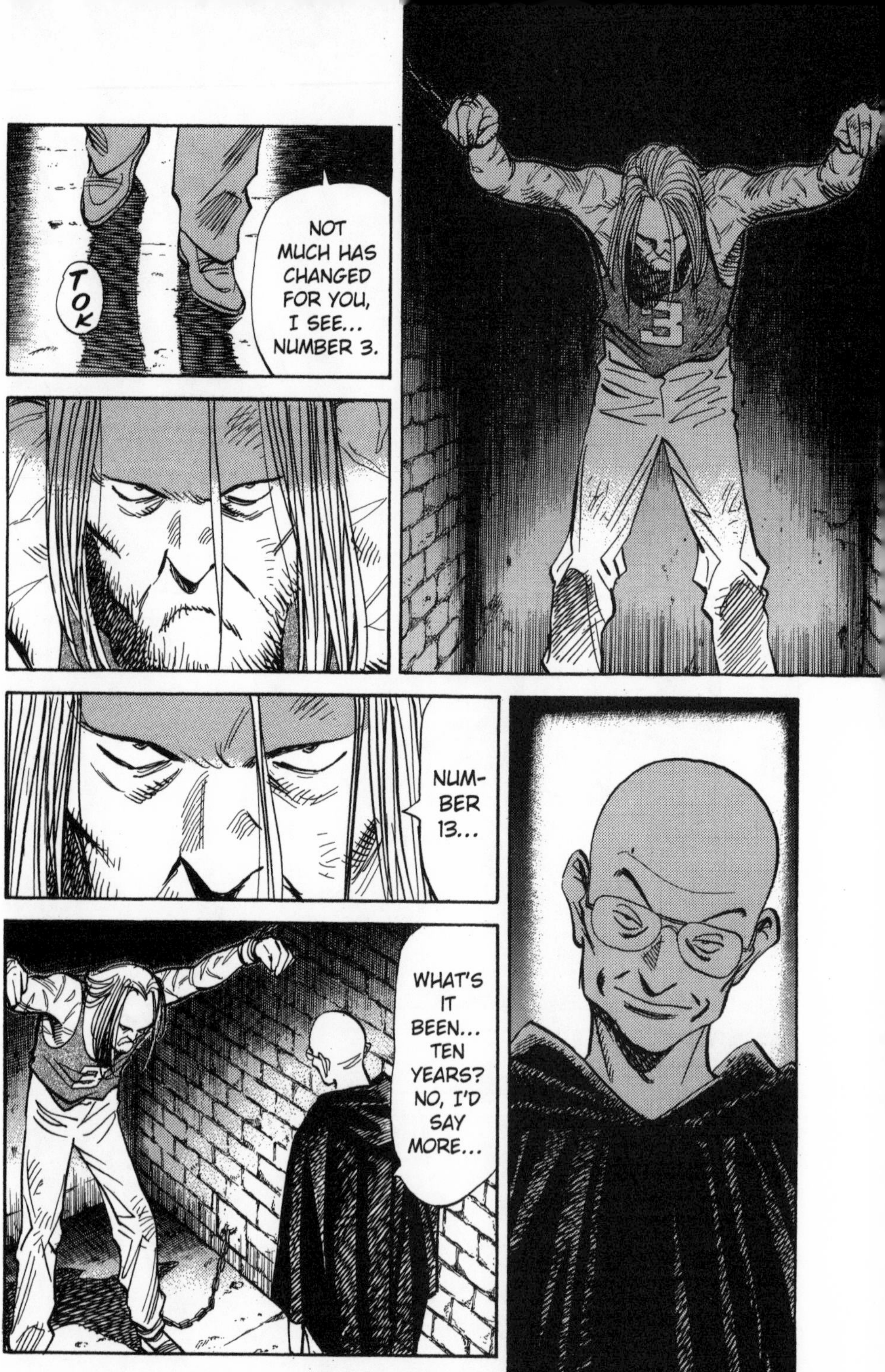
NOT MUCH HAS CHANGED FOR YOU, I SEE... NUMBER 3.
TOK
NUM-BER 13...
WHAT'S IT BEEN... TEN YEARS? NO, I'D SAY MORE...

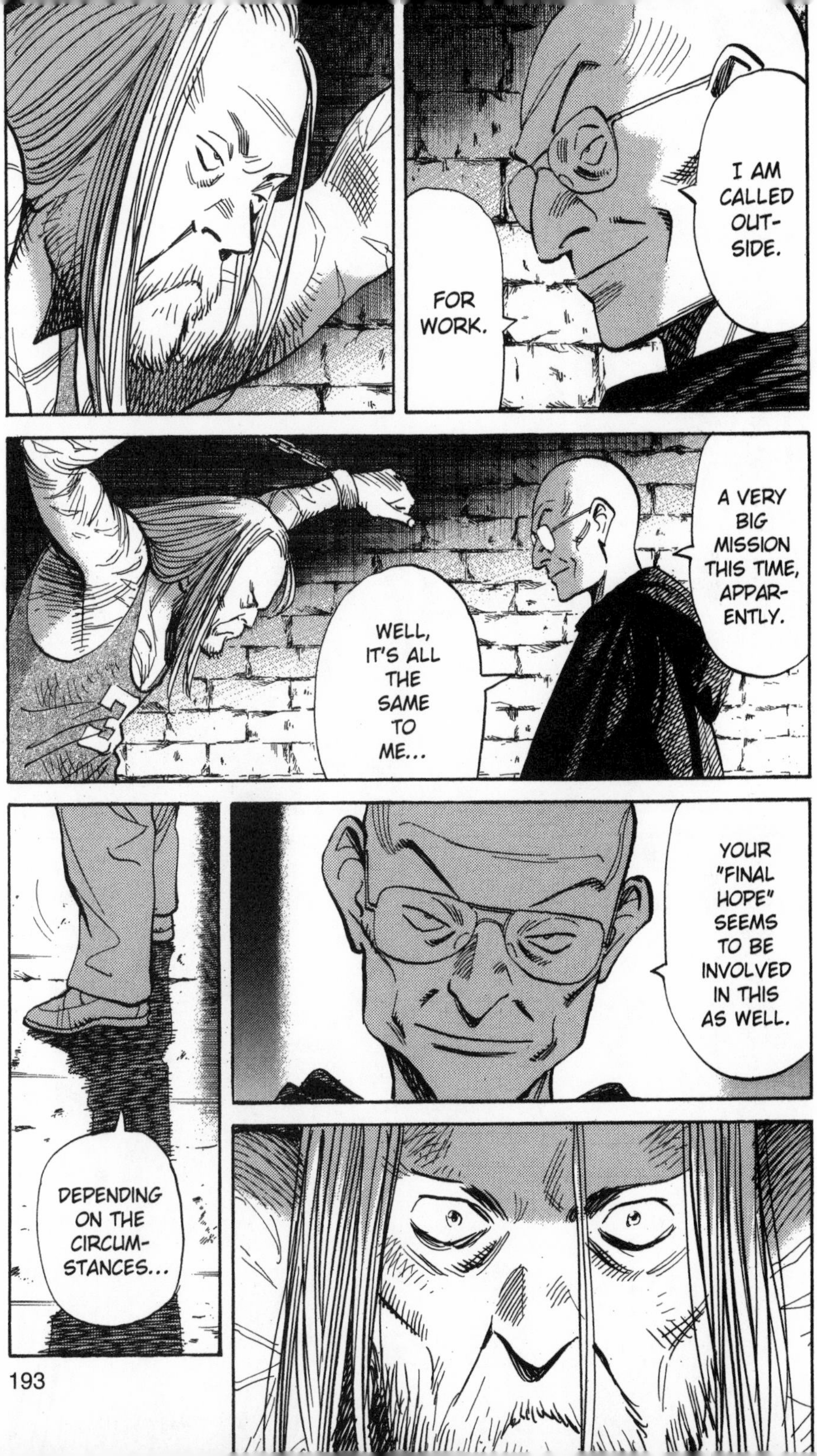
I AM CALLED OUT-SIDE.
FOR WORK.
A VERY BIG MISSION THIS TIME, APPAR-ENTLY.
WELL, IT'S ALL THE SAME TO ME...
YOUR "FINAL HOPE" SEEMS TO BE INVOLVED IN THIS AS WELL.
DEPENDING ON THE CIRCUM-STANCES...

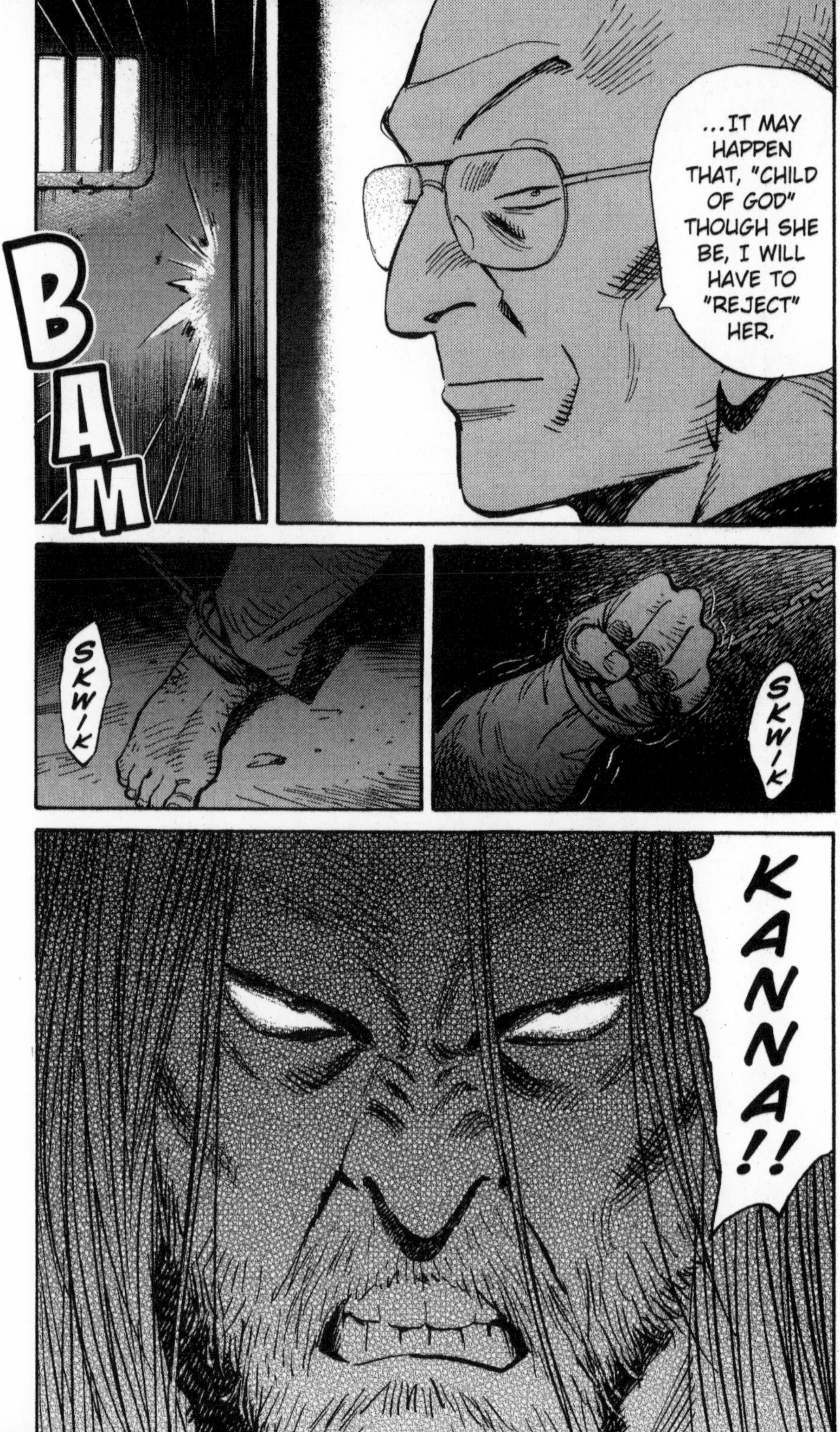
...IT MAY HAPPEN THAT, "CHILD OF GOD" THOUGH SHE BE, I WILL HAVE TO "REJECT" HER.
BAM
SKWIK
SKWIK
KANNA!!

Chapter 11 Test of Courage

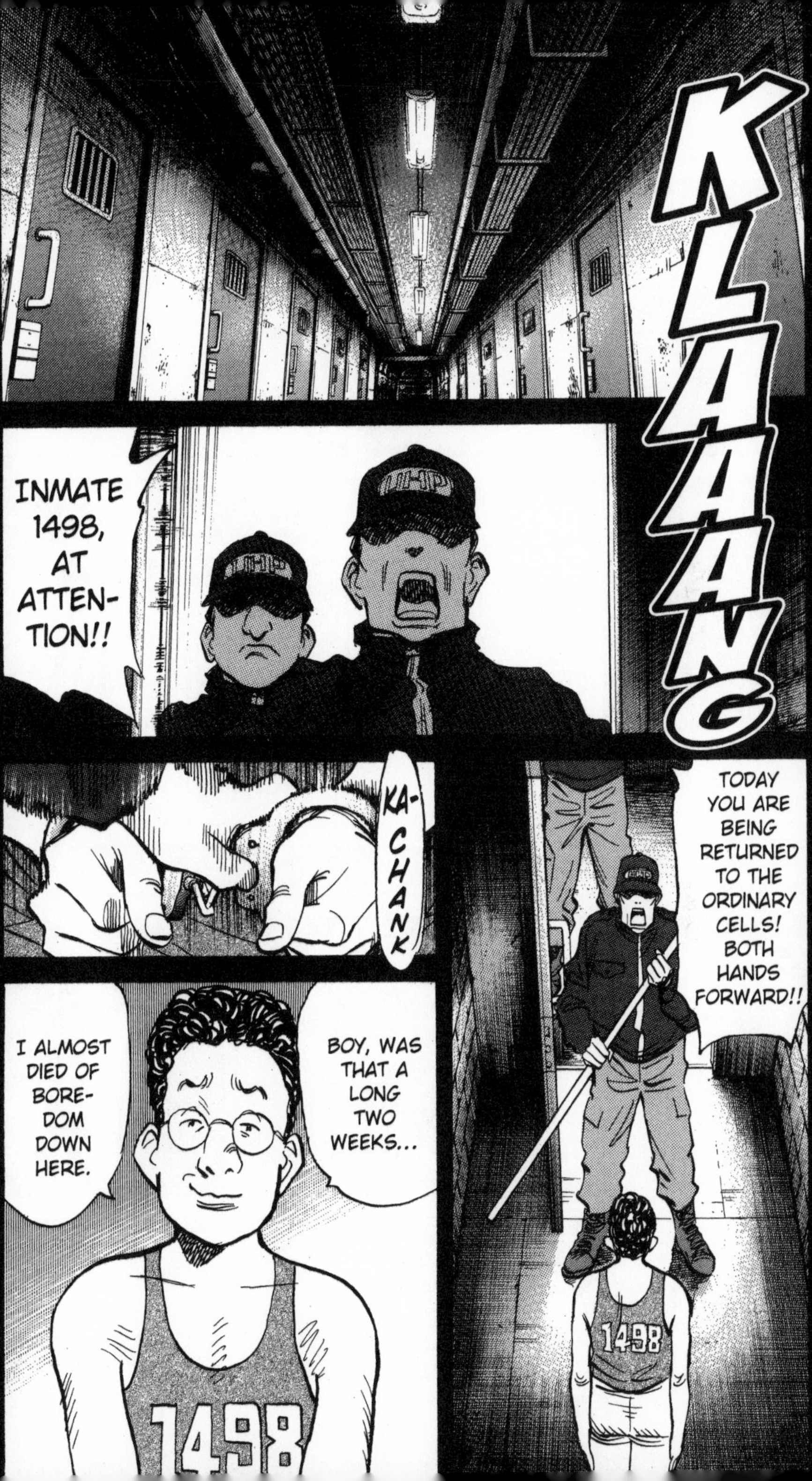
KLAANG
INMATE 1498, AT ATTEN-TION!!
TODAY YOU ARE BEING RETURNED TO THE ORDINARY CELLS! BOTH HANDS FORWARD!!
KA-CHANK
BOY, WAS THAT A LONG TWO WEEKS...
I ALMOST DIED OF BORE-DOM DOWN HERE.

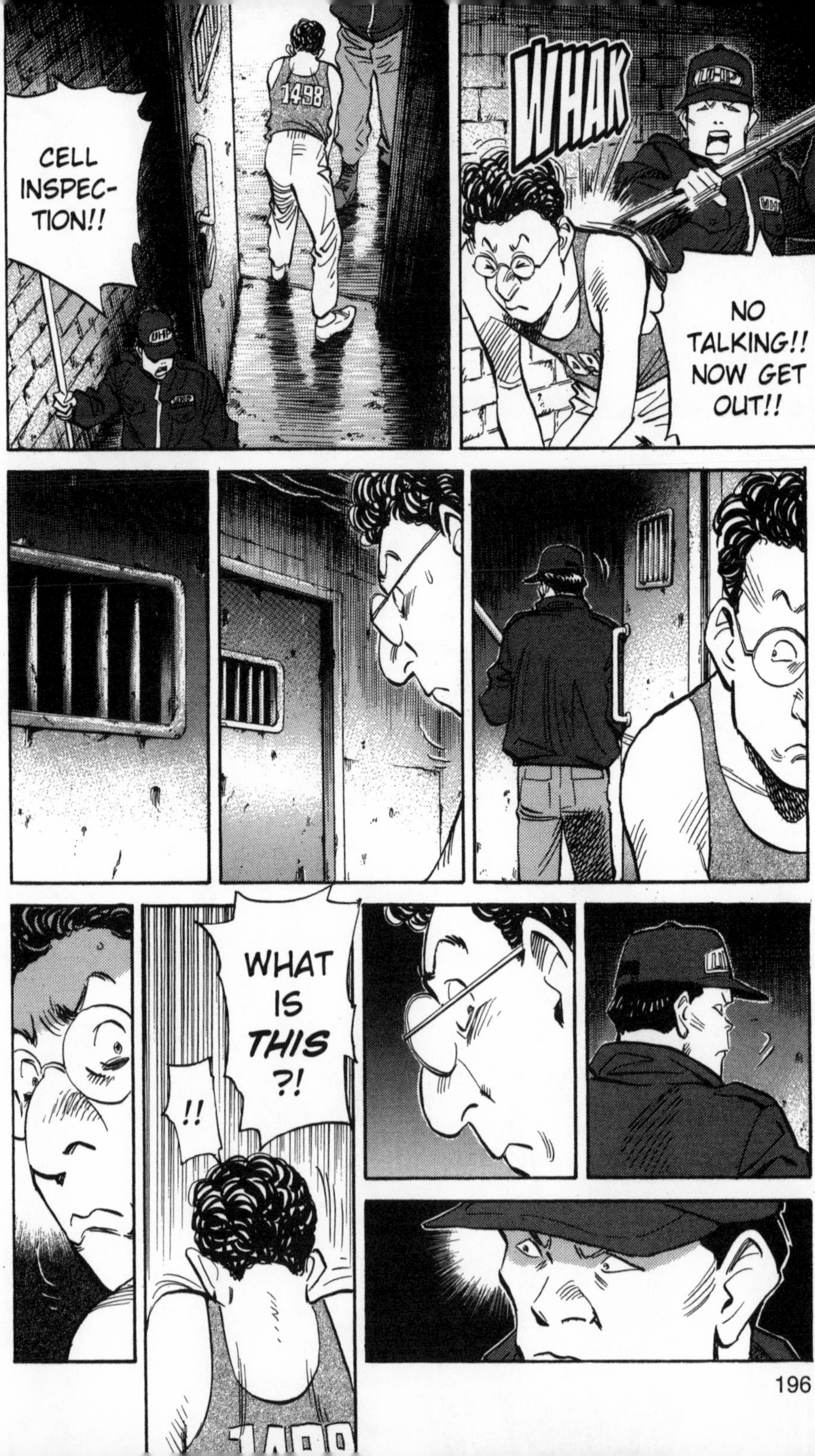
WHAK
NO TALKING!! NOW GET OUT!!
CELL INSPEC-TION!!
WHAT IS THIS?!
!!

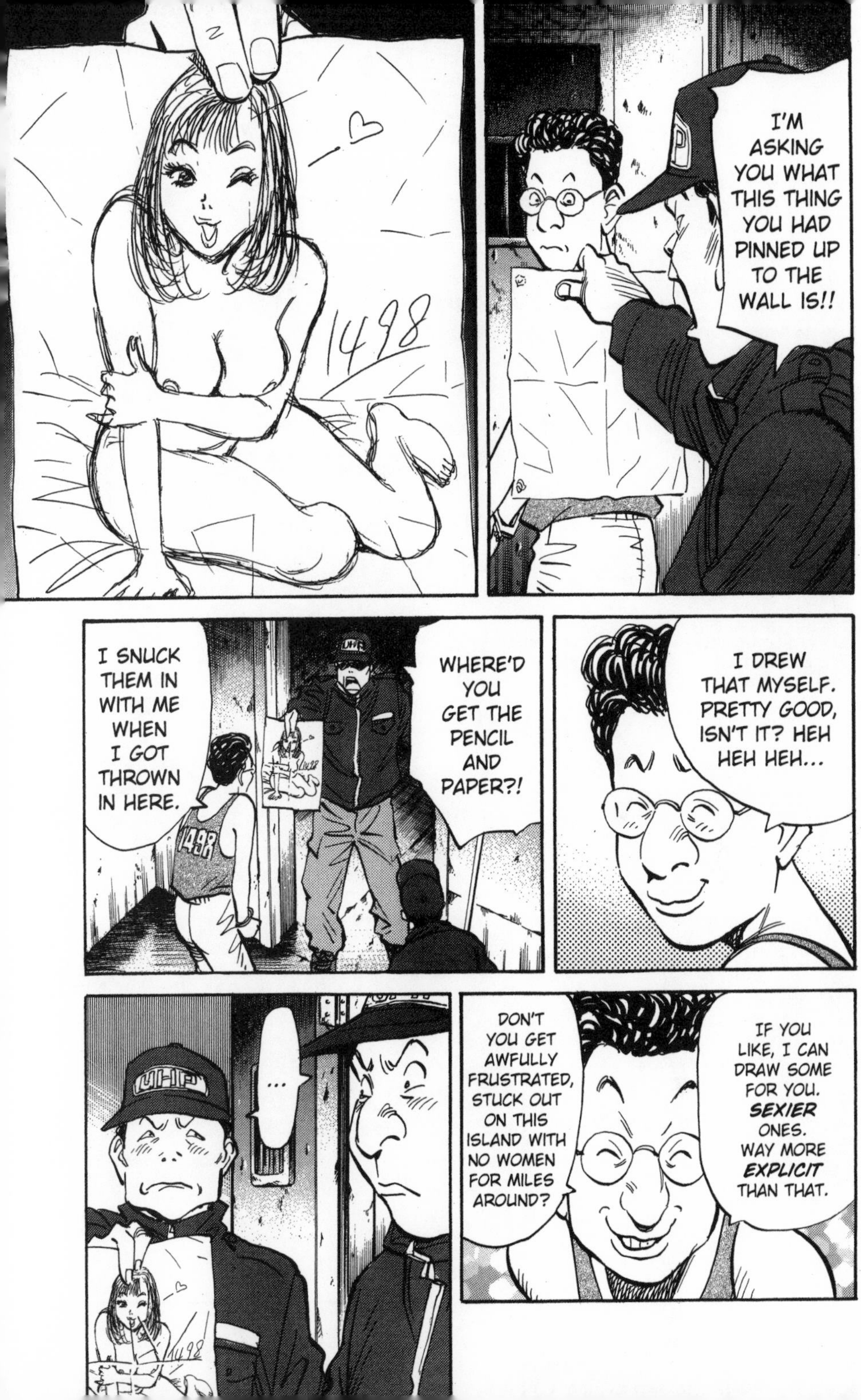
I'M ASKING YOU WHAT THIS THING YOU HAD PINNED UP TO THE WALL IS!!
1498
I DREW THAT MYSELF. PRETTY GOOD, ISN'T IT? HEH HEH HEH...
WHERE'D YOU GET THE PENCIL AND PAPER?!
I SNUCK THEM IN WITH ME WHEN I GOT THROWN IN HERE.
IF YOU LIKE, I CAN DRAW SOME FOR YOU. ***SEXIER*** ONES. WAY MORE ***EXPLICIT*** THAN THAT.
DON'T YOU GET AWFULLY FRUSTRATED, STUCK OUT ON THIS ISLAND WITH NO WOMEN FOR MILES AROUND?
...

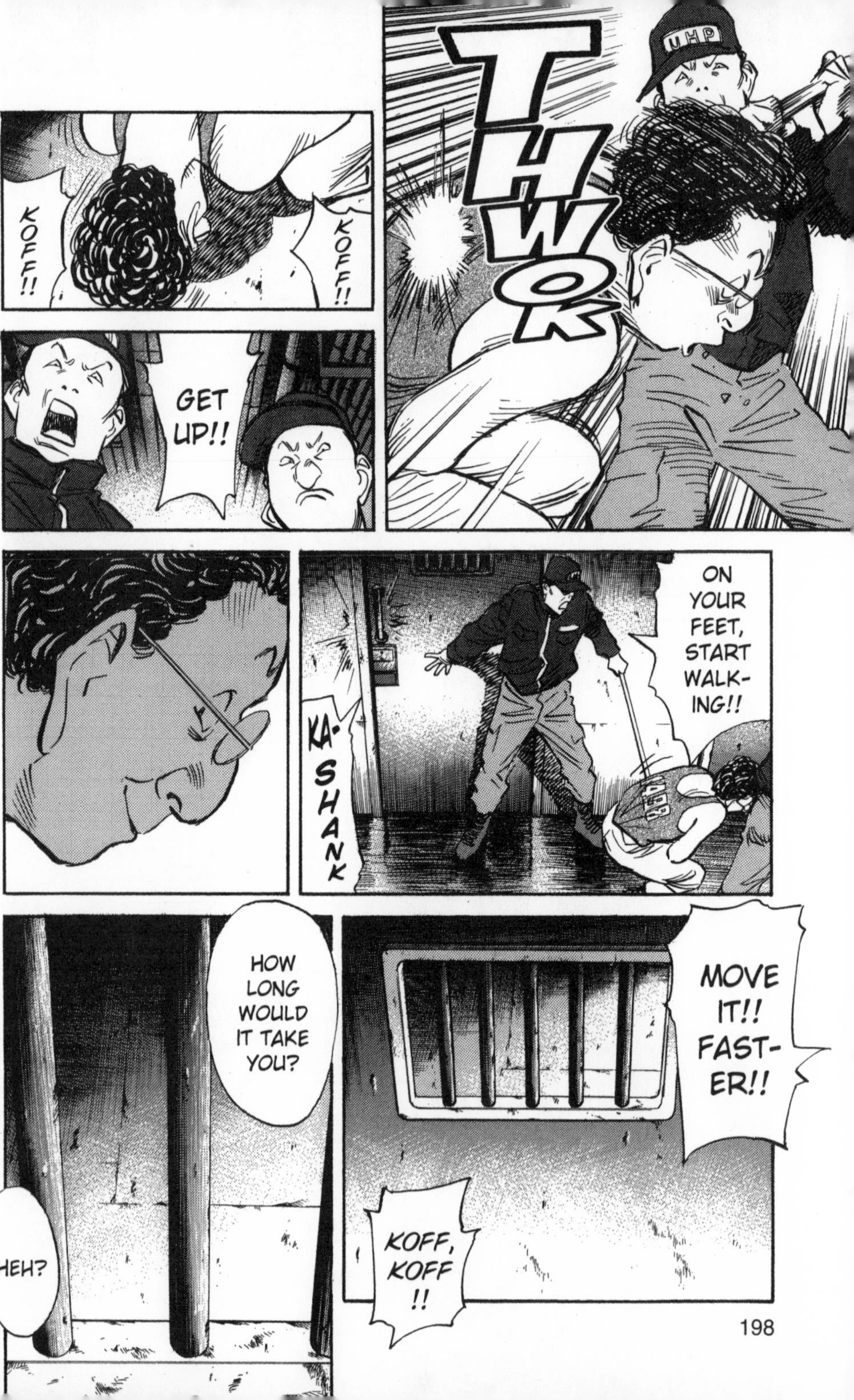
THWOK
KOFF!!
KOFF!!
GET UP!!
ON YOUR FEET, START WALKING!!
KA-SHANK
MOVE IT!! FASTER!!
KOFF, KOFF!!
HOW LONG WOULD IT TAKE YOU?
HEH?

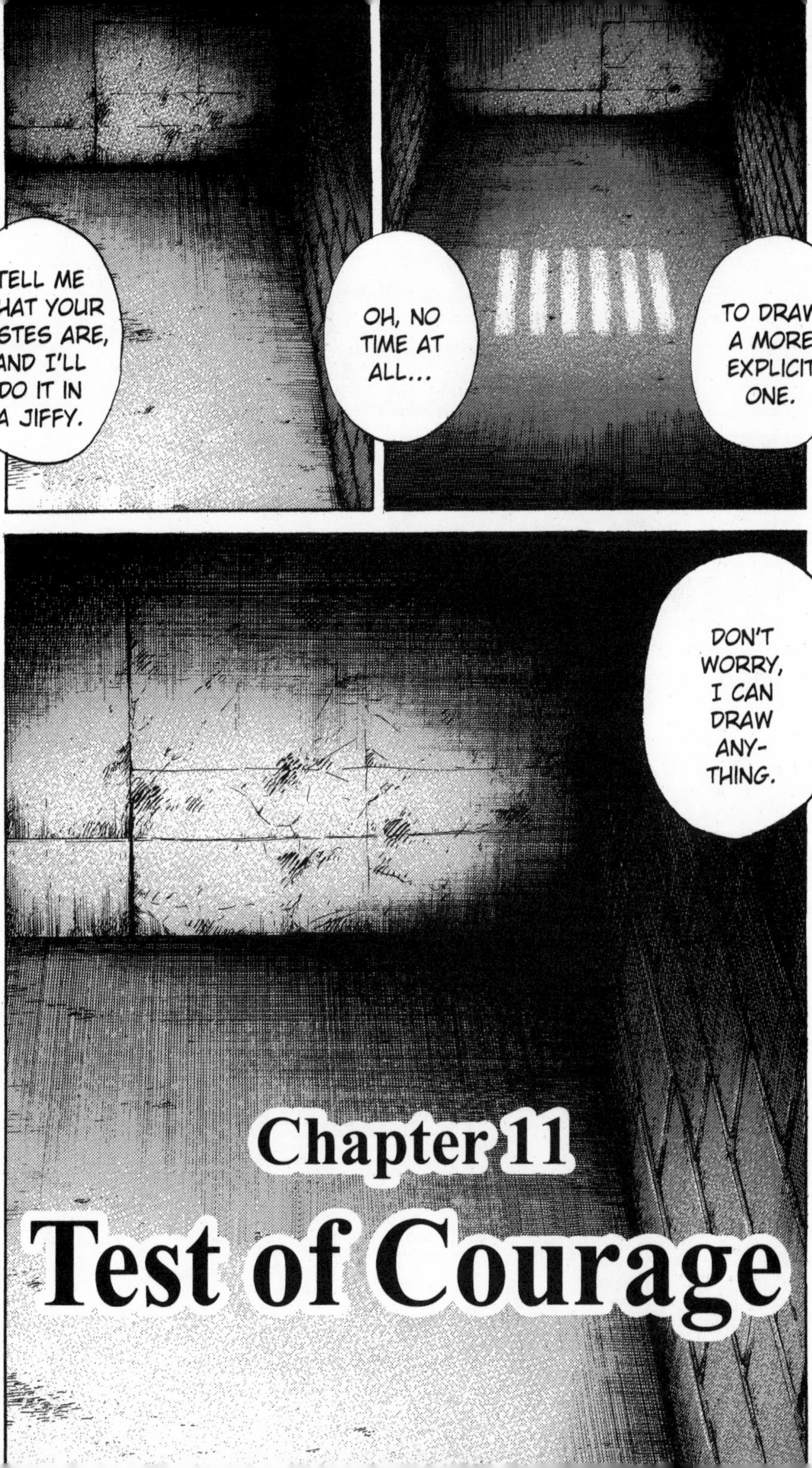
TO DRAW A MORE EXPLICIT ONE.
OH, NO TIME AT ALL...
TELL ME WHAT YOUR TASTES ARE, AND I'LL DO IT IN A JIFFY.
DON'T WORRY, I CAN DRAW ANY-THING.

Chapter 11

Test of Courage

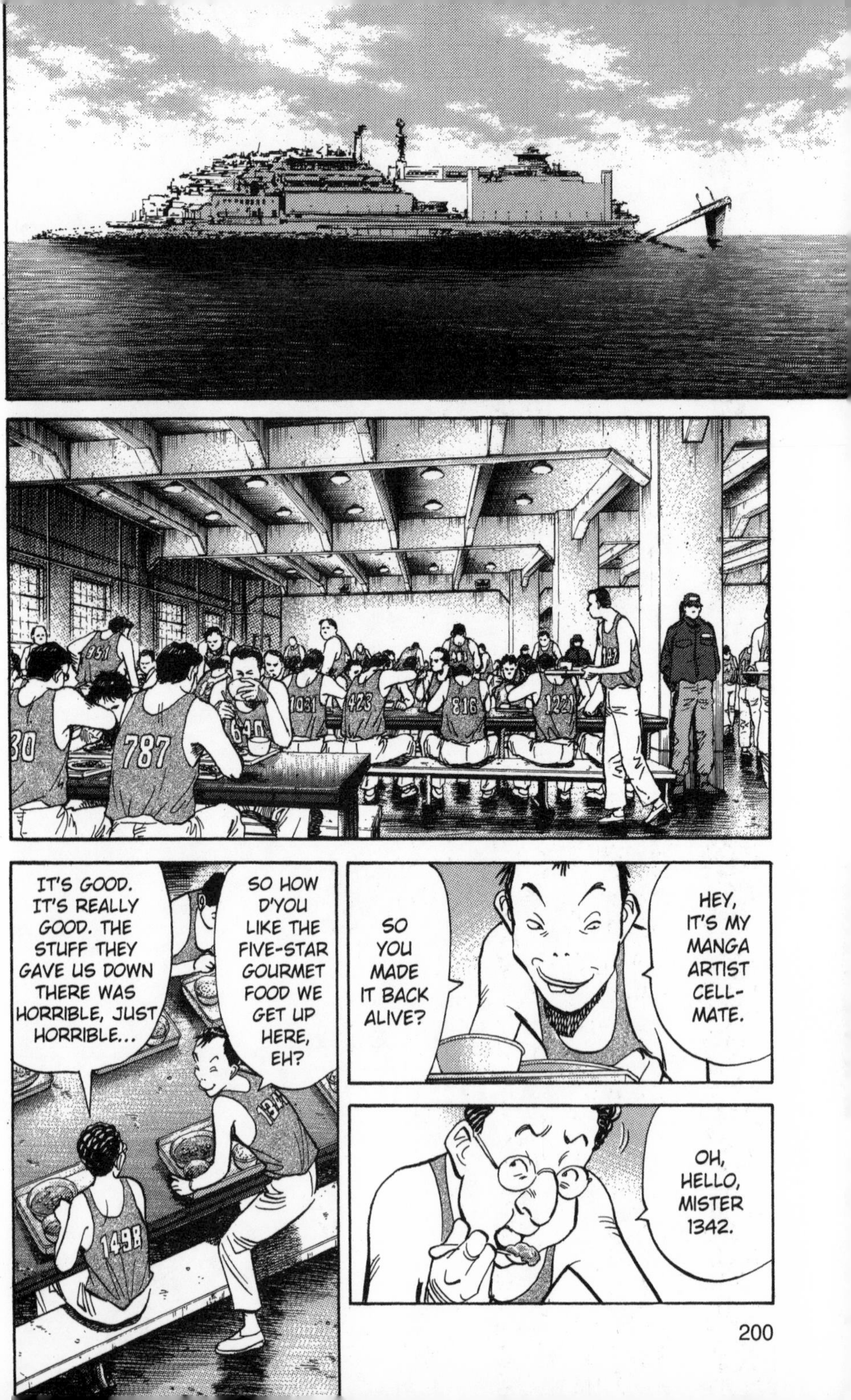
HEY, IT'S MY MANGA ARTIST CELL-MATE.
SO YOU MADE IT BACK ALIVE?
OH, HELLO, MISTER 1342.
SO HOW D'YOU LIKE THE FIVE-STAR GOURMET FOOD WE GET UP HERE, EH?
IT'S GOOD. IT'S REALLY GOOD. THE STUFF THEY GAVE US DOWN THERE WAS HORRIBLE, JUST HORRIBLE...

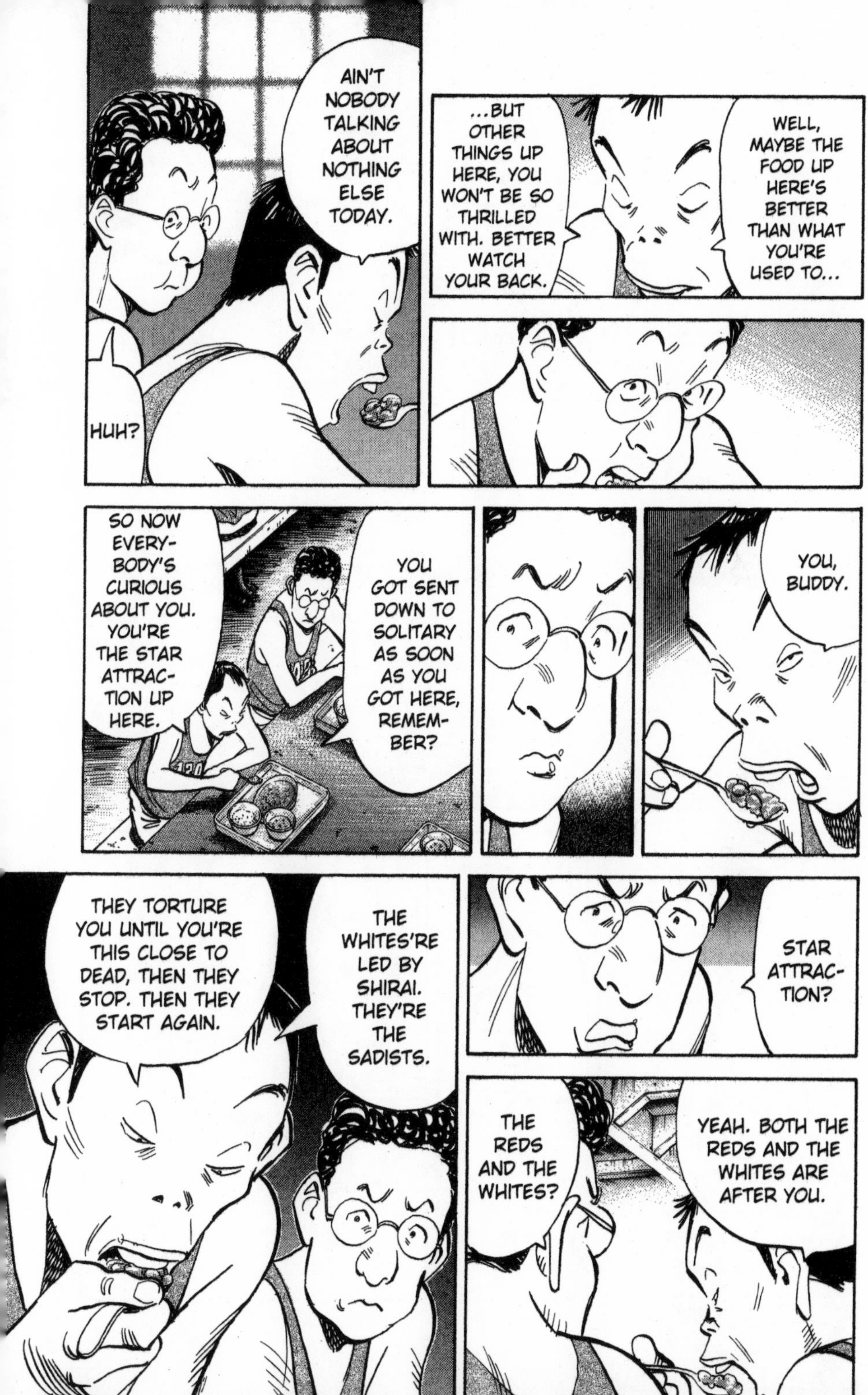
WELL, MAYBE THE FOOD UP HERE'S BETTER THAN WHAT YOU'RE USED TO...
...BUT OTHER THINGS UP HERE, YOU WON'T BE SO THRILLED WITH. BETTER WATCH YOUR BACK.
AIN'T NOBODY TALKING ABOUT NOTHING ELSE TODAY.
HUH?
YOU, BUDDY.
YOU GOT SENT DOWN TO SOLITARY AS SOON AS YOU GOT HERE, REMEMBER?
SO NOW EVERYBODY'S CURIOUS ABOUT YOU. YOU'RE THE STAR ATTRACTION UP HERE.
STAR ATTRACTION?
YEAH. BOTH THE REDS AND THE WHITES ARE AFTER YOU.
THE REDS AND THE WHITES?
THE WHITES'RE LED BY SHIRAI. THEY'RE THE SADISTS.
THEY TORTURE YOU UNTIL YOU'RE THIS CLOSE TO DEAD, THEN THEY STOP. THEN THEY START AGAIN.

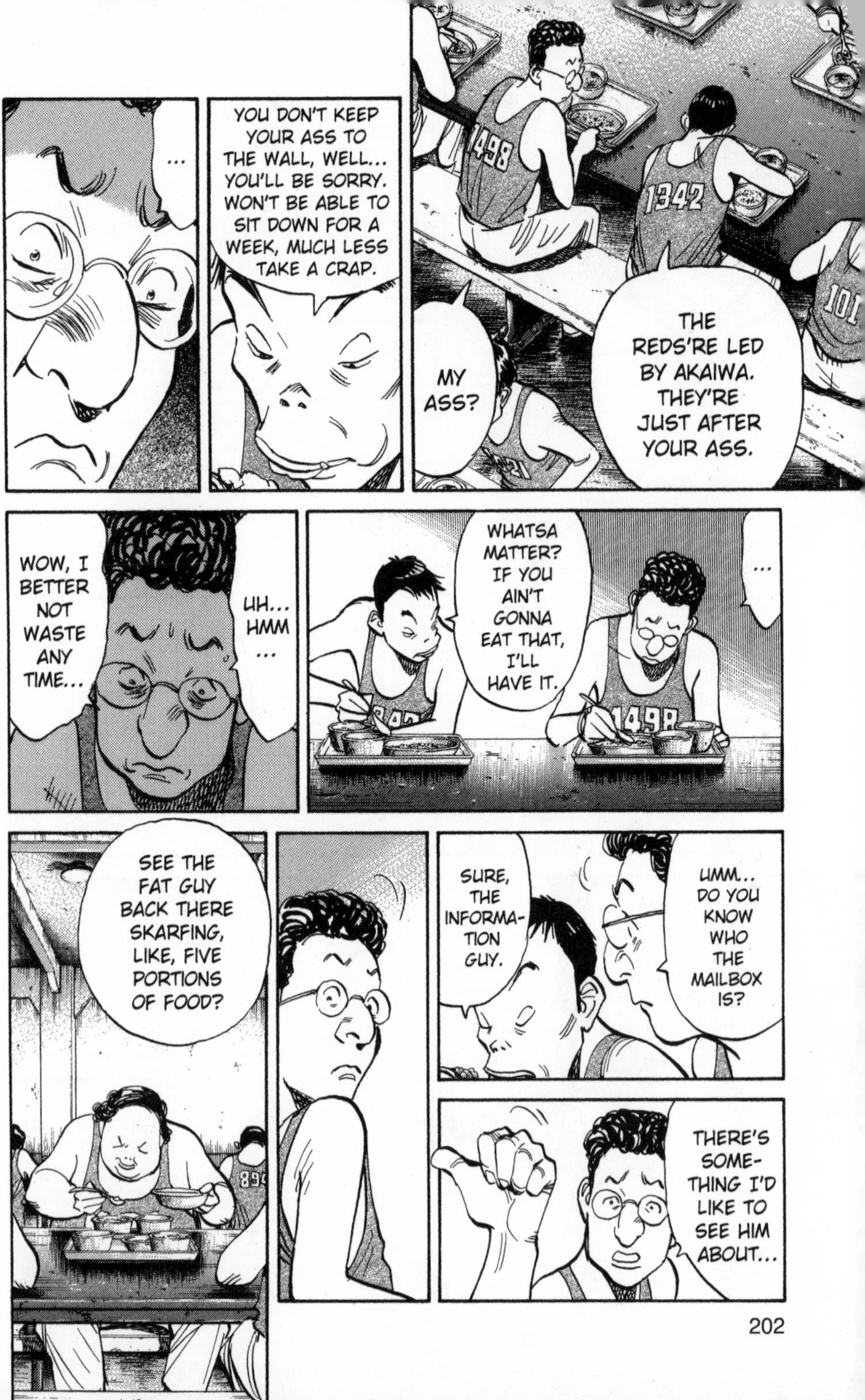
THE REDS'RE LED BY AKAIWA. THEY'RE JUST AFTER YOUR ASS.
MY ASS?
YOU DON'T KEEP YOUR ASS TO THE WALL, WELL... YOU'LL BE SORRY. WON'T BE ABLE TO SIT DOWN FOR A WEEK, MUCH LESS TAKE A CRAP.
...
...
WHATSA MATTER? IF YOU AIN'T GONNA EAT THAT, I'LL HAVE IT.
UH... HMM ...
WOW, I BETTER NOT WASTE ANY TIME...
UMM... DO YOU KNOW WHO THE MAILBOX IS?
SURE, THE INFORMATION GUY.
THERE'S SOMETHING I'D LIKE TO SEE HIM ABOUT...
SEE THE FAT GUY BACK THERE SKARFING, LIKE, FIVE PORTIONS OF FOOD?

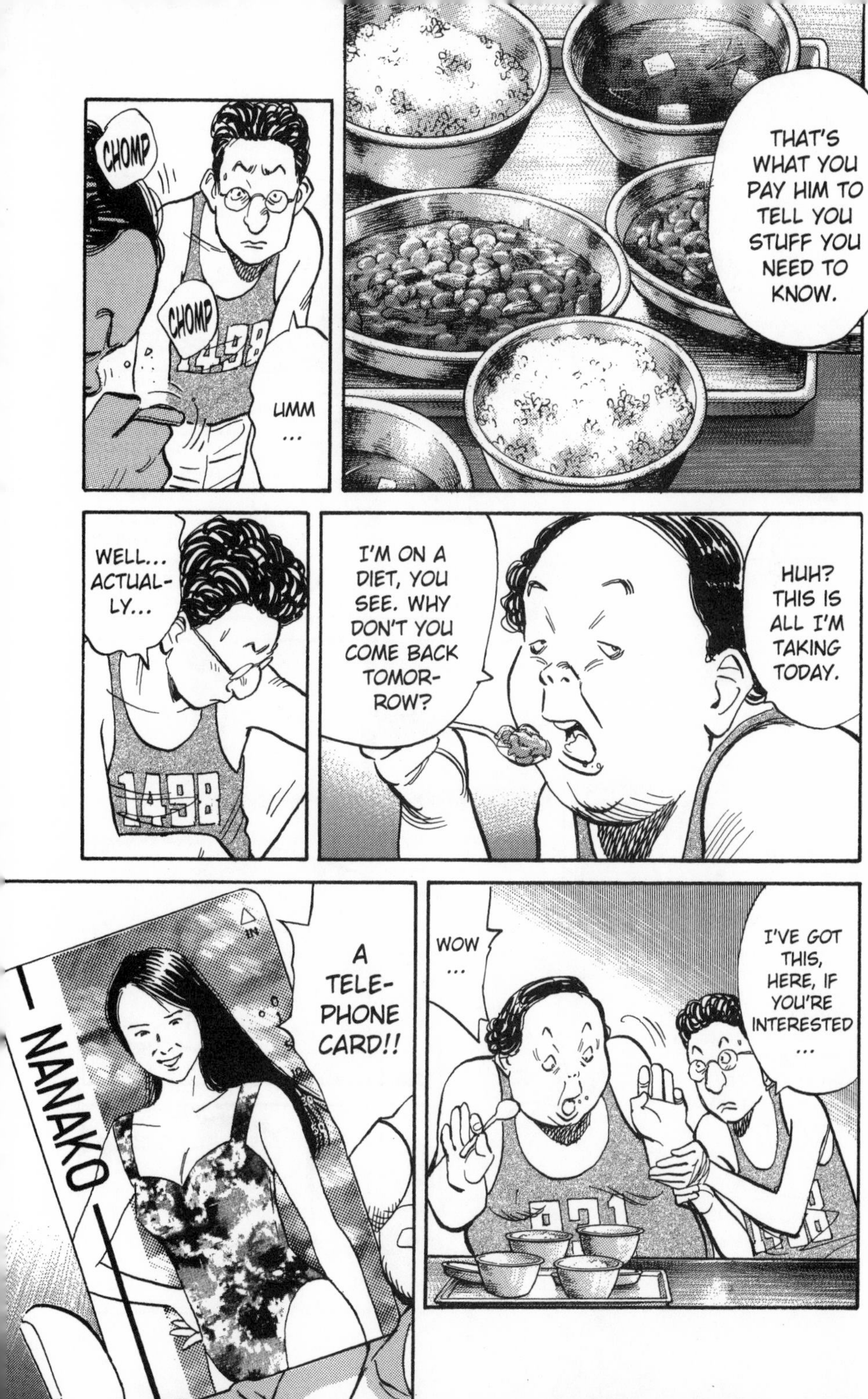
THAT'S WHAT YOU PAY HIM TO TELL YOU STUFF YOU NEED TO KNOW.
CHOMP
CHOMP
UMM ...
HUH? THIS IS ALL I'M TAKING TODAY.
I'M ON A DIET, YOU SEE. WHY DON'T YOU COME BACK TOMOR-ROW?
WELL... ACTUAL-LY...
I'VE GOT THIS, HERE, IF YOU'RE INTERESTED ...
WOW ...
A TELE-PHONE CARD!!
NANAKO

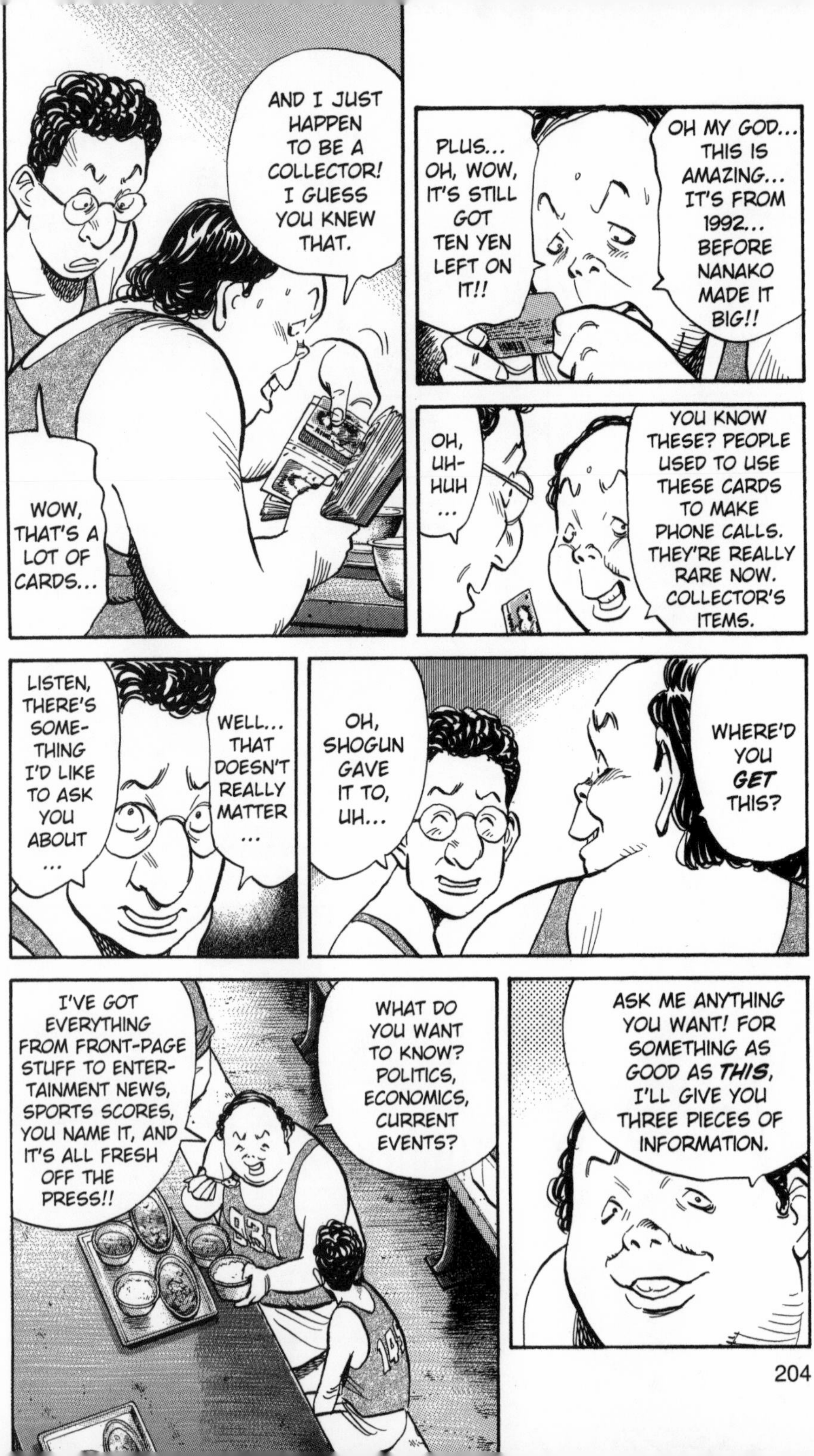
OH MY GOD... THIS IS AMAZING... IT'S FROM 1992... BEFORE NANAKO MADE IT BIG!!
PLUS... OH, WOW, IT'S STILL GOT TEN YEN LEFT ON IT!!
YOU KNOW THESE? PEOPLE USED TO USE THESE CARDS TO MAKE PHONE CALLS. THEY'RE REALLY RARE NOW. COLLECTOR'S ITEMS.
OH, UH-HUH...
AND I JUST HAPPEN TO BE A COLLECTOR! I GUESS YOU KNEW THAT.
WOW, THAT'S A LOT OF CARDS...
WHERE'D YOU *GET* THIS?
OH, SHOGUN GAVE IT TO, UH...
WELL... THAT DOESN'T REALLY MATTER...
LISTEN, THERE'S SOME-THING I'D LIKE TO ASK YOU ABOUT...
ASK ME ANYTHING YOU WANT! FOR SOMETHING AS GOOD AS *THIS*, I'LL GIVE YOU THREE PIECES OF INFORMATION.
WHAT DO YOU WANT TO KNOW? POLITICS, ECONOMICS, CURRENT EVENTS?
I'VE GOT EVERYTHING FROM FRONT-PAGE STUFF TO ENTER-TAINMENT NEWS, SPORTS SCORES, YOU NAME IT, AND IT'S ALL FRESH OFF THE PRESS!!

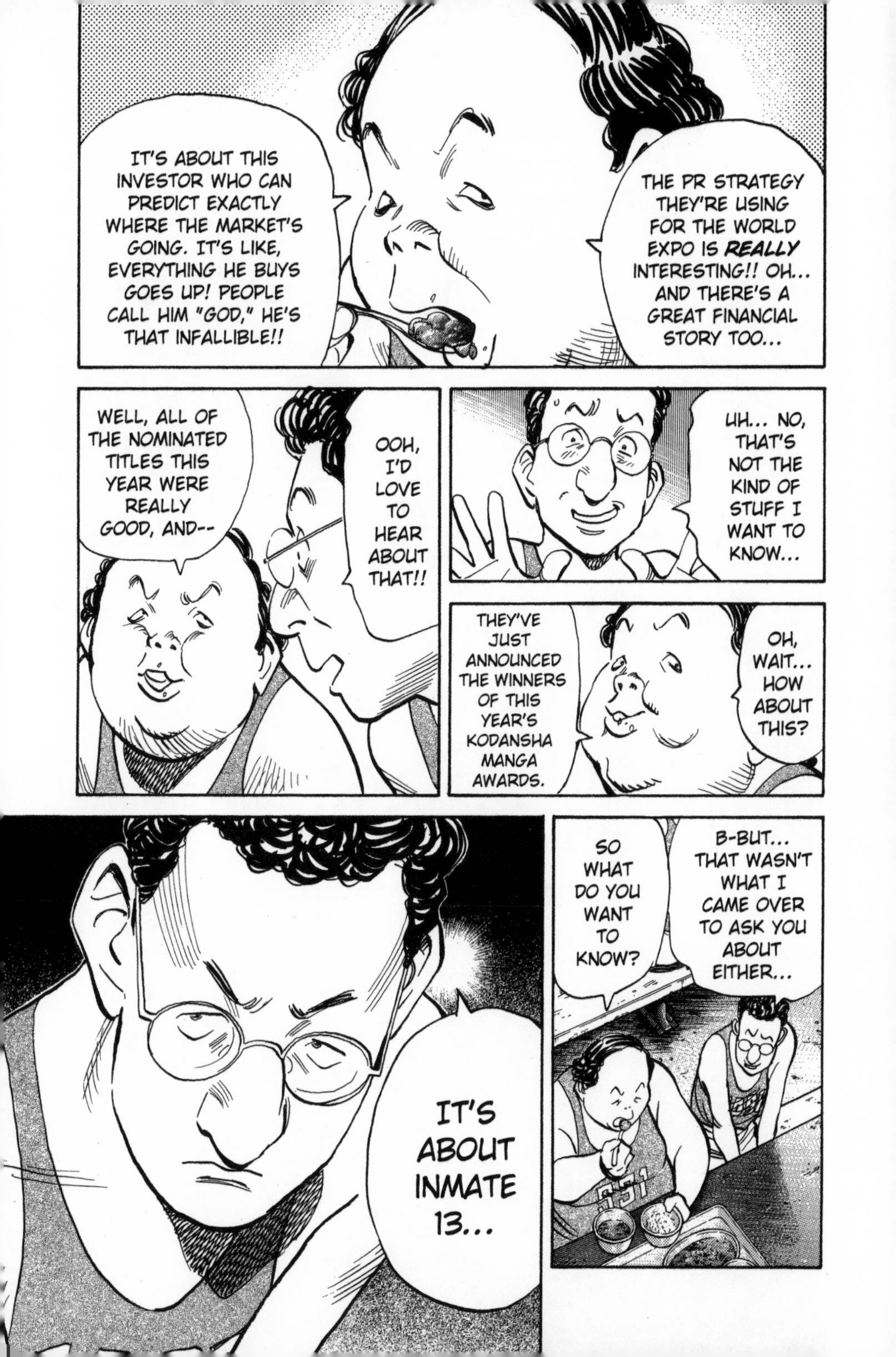
THE PR STRATEGY THEY'RE USING FOR THE WORLD EXPO IS **REALLY** INTERESTING!! OH... AND THERE'S A GREAT FINANCIAL STORY TOO...
IT'S ABOUT THIS INVESTOR WHO CAN PREDICT EXACTLY WHERE THE MARKET'S GOING. IT'S LIKE, EVERYTHING HE BUYS GOES UP! PEOPLE CALL HIM "GOD," HE'S THAT INFALLIBLE!!
UH... NO, THAT'S NOT THE KIND OF STUFF I WANT TO KNOW...
OH, WAIT... HOW ABOUT THIS?
THEY'VE JUST ANNOUNCED THE WINNERS OF THIS YEAR'S KODANSHA MANGA AWARDS.
WELL, ALL OF THE NOMINATED TITLES THIS YEAR WERE REALLY GOOD, AND--
OOH, I'D LOVE TO HEAR ABOUT THAT!!
B-BUT... THAT WASN'T WHAT I CAME OVER TO ASK YOU ABOUT EITHER...
SO WHAT DO YOU WANT TO KNOW?
IT'S ABOUT INMATE 13...

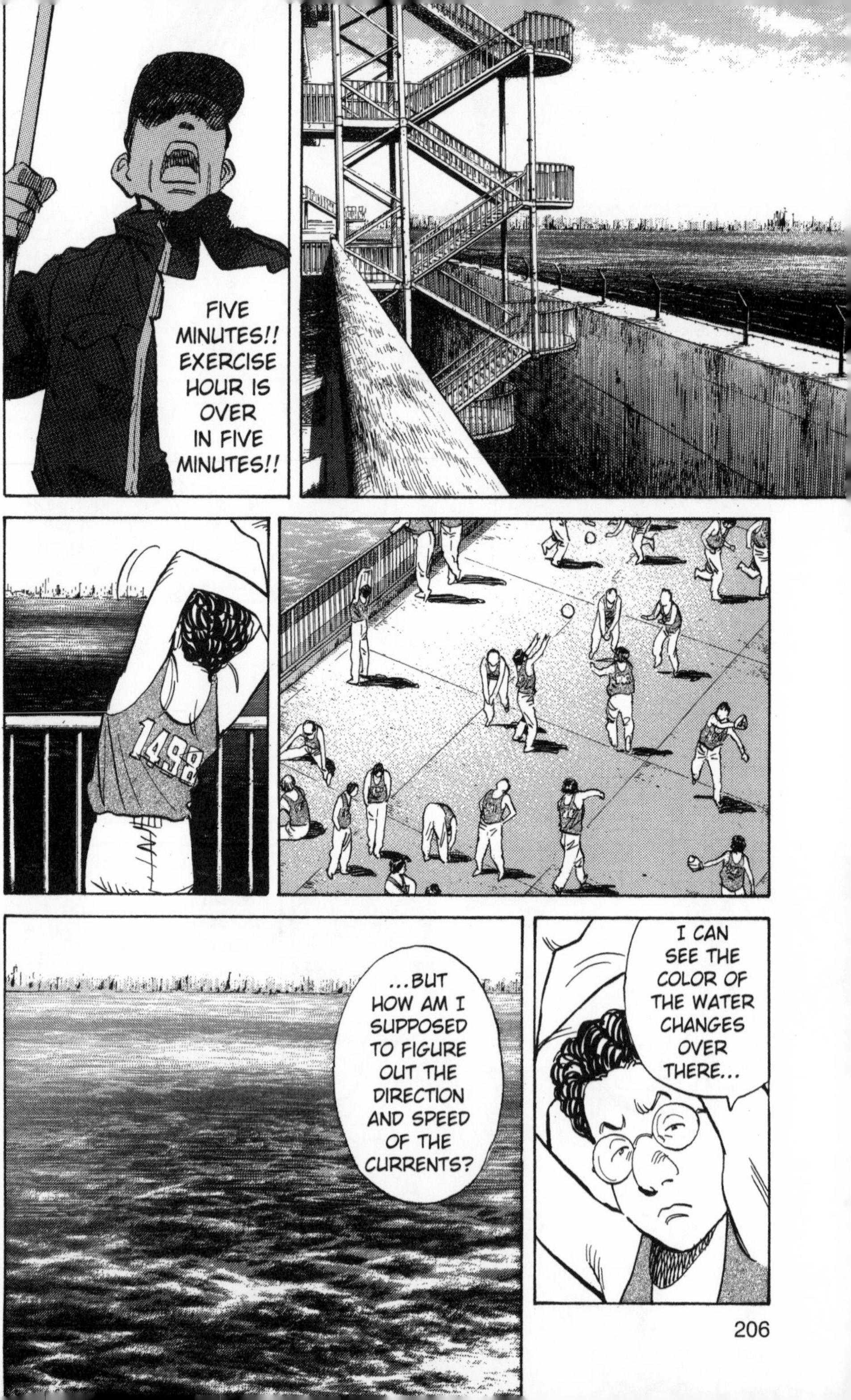
FIVE MINUTES!! EXERCISE HOUR IS OVER IN FIVE MINUTES!!
1498
I CAN SEE THE COLOR OF THE WATER CHANGES OVER THERE...
...BUT HOW AM I SUPPOSED TO FIGURE OUT THE DIRECTION AND SPEED OF THE CURRENTS?

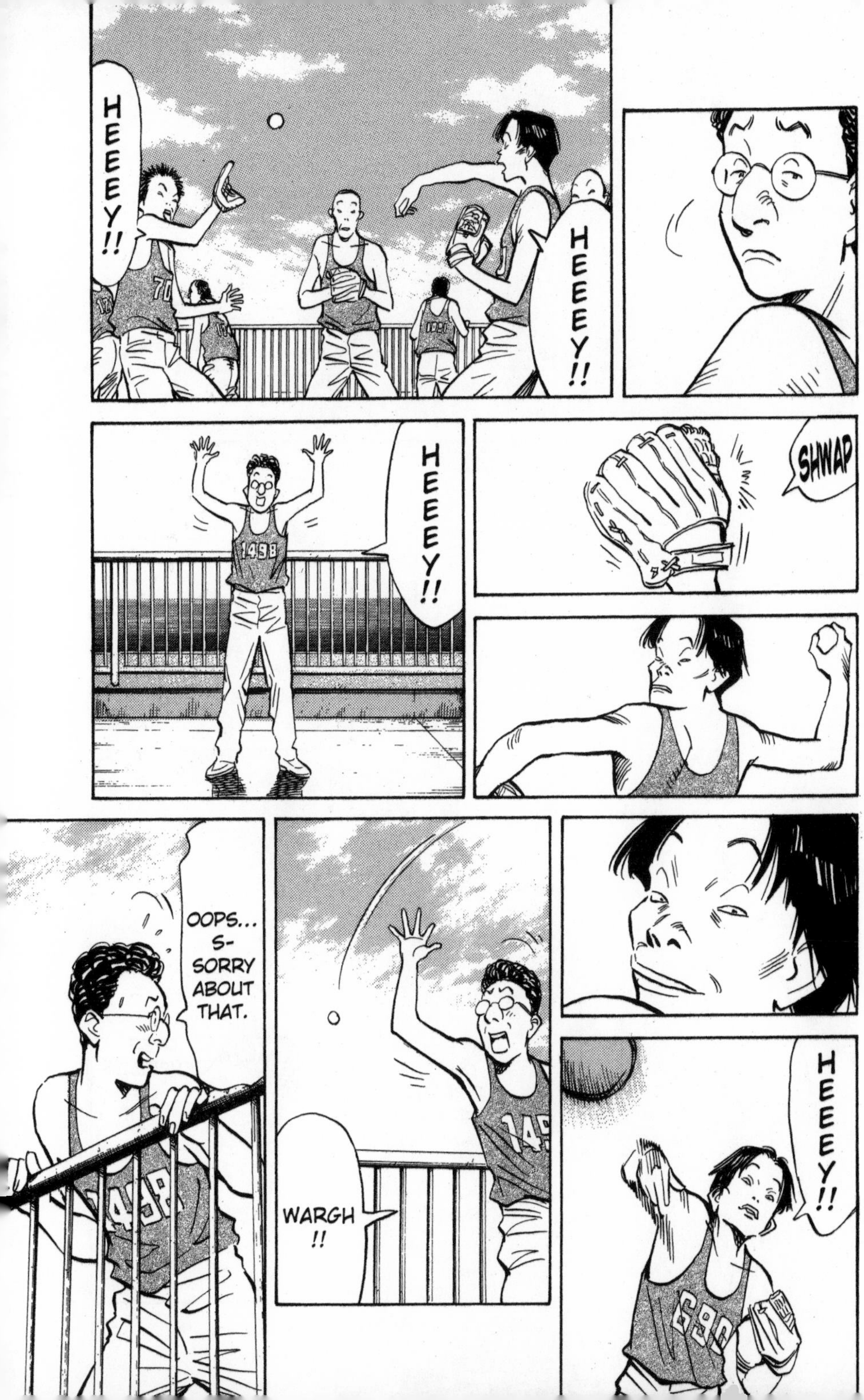
HEEEEY!!
HEEEEY!!
SHWAP
HEEEEY!!
HEEEEY!!
WARGH!!
OOPS... S-SORRY ABOUT THAT.

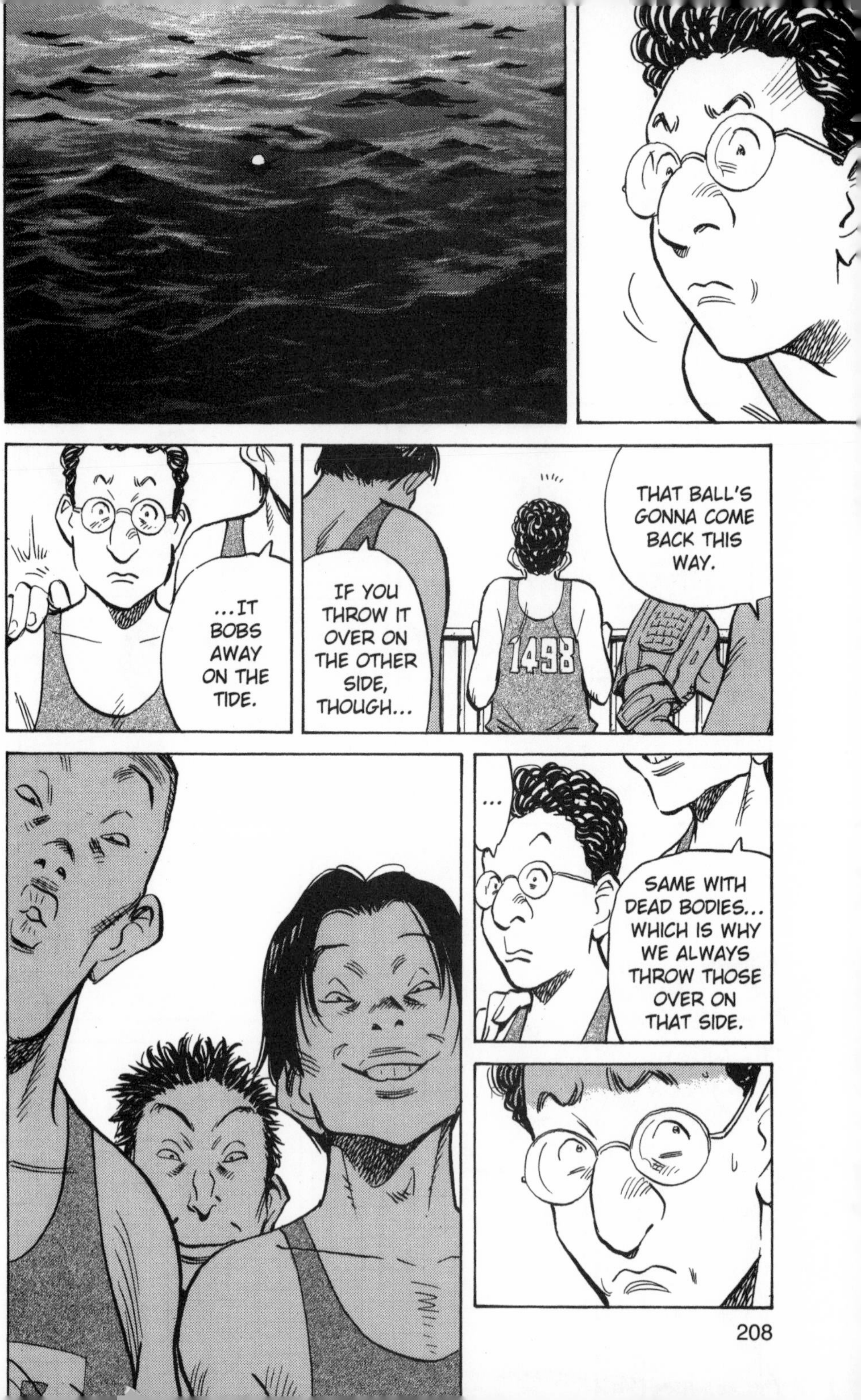
THAT BALL'S GONNA COME BACK THIS WAY.
IF YOU THROW IT OVER ON THE OTHER SIDE, THOUGH...
...IT BOBS AWAY ON THE TIDE.
SAME WITH DEAD BODIES... WHICH IS WHY WE ALWAYS THROW THOSE OVER ON THAT SIDE.
...

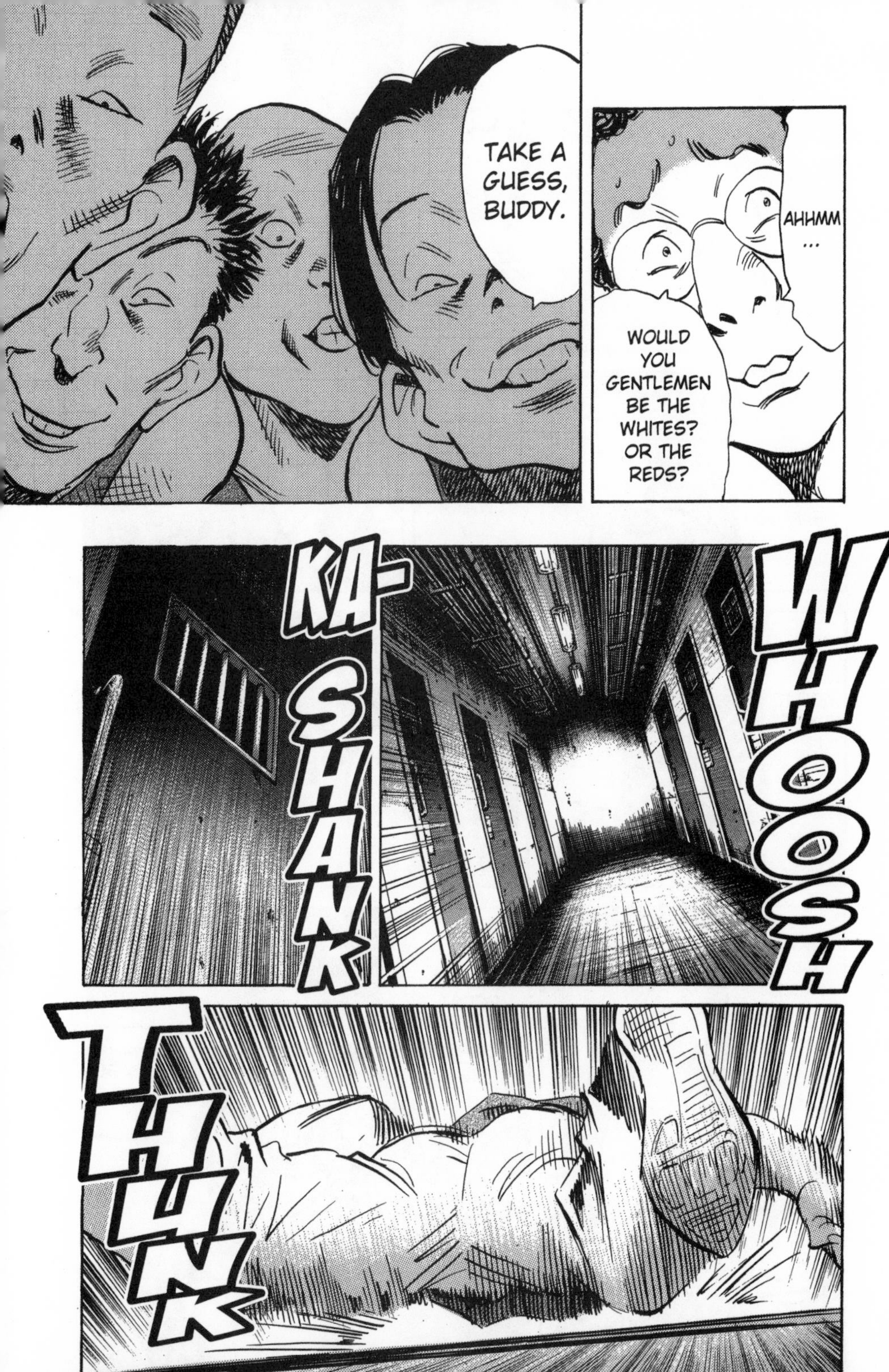
AHHMM ...
WOULD YOU GENTLEMEN BE THE WHITES? OR THE REDS?
TAKE A GUESS, BUDDY.
WHOOSH
KA-SHANK
THUNK

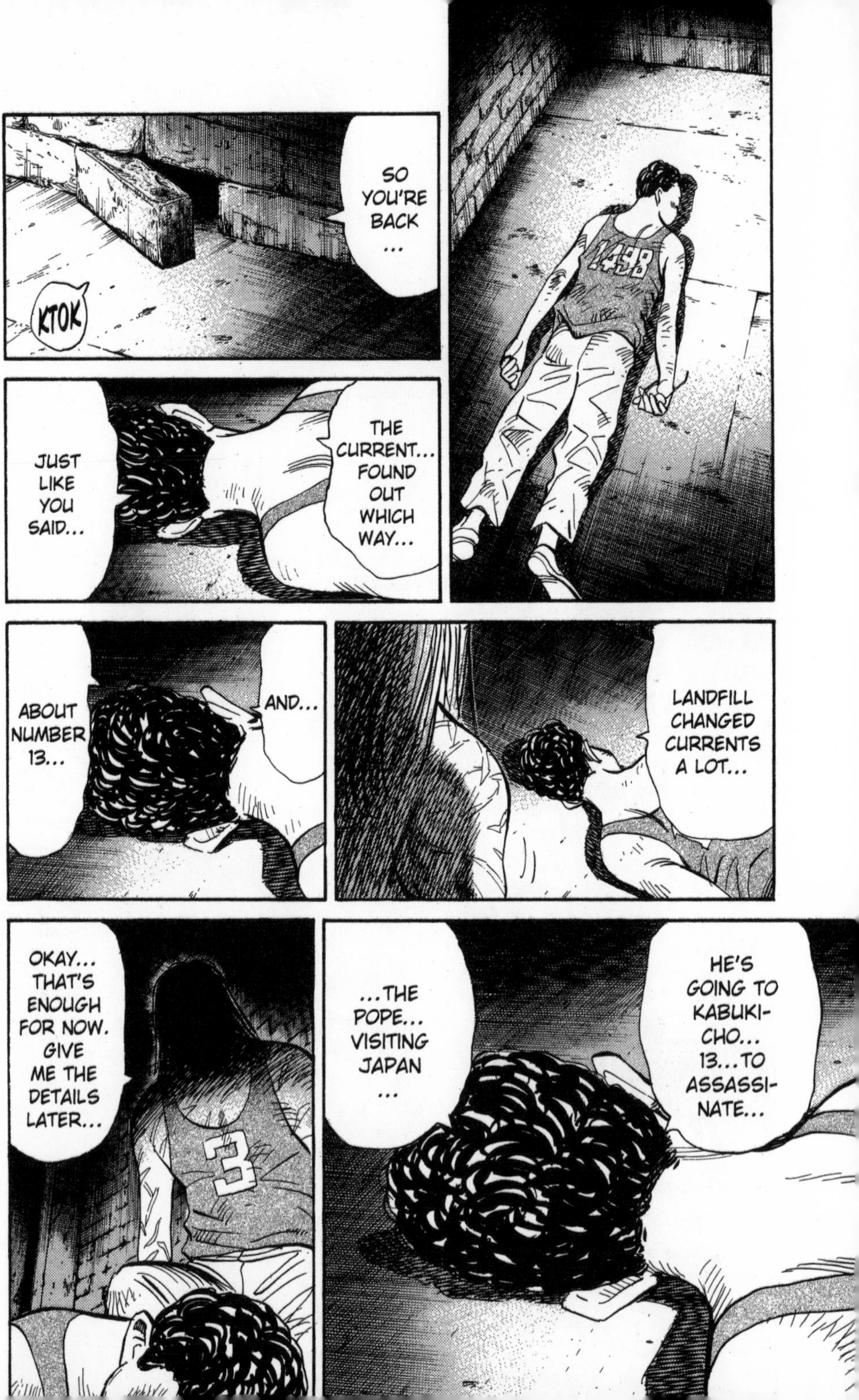
SO YOU'RE BACK ...
KTOK
THE CURRENT... FOUND OUT WHICH WAY...
JUST LIKE YOU SAID...
LANDFILL CHANGED CURRENTS A LOT...
AND...
ABOUT NUMBER 13...
HE'S GOING TO KABUKI-CHO... 13...TO ASSASSI-NATE...
...THE POPE... VISITING JAPAN ...
OKAY... THAT'S ENOUGH FOR NOW. GIVE ME THE DETAILS LATER...

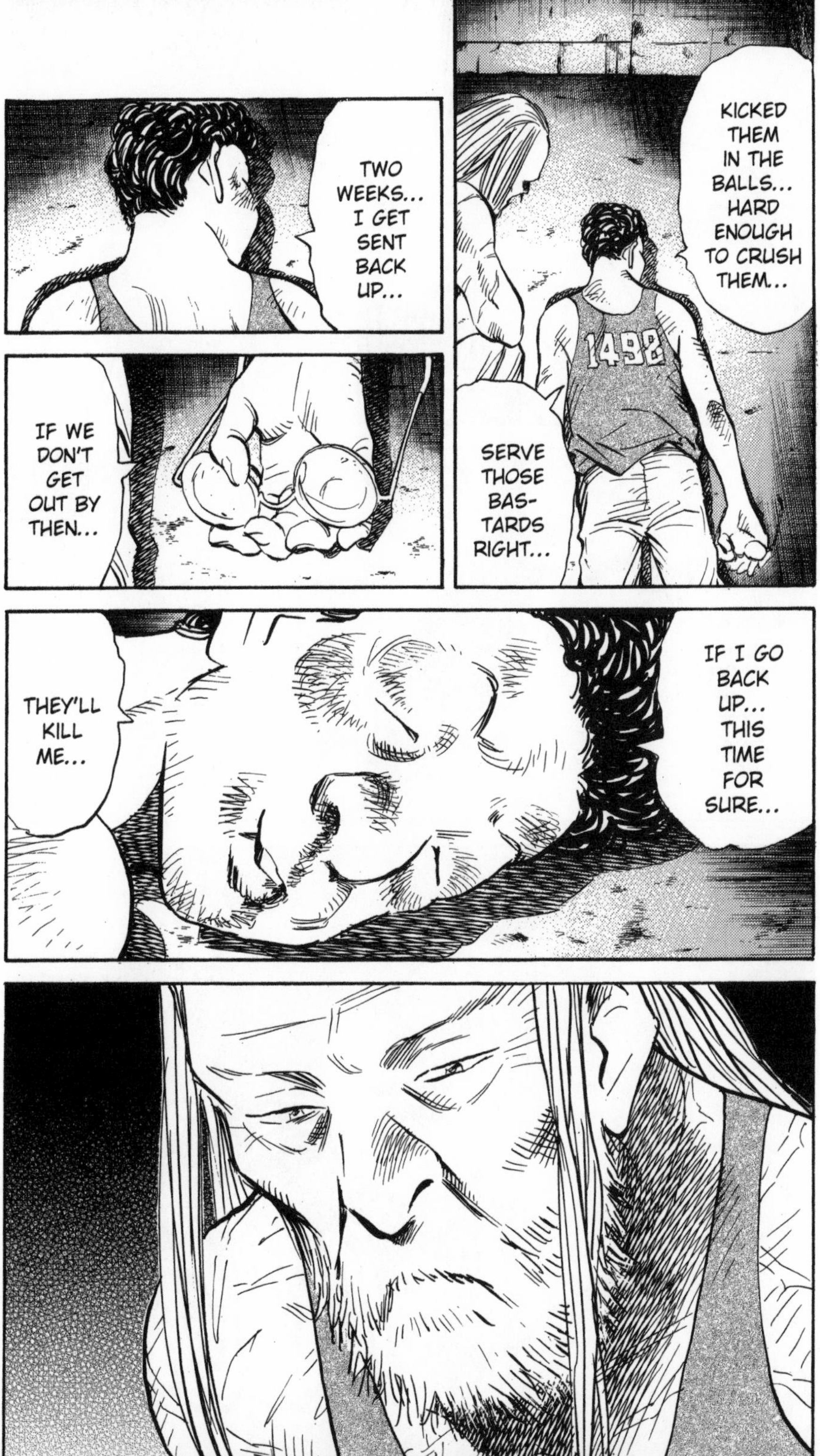
KICKED THEM IN THE BALLS... HARD ENOUGH TO CRUSH THEM...
SERVE THOSE BAS-TARDS RIGHT...
TWO WEEKS... I GET SENT BACK UP...
IF WE DON'T GET OUT BY THEN...
IF I GO BACK UP... THIS TIME FOR SURE...
THEY'LL KILL ME...

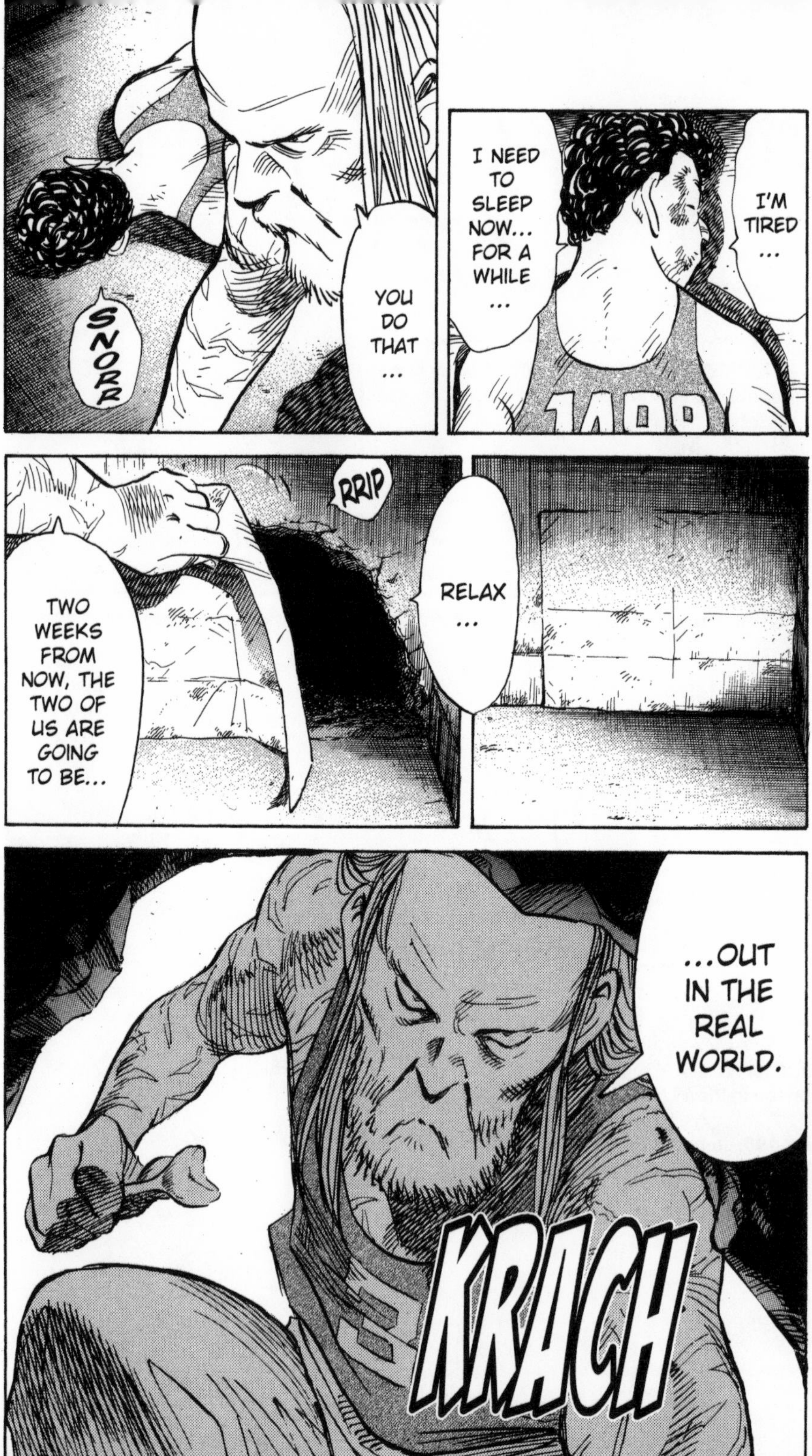
I'M TIRED ...
I NEED TO SLEEP NOW... FOR A WHILE ...
YOU DO THAT ...
SNORR
RELAX ...
RRIP
TWO WEEKS FROM NOW, THE TWO OF US ARE GOING TO BE...
...OUT IN THE REAL WORLD.
KRACH

TO BE CONTINUED

NOTES FROM THE TRANSLATOR

This series follows the Japanese naming convention, with a character's family name followed by their given name. Honorifics such as -san and -kun are also preserved.

Page 20: Sign reads "Uniform Dojo" and is an advertisement for an establishment where men can act out sexual fantasies with women dressed in a variety of costumes.

Page 44: Umihotaru is a man-made island in the middle of Tokyo Bay. It is a parking area on the Tokyo Bay Aqua-Line, which connects Kisarazu in Chiba to Kawasaki in Kanagawa, so drivers can bypass the capital. Umihotaru is where the Aqua-Bridge to Kisarazu meets the Aqua-Tunnel to Kawasaki.

Page 73: *Ashita no Joe* is a popular boxing manga created by Chiba Tetsuya and Takamori Asao, first published in Japan in 1968. *Touch* is a popular baseball manga created by Adachi Mitsuru, first appearing in 1981. *Ganbare Genki* is also a boxing manga, created by Koyama Yu, first appearing in 1976.

Page 90: Number 3 is the now retired-forever number of Nagashima Shigeo, Japan's "Mister Giants." Nagashima was fourth at bat in the Giants' lineup and their third baseman. He was thus known as "4-ban third," or "fourth up, third."

Page 177: Mandom is a Japanese brand of men's cosmetics such as aftershave, hair gels, etc., which ran a series of TV commercials starring Charles Bronson in the 1970s.

Page 180: Robert Vaughn is a popular American TV and movie star who portrayed the titular secret agent Napoleon Solo on the show *The Man from U.N.C.L.E.*, which first began airing in 1964.

Page 182: In addition to appearing in *The Great Escape* alongside Steve McQueen, Charles Bronson and James Coburn, David McCallum also co-starred with Robert Vaughn in *The Man from U.N.C.L.E.* as his Russian counterpart, Illya Kuryakin.

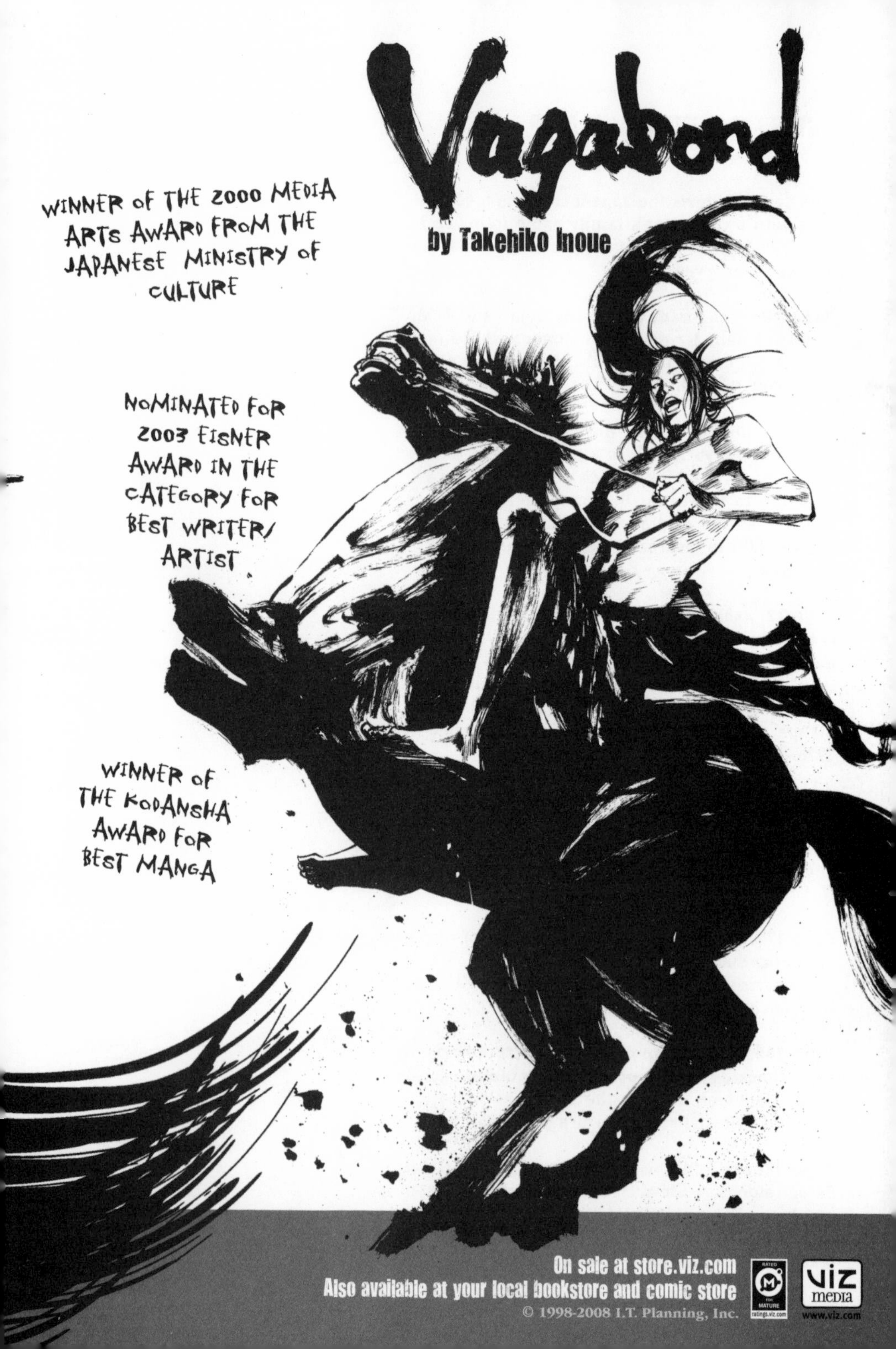
Vagabond
by Takehiko Inoue
WINNER OF THE 2000 MEDIA ARTS AWARD FROM THE JAPANESE MINISTRY OF CULTURE
NOMINATED FOR 2003 EISNER AWARD IN THE CATEGORY FOR BEST WRITER/ ARTIST
WINNER OF THE KODANSHA AWARD FOR BEST MANGA
On sale at store.viz.com
Also available at your local bookstore and comic store
© 1998-2008 I.T. Planning, Inc.
RATED M FOR MATURE
ratings.viz.com
VIZ media
www.viz.com